MEMORIES LIVE LONGER THAN DREAMS

Ronald Alway

JANUS PUBLISHING COMPANY
London, England

First published in Great Britain 1996
by Janus Publishing Company,
Edinburgh House, 19 Nassau Street,
London W1N 7RE

Copyright © Ronald Alway 1996

British Library Cataloguing-in-Publication Data.
A catalogue record for this book is available from the
British Library.

ISBN 1 85756 283 6

Cover design Harold King and Christine Jones

Printed in Great Britain by
Antony Rowe Ltd, Chippenham, Wiltshire

To those superb Welsh mastercraftsmen, all with the name of DAVID JOHN DAVIES, who went before me:
my great grandfather
my grandfather
And to my wonderful parents, Joseph and Anne Alway, and my dear Meg, my wife.

The true art of Memory is the art of Attention.
Samuel Johnson

Contents

Part One
Growing Up

1

My Early Life

It was a beautiful summer's day, so I am told – the black smoke from the batteries of coke ovens at the Bargoed by-products works was curling high against the clear blue sky, the never-ending coal trains clattering along the rails just fifty yards away from the front of my home, with their engines billowing smoke and steam, on their journey down the Valley.

Across the dirty, tar-laden, polluted River Rhymney, obscured by the trees and bushes of the Charity Woods, the recently developed Britannia coal mine stood out against the hillside on the other side of the Valley; the huge power station hissed with the escaping steam as the two huge derricks with their big winding wheels constantly turning, first one way and then in reverse as hundreds of tons of beautiful, black, shining steam coal were brought to the surface.

Every hour of the day and night this colliery sounded its deep throaty hooter, three short blasts of approximately fifteen seconds. It was the 26th day of July in the year one thousand nine hundred and nineteen, the hooter had just sounded the 10 a.m. time and, so I am told, I was born in the back upstairs room of Oak Cottage, Gwerthonor Road, Gilfach-Bargoed Glamorganshire in South Wales. It was a Wednesday morning, so my parents said. I was an innocent, bald-headed, blue-eyed baby completely ignorant of all that lay ahead, all the days of youthful happiness, the periods of sadness, the tears, the laughter, the hopes and disappointments.

It was a chapter in our time just seven months after the end of the greatest slaughter in history, the First World War. Everyone was affected and wherever one went you could not find one family not suffering the loss of at least one close relative, cut down in that useless, ghastly, imperial war.

My father Joseph Archibald Alway was the second son of George and Tracy Alway and was born at Alveston in the county of Gloucester

3

on 13th August 1885. I was his second son in a family of seven children, three boys and four girls. My father was a wonderful, kind, handsome man, a great thinker, self-educated and a brilliant athlete who, for some reason unknown to me in my early life, did not believe in more than one Christian name.

I would be 20 years old before he told me that he had been christened with the second name of Archibald, handed down from an elderly relative. 'He hated it,' I was told and for this reason he would not agree to any second name for any member of his family. In consequence I became just Ronald Alway and all through my young schooldays I was always called by my friends and schoolmates, Ronny Alway. The oldest member of our close family was my brother Gwyn, then came Edna followed by Joyce, Ronald, Toots, Trevor and Joan.

My sister Doreen was never called or addressed by her Christian name during her lifetime. In her very young life her stature was a little smaller than mine and my other brothers and sisters. My father always called her Tootsie-Wootsie and this name became attached to her and so it happened for the rest of her life she became Toots Alway.

South Wales at this time, the turn of the century, was booming with the industrial revolution, the coal mines and steel works. Accompanied by three mates – Bert Handcox, Phill Dineen and Bob Collins – living on fruit from the orchards, they walked all the way into South Wales to find work. They found their way into the Rhymney Valley and all three quickly found work and lodgings at Bargoed.

After some time, through his skills with football and cricket he became friendly with David John Davies, the eldest son of David John Davies (Snr), and Alice Mary Davies (née Webb) and they were to become my grandparents. He became friendly with Anne Davies, David John's sister, who was to become my mother. They were married at Gelligaer Norman Church, the parish church built around the year 1120, in the parish of Gelligaer in the county of Glamorgan on 12th June 1909. I can mention here that my father died in 1957 aged 72 years. My mother died in 1978 aged 92 years.

Of the first two years of my life I have little knowledge but I suppose, just like everyone else, I learned to walk and talk and started to grow up, but in later years when I could understand, I was told quite a great deal of what happened. The year 1921 came around and I was told it was one of the longest and hottest summers on the record up to that time. The giant private companies from across the border controlled everything and supported by an oppressive, diehard Conservative English government, put on the screws. The miserable basic wage of two pounds per week was to be reduced and so we experienced the first General Strike.

I was too young to recall any of the things that happened in those days; it was a sad and very unhappy period of life in South Wales. The term 'blackleg' became a well-known word; there were demonstrations and riots and all kinds of strife. One very well-known personality Winston Churchill, a minister in the government, hated by so many for the slaughter at Gallipoli, sent troops to the Valleys of South Wales to enforce their rule. These incidents will never be forgotten, soldiers with fixed bayonets confronting hungry miners and their supporters in the Rhondda Valley.

My father was a very capable man, skilled in many ways and, at the top of the garden at the rear of Oak Cottage, he built a big wooden framework and installed into the frame a pair of swinging boats, similar to the swinging boats at the sideshows and fairs. Shaped like canoes they were suspended on long iron rods. Two people sat at each end and pulled on a rope, suspended from the crossbar to gain momentum and speed. They were a source of great enjoyment and fun for the family at that time and, of course, for all of the neighbours' children around the area.

I still remember my first mishap. I was about three and a half years old and of course the inevitable happened. I was pitched head first out of one of those boats to fall about six feet on my head and was rendered unconscious. I was rushed up the street in the old big wheeled perambulator to the family doctor – Dr Turner. Old Dr Turner was a very well respected person in the neighbourhood and known by everyone in the village. Granny – Mrs Alice Mary Davies – had to be informed immediately of course. Known in the district as Mrs Davies-Quarry – she came along breathless and fussing over everything. It appears that by the time we reached the surgery I had come to and with the application of the common remedy of a cold compress, the old-fashioned iodine on the cut big lump on my forehead, and all the advice in the world from dear old Granny, I soon recovered to leave with a big headache.

In Wales at that time, with the Welsh language spoken by so many, the English language so often became mixed up with the mother tongue. In this language the noun or adjective depicting the occupational attachment to a person or the description or demeanour of anyone usually comes at the end of a sentence and in conversations amongst the villagers and the locals, people were referred to in this way just like my grandmother – Mrs Davies-Quarry – my grandfather being the operator of the local quarry.

There were so many referred to in this way, especially with so many Jones, Davies, Williams that we often heard of Mrs Davies Whisper, because her voice was so quiet; Mr Williams Co-op, because he worked at the local co-operative store; Mrs Jones Fat, being such a huge lady; Mrs Evans Crossroad, because she lived at the intersection of two streets etc. etc.

My playmates at this time were chiefly the two cousins, next door but one, at Ash Cottage, Billy and Effy Hughes, the children of my mother's sister Florence; Billy Crane farther along the street, with Hywell Rees-Mathews and Tegwyn Jones, the son of Thomas Jones Shunt, who worked on the railway, which was known at the period as the Great Western Railway. Just about this time work was commencing on the new road bridge across the eight tracks of railway to make and carry a new road to Pengam to avoid the narrow Gwerthonor Road, the right-angled stone arch bridge and the steep hill down into Pengam known to us as the Grammar School Hill.

The location of Oak Cottage was originally the entrance to the Gwerthonor Estate; confiscated land which had belonged to generations of Welsh crofters. It had become the property of an absentee English landlord granted to him by one of the English kings. Three giant trees dominated the area, all estimated to be in excess of 800 years old, a massive oak in front of Oak Cottage, the biggest ash tree I had ever seen at the rear of Ash Cottage and a great beech at the side of Beech Cottage. Hence the names of the three conjoined cottages built around the year 1830. There was no freehold land anywhere. All the land, woodlands, moorlands and fields were the property of either the Lord Tredegar or the Marquis of Bute, English lords, all confiscated and granted to them by one of the reigns of English kings. Royalties from everything above and below the land, iron, coal and ore mines, all growing crops, all structures and buildings, all goods taken or transported by road or rail, even to the horse and carts and cabs travelling along the roads, were paid to these absent parasites.

Rich black bituminous and lignite coal spewed out of both sides of the Valley. There were levels everywhere. This was the term given to any entrance on the sides of the hills to dig out this coal. Anyone apprehended taking a small lump or piece of the coal suffered imprisonment, and anyone, boy or girl under the age of 14 years doing likewise, risked being sent to a Borstal institution, a corrective services prison for minors. In the Bargoed area at that time (approximately 15 square miles) there were 3 lignite mines, 5 steam bituminous coal mines and as many as 50 levels.

The lignite coal was burned in every household and in one section of the coke ovens for producing coal gas; every home was lit either with coal, gas or paraffin oil lamps; gradually the street gas lamps were being replaced with electricity. This lignite coal, or house coal as it was commonly called, was a wonderful fuel; it was soft in structure and laced with golden yellow colours, when it burned as fuel in the fireplaces and grates of the homes. It was fascinating to watch as it expanded into small bubbles, releasing jets of gas, throwing out all kinds of red, orange, yellow and blue colours as it melted into the flames. At the rear of Oak Cottage it was all green open space at this period, the big fields, separated by hawthorn hedges spread out across the hillside towards a sunken lane known to us as Mathew's Lane, leading up to Mathew's Farm.

These fields during the spring and summer months were a picture. During the spring they all turned blue with the masses of bluebells, with the red hawthorn mayflowers standing out in lines across the landscape. Dispersed amongst the blue were clusters of cowslips and primroses and bunches of red petals from the field ragwort called by the children as Ragman's Bladders and along the hawthorn banks masses of beautiful violets. This area was a wonderful playground to us all, and where we helped with the gathering of the hay in the old hay cart of Mathew's, as each summer came to an end.

At this time I was nearing my fourth birthday and a council housing estate was being built on these wonderful fields; our wonderful patchwork playground was being destroyed. Building sheds, mortar mills and all kinds of equipment were blighting the area. These mortar mills, an antiquated affair, consisted of a big round iron bowl with two big stone wheels revolving around this bowl crushing the limestone for making plaster, mortar and cement. Many of these big stone wheels were cut and fashioned by my grandfather. The whole affair was driven, through a series of cogs, by a steam engine. Our playground now became the area of the new bridge. The new concrete mixers, the compressed air-driven saws for cutting the reinforced steel bars and timber fascinated my young mind, and again and again, my worried, cross mother came along to take me away from the area. Each time that I was missing at home they always knew where to find me.

It was the summer of 1923 and how well I can recall one tragic incident that I would never forget. My sister Joyce and her friends were playing 'jumps' off a four feet level of some scaffolding. One of these friends, Norma Allen, about seven years of age, jumped from the extreme end of the planks; she landed on some discarded timber used in the building of the bridge, a big six inch nail protruding from a piece of this timber penetrating right through her foot. She was wearing flimsy sandshoes only, footwear commonly called around the area as 'daps'. The nail went through the dap, through the foot and came out in her instep alongside the bone.

All the children ran away screaming and I, an innocent three years and 11 months old, placed my own foot against poor Norma's to take the strain whilst Joyce tugged at the piece of timber to withdraw the nail. By this time my mother and the neighbours arrived on the scene alerted by the screaming children. There was no such thing as an ambulance in those days so once again it was the big old high-wheeled perambulator and a race to the doctor. Poor Norma recovered but she would suffer for the rest of her life.

July 1923 arrived and my fourth birthday, a big event in my life. It was also the annual outing of the Tabernacle Welsh Baptist Chapel next door to Oak Cottage. It was usually a train journey to Barry Island, the big seaside resort five miles along the coast from Cardiff. On this occasion it was a special charabanc journey, three rickety, tin lizzy buses with solid tyre wheels. For me it was a thrill, the first ride in a charabanc; it was a bumpy journey, but it was so wonderful, and so much to come – rides on the donkeys along the sands, a paddle in the sea (something I had never seen before), picnics on the sands with lots of rides on the hurdy-gurdies and the merry-go-rounds. Tired and exhausted at the end of that wonderful day I was glad to lay my head to sleep and to dream of all the wonderful things in such a great big world.

After that fourth birthday in July and then the month of August for the school summer holidays and for me another big step in my life, to start school at Gilfach Infants School. The beginning of September 1923 was the first day and the start of my schooldays. Just like so many others I shed a few tears with doubts about it all but it was a new experience, being taken to school by my sisters Joyce and Edna.

Joyce had already moved up to the girls elementary school across the big school yard adjoining Vere Street. Edna, a little older was already established there. I suppose I was privileged to begin school shortly after my fourth birthday instead of waiting another six months, because the headmistress, Miss Gwladys Price, was a friend and neighbour of our family, and lived just 20 yards along the street at 4, Gwerthonor Road. She belonged to a family of three sisters and one brother; the other two sisters were teachers at Gilfach girls school, Misses Alice and Janet Price. The brother Moses was a local district councillor and a very influential person in the neighbourhood. Miss Gwladys Price was one of those eccentric persons whom I feared so much in my young days. I was always so afraid of her. She was a short, plump lady, with jet black straight hair in two long plaits hanging down her back to her waistline and tied at the ends with a black bow – always a black bow! Her face was plain and wrinkled, to me almost ugly. The clothes worn at all times were black, full and frilled, sweeping down almost to the floor giving the appearance to me that they were always five sizes too big, and to my young mind the tall ladies' Welsh hat worn so often on the top of her head made her well and truly the storybook witch.

Perhaps it was this appearance and demeanour that made me fear her so much. Her discipline was harsh on the small children and another habit we all hated so much, as we sat at the school desks, was the drumming of the end of a pencil, held between the finger and thumb, on the top of our heads. It was so painful and so often brought tears to my eyes and my fellow school mates. For the rest of my life I would always remember Miss Gwladys Price!

There was another personality I feared also as I grew up; this lady was Mrs Wyatt whom I truly believed was a witch. She lived in the next house to my mother's brother – David John Davies – my Uncle Dai, and she will come into my story as time goes on.

The hours at school at that young and tender age were long and tiring, 9.30 a.m. till 4 p.m., with 30 minutes for lunch or dinner, and I would run home every day through rain and snow making sure that I was not late, otherwise I would be sent to Miss Price to be chastised and head drummed. Everything was controlled by the big school bell, housed in a small tower on the roof of the school and tolled by a monitor, who had reached the age of seven years, before his or her promotion to the elementary school. The girls' and boys' elementary schools had similar bells also but all three were different tones and no excuses were accepted for not knowing the one to obey. There were three bells at 15-minute intervals to begin the day commencing at 9 a.m., three bells at lunchtime, one to announce the lunch break, another 15 minutes later and the third to line up to be marched into school, and the final one at 4 p.m. to signal the end of the day, the elementary schools' bell at 4.30 p.m., their end of the day.

There were seven teachers at my infant school dominated and controlled of course by Miss Gwladys Price, and Miss Price always taught the last six months of all juniors prior to them attaining the age of seven years and being promoted to the next school.

The daily routine at that young age was building blocks, plasticine, story telling, etc. and the compulsory one hour of each day of the subject referred to as 'Penmanship'. Each child for the whole period, with pencil correctly held and a straight back, from left to right using scrap paper, had to make continuous round circles conformed to each other across the page for practice and preparation for rounding all letters as one began to learn to write. No left-handers were tolerated; everyone was compelled to use the right hand only, and woe betide any boy or girl seen using his or her left hand if Miss Price walked into the classroom.

Many of those days were so enjoyable despite the obstacles and it was wonderful in the early spring and summer days to go on rambles to learn all about the flora and animals on the hillsides and across the moors. It was around this period, when the school day came to an end I would wander across the adjacent quarry to see my grandfather. To me in all my bewilderment my grandfather was superior to all others and, as I look back through my life I believe he must have been the most admired individual of all. He was always a source of wonder and perfection; to my young mind he could do things that no other man could do. Even then, with my ignorance and limited knowledge, I often thought and dreamed that perhaps some day I might be able to do all those wonderful things he did with his hands and tools.

He was a tall man with receding white hair, his forehead and deeply lined face were weatherbeaten and slightly red, which I believed came from the glow and heat of the forge. His chin was indented with the deepest dimple, shaping it into a perfect doughnut; this I believe was the inheritance he passed on to me. He still showed a line of perfect teeth each time he spoke or smiled, although I never knew how old he was; his powerful shoulders and muscular arms reached down to big, strong, wrinkled, gnarled hands from the constant handling of rocks and tools. He walked with a slight limp caused by a big slice of rock injuring his left leg in younger days; he was a superb craftsman, a master in all that he did.

Although I understood very little, as he spoke in his deep base voice, the Welsh language flowed out and rolled in a wonderful musical lilt from his tongue, every syllable correct with perfection and it fascinated me. He was a scholar taught by the old Welsh teachers and he possessed a great singing voice. He believed and practised the Presbyterian faith devoutly and each night before retiring to bed he would read out loud one page of his old Welsh Bible.

He always addressed me as Ron Bach – the word *bach* being the Welsh word for 'little'. At any time as I approached and he saw me, his first words in greeting were always *Sh'mai Ron Bach* meaning 'how are you little Ron', then came the instructions on where to stand to avoid obstructing any work.

My grandfather David John Davies (Snr) leased the local quarry, just like all the other property and land owned by the Marquis of Bute. On the south side across a wide lane were the infants and girls schools. On the north side, Maes-y-craig Street where he lived. On the east side, the boundary was almost reached and soon the working of the quarry would come to an end. The area covered about 10 acres, and three headings, or inroads had been made over the years into the Cambrian and Pre-Cambrian rock face, the oldest type of rock in geological records. This had formed three separate small valleys. It was on this final heading that work was being carried out.

The rock face was drilled with numerous holes by a compressed air drill bit from an air compressor, which in turn was driven by an ancient steam engine. The charge, detonated in these holes by the amazing skill of Grandfather, discharged a massive slice of rock. It was all manhandled with ropes and pulleys and swung into a cutting area. So often I watched Grandfather walk around the huge piece of rock after it had been hand trimmed. He would tap it and sound it putting his ear against it in many places, studying it carefully, examining the grain and cross-sections, then carefully in his uncanny way of finding the right spot, with a big stone hammer and a big chisel he would give it a mighty blow and that rock would sheer straight through as if cut by a knife. Again and again he would repeat the process reducing the rock to his required sizes.

All the kerbs and gutters of all the roads and highways were hewn by hand. Each kerb was 6 feet long, 6 inches high and 4 inches wide; the gutter section was 6 feet long by 1 foot by 4 inches thickness, so Grandfather cut dozens of those sections each day. In his working lifetime he had cut thousands of rock-faced sections, keystones and pillars for all the stone-arched bridges, high viaducts and buildings throughout the municipality. It was a hard, difficult job; everything was manhandled on frames operating on tramlines by ropes and pulleys. Two magnificent memorials still stand to his amazing work – the Bargoed and Hengoed viaducts. A Tory government in the 1950s started to demolish them both after their destruction of the Crumlin viaduct. The public outcry was so great, almost leading to violence, that they reneged, so these magnificent structures are left for everyone to see.

From the rock-face area where he worked, running down the heading, a tramline twisted and turned its way down to the rock-arched bridge carrying the main road through Gilfach and then on to the railway sidings. It was at the entrance to the overhead bridge that grandfather had his blacksmith's shop. It was to have been William Thomas Davies 'Smithy' – Grandfather's youngest son, my mother's brother – but sadly he had died in the slaughter at Gallipoli. Even before he moved to the Gilfach area around 1885, each day he walked through all weathers 15 miles each morning from Pontlanfraith to his work and walked back again each night. He told me this and many other things a little later in my life.

His day started at 4 a.m. and ended when he reached home between 11.30 p.m. and midnight every day except the Sabbath. He fascinated me with all the tales he told by the light of an oil lamp and a big coal fire when I was seven and eight years of age. I was spellbound so often as he fashioned the raw iron into so many wonderful things at his forge. One day each week, usually a Thursday, he broke off from the quarry to operate the blacksmith's shop. Of course I was always in trouble because so many times I did not go straight home from school and my sisters were sent to find me even at the tender age of four-and-a-bit.

I soon reached the age of five years, and I had lots of schoolfriends and, with orders from Granny I had to attend Sunday School also. Dressed in my sailor's suit, which was the fashion in those days, I was taken to the Gilfach Presbyterian Chapel in the main street of Gilfach. Beneath the big chapel, on the lower floor there was a big hall used for all kinds of functions in the village, so each Monday evening I was also taken to the 'Band of Hope', where we played all kinds of organised games and were often given during the interval a big slice of caraway seed cake and a bottle of 'pop'. This was the old-fashioned lemonade bottle with a glass ally for a stopper. We simply pushed down the glass ally with a finger or thumb to break the seal. The ally would fall down to the recessed neck of the bottle and then we enjoyed the fizzy contents.

One of my schoolfriends was a boy called John Law. He was very dark skinned with masses of tight, jet-black curly hair. He had no parents from what we could make out and he lived with what we believed to be his step-parents. He was always badly treated and brutally thrashed by his drunken stepfather. He became a very special friend to me and my mother often referred to him mockingly as the 'White Nigger'. He was uncared for in every way; his untidy clothes, often too big or too small, were never repaired and we believed they all came from Bratt's – the Jew, and his secondhand shop, often brought in from the rag and bone man. His boots were holed through the soles and down at heel. There were no socks in those times, all children wore stockings to the knee and poor John had none at all, and he was often hungry.

There were many children in similar circumstances during those times; the schools and teachers had to tolerate it and the bureaucrats cared little about it. They were too busy exploiting everyone and counting their ill-gotten gains, and then going through the hypocritical process of attending church three times on Sundays to give thanks for it all.

We had one very conscientious lady, the school nurse, paid for by the miners' welfare organisation through the local council health services. Her duties were never ending – trying to care for those children, keeping them clean, using paraffin washes for their contaminated hair, supplying and dressing them with donated clothes and shoes from jumble sales and auctions and then, sadly, trying to go through it all again later as those clothes had been pawned to obtain funds for drink.

On one of my visits across the quarry to see Grandfather, I took John along with me, although he would get into trouble for not returning straight home. When Grandfather saw him he was appalled and all kinds of adjectives rolled off his tongue in the Welsh language; he ordered me to take him over to Granny to do something about it.

My granny – Mrs Mary Alice Davies-Quarry – was a lady out of the nineteenth century, her white hair always ribboned around in tiers to a large bun at the top. Her clothes were always trimmed and hand laced high around the neck, with long flowing black skirts reaching to the floor. She too, often wore the red cloak of the Welsh national costume, but I never saw her at any time wearing the Welsh top hat, although she possessed three of them. It was always broad-rimmed floral hats at rakish angles held in place with long fancy hatpins. She was a dedicated believer in all of the old herbs and natural herbal remedies and there were dozens of mystery mixtures tucked away in the cupboards, cures for all ills and ailments. She believed, just like my grandfather, that to spread butter on bread to eat with cheese was a crime. It was bread and cheese only. She was an attractive lady, very thorough in everything and every task she did, very devout in her beliefs, full of kindness and compassion.

She would search from one end of the village to the other if she received information that there was some poor soul playing a tin whistle or other crude instrument to obtain a reward and when she found that person she would always press money into the outstretched hands. I believe she must have given away a great deal during her lifetime to benefit some other unfortunate being. My own reward from her every week, from the age of five years, was a threepenny bit each Thursday evening when she called, right up to her death. This threepenny bit was a lot of money to me, one penny deposited in the Christmas club at Chinock's shop, one halfpenny for sweets (usually a slab of toffee, or perhaps a gobstopper, some Red Indian eyes or ogo pogos), one halfpenny to replace my lost marbles or other treasured possessions, and one penny deposited in the old black teapot in the kitchen cupboard to save for a rainy day.

When John and I arrived at Granny's she, too, was upset with his state of affairs. She gave him a meal and repaired some of the worst areas of his clothes, then marched us off to see and dress down his step-parents. They lived in an area known as Llewellyn Street, one of the streets of the village with a bad reputation, and Granny certainly gave John's stepmother a dressing down. She did not expect such a bombardment from Granny, who made her promise that John must attend Sunday school with me and also Band of Hope each Monday and she would ensure John would be put in order.

During the next week John's clothes were put in order and Grandfather repaired and re-nailed his hobnailed boots. John remained a close friend until after his tenth birthday but things went wrong at home. His stepfather went to prison and John was sent to an institution outside Newport, being in need of care and attention, and I lost touch with him. To my surprise I would meet him many years later in 1941 on the rifle ranges in southern England, during the war. He gave me an outline of what had happened. He had become a professional boxer until he was conscripted in 1939. I was to learn later that he died in the Western Desert at the battle of Alamein.

Just before my sixth birthday in 1925, Grandfather retired from the quarry. The blacksmith's shop was dismantled and everything worthwhile was sold. The tramrails down to the railway sidings were pulled up and a road constructed down under the arched bridge, with a connector to the main road, for refuse carts to carry the local garbage from daily collections to a new refuse tip, burying the northern end of our wonderful Charity Woods along the edge of the river. The two inroads of the quarry were now being filled in with waste and slag transported along a small rail tramway from the Gilfach slag tip and the Hillside Park level. A bowling green, tennis courts and a children's swing area were to be constructed on the finished area by the Miners' Welfare Association. We were all so pleased that the third inroad was to be left and it filled with water from the rain making a wonderful winter playground for us all. From December till March it was continuously frozen hard with each heavy frost and with our hobnailed boots we had glorious long slides.

September 1925 and I was about to begin my final year at Gilfach Infants School before my promotion to the boys school. I was somewhat apprehensive about the last six months when I would come under the wing of Miss Gwladys Price so I tried to work hard and excel in every lesson, to avoid getting into trouble like so many of those other children in my class at that time. There were many squabbles and clashes with many of the rough and tough boys from different areas of the village. During the autumn and winter months the marbles time always came around and there was great rivalry between the boys for supremacy in all the games we played.

The most popular game of all was known as 'Little Ring', and there was no limit to the number taking part in the game. It was a great advantage to be the possessor of a half or three-quarter inch diameter steel ball bearing to use as a 'Tor'. A nominated amount of marbles 'up' was made to begin the game, and each player deposited that number of marbles in a twelve-inch diameter ring or a square about that size. From a distance of about 20 yards along a marked line each player, in turn, would roll their Tor to try and knock out marbles from the ring. The player who was successful obtained 'Shots' and became eligible to try and hit any other Tor at its stationary position where it had stopped after missing the massed marbles in the ring. If that Tor was hit, its owner was out of the game, and so it continued on, and the last person remaining in the game scooped all the marbles in the ring.

This game often went on for a long time, depending on the skills of the players and their accuracy in rolling the Tor. There were always many onlookers urging on and cheering their favourites. There were often disputes over chalky marbles and genuine marbles. If a player deposited chalkies in the ring and if one was broken by the rolling Tor, the person concerned had to forfeit 20 marbles in compensation.

There were all kinds of characters amongst my classmates, and one of them I remember so well. He was always late for school, missing the final bell, although through no fault of his own, and he accepted the punishment inflicted upon him without complaint. His father was a local gardener and he rented a small area for a market garden to earn a living. He was a very unpleasant person and disliked by everyone. If a ball accidentally found its way into his garden, it would never be returned. Generally the owner was too scared even to ask for its return from angry Mr Northcote. There were two children, Harold and Sylvia. Every morning and evening before and after school, Harold was compelled to collect his small barrow of horse manure from the droppings around the roads and fields. There was usually plenty around the area, with almost everything depending on the horse for all kinds of transportation.

Many times there was a shortage, and poor Harold was never allowed to go to school until he had obtained his complement of dung. We often helped him, and so many times my friends and I would find him up Gwerthonor Lane, waiting in the pouring rain, for old Garland, the coalman to bring out his four big shire horses so that he could obtain his barrow load and get to school in time. Both Harold and his young sister continued this daily task until they were 14 years old. I often loaned him my two-wheeled hand barrow and helped him repair his own when things went wrong. Poor Harold! He must have been absolutely sick of the sight of horse manure after such a long time.

As the winter approached in that year of 1925, in my young life I had never seen or experienced a very dark night. The skies to the north and north-east of the Rhymney Valley were a continuous blaze of light accompanied by a deep red glow. The Ebbw Vale iron and steel works were the biggest in the world during that period. The smelters and giant blast furnaces reflected their powerful red glow against the sky across the head of the valleys; adding to it also was the blaze of light thrown out from the 20 batteries of coke ovens at the Bargoed works. Oak Cottage, just like all the stone-terraced cottages throughout the region, had gaslight in two downstairs rooms – the living room and the front parlour. We did not need a nightlight to go upstairs to bed. With the curtains pulled aside the room was quite light each night to send us off to sleep. Any additional light we needed was always supplied by the faithful wax candle tucked into the old fashioned wee-willie-winkie candlestick. My parents, of course, were more privileged with their shining brass ornamental paraffin lamp. It was such a big advantage for anyone to go places, visiting or shopping at night. The poor street gaslight would not have helped very much and, sadly, we were going to miss that wonderful skylight so much in the years ahead when the big downturn in industry began.

I would lie awake at night so often, especially at weekends, to listen to the wonderful singing echoing and re-echoing across the valley. Groups of young men and women on their way home along Gwerthonor Road to the adjacent villages of Pengam, Fleur-de-lys, Hengoed and Penpeter, after the evening out in Bargoed town, singing in unison all the popular songs of the period, their choral voices blending into the high and low notes with perfection as they walked along. It was such a common sight at all times of the day to witness someone bursting into song in the streets as they went about their business. Strangers and visitors to the district often thought those folks were mad or inebriated but it was a wonderful custom that went on, and one that I hoped would never go away.

We had no such modern amenities as radio, or television; we had to make or provide all our own entertainment except for three cinemas, the New Hall, the Palace and the Hanbury all showing silent films (the talking pictures had not yet arrived) and one roller-skating hall, where skaters just went around and around in one big circle.

We were privileged at Oak Cottage: we owned an ancient His Masters' Voice clockwork gramophone. It was a neat square polished box with a metal disc turntable covered with green billiard cloth felt on the top; it had no lid to keep off the dust. A mechanical brake, operated by a small lever started and stopped the revolving disc, and from the far corner emerged the big metal horn to emit the sound. The turntable was operated from a powerful clockwork motor beneath, with a big winding handle to wind up the spring. Each time it was played it was cranked and wound up, and the needle, held by a set screw in the hinged head, was changed. We could purchase a small box of needles, contents one hundred, for the price of sixpence. We possessed about fifty wax records and that wonderful gramophone certainly worked overtime every evening until the spring finally broke down. We compromised later and inserted a 'meccano' clockwork motor inside and, by means of a rubber band, operated the turntable. The correct speed varied continuously, but we could still hear all those old songs from the overworked scratchy records.

We were all sorry to see it go when the end of its days came around and it was given away to the rag and bone man. My father also was privileged to own a bicycle, the latest model of that period. I well remember the specifications of that bicycle. It had 28-inch wheels, high handlebars with a single caliper front brake. The rear mudguard supported a large carrier complete with leather hold down strap and the very latest Sturmney-Archer three speed gears operated by a small lever on the crossbar. It was his usual practice about the beginning of October to set out with five or six of his friends to ride to the Wye and Severn Valleys to obtain the big Blenheim apples from the orchards in those areas. Usually at daybreak on a Saturday they would leave, complete with a number of pillowslips for containers. It must have been a gruelling day for them all, but it was good to see them safely return, with their carbide cycle lamps burning as darkness fell, one full pillowslip across the crossbar, one on the handlebars, one on the rear carrier and another tied securely on their backs, and we appreciated those apples so much.

Our first big event to add to the excitement of those youthful days was Bonfire Night on 5th November. A huge communal bonfire was prepared on Gummer's Field; all the rubbish imaginable was collected and supplied from around the village. Perhaps it was an annual event because it was an excuse to get rid of all the burnable rubbish.

My two-wheeled handcart was used also by my friends and me. Carting around the neighbourhood a stuffed-straw guy, we usually succeeded in obtaining a few pennies to help the fireworks show. The Miners' Welfare Association donated a sum of money for fireworks and all the children usually had their sixpenny worth. Ten little demons – small bangers – for one penny, a small Catherine wheel for one halfpenny, and a skyrocket for three halfpence. Many children had nothing, especially from the large families, and they had to be content just to view it all.

My friends and I preserved and kept one little demon for the following day, to use in order to blow a concave in the bottom of a small mustard or Oxo tin. The procedure was to place the demon firmly in an upright position, light the blue fuse paper, quickly place the tin over the top, stand clear and let it explode. It expanded to a uniform round in the base of the tin. A few nail holes made in the expanded roundness and the separate lid and we had perfected our 'winter warmer'. A piece of smouldering rag inside the tin completed the job. A swing of the tin or allowing the wind to blow through kept the rag glowing and helped to keep our hands warm on the coldest days, especially in the frost and snow, as we used our hands to play marbles and conkers.

Conkers was a very popular game during the early winter days. There was an abundance of horse chestnuts available in the woods which, of course, we eagerly gathered or knocked them down off the trees, removed the husks, and kept them in our conker bag. After piercing a hole through the sturdiest conker and inserting a length of string complete with a knot at the base, the custom was to challenge an opponent. Three blows each in turn with one's own conker in an attempt to break the opponent's conker; the loser with a broken conker forfeited five conkers to his opponent who was so proud of his win.

Our second annual big event – the Night before Winter called by the children in the Welsh language Nos'n-Gyer, or more commonly referred to as 'Ducking Apple Night' – came round on the last night of November. It was a great occasion to which we all looked forward. My brother Gwyn, sisters Joyce and Edna and myself had already been to the chestnut trees at the top of the 'jungle' and Mitchell's fields at the beginning of the month to collect a big bag of chestnuts. Tom Carter from next door would come along with his squeeze box melodian; Crane brothers, Bill and Fred and sister Edith and other neighbours turned up that evening for the celebration.

After supper that evening, usually the traditional meal of faggots and peas and other delicacies about 7.30 p.m., with a huge warm coal fire burning in the grate, we would begin ducking the apples. Instead of floating them in a bowl of water, we suspended them by a string attached to the strong stalk of those big Blenheim apples. Hands behind our backs we would attempt in turn to take a big bite out of the apple. The biggest bite of the evening was awarded the prize, a big slab of Mrs Wyatt's toffee. The evening's entertainment continued with roasting the chestnuts on the hob, with all the excitement running high, as the chestnuts popped and exploded, announcing that they were well and truly done. Tired and exhausted and having eaten too much, I was allowed to stay up until midnight and then off to bed.

Almost asleep I could hear the hiss of the steam and the whistle from the Rodney, the 12.15 train from Cardiff on the Great Western Line, the last passenger train of the day, and the sounds of song and revelry coming from the open carriage windows as it passed under the almost completed new bridge in front of Oak Cottage. Across the river, there was the answering whistle from the other Rodney on the Brecon and Merthyr line from Newport to steam into Bargoed station on time together at 12.20 a.m. It was the end of another day.

All the old unpleasant diseases were rife throughout the country during that period. The modern cures of medicine, injections and inoculations to prevent these things were not yet discovered, except for vaccination against the dreaded smallpox disease, and even this

19

was causing trouble, resulting in vaccine poisoning etc. Every person who had received a vaccination carried a red ribbon around his or her left arm, a warning to avoid any bumps or jostles by another person. Scarlet fever, diphtheria, smallpox and so many other diseases were a common event, but all our family managed to keep free of them except Toots, who would go to an isolation hospital with scarlet fever, and sister Joyce to suffer all her life from the effects of vaccine poisoning against smallpox.

My father was so upset and angry he would not allow any other members of the family to be vaccinated after that incident. Perhaps I can believe that it was all the old herbal medicines of dear old Granny and Mrs Wyatt that kept us immune from these scourges.

At the end of November that year of 1925 I was confined to bed with the common complaint of measles. I believe everyone must have had measles at some stage of their lives. I recall so well those two weeks I spent in bed getting over that awful disease. My mother moved the bed across the room as close as possible to the window, so that I could look out and view the passing scene each day. The new bridge was completed but the roadworks across the railway lines were still unfinished and work was continuing.

The road had to be built up approximately 60 feet – to meet the end of the concrete abutment end of the bridge. Mutton Tump, the top side of the Charity Woods, was cut in half by the new road and from the grounds of Lewis's Grammar School, 500 yards to the south, the soil was being excavated for new sports fields and this soil was being used to build up the road. I could see the small steam engine, all day long, pulling its full load of earth, contained in three tip wagons, known to us as 'dandies', up the hill, depositing it and then running backwards on the tram rails to be refilled.

I could view all the other colourful characters that came along Gwerthonor Road at all times each day. Every morning the first to appear around 7 a.m. would be Dai Isaacs, the milkman with his horse and milkcart usually containing three big milk churns, stopping at each door. With the familiar call of Milko, someone would appear with a jug or container to obtain their daily supply of milk. At 10 a.m., Stan Davies with his horse and bread van with all the fresh long loaves of high top bread, cottage loaves, the Welsh round bakestone batch loaves and the big brown varieties.

Around 11 a.m. was the daily round of the ash cart. With all the numerous coal fires each household would deposit at the kerbside their daily buckets of ash from the grates and fireplaces, along with any other rubbish or throw aways. This was a continuous service daily except on Sundays, Christmas and Good Friday.

On Tuesday morning came the oil and hardware man – John Morris, his big decorated four-wheeled cart had three open sides, with the paraffin tank at the rear for easy access to the tap to fill the customers' tins and bottles. Hanging in that cart and visible through the open sides was everything imaginable – brooms and mats, tools, tin buckets and dishes, tin baths and bowls, carbide lamps with packets of carbide, gas mantles, miners' lunch tin 'tommy' boxes, anything and everything in hardwares.

Tuesday afternoon about 2 p.m., Peters, the fisherman came; you could smell him approaching along the road. Haddock and hake, plaice and herrings, kippers and bloaters, plenty of cod, jellied eels, cockles and mussels. The aroma of old Peters and his fish cart had almost drifted away when along the road would drive and come into view Vicar Hughes, the Gelligaer Parish Church of England vicar, in his beautiful trap pulled by a wonderful white horse, on his way to Maes-y-craig street to one of his parishioners who groomed the horse and cleaned and polished the shining black paintwork on the trap. I disliked Vicar Hughes, just like so many of the other boys, because he caused so much punishment to be inflicted upon us when we attended Gilfach Boys School.

In those days every schoolboy wore a cap, a tight-fitting affair with a small peak. Anyone who failed to touch his cap in a salute as he passed by was immediately reported to the headmaster Trefor Cadogan Jones – T C Jones – known to us, and always referred to as Gaffer. With each report it was six cuts across the bare backside and there were no excuses accepted and it was so painful! I received that punishment many times for failing to carry out this ritual. My father ordered me not to recognise him in any way, and I dutifully carried out that order with so many of the other boys. In the words of my father as I remember so well, 'You are a far better honest youngster than that sly grog shyster, do not under any circumstances lower yourself and salute him.' Vicar Hughes, a name I shall always remember from my childhood, was notorious with the things that went on. I was 14 years old when he was finally defrocked and disappeared from the district.

On Wednesday the noise of a horn, blown on the bone-horn, heralded the approach of the rag and bone man. He was a one-legged character with a half pegleg below the knee, ready to cheat anyone at the first opportunity. Money was scarce and the poverty of everyone often induced people to part with some object or piece of clothing to obtain a few coppers to help them along.

All of us as young boys often visited the refuse tip for scrap iron or some metallic object to trade with this man. Ironically his name happened to be another 'Jones'. We often followed him to find out what he did with many of the things he collected. All the clothing, wearing apparel, or shoes went to old Bratt, the Jew, and finally appeared on sale in his secondhand shop and pawnshop.

On Thursdays, adding to the scene with all the passing carts, the old Fords, Austin and Morgan motor cars, the tinker would pass by, pushing his workcart along and ringing his bell to obtain odd jobs. This cart was an ingenious affair fitted with all kinds of gadgets. It was pushed along with a pair of handshafts. When it was stationary, gaining pressure by pushing down on the shafts, two supporting legs lifted the wheels clear off the ground, and two other hinged legs dropped down to give it firm support and make it a portable workbench. A small treadle on the side, with its treadle arm, was linked to the cart wheel and a leather belt revolving around a spline on the wheel, in turn, with its large diameter turned a grindstone very speedily for sharpening knives, scissors and implements etc. One hinged box lid opened to reveal a shoe last attached, to re-nail or repair boots and shoes. Another box contained all shapes and sizes of metal templates, just like a modern panel beater, to repair almost anything in need of repair, and to patch and sharpen all kinds of things in need. The tinker was always in demand, he was well liked and he did a roaring trade.

On Friday, Peters the greengrocer (the brother of Peters the fish) with his horse and cart, also came with all kinds of fruit and vegetables with the big brass scales to weigh the sales, and the bundles of paper bags hanging from the side of the cart. Each day and all day, there was something interesting as I looked out of that front bedroom window when I was confined to bed with those dreaded measles. On the Saturday, too, I saw the monthly round of the gasmen, Mr Sharp, and Mr Court, the company staff, two powerfully built men going through their ritual. At distances of 12 feet between the joints below ground of the main gas pipe, they would drive a black-pointed metal bar into the road with a huge sledgehammer, one man holding the bar to obtain a start into the ground, whilst the other delivered the blows. When the necessary marker was reached, a mark was painted on the bar. It was loosened and removed and a meter placed over the hole to test for leaks. If a leak was registered on the meter, they would return, dig up the road and repair the joint. This went on seven days a week around the whole district nonstop, and it seemed to work out that each section was tested regularly once each month.

I recovered from the measles and went back to school once more before the arrival of Christmas. The week before Christmas was always a busy time. My mother prepared all the year and stored away the currants, sultanas, raisins and other necessary ingredients for the Christmas pudding and cakes. One special day was set aside by the Gwalia bakehouse before Christmas each year to bake all the Christmas cakes for the locals. I went along with Joyce at 7 a.m. on that special day to collect, on loan, seven big long bread tins, paying sixpence deposit on all the tins, to be refunded when they were returned. At home my mother had already prepared all the mixings for the cakes; the yeast had been added, and the huge earthenware pan was standing on the cast-iron stand in front of the fire. In the reflected warmth those magical ingredients were allowed to rise. The tins were carefully filled, covered over with a white cloth, deposited in my cart, and off to the bakehouse once again to be baked, the price – two and a half pence each for baking. After school that day, back to the bakehouse again, Joyce carefully checking the names on the greaseproof paper, then, back home again with those wonderful cakes. All the tins were washed and cleaned and we returned once more to collect our deposit. It always seemed to be the same number of seven cakes each Christmas, all baked in the big seven-pound tins and they would last the whole year until Christmas almost came around again.

The Christmas puddings were usually boiled in two batches. The number was ten in all, five at each boiling. Once again my cart would come into use going along to Granny's to collect the big cast-iron cauldron. It accommodated five large puddings at each boiling. My mother toiled all day on both those boilings, two separate mixings, then the yeast rising in, the big white basins, all the pudding cloths and then keeping a big fire going to keep them on the boil for eight hours. For us all it was worth it so much, we did appreciate and enjoy those wonderful Christmas puddings. Christmas for me, at that tender age, just like any other child, was an exciting and wonderful time. The day before Christmas day arrived, I collected my Christmas club proceeds from Chinock's shop – a variety box of Rowntrees chocolates and toffees paid in full, two shillings and sixpence! Granny gave me a whole half-crown, another half-crown from Uncle Dai and a shilling from my parents. I had the huge sum of six shillings to spend on that

Christmas eve. The shops remained open until 10.30 p.m. and all the family went into Bargoed town to enjoy the festivities.

There were the big toy departments of the Emporium and the Big Bon Marche to visit. Ile's the saddlery and gifts, Peacock's Bazaar with nothing in excess of threepence, Woolworths with nothing in excess of sixpence, the Penny Bazaar and Brobyns and Rutter's the big fruitiers. My important buy would be three packets of Trix, with separate accessories, from Woolworths, for the sum of four shillings. Trix was similar to Meccano; to me I thought it was superior. Each metal strip, in different lengths, had three bolt holes horizontally, unlike Meccano with a single hole. From that time onwards I always saved every penny I possibly could to purchase an additional packet to enlarge my constructions and by the time I reached 14 years I had a wonderful Trix set.

In later years my destructive young brother Trevor, who had a mania for pulling everything to pieces and then failing to put them back together again, gradually disposed of and lost much of that wonderful Trix building set.

Later I went to bed that Christmas Eve to hang my long stocking on the rail at the bottom of the iron bedstead. I shared that bed with my brother Gwyn. He was seven years senior to me and I still remember that I could not understand the reason why he did not hang up his stocking for Father Christmas. When I asked the reason why, I was told that Mum was repairing a hole in the heel and she would hang it up later after we had gone to sleep. Innocently, I believed it all!

Christmas day that year was free of snow and all the family activities were indoors. I was up and around at 6 a.m. of course to examine my stocking for contents of fruit, nuts, Christmas crackers and sweets and I found the best present of all, the annual of the *Boy's Magazine* issued at Christmas time, containing all the special stories, anecdotes and hints of the previous 12 months from the weekly editions priced at one penny. I purchased that book every week from that time onwards, as my reading improved, until I was 15 years old. Every Friday evening at 5 p.m., rain, hail or snow, I would run all the way to the papershop to get my copy. I kept them all so carefully, they were so valuable to all the boys at that time, and on many occasions later I swapped or traded them for various things I wanted and did not possess.

The other publications for boys during those young years were *The Rover, The Wizard, The Thriller* and lots of different *Comic Cuts*, but they did not interest me; my favourite was *Boy's Magazine*. Many times it was such a relief for me, after racing all the way to the papershop, to find that familiar pinky-orange paper cover on the shelves. After examining all my treasures in that stocking, I lit the fire and from that early age, during holidays and weekends I always lit that coal fire and placed the big cast-iron kettle on the fire to make the tea, and without fail I would always carry up the stairs to my parents, a hot cup of tea. We had no electricity to make toast with electric toasters; we could make the toast on the griller of the old gas stove but it was the toasting fork for us, always, in front of the red-hot coals. This made it so deliciously and that wonderful aromatic smell of fresh toast floating through the house was a great appetiser and rings through my memories of all those days gone by.

We had plenty of holly hanging everywhere throughout home; there was a never ending supply for the taking in the woods around. We had no pretty lights or a Christmas tree, our decorations were simple paper lanterns and coloured paper chains all made at school. Ivy was never allowed inside any home. The old Welsh folk were very superstitious and ivy was considered a poisonous curse; it grew everywhere and was regarded as a pest. All my life I never discovered or found the reason for such a terrible hate of this plant. I can only assume it was the old superstitious tales handed down through the generations that made everyone reject it so vehemently.

Christmas night was another exciting evening. Having eaten so much all day long I still tackled the roasting chestnuts on the hob and played Ludo and Snakes and Ladders with the other members of the family. I believe they must have been the only available games. There were the usual carol singers around the streets in groups carrying their carbide lamps, and we had a visit from many of them, singing at our front door. I was hoping for a very heavy frost and some snow that night and – yes – it came. Boxing Day morning gave us a mantle of white and everything was frozen. We had no hot water on tap, our hot water was supplied by a gas geyser. When the tap was turned on it released the gas in the pipe to escape, and it ignited into a small flame from a tiny pilot light. It was an antiquated affair but it seemed to work all right with very little trouble.

During the winter months and through the heavy frosts the cold water pipes feeding the homes usually froze. Everything was lead piping and I suppose being soft and malleable the lead expanded with the ice, although there were many bursts when the thaw came. Patiently, on many frosty mornings the faithful big iron kettle full of boiling water on the fire, was used to thaw the pipes so that we could replenish our water supply. Almost before I was ready that Boxing Day morning, the Crane brothers and many other friends were calling outside the front door. It was to be a big day at the quarry with the long wonderful slides.

The week-long Christmas holiday from school was to be one of the most enjoyable times of my infant-school days. My young mind was not yet able to construct a sledge for all the snow-covered frozen days but this was not very far away. In the meantime I borrowed Tom Carter's sledge from next door. Tom had left school at the age of 14 and he was working with his father Joe on the crushers that broke down the huge pieces of steam coal into what we called 'small coal'. These were then stockpiled into a big concrete silo and fed by hand-operated hoppers into the aerial buckets at the staging point across the river at Britannia Colliery and then carried along the ropeways to feed the Bargoed coke ovens and by-products works.

Tom was a very kind person and he would do anything for me; his sledging days were over so he offered me his big sledge whenever I needed it until the time came when I could build my own. All day and every day in that wonderful frozen snow it was perfect sledging down Mutton Tump with all the boys. At the end of the sledge run we had to build a big snow mound, at the point where the slope ended and the woods began. This was vital to crash into to break our speed and prevent us speeding on through the woods and into the river. Again and again we would crash into that mound, coughing and spluttering amongst the powdery snow as we stopped dead. It was so exhilarating and wonderful, the time simply flew by and, of course, again and again, Joyce would be sent over the bridge to collect me and get me home for dinner.

2

Early Schooldays and Unusual Jobs

New Year's Day arrived, the beginning of the year 1926. It was to be a bad year, a sad year with all the things that would happen. It was the start of the awful big depression, the beginning of the massive recession and downturn in industry and trade throughout the world. On New Year's Day it was a regular custom to visit the various traders who carried on business in the village. The custom was to 'throw out money'; it wasn't very much, usually a small bag of halfpennies and farthings. The day before, that is New Year's Eve, we would know the appointed time when this event would take place, always between 8.30 a.m. and 10 a.m. I have never known where this custom came from but the children everywhere from all the streets around would gather around the area of the trader at his appointed time. He or she would quickly rush out of the shop, call out 'Happy New Year' in the Welsh language and then throw and scatter the bag of coins into the crowd of children. Then an immediate stampede and rush and scramble to try to obtain some of the spoils. When all of the treasure was gathered up and taken, the children would move on to the next trader. I was too young to enter the fray but my turn would come. My brother Gwyn and sisters Joyce and Edna were in the scramble to get some reward. I remember so well in later times going round in turns to Browns' the fish and chip shop, Cross's and Jones the sweets and general stores, Rutter's the fruit shop, Chinock's, the Gwalia bakehouse and store, Olivers' the oil man, O'Brian the corn merchant, Lizzy Anne's the drapery, Thomas and Evans the cake shop and many more.

I began my last six months at Gilfach Infants School at the end of the Christmas holiday under the guidance and discipline of Miss Gwladys Price. I was much bigger and stronger than the majority of

27

my schoolmates at that school. With a close cut up the back and sides of my head, operated upon by my father with his hand clippers, and my school cap crushed down on the top of my massed curly hair, dressed in a new blue knitted jersey with three buttons at the neck, short trousers with a big patch on each seat, long black stockings to the knee, and hobnailed boots, I started, with a little apprehension, the final term. After the first week, being stronger than many others, along with a schoolmate named George Rirby, I became a monitor.

I had to get to school each day now at 8.30 a.m. The cleaners and school caretaker would light the big coal fires in each classroom. Our duties consisted of refilling and keeping filled all the big coal buckets in each classroom. We used a big, solid-tyred four-wheeled trolley to carry the big buckets from the coal dump and we had to ensure that the fires were hot and blazing when school commenced or face the anger of Miss Gwladys Price. I had to learn how to ring and control the big school bell. The long chain hung down from the belfry in the centre of the small assembly hall. A steady pull on the chain would tilt the bell and allow the clanger to peel the sound then, the momentum of the big bell was allowed to swing back to its vertical position and sound the second peel and then the performance was repeated. It was difficult at first to gauge the correct interval when the bell rang its second peel but I soon got used to it and became quite an expert.

The 9 a.m. toll, 9.15 a.m. and 9.30 a.m. each morning, lunchtime and at the day's end – all these duties, including keeping all the blackboards clean for Miss Gwladys Price, and all my desk work, made it a long day. I worked hard and progressed very well but so often I received that awful drumming on the head with the end of the pencil when anything was wrong or incorrect but I put up with it and accepted it as one of those unhappy things in life.

March the first arrived, a big day in Wales – St David's Day. Leading up to this day all the schoolchildren had to learn word perfect many of the old traditional poems and songs of the departed bards and the poems and verse of Ceiriog and Islwyn, and prizes were given by the Welsh education authorities to each school for distribution in small eisteddfodau of music, song and verse. On that particular day we went to school at 8.30 a.m. In my position as monitor, I had to be in attendance at 8 o'clock. Everyone would be dressed in their best Sunday clothes and each and all, wearing a small leek or a daffodil as a buttonhole, had to assemble in the school hall. When the eisteddfod ended and the prizes distributed that morning, the remainder of the day was a half holiday. All the parents too, if they wished to come along and attend, were welcome.

About that period in that year of 1926 a letter came from California written by my Aunt Dot, my father's sister Dorothy some ten years older than him, to announce that in the following summer of 1927 she would be sailing across the Atlantic in one of the big ocean liners to pay us, and all the other members of her family, a three-month visit.

It appears that her previous visit had been during the late months of the year 1921 and I was too young to remember but at that time I was told there was a little controversy, because again and again she begged my parents to allow me to go back with her, for her to rear me and live with her in America. It appears also that I must have been a golden-haired, blue-eyed toddler with a mass of curly hair. Aunt Dot had no children and I believe she must have been a prominent, influential, well-off personality in the district where she lived, for even during those early years, she constantly spoke of driving everywhere in her luxury Ford motor car. She wanted to take me back with her so much, to bring me up, and anything or everything I needed I could have. My mother told me that my father wavered somewhat considering his own childhood and he was prepared to let me go but my mother refused to part with me.

Every birthday and Christmas time from then until she died, she sent me an expensive present, and so often a little jealousy crept in amongst my brothers and sisters. One of those gifts I kept and looked after so well, until I was 20 years of age and departed for military service, but it was broken and ruined by my young brother Trevor during my absence. It was a model of a complete electrical power station with all working movable parts and it would generate and supply enough power to light 23-volt bulbs. It was driven by a working steam engine from eight small steam boilers heated by a spirit lamp. I used it all through my youth, as it was my pride and joy, and I spent so many happy hours with it driving all kinds of wheels and models that I made from my Trix construction sets.

There was mention once again in this letter of 'Spalway', the name by which she always called me and the words also that she hoped this time that I would be coming back home with her. This became a big worry to me now and I continuously thought about it. I did not want to leave everyone and all my family and friends. It hurt me so many times when I did something wrong and my mother apprehended or chastised me and, jokingly, although I did not know, threatened to send me to America. It was an inward fear that stayed with me for a long time.

The summer approached in the first half of that year 1926; it was to be a glorious warm summer but industry was slowing down, unemployment increased so much and, once again, there were the sounds and threats that the minimum wage rates were to be reduced. There were murmurs of discontent everywhere, people could not live on the miserable sum of two pounds five shillings per week and large families were desperate. I still enjoyed the two annual outings that early July, the first with the Presbyterian Sunday School to Barry Island and the second with the Welsh Tabernacle located next door, on this occasion by train to Penarth. On this trip we had to walk down the new road from the recently completed new bridge and across the river to Pengam(mon) railway station to catch the train.

This railway line was the Brecon and Merthyr Railway. To me it was, and always will be, one of the most beautiful and scenic railways in the world. It has all disappeared now, destroyed, discontinued and ripped up by a decadent English Tory government to cut costs sometime after it had been nationalised and state owned to form part of British Rail by the previous post Second World War labour government. On this wonderful trip we travelled down the east side of the Rhymney Valley, through the tongue twisting Welsh-named villages of Maes-y-cymmer and Pontlanfraith and across the long, high steel viaduct east of Llanbradach and Ystrad Mynach to Caerphilly.

From the carriage windows we could see the old picturesque Caerphilly castle and through the long tunnel, skirting below the fairy castle – Castelle Goch – the red castle, bypassing Cardiff, and on to Penarth. Penarth was a very nice, busy seaside resort but disappointing to us as children as it had no sandy beach. The beaches were entirely pebbles, round, oval and smooth, about the size of a hen's egg, about 18 inches in depth. Below the main promenade the authorities had constructed three square concrete pools on the pebble beach. With the incoming tide they filled with sea water and as the tide went out they remained full enough for children to paddle instead of going down to the waves. That morning the tide was out, I was dressed in my best white short trousers and a white knitted jersey with a sailor's collar. Young, carefree and excited I ran around the concrete edge of one of those pools. Unknown to me it was slippery and wet with the receding tide. I fell head over heels into that pool; the bottom was inches deep in mud, and when I was pulled out my white suit was black with mud and ruined. I ruined my day, and my poor mother's day also! I had no replacement clothes on hand and I was left with my father and others, whilst mother went into town to buy more clothes for me. I was glad to get home. What I believed was going to be a wonderful day turned out to be a disaster.

The end of my infant schooldays came that July, and the whole month of August was the school's summer holidays, just before I was to begin my early days at Gilfach Bargoed boy's school. The Welsh language is a wonderful, rich, soft musical language to anyone who knows and understands it. It varies and changes its mode to avoid the pronunciation of harsh consonants; the town of Bargoed, for example, when modified by the word 'Gilfach' introduces a mutation, so instead of pronouncing the harsh letter 'B' after Gilfach it changes to the letter 'F', which in turn is pronounced as the letter 'V'. It all sounds so complicated, but there is no letter 'V' in the language, the letter 'F' is sounded as 'V' and the double 'F' is an 'F', so our village was Gilfach Fargoed.

Industrial turmoil began in that year 1926 and another big national strike began over the reduction in wages. Money was to become so scarce now, there were no wages, allowances for children only to avoid desperate poverty and hunger. My sisters Joyce and Edna went to Bourneville outside Birmingham to stay and live with the Butler family, who volunteered to take them until things improved. They were friends of ours, who were officials at the Cadbury's cocoa and chocolate works in Bourneville and not affected by the turmoil.

My brother Gwyn was attending Lewis's Grammar School at Pengam. He was a brilliant scholar – he had won a rich scholarship to keep him there – and my parents did not wish to upset his progress. His whole environment was built around books and study and so often through my schooldays we clashed, because he could not understand why I did not swot and study before examinations. When I was taught anything I digested it thoroughly and I relied on my memory for all examinations. All through my schooldays it pulled me through into the top ten in every class. In those days it was always merit that counted in everything.

Gwyn and I were entirely different in that way. I preferred to be outdoors doing and making all kinds of things with the skill of my hands, thinking and working out in my mind all kinds of different projects. My sister Edna also was attending Hengoed Girls Grammar School and Joyce too was shortly to attend this school, so things were very difficult for us all. The beginning of August 1926 I went to Granny's place to stay to help out with the financial troubles now affecting the family and just prior to this move I obtained two separate jobs at sixpence each, carried out and completed each Saturday.

That first job was rather odd and most unusual for any small boy of seven years to fulfil. Sister Joyce had performed her duties in this particular job for a long time and, as she was leaving the district, it was passed on to me and I shall try to describe it in my own way. I have mentioned many times previously Old Bratt the Jew, a well-known local character who owned and operated a secondhand shop and a pawnshop combined. Eli Bratt was a typical 'Shylock', as whatever he bought or sold he always seemed to obtain his Pound of Flesh.

He was a bald, wizened, black-bearded old man, always dressed in the same old clothes year after year. His nose was long and peaked, so familiar to his race, and he walked with the aid of a crooked, curled walking stick, with a shiny silver grip. He lived alone in the last house of Gwerthonor Road, on the bend and at the top of Grammar School hill. He was a devout orthodox Jew and he kept rigidly and strictly to all the rules of his religion. His Sabbath began at midnight on Friday and ended at midnight on Saturday. His shop always remained shuttered and closed all day Saturday.

On the first day I took over from Joyce I had to go along with her to learn the routine, so my first job began. When we arrived at Old Bratt's house at 8 a.m. the first Saturday, the first rule was carried out. We had to knock with the big front door knocker six times only. This indicated to Bratt the business of the caller; no other knock would be answered or recognised throughout his whole Sabbath day. Bratt withdrew the bolts of the door and opened it ajar to view his callers. He knew that I was Joyce's brother, and she explained that she had to go away and I would take over and stand in for her during her absence, and it was accepted by Mr Bratt. He was wearing his little skullcap on the bald head, an ornamented cloak around his shoulders, and carrying his huge religious book, from which he read, and chanted, all day Saturday.

The house was dark and smelled musty, all the curtains were drawn as always as we walked along the entrance passage to the middle living room. Many candles were burning in that room, to me it was a room of mystery and secrecy. There was some old furniture and oddments around the room and one big leather armchair draped with coloured cloth and beads where Old Bratt sat and went through his ritual each Sabbath day. I received the instructions now from Joyce. Firstly, under the supervision of Old Bratt, we opened the back door. There were six heavy bolts, two at the top, two in the centre and two at the bottom, and the window at the side in this small kitchenette was covered with heavy iron bars.

Opposite the back-door entrance was the building for storing the coal (all the buildings possessed them) and known to us as the coalhouse. It was replenished and filled by the coalman from a small outer trapdoor facing the back lane. We filled the big bucket with pieces of coal and a bundle of sticks from this coalhouse and carried it inside to the living room. I must explain also, sticks were sold in the shops and oil shops in bundles of ten, approximately one foot in length and about one inch square, all bound together with a length of thin wire. Old Bratt sold the bundles from his own shop priced at threepence per bundle. They were obtained from a local stickman who bought all the disgarded Norwegian pine pit props for this purpose. We now set and lit the living room fire, waited until it was burning well, piled it up with extra coal, filled the big kettle and placed it on the iron hob to heat.

We left the premises and heard the big bolts pushed home behind us. Closing and bolting his doors was the one and only manual task performed by Mr Bratt during the Sabbath; we never discovered if he ate anything but we knew nothing was ever cooked, although he always had an old boiling fowl steeped in a big iron saucepan, during all our visits. We returned at midday to perform the same important six knocks, poked the fire, restacked and refuelled it and left again in the same way. At 4 p.m., once again we knocked on the door, poked the fire, refuelled it for the last time and left the premises. Our payment was one whole sixpence, to go through this routine each Saturday. Old Bratt would chant and read his religious works all day, he would perform no other task but bolt and unbolt the doors.

I did this job continuously for almost a whole year through all the inclement weather and winter days until Joyce returned and carried on once again. I have wondered all my life why all those stupid things go on; a person was not allowed to poke the fire on a certain day according to the religious rules, yet it was quite permissible to push home heavy bolts on a household door. Perhaps from that early age, that is the reason why I became a radical and rebelled against such stupidity and the destruction of things so precious from the past and the progress and beauty all around us.

My second job, which also earned me another sixpence, was in connection with my Uncle Dai – David John Davies – always referred to around the district as 'Dai Wasp'. Uncle Dai was a big powerful man, the eldest son of my grandfather David John Davies-Quarry, and of course my mother's brother. He was also a very skilled person and deeply involved in the mining industry. He was the chief 'overman' of the Britannia Colliery, that is, the third in seniority after the manager and under-manager. He was also the chief of the mining rescue team in the Rhymney Valley and on call at any time if a disaster occurred in any of the deep mines in the district. He obtained the nickname 'Dai Wasp' from the miners because of his efficiency, flitting from one district to another in the underground areas to ensure that everything was carried out properly and safely, but he was a very well respected man.

In his capacity as chief overman and an influential member of the management, he was permitted to carry home each day a 'block'. This block was cut off from an 8 or 10-inch diameter pit prop, which was split and cut into sticks to kindle the household coal fires. He was also privileged to have delivered regularly each month, free of charge, one ton of the best steam coal. A whole imperial ton could not be burned by one household in 28 days, so of course my cart was always around on the darkest nights, to cart away, secretly, down the back lanes to Oak Cottage, and deposit in our own coalhouse.

Every Saturday morning after Bratt's job was done, I made my way to 41 The Drive, Gwerthonor Site, to chop those blocks into the required sticks for kindling and lighting the fires. I would cut one full tea chest of those sticks, obtain payment of sixpence from Auntie May, then make my way back to Granny's and as things were so bad, I gave the two sixpences to my mother to help out and she, in turn, ordered and had delivered the one penny weekly *Boy's Magazine* in return.

That month of August 1926 was a beautiful warm sunny month and, as it was the school holidays, I was involved with the Stuckey brothers, Simon and Glyn next door, and all my schoolmates in that district called the 'Sloggers'. We had to provide our own entertainment, so it was often long treks up through the farms and across the mountain moors to an area we called 'Quarry Mawr'. This quarry had been used for hundreds of years to supply the stones that built both the miles and miles of dry stone walls which were used as fences dividing the areas into fields for pasture and stock, and all the old crofters' cottages which were burned down and destroyed by English invaders, of which only a few ruins remained. The old road to the area had been built originally by the Romans around AD 60 but it was still called the Roman Road. It had many offshoots and one of them branched off to the old original Roman Camp at Gelligaer. It was the

34

highest prominent area on the west side of the valley and in later
years, the Normans built the Gelligaer parish church in the year 1102,
where my parents were married many centuries later.

Across the valley to the east, we could see the highest point,
Bedwellty Norman church and, to the south east, the Tudor church
on Nynydd Islwyn. All were used as signal points to warn off
approaching travellers or English intruders entering the valley in
earlier times. Quarry Mawr was a wonderful place where I spent
many, many hours of my schooldays. The floor of the quarry had
become a huge, deep, crystal-clear pool; the pure mountain water
seeped through the rocks and dripped down to the pool below. This
was the place where I learned how to swim. It was completely sheltered all around by the high rock walls which kept out the wind and
the sun shone directly on to the pool all day long.

Day after day during those warm days we would trek the five
miles or so to that pool, complete with a packet of sandwiches for
refreshment and a bottle of homemade ginger beer, usually purchased
from Mrs Wyatt from her choice variety of five delicious flavours:
stinging nettle, dandelion, burdock, elderflower and wild sloe. I must
digress at this point and write in remembrance of old Mrs Wyatt, that
amazing lady, feared so much, whom I believed in those young infant
schooldays was a true witch. To our knowledge, she had no offspring
or relatives of any kind. She resided in the next house to my Uncle
Dai, 39 The Drive. I would never go alone to her door and over the
years I collected bundles and baskets of everything she required for
her ingredients but I would not deliver them unless my sister Joyce
or my mother came along with me.

Her husband had been killed in the First World War and she
received a miserable pension, using my mother's words, of ten shillings per week to live on. This amount was not enough to exist on
alone, so she supplemented her income by dispensing all her mystery
herbs and medicines and selling her wines, ginger beers, slabs of
toffee, homemade sweets, jellies, jams and so on. Her living room was
the back kitchen, her bedroom upstairs, the parlour downstairs was the
place she dispensed and sold her wares, the middle room was full of
big earthenware pans, bottles, demijohns, containers, brown paper
packages and other storage containers, fermenting wines and mixtures. She made and bottled numerous kinds of homemade wines,
including parsnip, elderberry, potato, wild slough (slow)*, blackberry

* Local children's slang for sloe.

35

and rhubarb. They were sold to the neighbours and residents of the village for the price of six shillings per bottle. My father always purchased for Christmas each year a bottle of the wild sloe; it tasted something like whisky with a slight plum flavour, and it was considered an excellent tonic.

As I grew older, along with the Crane brothers during the autumn, I picked many baskets of the sloes from the woods around for Mrs Wyatt, for the price of sixpence a basket. The sloe was a very small plum a little more flat than the damson in appearance; when it was fully ripe it developed a pale purple of damson colour. I guess it must be related to the small damson plum in some way. Another crop we collected for her regularly was the crab apple and the winberry; the crabs grew so abundantly in the local woods and the winberries on the mountainsides and on the moors amongst the tall bracken.

When fully ripe at the end of September, the crab apple is delicious and as children, to us far more tasty than the orchard apple. We picked the crab apples for Mrs Wyatt before they matured and from these apples she produced the most sought-after, wonderful crab apple jelly. Despite my own apprehension for Mrs Wyatt, she was a kind lady full of compassion, and always on hand if anyone was sick or seriously ill, her ingredients, cures and herbal medicines were always readily available. One particular remedy I remember well because I was doctored with it on a number of occasions.

This remedy was warm goose grease applied to the chest with a bread poultice to release the congestion caused by a heavy cold. Added to the grease was some secret mixture; it did the job, and certainly worked well! Mrs Wyatt was also a devoted follower of reading the tea leaves in the residue of the cup and she was welcome when the neighbours and residents gathered for their cups of tea so that she could read out their fate and fortune in their superstitious ways. At any time she could supply all and every recipe for cakes, puddings, and all the cooked foods, if anyone requested them, and her advice was never ending.

Many things she kept secretly, and would not disclose to anyone the methods, additives and ingredients or the making of all her homemade confectionary, wines, and all those wonderful ginger and root beers. Mrs Wyatt died just prior to the Second World War. All her mourners were local residents and neighbours, there were no next of kin and she carried all her secrets with her to the grave.

On our way home from our swimming excursions our brown paper bag, now minus the sandwiches, was often used to collect the winberries. They grew on a small bush rarely higher than one foot in height and they cropped heavily if they were out of the way of the mountain sheep. The berries were a deep purple in colour about the size of a blackcurrant, with a flattened top where the stalk attached to the bush. They had a delicious taste difficult to describe, the flavour was entirely different from any other berry that I have known and the juice was the colour of a deep mulberry. They were in great demand because they made wonderful pies and tarts and the only drawback with them, although we did not mind, was picking them. It was very tedious and it took a long time to fill the bag or container.

Every boy carried a pocket knife of various types and sizes. It was considered a recognised and much common practice, far more important to us than a handkerchief and, of course, there was no such thing as wristwatches; the only watches that we ever knew of were the ones worn by men on the end of a chain and tucked into the waistcoat pocket. The pocket knife was a tool for almost everything in our youth and my own pocket knife was a combination affair; it had been given to me by Tom Carter. It contained two blades, a tiny saw, a tin opener and a sharp-pointed awl.

During all my ramblings with the boys from the 'Sloggers' we usually put those knives to good use. I received lots of instructions in making the dolly clothes pegs, the pea whistle and the pea shooter. The pegs were made from holly branches. We would find suitable offshoots of the holly about three-quarters of an inch in thickness (these offshoots were always straight and true), and cut off the sections of about six inches and shape them accordingly. When one dozen had been completed a long twig was pushed along the forks to hold them all together, then they were carried home to be finished off with a band of tin secured by a small nail around the top of the splayed forks.

There were no spring pegs during those times; no one would ever buy pegs, they were all homemade and Mum always had a good supply. The pea whistle was made from the thick elderberry twigs, the elderberry was the most suitable, although the willow was quite good, but preference was given to the elderberry. When it was freshly cut and soaked in water for a few minutes the inner wood core slipped out of the bark exterior easily, then all we had to do to complete the whistle, was to cut the holes, shape the mouthpiece and the splines along the wood. We could now blow into the mouthpiece moving the inner wood core backwards and forwards to vary the piercing whistle. The pea shooters were always plentiful and made by cutting the stems of the wild hock, a plant that grew very similar to a big thistle, with a long stem and big broad leaves. The stem was hollow, just the correct size to use the big hawthorn berries as missiles.

During the last week of August of that year 1926, things were going from bad to worse, and evidence was beginning to show that many folk were going hungry; there were no wages and no relief. Almost three miles along the road south from Gilfach there was situated the small village of Tir-y-beth. All the houses, street after street of conjoined terraces, had been erected by the Powell-Dyffryn Company to lease and rent to the imported migrants from Ireland and across the border from England to work in their mines after the First World War. There was no school at Tir-y-beth and all the children over the age of seven years had to walk to Gilfach boys and girls schools each day through every kind of weather.

Many of their parents were almost destitute and evictions from the houses were becoming a common practice. A big public meeting was mooted by all the local Gilfach residents. The town crier went through the village ringing his bell and orating the message in all the different streets and residential areas. They decided at the meeting to organise a big food and soup kitchen because things were so bad. From collections and a large grant from the miners' organisation the food kitchen was set up in the big hall beneath the Gilfach Presbyterian church.

From that time onwards until December 1926 over one thousand children from Gilfach, Pengam, Cascade and Tir-y-beth were given three meals a day in that hall. Everyone gave their time and labour to assist in the food hall and I still have many vivid memories of what happened during those winter months. Many of the young boys and girls from Tir-y-beth trudged through the snow in bare feet, because they had no boots but they reached that hall for breakfast each day before the start of school and then were ushered by the teachers in line to thaw out their feet before the classroom fires. I remember, too, many, many times carrying to school some leftovers and toast crusts in a jam-jar container for some of the boys who were my classmates, the ones who had failed to get there for breakfast because of something wrong at home and they had not eaten anything since midday the day before. This often happened on Monday, because there was one meal only on the Sunday at midday.

I had used my hand cart to bring many things from home now that I was staying with Granny and Grandfather, my Trix building set stowed away in a wooden cast off orange box, a clockwork train set that wound up with a key to pull four carriages and a guard's van around the oval track, all kinds of odds and ends and many other possessions. The hooters from all the surrounding collieries were now silent, everything was on stop, the sky-lights at night had dimmed, and, for the first time in my life, I experienced long dark nights as I looked out of the window and across the valley to the north as I lay in bed in the back bedroom in Maes-y-craig Street. Grandfather was becoming poorly now, I guess the strain of the long hard life must have been starting to take effect. He would never tell me how old he was and I did not like to ask but I had seen written in his old Welsh Bible along with so many other names, David John Davies April 26th 1844 so I assumed, with my faint knowledge of mathematics for a seven year old, by subtracting with a pencil and paper 1884 from 1926, he must have reached the age of 82 years. It was at this time also, one Sunday afternoon, that I saw an aeroplane for the first time. It caused so much excitement that day, everyone rushed out of doors, and all eyes were gazing skywards to see this wonderful plane flying across the sky, although it was only a wood and canvas affair probably left over from the war. Everyone takes it for granted nowadays, with jet liners speeding through the skies but for me it was a red letter day in my life and the beginning of all those wonderful things that lay ahead. I read so many stories of aeroplanes and war planes in my *Boy's Magazine* but little did I know that in my lifetime I would actually see pictures of a man landing on the moon.

Another great thrill for me that September was to see a hot air balloon travelling through the sky from Bargoed Park to land across the valley for the opening of Blackwood Annual Show. Grandfather explained everything to me about this balloon. The heat to make it rise, carrying two occupants in the wicker basket slung below, was generated by a container filled with carbide, a system of dripping water on the carbide released the gas to ignite and make the hot air to fill the canvas balloon and float through the air. It seemed to drop so often but a boost of flame from the gas soon sent it skywards again.

It was about this time that we began to break the law. We had no alternative in order to help people around the neighbourhood. We had to take the risks irrespective of the consequences. The Crane brothers' grandfather – Tard (father) Davies as they always called him – was in charge of the Gilfach Level, situated on a hill outcrop behind the Gilfach Infants School. It was owned by an English Mining Company and, just like all the other industries, was at a standstill with the General Strike. Unless we crossed through the woods and fields, there was one access only north and south, to this level, a sunken lane, wide enough for the coal carts and their shire horses to get in and out. There were many tall oak trees in the area and our raids on the level went off like a military exercise. The trees were used as lookouts. It was no trouble at all for the young boys to climb to the top of those trees with a pea whistle in our pockets and use the warning call if any person in authority was in the neighbourhood. It was always a recognised sign that the distress or warning call on the whistle was a copy of the peewit bird call. This bird was a local inhabitant of the woods and moors and when disturbed made the distinct peewit call as it flew away and it was so easy to make a mock call with our whistles.

Our greatest worry was Noah Thomas, the policeman for the area of Pengam and the lower end of Gilfach. Everyone hated him, he was so sly with every movement he made, and he was distrusted by everybody. It was his greatest delight to chastise and clip around the ears all the innocent youths of the district on the slightest provocation. The main areas of Gilfach were covered by Thomas Folland but he was very slack in his duties and we usually knew all his movements. His routine never varied, so we could handle him in our own times accordingly. There were three policemen in the Bargoed area and one industrial police constable who roamed from mine to mine, and around the outcrops and levels, but the grapevine was so strong and everyone so loyal, the word was soon passed around when he was in the vicinity, so our greatest concern was Noah Thomas. Tard Davies knew what was going on but said nothing. He was loyal to the neighbourhood, so across those fields for hours on end we carried buckets and containers of lump coal depositing them in various coal houses and sheds around the district, making sure that no resident of our district would fail to have some heat and warmth and cooking fuel.

The older boys, and the men skilled in cutting and extracting coal, simply went into the level, loaded a 'Dandy', pushed it to the level entrance and we quickly disposed of it across the fields. This working bee arrangement worked well, the time was made, everyone cautiously turned up from all directions, the lookouts were posted, all the information about the copper was received on the grapevine and the job was done efficiently and quickly. We had no qualms about it at all, it was our land by birthright and our coal, not the property of absentee landlords, so we did it for all our close local community and countrymen.

The September of 1926 was the beginning of a new era for me, the beginning of school at Gilfach Boys school. I had just 50 yards to go from Granny's home in Maes-y-craig Street, and slip over the boundary wall into the school yard. My teacher, to begin, in standard one was Miss Doris Davies-Black referred to again in this way in the local fashion, being the daughter of Fred Davies the local undertaker. She was born and bred in Gwerthonor Place, the road adjoining Gwerthonor Road, and of course she knew everyone, all the boys she taught, their parents and grandparents, as was the custom of everyone knowing the natives of the area.

I was very fond of Miss Davies, she was kind, considerate, and helpful in every way and I soon progressed very well in all my schoolwork. I was just seven years and one month of age at this time and I had done more things in my life at this tender age than the majority twice my age. Life was getting much tougher now with all the bigger boys of the school up to the age of 14 years, and there were many bullies amongst them, which I suppose would be a common thing with anyone's schooldays but I managed to hold my own and get by. I always had help and protection from the older Stucky brothers who lived next door to Granny, the Powells of the 'Sloggers' area, a family of ten sons and two daughters, with five of those boys between the age of seven and 14 years, and there was also Francis Court and Lera Sharpe the sons of those two huge, powerful, local gasmen.

I had permission now also from Granny to go to the penny pictures on a Monday and Saturday afternoon. This was a great treat in our young lives. At 4.30 p.m. on Mondays as soon as school ended we would run all the way to the Palace Cinema in Bargoed to follow the silent picture western serials; breathless and excited we would get there to just miss the first five minutes or so of the picture. On Saturday afternoon at 2.30 p.m. much more leisurely we would make our way to the Palace once again. On these occasions there was one important stop that was rarely missed. We would call at Brobyn's the fruitiers, in High Street, and, for the price of one halfpenny, we obtained a large paper bag of cut apples.

The proprietor of the establishment had a system with all his fruit that was partly affected by bruising, rot or other problems, towards the end of the week. The affected fruit was cut to remove the sections that had turned bad or rotted, and the sound part of the fruit retained and placed in a special bin. To us all as young boys we considered it a wonderful bargain to obtain a large bag of these cut apples and pears – although they were usually brown from the exposed mutilation, for the price of just one halfpenny, and we had a wonderful feast as we

41

cheered and cried out in the excitement of watching those thrilling silent films. I always made it back home again in time to fulfil my duty with Old Bratt's fireplace and obtain my wages of that huge sum of sixpence.

During those troubled times everyone, young and old, were smokers of either a pipe or cigarettes. All the cigarette packets contained a picture card that made up to a series of 50 to complete the set. These cards were in great demand among the children and, as a result of this, games developed in order to win those cards and perhaps add to the collection or complete a set. The first of those popular games was called 'Pecks', and just like all the other boys I became involved because I was an ardent collector of those cards. The game involved many competitors who sought eagerly after those picture cards and a number of cards were nominated to 'put up' to start the game. The number of cards nominated and agreed upon to play a game were divided up into pairs, trebles or fours and placed at a ten-degree angle, face inwards, against the concrete or brick base of the school wall. From a distance of three yards, each player, in turn would peck or propel his own master card, held between the index and second finger, at the line of cards along the wall. All the cards that were knocked down and lying face upwards became the possession of the pecker and so the game went on until all the cards were knocked down and claimed.

Another game was called 'Blows', again a number was nominated and the pile of cards placed face down on the school brick windowsills. Each player was now allowed one puff from the left or right of the pile to try and turn over the cards, face up. That player kept any cards he turned over and the order of taking part was made by the toss of a coin. With all these games, football, handball, marbles and so many others there was never a dull moment in the school yard during those recreational times before and after school.

Another popular game we played so often, I must mention, although it was banned on the school premises because of so many broken windows, was called 'Dog and Cat' or 'Dog and Catty'. In order to play this game we cut a straight strong stick about three feet in length, and a small stick of the same thickness, about six inches in length. The smaller stick was sharply pointed at each end with a pocket knife, and called the 'cat' or 'catty', the long stick was the dog. A line was drawn as a boundary or starting line and, from any position behind this line the competitors in turn tapped the pointed end of the 'cat', with the dog stick to make it jump and fly upwards. When the 'cat' was in its upward flight an attempt was made to hit and drive the 'cat' as far as possible with the dog stick. The distance of the drive was paced out by jumps, as far as possible, by the biggest jumping opponent and added to complete the score of the team. Three attempts or hits were allowed to each player and all misses were his bad luck and failed to add to the score.

September also, was a busy time for many other things and pastimes after school. There were blackberries and winberries to be picked, the annual trek across the moors and through the woods for the sloes and crab apples for Mrs Wyatt and our winter supplies of filberts – the hazelnut. It was usually a race between the squirrels and ourselves to obtain big supplies of filberts from one of our special areas. Across the moors, west of our swimming area, Quarry Mawr, at some time in the past, a large wood or plantation must have been established by some hard-working farmer or crofter, and it continued to grow, expand and flourish over the generations.

We could usually pick and collect a full pillowslip of nuts in about half an hour, and I suppose we were always greedy in the picking by looking for the 'Peggy' sixes up to the 'Peggy' tens. To give a more simple explanation, the nuts grew in clusters of pairs, trebles etc. up to the clusters of ten, and they were referred to in our way of speaking as peggy two, peggy three, peggy four etc. The greatest cluster we ever found was ten and this was exceptional. The days were getting shorter, it was almost five miles each way so we had to hurry to obtain our supplies and get home before dark. If the weather was too bad and we were unable to get there, we had to be satisfied with our collection along the hedgerows and in the woods. We carried them home, tipped them out in the shed and allowed them to dry until the husks fell away to give us a good supply of beautiful hazelnuts for Christmas and the winter months.

Amongst all the different characters and individuals who lived in our village of Gilfach, there was one other person I must mention and write about because he came into our everyday lives so often as I grew up. His name was Davy Bennett. He was a tall, thin individual, well liked in all his simple ways, and always wearing the appearance of a permanent smile on his face, displaying a row of big buck teeth. According to my mother he was about 40 years of age with a mind of a two year old. He was unfortunately referred to and denigrated as the village idiot.

The explanation from mother once again, 'He fell off the table when he was two years old and damaged his brain.' All people like Davy, during those ignorant years, were taken away and locked up in a lunatic asylum for the rest of their lives. Davy had been carried off to Bridgend Asylum many times but he always escaped and found his way back to Gilfach. The authorities finally allowed him to stay with his parents in Thomas Street. He must have had a bed or couch to sleep on but he wasn't wanted by his parents. He was neglected and uncared for and it was the local residents and church authorities who gave him food and clothing.

He was a regular caller at Granny's home, and to Oak Cottage where he always received something to eat, and his attraction and fascination at Granny's was a West African Red Parrot in the big cage hanging in the back kitchen. This parrot was talkative and could repeat and mock anything. His visit to Oak Cottage was always a request for a 'piece' – a piece of bread and jam – and sometimes repairs to his 'Bowly', an odd term perhaps to use for this article but this was its common name and where I was involved. Davy was a constant follower of the steam road roller. Everyday and all day from morning till the end of the working day he kept up with a steam roller and often, to his great delight, was given rides on the machine. It was his greatest joy and fascination.

Davy also carried with him wherever he went the 'Bowly', and a 'Guidor'; this was the term given and used by the children and I can smile as I try to explain it because it was a toy used in no other place but South Wales, that is, of this particular variety. In the coal mining areas with plenty of coal and iron etc., everyone used iron buckets. There were no such things as rust-proof galvanised buckets for containers. When they became badly dented, rusted, or holed they were discarded and carried away by the garbage men and dumped on the refuse tip. This particular bucket had a high-looped handle made from half-inch iron slightly concaved in order to carry it more comfortably, with a small loop at each end housed in a hasp, allowing it to swivel to either side of the bucket.

We made many visits to the tip to recover these handles, they were so useful to us and we could utilise them in so many ways, and of course, they were free of charge. When the loops had been straightened with a few blows of the hammer we took them along to the railway sidings to get the concave straightened also. I feel guilty now about the crude and dangerous methods we used to remove the concave. Our friends, the gangers, with the shunting wagons, would willingly place those straightened handles along the railway rails and allow the loaded 30-ton wagons to ride over them compressing them into perfectly flat, three-quarter inch pieces of iron. Grandfather was our next client and, with the kitchen fire, now that his forge days had ended, and with the anvil in the backyard, he would fuse those pieces into a perfect iron hoop, which was to become the 'bowly'.

Another piece with a right-angled bend of three inches at one end became the 'guidor'. The guidor pushed against the bowly made it revolve and the harder one pushed the faster the hoop would go, and when it was allowed to free-wheel it could be steered by the guidor. The pranksters and bullies of the village often stole and hid Davy's bowly and so often he would come along to Oak Cottage in tears and crying for me to get him a replacement and so I had to do my good deed. These straightened iron handles also made the runners on the sleds we made to sledge down the slopes in the snow. Turning the sled upside down, thoroughly wetting the iron runners and leaving them out at night they became coated with ice which helped us to speed down hill in the snow.

October of that year slipped away and Bonfire Night arrived in the usual way with our local celebrations. It must have been around 3rd November, with all its dreary days of rain, low clouds and mist. From memory now it was a Thursday evening, the rain was beating against the kitchen window with a driving wind from the north, the old pendulum mantle clock with the fading face numbers, sitting on the centre of the mantelpiece was ticking away the seconds faithfully as it had done for so many years. The fire was blazing hotly in the big grate; Granny had just heaped on more coal, and the big cast-iron kettle on the hob was steaming away with a slight singing purr. The oil lamp was burning brightly on the kitchen table; the highly polished brass base and fluted oil tank was gleaming in the reflected red fire-light. That beautiful old oil lamp with its bulbous chimney and its decorated outer-glass scalloped surround threw shadows across the old Welsh dresser against the wall, picking out the rows of china plates and the big glazed tureen as they leaned against the old oak timbers.

Granny was sitting in an upright wooden kitchen chair on the left of the fireplace, her usual place, as she darned and mended an article of clothing. Grandfather had been confined to bed for some three days, not feeling very well, but now he was sitting in his big oak armchair on the right of the fireplace, a pair of steel-rimmed glasses on the end of his nose. He had just finished reading the *South Wales Echo*, the evening paper, and on his lap, as was the custom, he had taken up his old Welsh Bible. On occasions such as this he seemed to enjoy his pipe. He wasn't a heavy smoker but he possessed a variety of different pipes hanging in a pipe rack at the end of the high mantelshelf, just clear of the tapestry and lace surround that was draped around the edge of the mantelpiece, with all the little tassel balls moving with the rising heat from the fire.

His tobacco was stored away in a brass tobacco tin sealed down with a tight-fitting lid, highly polished of course – Granny would see to that – and sitting in a special place on the mantelpiece. The tobacco was 'twist'. Commonly called that name, it was thick black plugs of tobacco just like sticks of liquorice, cut into small pieces with a knife, and rolled between the palms to fill up the bowl of the pipe. It was slightly aromatic, but it often caught you in the throat if you experienced a strong whiff of it, and it made you cough. Down by his side on the end of the cast-iron stand in front of the grate, there stood a brass container shaped like a mug and filled with homemade, tightly rolled paper tapers used to light his pipe whenever he needed them. These tapers were rolled and kept in plentiful supply by the ever busy fingers of dear old Granny.

I was sitting at the kitchen table, my clockwork train set going around and around its oval track. The pendulum clock had just given one strike, the time just after 8.30 p.m., and almost my bedtime at nine o'clock. Grandfather had lit his pipe. He turned in his chair and he said to me, from what I remember now something like – 'You are fond of the trains Ron Bach? Do you know that we were connected with the first steam engine that was invented and built a long time ago?'

I pricked up my ears when he asked me this question because I did not know what he meant. I told him that I was a keen collector of the steam engine numbers just like many of the other boys and, at home I had recorded the numbers of some 21 tank engines from the Brecon and Methyr line and many more of the goods-class engines that pulled the long lines of coal wagons down the valley on the Great Western Line. The tank engine fascinated me, referred to as the tank engine because it was built with a long oblong tank with square sides. The front opening with its two handles were all made of solid brass, the funnel and the centre steam dome was brass also and all the various handles and plates around the engine were made of brass. The engine driver and the fireman kept all this brassware highly polished and it gleamed with the sun's rays striking it at different angles as it puffed along on its two-three-two wheels on that wonderful Brecon and Methyr line, one of the most picturesque railways of the world.

Grandfather then beckoned me to him for what I believed to be an explanation of the question. He opened his Bible to one of the notary pages and he pointed out to me amongst some other signatures the signed names of Richard Trevithick and Andrew Vivian Trevithick 1805, and he said or words to the effect, 'Have you heard of this name Richard Trevithick at school, or do you know anything about him?' My answer of course at that young age was in the negative. With a few Welsh syllables rolling off his tongue, something I did not understand, he said, 'I must tell you something about it.'

'My father's father, was an iron smelter and an engineer. His name, just like mine, my father's and my son's – your Uncle Dai – was David John Davies. He spoke Welsh only, he had no knowledge of the English language; he lived at Penydarren just outside the town of Merthyr Tydfyl and he was the chief smelter and engineer at Homfray's Penydarren Iron works. This man, whose signature you see written here, was a very clever man, he was born in Cornwall, and many Cornishmen at that time could understand the old Welsh language. Sometime around the year 1800, he went to London, and with his cousin Andrew Vivian Trevithick, the other signature here, they built the first steam carriage to run between Holborn and Paddington. The roads were so bad and hopeless, the carriage became damaged and broken, although the pressure steam engine was a success. He came to Merthyr Tydfyl about 1802 and lived with our family at Penydarren. He was encouraged to use his skills at the iron works and, with my grandfather's skills also, as his chief assistant, he perfected and invented the first steam pressure locomotive in the world. They laid a steel track, all smeltered and rolled at Homfray's iron works, on small steel bars, tree trunks and strong branches, two feet six inches wide, all the way from Penydarren to Abercynon, just over ten miles in length. By February 1804, Richard had finished the locomotive engine and during that month they coupled five wagons loaded with ten tons of iron ore to that engine. They then added more wagons, and the 70 men from the Homfray works clambered on to those wagons.

'That wonderful locomotive pulled them all along the prepared railway track, at a speed of five miles per hour, all the way to Abercynon, over ten miles. It was the first railway in the world, ten years before George Stephenson's Puffing Billy and before James Watt. Richard was the first man also to patent the use of iron to build ships. They all thought he was mad, believing any ship made of iron would immediately sink.

47

'In the year 1819 his pressure steam engine propelled the first iron-built ship, the steamship *Savannah* across the Atlantic Ocean. He went to South America to use and install his pressure steam engines in the silver mines of Peru. He fell ill with the climate and conditions and returned to this country, and he came back to Penydarren and stayed with my grandfather's family – our family. He died penniless, and a sick man in 1833, about 10 years or so before I was born. All our family, friends and countrymen, helped to petition the English Parliament for a pension and reward, for what he had given the country and the whole world, but he was ignored.'

I felt so proud that evening to hear this wonderful story and Richard Trevithick became one of the greatest heroes of my schooldays. In 1930, when I was 11 years old, I was encouraged by my teacher Jim Watkins at Gilfach School to enter the school essay that I had written on the 'Steam Age' in the Annual County School Essay Competition. I won first prize, the huge sum of ten guineas. I had never had so much money in all my life! It was as a result of Grandfather, Great Grandfather and Richard Trevithick! Richard Trevithick is remembered now by a stained-glass window in Westminster Abbey, paid for and inserted by the grateful citizens of Cornwall and South Wales, ignored and forgotten by the pompous English Parliament, after he had given so much to the world. Less than 100 years later Great Grandfather's railway track from Penydarren to Abercynon became part of the railway track of the Brecon and Merthyr railway.

Every time I clambered over the arched viaducts to pick out the numbers of the tank engines, and each time I rode in those ancient carriages, with their separate compartments decorated with framed pictures of that scenic railway, I felt so proud it was my railway – my great grandfather's railway! In my old age now, with all the modern electric and diesel trains, the fast bullet trains, and all the millions of miles of modern railways in every country of the world, I can ponder and wonder, because it all began just a few miles away from where I was born, on the railway track smeltered, milled, rolled, and crudely laid, by my great grandfather, David John Davies.

The end of November and the first night of winter came around once again and I was looking ahead for Christmas. During December of that year, 15 banks of the huge coke ovens closed down, and much of the by-products works were dismantled. I was beginning to understand that petroleum and the use and discovery of huge reserves of oil throughout the world was making the use of coal decline. It was also a ploy by the big companies to beat the rising demands of the miners. Their money could be switched to the cheap labour oil-producing regions of Persia and the Middle East. There were 97 different by-products from coal. The patent chemical garden fertilisers, and everything from margarine oil to benzine. There was also a small distillation plant that produced high-grade petrol from coal in the Bargoed work site, the first in the world at that time, and the greedy company directors, all lords and dukes from across the border, had it destroyed. It was blown up with explosives: they were afraid of competition with their new riches from the Middle East and the growing demand for oil, as the internal combustion engines of cars, transport and machinery began.

I was getting on very well at school with Miss Doris Davies-Black. Everything was based on merit, nothing else mattered. At the end of each term we had the terminal exams and each class at every standard was divided into A, B, and C. The brighter pupils were graded in A and the not so good in B and C. My class at this stage was 1A and I came second in my class for that term. My brother Gwyn of course was so pleased. He was considered to have the academic brains of the family but I proved my worth and I was going to improve even more.

My present for Christmas, as the end of that unhappy year of 1926 drew to a close, was a football and, as conditions were so bad, I had a feeling that my grandfather had something to do with it. Granny and Grandfather had been thrifty all their lives and they received, using Mum's words once again, a miserable pension of nine shillings and sixpence per week for the loss of a son, William, in the war. I was sure they must have contributed the greater part of the funds to purchase the ball, although I know the price was just seven shillings and sixpence.

It was the first among the young boys of our district. We usually played with a small rubber ball, and often a compressed bunch of newspaper, tied up and rounded into the shape of a ball. Tom Carter now helped us and coached us all; he was a brilliant player at every position on the football field. We also obtained the help of George Gummer the son of Geo Gummer (snr) who rented the field where we played. It became known as Gummer's Field. My father came along often, and taught us how to control the ball, the correct way to kick the ball in our instep instead of the toe, trapping and heeling. He organised the formation of our team and each Saturday afternoon we played against one of the other villages of the district.

The Hughes family, my mother's sister Florence, moved away to the Coventry industrial area in the English Midlands at the end of December, hoping they could improve themselves. As a result we had a new neighbour – Stan Davies and his wife Caroline. He was the local co-operative bread roundsman with his horse Mary, and the colourful baker's cart. The motor car was improving and developing so much, Coventry was becoming a huge production area for petrol engines and the Hughes wanted to be part of it. Sadly for me it was the last time I saw Billy and Effy Hughes, my cousins, I cannot ever remember meeting them again.

The Prices – Miss Gwladys, Janet and Alice – purchased their first motor car that December also. It was an Austin tourer type with celluloid windows all around the sides, and a canvas removable top. We were invited to have a ride and Noah Thomas, the bobby, was there giving all the advice in the world, what to do, and how to go about things, and in my young mind the sly silly old fool knew nothing at all about it.

Gwerthonor Road, along with another secluded road called Hillside Park, was one of the snob and elite residential areas of the village. Ironically we had nothing and lived at the Gilfach end of that road. Noah Thomas took particular interest in this road because so many of the influential residents of the area lived there. Using one of my mother's funny expressions once again, 'He wanted to keep in with them and rub noses with them all.' At that time I could reel off and name every resident along that road, and I can still remember such people as T C Jones, the 'Gaffer' of Gilfach school, Hughes the parish vicar, Mr Tegwyn Mathews the district manager of the Great Western Railway, Mr Wright the 'Gaffer' of Lewis's Grammar School, Major Perrott the one-armed PT instructor at the Grammar School, and two English Justices of the Peace, who had no mercy for anyone brought before them at Bargoed police court.

As young boys we had to be quiet and correct making our way along the road to the railway station for the newspapers, or to the lower end of the 'jungle' and Green Meadow, in case Noah Thomas was on the prowl. We would certainly receive a heavy clout across the head if we were caught peering through the front garden hedges or through the gates, or even loitering anywhere along that road.

New Year's Day arrived, the beginning of the year 1927. It was going to be another sad year, so many things were about to happen suddenly, incidents we could not foretell. Our New Year rituals went on in the same old way, although with the 'throwing out of money' the amounts were greatly reduced. The tradespeople had experienced a bad year also, with little trade due to the lack of spending power by the residents. A few of the small shops closed down, and the corn shop and the china shop in Gwerthonor Place put up their shutters for the last time. The Penny Bazaar, the Big Bon Marche and many other shops in the Bargoed area closed their doors for the last time. Joyce and Edna, my sisters were still absent in Bourneville but the big strike had at last come to an end.

My hand cart was in use once again, when I moved the last of my personal things from Granny's place back to Oak Cottage. The Prices also moved house, and vacated their home in Gwerthonor Road. Their home was sold to Mr Gonton, the new manager of the Gelligaer Urban District Council public bus transportation service. The bus service was being modernised with lots of new green buses as the motor car industry increased and progressed.

The Price family now moved into Gwerthonor House. It was the biggest house in the area, the residence of the Gwerthonor Estate and originally occupied by the local squire whose power and influence controlled the district and represented the Marquis of Bute. I was to become involved with this move along with my father, and once again my devoted hand cart would be used to carefully carry the various small valuables and china. All the bigger furniture and possessions were packed on the Garlande's four-wheeled flat coal cart, especially washed down for the occasion. It was pulled along by one of the quietest of the big shire horses dressed up with all its best horse brasses, polished harnesses and reins.

Gwerthonor House had always been a mystery to me and all my young friends. I had never been inside the place before. On the north and west sides it was protected by a high, thick, massive stone wall fully twelve feet in height. The top of this wall for its whole length had a thick heavy layer of mortar and embedded in that mortar, and protruding in all directions were sharp-pointed pieces of jagged glass, so that it made it difficult for any intruder to get over the top. Along the eastern and southern sides an eight-feet-high wrought-iron fence bordered the perimeter. The top of that fence had sharp ornamental spikes, and the distance between the upright rods was just four inches, so mischievous youths, like me, could not even get their heads through the limited space. Inside the fence on the eastern side there was a thick hawthorn hedge and on the south side a high cultivated laurel hedge, tended and cultivated for the laurel berries. Our intrusions into the mysterious areas behind the fences were nil. We would not get in despite all our youthful efforts to raid the beautiful apple trees that grew inside.

The wall to the north contained a big, arched oak door with heavy bolts through the timbers, and a large peep-hole operated from the inside as a slide opening to the side.

The stables entrance at the end of the wall was protected by a huge iron gate matching the iron fence, although much higher as it swung on the big hinges anchored into the end of the wall. The big arched door on the northern side opened inwards to a long, wide, flagstoned path leading to the big front double doors.

Another smaller arched door on the eastern side was the servants' and tradesmen's entrance, which opened inwards, also leading to another smaller flagstone path up to the side and the servants' quarters. I made many trips with my cart under the supervision of my father during that move, and I received a good insight into all the details of that old house for the first time. It consisted of four levels, the cellars, the ground floor, the first floor and the attic bedrooms with their small dormer windows protruding from the roof, I presume used by the servants over the years. The cellars were cold and clammy, with big slate slabs protruding along the sides to hold and store all the food etc., and big stone steps leading up to the ground floor.

A big, wide, straight hall ran from the stout double front doors through the centre of the house meeting about half way along its length, a wonderful, wide, oak, curved and beautifully carved staircase leading up to the first-floor landings and bedrooms. Two big oak doors led off this hall on opposite sides into two large rooms, with huge bay windows, looking out on to the cultivated lawns and gardens and the apple orchard beyond. Other doors opened into a dining room, a drawing room, a morning room, and a big old fashioned magnificent Welsh kitchen with an enormous fireplace, with hanging chain spits, and side ovens, and two wonderful old beech Welsh dressers along the walls. The mantelpiece over the fireplace was adorned with a woven tapestry and lace surround secured with ornamental brass studs embedded in the timber, and each tassled frilly end carried a small brass ornamental ball so that it hung well, in a vertical position. I can still remember going to the trouble of counting those little brass balls, a total of 88 balls, I distinctly remember because of the double eights.

The mysteries of that house were no longer a secret to me now, I could tell my friends what was inside. From that time onwards along with my parents I would become a regular visitor over the following years. The Price family paid for that home, with all its magnificence, the total sum of £750 in the year 1927. When the last member of the family, Miss Janet Price moved out and died in the 1980s, the place was sold for £300,000.

When school began again in the new year of 1927, I was in hot water once again. On Boxing Day previously, accompanied by Billy Crane, we were making our way to Gummer's Field when we passed Morrison the Justice of the Peace living in Gwerthonor Road with his wife. We were not wearing caps at the time because it was the holidays. Morrison owned a three-wheeled Morgan runabout motor car – two wheels at the front and one at the rear. He drove this vehicle to his occupation as manager of the Bargoed branch of the Bank of England and of course all around the district. He was a big-nosed Englishman with horn-rimmed spectacles and he hated all Welsh-speaking citizens, classing them all as ignorant and beneath him – Mother's words again – 'a peaked nosed snob'.

As he passed Billy and myself, we ignored him and the pompous old fool reported us to Noah Thomas, and he of course in turn told T C Jones the 'Gaffer'. The first morning back at school Billy and I were named at Assembly, by the Gaffer, to attend his office before classes began. We pleaded ignorance that we had not even seen the man, but excuses were never accepted. On that cold January morning on the first school day, across the desk we bowed, held down by the nape of the neck, in all our sweet innocence bare backsides upwards to the sky, to receive six heavy cuts from old Jonesy, his tongue hanging out from the side of his mouth as he lashed us in his sadistic way.

We suffered a great deal that day sitting on the wooden seats of the school desks, and that evening I complained to my father and Billy complained to his father also. Fred Crane, Billy's dad was a jovial, short plump man, and he adored his family. Billy had displayed to him a nasty weal across the lower back. Old Fred went mad. I had never seen him like this before. He stormed down the road to throttle Jonesy, my father rushing after him to try to subdue him. Corporal punishment was allowed in the schools and we did not want the Black Maria around to carry Fred off to the lock-up if he confronted the Gaffer. What hope would he have, or any leniency, if he came up before Morrison!

My father explained all this and managed to subdue him, and he went home. My father laughed about it all, and he told me to stick it out, and he said, 'Next time rub some resin on your behind to take out the sting.' Resin was a lump of material that musicians used to rub the strings of a harp or violin but it was a common practice with all the boys to rub it on the palms of their hands to lessen the sting from the cane. I, too, soon borrowed and obtained a piece of resin from one of the boys. I was prepared!

The month of January was a bitterly cold month, and we continued in our young innocent ways to break the rules and the law in so many ways. The Gilfach level was working once again and we still thieved the coal and the workmen collaborated with us and helped us remove it, whenever we received information from the Crane brothers that their Tard Davies was not around.

From the area of this level, a stream ran out of the hillside, permanently tinged rusty red in colour, and probably caused by passing through the iron ore areas under the surface. This stream, was known to us as Nant Brook, the Welsh word *nant* actually meaning 'a stream'. It flowed past the rear of Gilfach Girls School, along the back of Mrs Wyatt's home and down beneath Gwerthonor Road to the new road bridge across the Great Western Railway. At this point it entered a brick arched tunnel under the railway tracks and the road extensions, to flow out into the Charity Woods, a distance of approximately 100 yards, and then flowed on and into the Rhymney River. This tunnel became a secret passage for all the boys of the Gwerthonor area and a short cut down to the woods. From the top of the New Bridge we had a clear view in every direction along Gwerthonor Road, up through Gilfach, and across the railway sidings to the river. Through those years our tunnel was a secret passage, and even stupid Noah Thomas knew nothing about our excursions through that tunnel and all the things we got up to.

If anything was planned we always tried to have one boy up on the bridge to sound his peewit alarm if any suspicious person or Noah Thomas approached. Climbing the steel standards and supports of the aerial ropeway buckets, we were able to grab the tip handle at the bottom of the moving buckets and hitch a ride across the river. On the other side we could now climb the slopes of the tipped slag which extended down to the river's edge. At the top there were big concentrations of stockpiled Norwegian pine pit props or supports, eight and ten feet long, six to ten inches in diameter. We would release the chocks holding a section of this timber and allow them to roll down to the river's edge. One by one we would wade and ferry them across the river, carrying them up through the woods out into Nant Brook tunnel and conceal them in that tunnel from the point where the penetrating daylight ended to the other end where the daylight began. Whenever we needed one, under the cover of darkness, we would smuggle them up the back lanes to various backyards. We cut them up with a big cross-cut saw and made them into all kinds of things, cricket bats, barrows, and carts, garden sheds, sticks for firewood, anything and everything we needed.

Over the years we must have taken hundreds of those pine logs and no one in authority even knew or suspected anything.

My mother's young sister, Mathilda – my Aunt Tilly – died at the end of January that year; it was a sad and tragic affair. Aunt Tilly had married a man by the name of Robert Layman at the age of 18 years, defying the wishes of Granny and Grandfather, and in opposition to all the family. There was some special reason for the opposition but I was never able to find it out. Even my sister Joyce did not know, and this was unusual because she seemed to know the details of everything that was going on with everyone throughout the neighbourhood.

Many times during the big Strike I trekked all the way to Tir-y-beth where Aunt Tilly lived to help her, pulling my hand cart full of coal. It was filled up from Uncle Dai's coal house. Uncle Dai would not go anywhere near her home. Very often I had found her in tears, her face bruised and on one occasion wearing a black eye. There was anger all around when I reported these things to my mother, and Uncle Dai and my father many times reached the point of taking the law into their own hands with Layman, but they avoided it and sadly it was too late. Aunt Tilly living with Layman had very little, because he became a violent drunk smashing everything and he constantly beat her in his fits of drunken rage. The family begged her many times to come back and live with Granny but she would not do so, she maintained that she had married Layman foolishly and she would not leave him. There was an inquest as a result of her death and the verdict was 'accidental death due to a fractured skull caused by falling down the stairs'. Layman gave evidence at the inquest of having found her after she had fallen down the stairs, and it was accepted by Morrison the JP acting in the capacity of coroner.

We were unable to produce any evidence to the contrary but we have always believed that Layman threw her down the stairs and kicked her in the head with his heavy boots. It took a long time for my mother to get over that tragedy, with a further sad blow just a couple of months later.

Remembering so well the death of Aunt Tilly, and shortly after her burial, another unfortunate incident happened in early February of that year 1927. Joyce had returned from Bourneville and I lost my weekly earnings of sixpence from Eli Bratt when she took over the task once again. It was a very bad day. It had snowed continuously for two days, and during the night the strong northerly wind had piled the snow into a huge drift right up to the upstairs bedroom windows, completely covering the front downstairs window, and the front door. I helped my father and brother Gwyn dig ourselves out that early morning to make a clearance to the road. The roads also were almost three feet deep in snow and everything had stopped. There was no transport of any kind and no milk supplies from Dai Isaacs the faithful milkman. I struggled through the snow that morning in the company of Joyce, in case there were more drifts, and she might be unable to get through to Old Bratt's place at the end of Gwerthonor Road, but we made it safely to his front door. Our usual ritual, heavy knock six times on the big door knocker, was unanswered. We repeated that knock about a dozen times but there was still no answer. Everything was silent with the deep snow. Finally we gave up and made our way back home and reported it to our parents. My mother, with all her instincts and knowing all the same regularities of Eli Bratt, was convinced that something was wrong. My parents decided that we go back once again, to try once more, and if there was no answer I should go down the Grammar School hill to the Pengam square to find Noah Thomas and report the matter to him. Noah Thomas lived in Pengam Street just off the square. I was familiar with his address, as every boy in the district knew where he lived. He knew also of our weekly Saturday errands to Eli Bratt's house, because there was very little about Gwerthonor Road that the cunning old fool did not know.

I told him what had happened and the instructions given to me to report the matter to him. I even got some praise from him – I was a good lad for letting him know promptly, and he told me to go home to get my dad in case he needed help, with the weather being so bad, and to meet him at Bratt's house in 15 minutes' time. I made my way home through the deep snow once again, and my father protested a little saying words or something from my memory now, 'What does he want me for, there's probably nothing wrong with Bratt?' A little persuasion from Mother and we trekked through the snow once again to rendezvous at Eli Bratt's home. Noah Thomas was there, he had already pounded the door without any reply. I explained to him the sequence of our knocks, one thing the old fool did not know! The only thing we could do, he at last decided, was to get inside to see if anything was wrong, and I told him it was impossible as everything was barred and bolted. We waded our way through the deep snow to the rear of the house by way of the side lane. All the windows were heavily curtained so that no possible view could be made inside the place. Beneath the end window on the left-hand side there was a skillion roof which covered a scullery area, off the back kitchen and near the back door. I knew this and I told Noah Thomas the window above was at the top of the stairs that led off the passage from the front door. 'Well my boy,' he said, 'you have to get in through that window, get down the stairs and unbolt the front door for me.' My father found a sweeping brush, half buried in the snow leaning against the back wall. Using the long handle he pushed away the deep snow from the edge of that roof as far as he could reach and, with the help of Noah, I was hoisted up until I got a foothold half on the spouting and half on the roof. The sweeping brush was passed up to me and I pushed the snow away over the edge to make a path to the window above and I clambered up to the stone sill. The old fool, Noah Thomas, shouted up to me, 'You young devils like breaking windows, so use the brush to smash the window, clear the glass away, get inside and open the front door.' I was scared getting through that window as I pushed aside the curtains and eased myself through on to the wide sill inside. I ran down those stairs as fast as I could go with my heart in my mouth, shot back the bolts on the front door, pulled it open and rushed outside.

Noah Thomas went inside with my father and sure enough Old Eli Bratt was slumped in his big armchair lifeless and dead. I wasn't allowed inside. I was sent once again by Noah Thomas to tell Folland the Gilfach bobby what had happened and to alert Fred Davies-Black, the undertaker. My father was told to call into the home of the Pengam doctor, on his way home along Gwerthonor Road, to report that Noah Thomas needed him urgently at Bratt's house. There was an inquest held on Eli Bratt's death and the verdict told us that his heart gave out and he succumbed accordingly.

My mother said to me later, with one of her funny but serious expressions, that 'Mr Bratt was buried in Caerphilly cemetery standing up, so that he could walk to the other side. He carried a chicken sandwich made from a boiled old fowl, a small rock to knock at the pearly gates, and a copper coin to pay his fee to pass to the other side'. I believe that this was actually true and a common devout practice performed by the followers of Mr Bratt's extreme religious beliefs. Mr Bratt's religious organisation took over his estate and all his possessions, including the secondhand shop and pawnshop, and it makes me smile now as I remember my mother saying once again,

'They would have found much more if Noah Thomas's thieving fingers had not found their way under the mattress.' This was the end of an era with the passing of Eli Bratt and the end of that strange and unusual sixpenny job for sister Joyce and myself.

3

My Greatest Idol Dies

April of that year brought another unhappy blow to our family; it hurt mother deeply and it upset me so much. My granny's birthday was celebrated each year with a birthday cake, made by my mother and a jug of stout purchased and collected by my father from the Jug and Bottle at Gwerthonor Hotel. Granny always believed that stout was a wonderful 'pick-me-up' and a tonic for the old and aged. This birthday in April each year was always a special day and had only just passed by when, one week later, Grandfather, pottering around as usual in the backyard, suffered a seizure and died instantly. It was a bitter and sad blow for me, all my bits and pieces, all odd jobs I wanted done, and all the things I wanted to make, had come to an end.

Grandfather had always been there so willingly, without any fuss or bother, anything I needed, anything I wanted, all the help and advice I required, it was all done immediately. The man I had admired so much throughout those young innocent days of my life was no more.

Grandfather's funeral was the biggest I had ever seen in the Bargoed and Gilfach districts. The funeral procession was headed by Fred Davies-Black and his magnificent six-wheeled hearse pulled along by six wonderful black horses. Whenever it was used the hearse drew the residents from the whole area as spectators and to pay their tributes. It was such a beautiful and sombre vehicle. Fred Davies-Black always took the driver's position high up at the front where the turntable joined the shafts resting on its lower two medium-sized front cartwheels. His seat was almost a throne, with polished silver metal ornamental lace around him. Dressed in a top hat, long black tails with breeches and black leather leggings down to his black boots, he held the reins of his paired horses in his lap.

The body of the hearse was carried, supported and cradled on four thick, silver-studded leather straps, two at the front and two at the rear, anchored to the chassis of the carriage, allowing it to swing and sway gently with the movement of the wheels, and centralised in between four big cartwheels with painted black spokes, silver hubs and silver rims. The glass all around was etched in lace designs with an ornamental door at the rear to enter and exit the shrouded coffin.

Below this rear door there was a fancy running board with a silver metal decorated back support and arms, almost like a park bench. The two assistants of Fred Davies-Black sat on this seat, dressed up in the same way, top hat, tails, breeches, leggings and boots. The whole top of the vehicle had a nine-inch ornamental silver metal fancy fence running around the perimeter to hold and contain all the floral tributes and wreaths on the top. This magnificent vehicle was pulled along by six paired black horses. The horses' manes and tails were dressed and tied up with black and white ribbons. Beneath the neck of each horse, at least twelve polished silver horse brasses, with their leather supports, stood out in rows against their shining black coat. All the leather buckles, all the chains were silver, and around the shining black polished leather collars of each horse, dispersed in between polished silver staples were threaded rows of golden daffodils, the trumpet of each flower bobbing as the horses moved along.

Behind the hearse walked Uncle Dai and my father. I followed behind with my brother Gwyn, then came the 20 ladies from the choir of the 'Babel' Chapel Pontlanfraith, all dressed in the Welsh top hat, the red cloak, skirt and high-laced boots, the national costume. It was the first time I had seen ladies in a funeral procession. Ahead of the hearse, all alone, walked Noah Thomas in uniform strutting along like a peacock. Behind the choir ladies came the column of men, all the relatives, and residents from Pontlanfraith, Ynysddu, Wattsville and Risca and the whole Bargoed district. The column strung out from the Gilfach Calvinistic Presbyterian Church where the service began, to the new bridge, about half a mile in length. At the rear came Miss Gwladys Price's car with the hood down. Miss Price sitting up behind the wheel, her top hat sticking up on top of the big hair bun, with Janet by her side. In the back seat sat my mother, Aunt Ethel my mother's sister, and Joyce and Edna. Following behind was Folland, the bobby. The whole procession was on its way to the Pengam cemetery, and as they marched the whole column in unison broke into song, singing the Welsh hymn *Cym Rhondda*. That beautiful hymn reverberated and echoed across the valley, almost one thousand voices singing in perfect time all the way to the cemetery. I did not know I had so many relatives and antecedents, so many Davies – from cousins so many times removed, to great great uncles – and all the Webbs and their side of the family. The name 'Webb' was my granny's maiden name. They all turned up from the Sirhowy and the Rhondda Valleys, and it was a wonderful tribute to grandfather. I was barely eight years old and I shook hands with so many people, many of them great big powerful men, rugby players from all the football clubs of those valleys, and from Newport on the coast to Pontypridd and Merthyr in the Rhondda Valley up to Brecon and the Beacons in the north.

My brother Gwyn at Lewis's Grammar School obtained a carved piece of oak from the manual and woodcraft rooms, and the craft teacher cut into that board Shakespeare's famous words:

> David John Davies
> Nothing in his life
> became him like the leaving of it; he died
> as one that had been studied in his death,
> to throw away the dearest thing he ow'd
> as 'twere a careless trifle . . .

A small headstone was placed at the head of his grave some time later and this board set at the foot of the stone. Sixty years later in 1986, when I visited the grave with my sister Joan, the board was still there, cracked, weathered and rotted. The words were indecipherable, it was the end of that great tribute paid to a great man such a long time ago.

With the death of Grandfather, this was the first time I had seen my mother cry. I guess there were many tears at different times but she always concealed them or hid herself away. During those first 20 years of my life from 1919 to 1939, as I grew up at Oak Cottage, there were so few occasions when the tears flowed and I remember them all as I pay homage now to that wonderful lady. There was the time she cried with the pain and suffering of my sister Joyce, so near to death from vaccine poisoning, which affected her all her life. The death of Granny and the incident when little Toots fell off a horse and broke her nose, and the day I departed for military service and war, at the age of 20 years. She was always looked up to and considered the most beautiful lady in the whole district. Everyone rich and poor, right down to the biggest ruffian in the area, always raised their caps or their hat to my mother. During my lifetime, I had never seen her use makeup except for cold creams, often the recipes of Granny or Mrs

Wyatt. She had a flawless, peaches-and-cream complexion. I had never known of any visit to a hairdresser as there were no hairdressers in the area then. The only hairdressing implement that I knew of were the metal curling tongs placed in the fire, wiped with a cloth and allowed to cool to the required heat, and rolled, often leaving behind singed hair. Mother always cut her own hair, often with the aid of my sisters. It was natural, wavy, and fair, always decorated with hairpins and all kinds of fancy slides. She had an obsession for large funny floral hats, at least they were funny to me! And just like Granny she was very, very superstitious, just like all the old folks. She would be upset and appalled if two knives crossed on the table, she would never look at the moon through a window, and I have heard her scream out if any of the children brought ivy anywhere near the home. Table salt was unheard of during that time. Salt was always dispensed from a small dish in the cruet, by a small spoon. We were not allowed to dispense it on anything on the plate in case of a spill. She always handled it herself. Then there was the black cat theory, and the broken mirror, and so many more. She had all kinds of funny witty sayings, many of them half in Welsh and half in English, and she was always so kind, gentle and overflowing with compassion. She had an uncanny knowledge of everyone in the whole area, she knew the parents, their antecedents, even down to the birthdays of all the children. Scores of times in her later life, so many people who had moved away from the district, came back to see her and consult her about some relation, incident or happening from those cruel, tough and often unhappy days after the First World War and during the 1920s.

She was so gentle but also extremely tough. Many, many times she tumbled and fell down the stairs at Oak Cottage catching her foot in those long, wide dresses and skirts. So often we have picked her up bleeding from the fall, and she would laugh about it. Sadly, a fall was to lead to her death. Her last fall put her in hospital just after the age of 90 years and she never recovered again.

After the death of Grandfather in April 1927 the home in Maes-y-craig Street was at an end and many of the old possessions and furniture were sold. I suppose at that age and during that time we did not appreciate all those wonderful old things. Grandfather's old Welsh Bible was given to me, as he had told me before he died requesting that I take care of it. I took it home to Oak Cottage, carefully wrapped it up in brown paper and I deposited it in a right-hand cupboard adjoining the fireplace in the front room. It remained in that cupboard, untouched, for 20 years. It was thrown out as rubbish unknowingly by my sister Joyce during my absence, when everything was sorted out after my father's death.

That Bible was a piece of history, it was one of the first translations made and printed in the Welsh language. It contained all kinds of wonderful anecdotes, events, poems, verses, and signatures in the beautiful script writing of many famous people. Today it would have been priceless, and instead of finding its way to the refuse dump, it should have been on show, for everyone to see, at the National Museum of Wales, a wonderful relic from the past compiled, translated and hand printed sometime between the years 1750 and 1770.

Granny moved from Maes-y-craig Street now to Uncle Dai's home in the Drive and she lived with him and his wife Aunty May, and their daughter, who was born later. Her name was Mair, the Welsh translation for Mary.

Uncle Dai took many of Grandfather's tools and the old anvil from the backyard – I have never known what happened to that old anvil! My mother took much of the old china and the magnificent coloured vases, one of Grandfather's brass oil lamps, the tobacco tin and the taper tin and a wonderful old corner cabinet. All those priceless articles were thrown out in later years in ignorance by my sisters and they always regretted it. The corner cabinet was a magnificent piece of furniture. It was made of red cherry wood, with inlays of sycamore, beech and oak. The single door at the front was divided into triangles with inlaid beading, the corners of the frame contained four colours of the old coloured glass, red, green, blue and gold. The top had a beautiful carved scrolled face and cut into the timber at the rear of the scroll that famous name to me – David John Davies. This David John Davies was my great grandfather. He made this cabinet sometime between 1765 and 1770.

Ironically once again, my mother sold this cabinet to a dealer, calling around the doors, for the huge sum of one pound, today it would have been worth 30,000 times that sum. Grandfather's old oak armchair went to my father and he used it until he died. The old armchair I shall always remember! It brings back so many memories of the days and nights I listened to him talk, laugh and sing, which makes me add to those lines of reveries of days gone by, and quote from an old poem, written by a person called E Crook in 1880:

> In childhood's hour I lingered near
> the hallowed seat with listening ear
> And gentle words that grandfather would give

to fit me to die, and teach me to live.
He told me shame would never betide
with truth for my creed, and God for my guide.
He taught me to lisp my earliest prayer
As I knelt beside that old armchair.

My last journey from Maes-y-craig Street was with my faithful hand cart carrying Polly the West African parrot. The cage was covered by the curtains made by Granny. The same curtains that were drawn around the cage at dusk each evening and drawn back again at 6 a.m. every morning for so many years. Polly was to take up residence at Oak Cottage. I never knew whether Polly was a male or a female bird, but it was a wonderful old bird capable of saying and repeating anything. It called us all by our Christian names including Mum and Dad. It announced every caller who came to the door, and mocked all the local characters who passed by. Morris, the oil man, was Polly's greatest admirer of all and he pestered and cajoled my mother for a long time trying to make her sell Polly to him. We kept Polly for three years then finally my mother gave in and sold old Polly to Morris for the price of three pounds. Morris kept Polly for approximately 18 months and it died in a violent electric storm in the winter of 1931. I did know the full history of old Polly, but I cannot recall now how long it lived with Granny and Grandfather, but that wonderful bird must have been at least 70 years old, so it brought to an end another chapter in the life of Alice and David John Davies.

The time was now approaching for the expected visit of Aunt Dot from the USA. My younger brother Trevor was now a two-year-old toddler, Toots was five years old and sister Joan had not yet been born. The Carter family next door at Beech Cottage were considering moving to a larger house. Mrs Carter and her husband Joe were finding it difficult to accommodate their grown-up family. There was Tom, Hector and Aubrey and the two girls Kathleen and Barbara. They were all in employment except Barbara, who was still at school and she would be leaving at the end of the school year.

In the middle of May that year we received a letter to say that Aunt Dot was in Bristol with sister Alice and she was on her way to South Wales. I felt uneasy when the day arrived for the visit of Aunt Dot. I was all dressed up in my Sunday clothes. It was a Tuesday morning; the whole family set off to meet the 1.15 p.m. train at Pengam(mon) station, on the Brecon and Merthyr line. I was pushing my hand cart once again to carry the luggage, Trevor was pushed along in the wooden pushchair, Mother wearing her biggest and most colourful fancy, floral hat, Father in his best bowler hat, wearing striped trousers and spats, his watch and chain proudly displayed hanging across his front, from his right and left waistcoat pockets. Spats, by the way, were a pair of soft felt gaiters worn over the upper of the boot and buttoned around the ankle and lower calf, underneath the bottom of the turn-up of the trouser leg. Toots was helped along hand in hand with Edna and Joyce, Gwyn was with me and, as usual, telling me all the do's and dont's of how to conduct myself. We all trekked along over the new bridge and down the road to the station as if we were heading for a garden fête. The pushchair I mentioned was a wood and canvas affair, similar in many ways to a deck-chair and it folded up in the same way. The four wheels were cast iron with solid rubber-tyred rims, the axles were slightly bent with so much use over the years, so the four wheels wobbled badly as it was pushed along towards the station.

Access to the station was made by a long flight of stone steps leading down to a platform from a bridge which carried the road across the railway lines and travelling uphill in the direction of Cefn Forest. My hand cart was parked on the bridge at the top of the steps, whilst we all congregated on the platform for the arrival of the train and the very important passenger from the USA – Mrs Dorothy Cunningham.

The 1.15 p.m. train from Newport arrived dead on time, the polished brass accessories of the tank engine gleaming in the spring sunshine. Then came the familiar sound of the slamming carriage doors as all the passengers alighted, my mother and father now fussing around as Aunt Dot's figure appeared from one of the carriage compartments. The porters were there also lifting out the luggage and dancing attendance on this unknown elegant immaculately dressed lady. She greeted us all one by one with a great big hug, and it gave me the opportunity to study her from top to toe.

She was dressed in a beautiful long fur coat and carrying a pair of fur-backed kid gloves. Her frilly dress was much shorter than the local custom of our area, with my limited knowledge of fashion, showing expensive silk stockings and patent high-heeled shoes – something else I had only seen before in newspapers and magazines. Around her neck she wore at least five rows of pearls, each row hanging a little below the other. Her head was adorned with a big wide-brimmed hat, with a wide brown ribbon encircling the crown ending in a big bow over the left ear. The whole affair was pinned with a pearl hatpin through her permanently waved hair. Her face was painted and powdered with makeup, displaying rich red rouge-coloured lips. Anyone wearing rouge on their lips during this period was considered immoral and a poor type. However, this was Aunt Dot in all her finery and, adding to the atmosphere, was the smell of sweet perfume drifting along on the gentle afternoon breeze.

The porters handled the luggage, consisting of a big tin trunk and two big portmanteaux. They carried them up the steps and deposited all three on the footpath, and then received their tip. It was left to me and brother Gwyn to do the rest. We loaded the luggage on and into my hand cart, Gwyn steadied it with his hand as we moved along, and I had the task of pulling the cart all the way home.

My parents went ahead with Aunt Dot all engrossed in conversation. Edna took the hand of little Toots, and Joyce had the task of pushing along the wooden pushchair, containing Trevor, and its stubborn wobbly cast-iron wheels. Our whole party received the stares of all the passers-by, with all the usual nosey whispers concerning the very important person in our midst. We arrived home about 2 p.m., and I had to go back to school. I had already produced a note that morning to the Gaffer asking to be excused for a short period to go to the station. It was approved providing that I returned to school and reported to him as soon as the mission was completed.

Everything had been prearranged at home. Edna and Joyce were to sleep at the Price's home, Toots went to Granny at Uncle Dai's place, Gwyn and I slept in our own room, my parents and Trevor had the girls' room, and Aunt Dot was given the VIP treatment to occupy the back bedroom.

As there was no mention made to me this time about returning with her to the USA, I believe Aunt Dot had given up, so I felt more at ease and we had a wonderful time on her visit. On Friday of that week, my father paid another visit to the Gaffer to tell him that I would be absent for the whole of the following week because I was to accompany the family to visit all the relations in England. This explanation was necessary and important during that time, because if any child was absent from school for any period longer than three days, and the parent had not given a reasonable explanation or produced a doctor's note, the truant officer – the school bobby as we called him – would be banging on the door, and physically hauling the child off to school, and the parent would be brought before a Justice of the Peace in the local court and quite often jailed.

Joyce and Edna would now return home and along with Gwyn they would look after themselves and little Toots until we returned. On the Saturday morning, my father, mother, Aunt Dot, Trevor in the push-chair, and myself set off once again to catch the 10 a.m. train to Newport and then on to Bristol.

Gwyn had the task, this time, of pushing my cart with Aunt Dot's luggage, everyone else, including myself had to carry their own. This journey was to be the first in my young life out of South Wales. We had a compartment all to ourselves and to me it was an exciting and wonderful journey. I sat next to the window that morning as the train puffed, hissed and snorted across the county, known in those days as the county of Monmouthshire. In my mind's eye now 62 years on, I can still picture those wonderful oak panelled carriages, all divided up into eight separate compartments. The velvet bench seats and buttoned backs across each side from window to window, the brass baggage racks above with their loose cord netting, the centre mirror on each side separating four picturesque panoramic framed views of a well-known historic site, or object, along the railway tracks. The thick leather strap hanging loosely, used for the lifting and lowering of the door window, with the long centre line of brass eyelet holes worn with the constant use of being anchored on a heavy brass pin, to control the level of the glass opening.

Across the top of each and above the doors was the communication cord showing approximately one foot length of brass chain as it entered the brass tube on either side and the warning brass plate below inscribed with the penalty of five pounds for improper or false use. The heavy brass sliding latch to open the door and above in the centre of the ceiling, the tiny pilot light to light up the gas mantle protected behind a glass dome. The gas was turned on and controlled by the guard as we entered a tunnel, or when darkness fell at evening time.

The train steamed on through the hills and across the valleys cross-ing the mighty Crumlin viaduct spanning the Ebbw River and across the Ebbw Valley. I had never been so high up in all my life. I could look down and see the flowing water and the tiny human figures 200 feet below. That wonderful, magnificent feat of engineering has gone too, destroyed and torn down by the orders of decadent English politicians to cut costs when the Brecon and Merthyr railway was destroyed under British Railways.

We arrived at Newport station and the porters were in attendance once again. Under instruction from Aunt Dot, we had to change platforms on to the Great Western Railway to take us on to Bristol.

The train steamed on through the long Severn tunnel into Gloucester-shire and down to Bristol. Aunt Alice, my father's sister and her husband, were there to meet us all. It was a new experience for me, I had never been to a big city before. I had passed through Cardiff on the train to Barry, but I had not been out into the busy streets. We had two taxis to transport us all to Aunt Alice's place, the old Austin cabs carrying four passengers in the rear seat and a small stool which swivelled from the side to seat a child or small person.

The canvas roof fixed to the driver's windscreen stretched over the top with a small celluloid window in the rear. The luggage was deposited at the side of the cab driver, with a leather strap hooked across the opening to prevent it falling out. My eyes were everywhere trying to see everything as we drove through the busy streets passing all kinds of vehicles I had never seen before, including the big old double-decker buses, with the rear open stairway exposed to the weather as it twisted around to the top deck.

We stayed two days and three nights in Bristol. During that time we paid a visit to the small town of Alveston for Aunt Dot and my father to call on some of the old folks from their younger days. My grandparents on my father's side, who had lived there, were both deceased, so unfortunately I never knew anything about them. I did meet my father's brother Hedley, who had made a special journey from the Swansea Valley in South Wales in order to meet up once again with sister Aunt Dot. I was taken all around the docks area of Bristol and Avonmouth, and I saw the big ships from all over the world. Bristol was such a busy port then, so for me it was just like another world.

We caught the train again on Tuesday morning to travel to Swanage on the south coast to pay another call, this time to Aunt Fran my father's sister. I had a wonderful time at Swanage, the weather was so good, the sands were beautiful with all the lines of bathing huts along the shore and deck-chairs everywhere. I even had a dip in the sea, rides on the merry-go-round, and a ride across the sands on a donkey. Aunt Dot bought me a huge stick of peppermint candy rock, with the name Swanage Rock written right through the stick. When-ever a piece was broken or cut off the name still showed in bright red colours. There were ice-cream barrows everywhere and lots of barrow boys selling cockles, winkles and mussels. They doled them out in small china saucers and even supplied the large straight pin to pick them up and eat them. They all did a roaring trade, but I did not like them at all. I was more interested in the ice-cream cornets.

It was a sad time for me to travel home once again to go back to school. We said goodbye to Aunt for the last time. She gave me a nice present, and gifts for all the other children. The present was the 1927 annual of a book called *The Winner for Boys*. It contained all kinds of exciting stories and I treasured it, but it was disposed of, like many of my other treasures after I had departed for military service at the outbreak of the Second World War. I corresponded and wrote regularly to Aunt Dot after she left for the USA. I was to learn that she was divorced from her husband, she then remarried and went to live in California. It appeared that her second husband had two sons by a previous marriage so she had a family of her own. We were to learn also, as the years passed by, that she was killed in a tragic car accident in the year 1938. In January of the year 1941 I was surprised to receive a letter from the oldest boy David. It had been sent to Oak Cottage, and my mother forwarded it to me while I was stationed at Byfleet in Surrey.

He explained to me about the sad end of his stepmother – our Aunt Dot. He wanted to know all about the conditions we lived under at that time and offered to send me anything I requested in the way of gifts, cigarettes or money. I wrote a long letter in reply detailing all the serious situations we were experiencing in the Battle of Britain and the worrying thoughts of the expected Nazi invasion, the massive bombing and the little rest and sleep we had keeping alert and ready for any Nazi onslaught. I did not mention anything about his offer in the letter and I never received a reply. It was the end of another family connection.

The month of June passed by that year in the same old way, the industrial situation was worse, and unemployment increased. The coal miners in the district were all on short time. The Gilfach and Pengam lignite mines shut down and became derelict, and the huge seams were being exploited and worked from new mining roads and underground workings from Bargoed colliery. It was a big blow and as a result many men lost their jobs, and many of them drifted away to the English Midlands with their families.

In July I had another birthday. I had reached the tender age of eight years. It was the time for the end-of-year school examinations and I achieved the second place in order of merit, so I was quite proud of myself and got further praise from brother Gwyn. The Gaffer, Trefor Cadogan Jones, announced his retirement. He had been headmaster of Gilfach Boys School for 50 years. Everyone was glad to see him go. There were 600 pupils at the school, and we were ordered to contribute one penny each towards a farewell gift. It was like drawing a tooth from every boy who had suffered a sore backside so many times. However, everyone paid up and Jonesy was presented with a clock from the proceeds of exactly five pounds. At the presentation there were so many subdued and undertoned remarks from the ranks of boys, many of which the sadistic old devil would have no desire to hear. The new headmaster appointed was Mr Thomas Garnet, the teacher of standard 5A, the class in which all pupils sat the eleven plus examination for promotion to a grammar school. Mr Garnet had survived the horrors of the trenches, and the Middle East of the First World War. He was a fair and reasonable man, each boy had a fair trial before any punishment was dealt out, and many of the usual lashings and canings were avoided by fair explanations and reasonings. He was a tall, stout, powerful man aptly described by Shakespeare's words in 'Seven Ages of Man' – 'A fair round belly with good capon lined' but he was well liked and respected and all the boys in their own way approved of him.

The new Tir-y-beth School was completed and it would be opened for the new school year at the beginning of September. Gilfach Boys and Girls Schools would lose 200 pupils, the children from Tir-y-beth and the surrounding districts would no longer walk through all the inclement weather to Gilfach School. Another big step also, the new school would have a section for instruction in all the trades. All the pupils from Gilfach School, having attained the age of nine years would attend one day each week to learn the first stages of woodwork, bricklaying, tiling, plumbing, plastering, weaving, knitting, cooking etc., to prepare them to proceed through the stages of the City and Guilds courses and examinations, and further detailed instruction if they passed to go on to a grammar school.

The month of August was the school summer holidays and as usual I went on the two daily outings to Barry Island. So the year had been good to me with my week's holiday included with Aunt Dot. I was growing up!

My brother Gwyn was sitting the Central-Welsh Board Senior examination and the London Matriculation in July, and the results came through at the end of August. As it was forecast and expected, he came out on top of all the others with credits and five distinctions in all the subjects. Gwyn spent all his spare time in the local library. He read everything that came his way and any spare minutes of his time he was engrossed in a book. For the next two years he would specialise in Chemistry, Physics and Pure and Applied Mathematics.

He had already won a place at Cardiff University to commence when he attained the age of eighteen years.

I spent almost a week with my father when he finished work each day and arrived home at 2.30 p.m. during the first week of August. We were dismantling lots of wooden buildings in the grounds of Gwerthonor House, now the home of the Price family; using my faithful hand cart we carted load after load of timber, boards, and studs back to Oak Cottage to build a big chicken house and a covered run at the top of the garden. We needed the eggs now and the possible profit from the sale of any surplus. It was at this period also my friends and I got into trouble with that pest and tyrant Noah Thomas, although, once again we were completely innocent.

On two occasions during the week and on weekends, Percy, the middle-aged bachelor son of Garland the local coal hauler, would take the shire horses and a pony to the fields to graze, from about 4 p.m. till early the next morning. The grazing areas were the fields adjacent and around the Charity Woods and Mutton Tump. It was our custom also to go to the woods to cut and collect pea sticks for our parents in order to train and support the tall marrowfat peas planted in the gardens and vegetable allotments. On one particular evening I was on my way home with a load of these pea sticks and away from the area where the horses were grazing. Garland's pony had somehow got out of the field on to the main road, and it had shied at a passing noisy vehicle and caused a slight accident. As usual Noah Thomas was roaming around in his sly way looking for a victim, and he was just a short distance away. My three friends Billy Crane, Vernon Evans and Harold 'Dicko' Lewis were crossing Mutton Tump from the woods with their own load of sticks. Noah Thomas rounded them up, recorded their names and addresses and informed them that they would be issued with a summons for riding and chasing the pony, making it jump the fence and causing the accident. They protested their innocence in vain. The following Friday morning three innocent boys were up before Morrison the JP. Billy was six months older than myself, Vern was nine and Dicko was eight years and two months.

They protested their innocence once again with the support of their parents and swore that they had nothing to do with the pony. Noah Thomas reeled off a pack of lies about the whole affair and blamed them as the cause of all the trouble. Morrison accepted everything that Noah Thomas said, and the three boys were each fined one pound and put on probation for one year. That order included that if they committed any offence during that period, they would be liable to be

71

sent to an approved Borstal School for a minimum period of two years. Perhaps it was just my good fortune that I had already taken my load home otherwise I would have been a victim also.

This was the exploitation and unfairness that we lived under during the 1920s. The incident hurt me a great deal, something I would remember all my life. All the boys of the neighbourhood and their parents swore that some day they would get even with that dishonest fool Noah Thomas. My father was fuming when he heard about it because he knew too all the boys were innocent. I could never repeat what Fred Crane, Billy's father remarked about that dishonest tyrant because he and the other parents had to find the money to pay the fine.

The August holidays were looked forward to eagerly by all the boys. Some of our time, mixed up with so many other things we did, was spent catching rabbits and rats. We could obtain a bounty of one penny for every rat-tail we produced to the local council health authorities. Our method of catching rabbits was extraordinary, perhaps rather dangerous for children, but very successful. The rabbit was a delicacy, with money so scarce and meat so expensive, it made many a hearty meal. During those times every man and boy wore a flannel shirt, which was warm and cosy, although sometimes a little irritable on the bare skin. All the men followed the fashion of the time with the collarless neck holding a white stiff collar, held in place by the back and front brass collar studs. Welsh flannel was a well-known cloth and it was a busy prosperous industry in Wales. There were plenty of pieces of old flannel from worn out and discarded shirts, so we made use of this flannel to catch the rabbits and rats. We would make our way to an area of well used occupied burrows with big pieces of carbide wrapped in flannel cloth. The carbide and cloth rolled into a ball was placed in the entrance to a main burrow. It was partially blocked leaving a small space only sufficient to push in a piece of long rubber hose connected to a bicycle pump. All the other burrow entrances were blocked, leaving one only free for the rabbits to escape. Water was poured onto the flannel-covered carbide which quickly soaked, reacting with the carbide to release the gas. One of the boys quickly operated the pump for a short period to drive the gas through the tunnels. Acetylene gas is heavier than air so it went down and settled into the burrows quickly. The rubber hose was then pulled away and a lighted match thrown at the burrow's entrance causing a big explosion to rip through the underground passages. The other boys would encircle the free burrow entrance with sticks and bags to knock over and catch the dazed rabbits trying to escape, to make our catch a very successful one. We shared out the spoils between us equally and fairly.

Along the river towards the local refuse tip, the settling ponds from the sewers were not very well maintained and looked after, and most of the effluent found its way into the black oily polluted Rhymney River. With food from the tip and the sewers, the rats bred in holes and underground passages in the soft black earth, and in this area we had a thrilling time exploding them out, axing off their tails to take along to claim the bounty.

In front of the tradesmen's entrance to Gwerthonor House in Gwerthonor Place, facing the main road, there was a big old stone building, which we always called and referred to as the Old Barn. It had been built long before the turn of the century for the storage of corn and meal etc. It had no windows, but long vertical six-inch cavities at regular intervals around the walls which could be sealed and shuttered from the inside. The floor was originally paved with big flagstones, but one by one they had disappeared, been stolen or carried away. The roof leaked badly, the slates were broken, missing, or blown off by the wind. This building was our headquarters for all the boys of the district, where our plans were made for all the things we intended to do, all our games, and in general a meeting place where we found out what was going on each day, and where we waited in the rain for each other to go to school. It was the place also where Noah Thomas made his first call if anything was wrong in the district, so that he could persecute or apprehend anyone for the slightest thing, usually something we knew nothing about in any way. It was his common practice also to storm into the building hoping to catch someone with a catapult or a shanghai in his possession. Catapults were illegal and anyone caught in possession of one was liable to a heavy fine, this applied also to any gun, or air gun, dagger, or dangerous knife. There was no vandalism or destruction or stealing by our schoolmates. We helped each other in every possible way, but we were hounded, exploited and persecuted all the time.

Syd Walters, the father of two of the much older boys, Ken and Lew, owned one of the local general stores in Gwerthonor Place and he kept a number of horses at the rear in some of the old buildings. He had sold the horses, deciding not to use them any more, leaving one of the larger buildings empty and unused. We were all so sick and tired of being constantly picked on by Noah Thomas at the Old Barn that Lew put forward a suggestion that we ask old Syd for permission

73

to use the building, voluntarily clean it up, and put it in order, pay small rent and use it as our secret headquarters and clubroom. It had an added advantage also, as access to it could only be made through an arched passageway next to the shop and anyone entering or leaving would be looked upon as going into or leaving the back of the store. It would be an ideal place, private and unknown to Thomas, where we could be free from any interference. Mr Walters agreed to the suggestion and he would allow us to take it over for the weekly rental of three shillings. We canvassed the idea with the boys in the area. There were about 50 boys in all, between the ages of 8 years and 15 years. They were all welcome, each paying one penny per week for the membership fee. Secretly, and away from prying eyes, all the boys enthusiastically joined in the big clean up. Our pine logs from the Nant tunnel appeared as if any magic; benches and seats were soon made up.

There was a fireplace in the building, and we had plenty of coal – Tard Davies' level was only 500 yards away. Two hurricane lamps were produced, and again we had plenty of paraffin oil to supply the fuel. We could obtain ample supplies of colza oil used in the miners' safety lamps at the local collieries. Colza oil was a much slower burning oil than paraffin, produced as a by-product from the local coal. It was far less volatile than paraffin and much safer.

We had frying pans, produced by some of the boys for making potato chips, a dart board, hookeye playing cards, bone jack stones used for the game we called Jack Stones, picking them up, tossing them and catching them on the hands etc. Our headquarters was complete, it was almost home from home, and it was made a strict rule that if anyone betrayed the situation or conveyed the slightest information to Noah Thomas, he would be blacklegged for the rest of his youth.

For a long time stupid Noah Thomas, again and again made all kinds of inquiries about what had happened to the boys from the Old Barn but no one seemed to know. He always received the same answer, that probably the boys did not go there any more. Walters' back building remained our headquarters, club and meeting place until 1934. Many boys left after leaving school but younger ones took their place. Alterations were made to the building that year and it was formed into a working men's club, which was later nicknamed the 'Nazi'. It remained the club until the end of the Second World War. It had grown so big in membership that they took over the roller-skating hall and premises next door to the Gwerthonor Hotel. It still carries on in the same premises nearly 50 years on and is still known as the 'Nazi.'

Now established in our club, we organised a working bee to dig out a big section of the Nant Brook, south of our tunnel in the Charity Woods, before it entered the Rhymney river. We dammed the walls and created a big pool and made it a great swimming area before the end of the school summer holidays.

In September 1927, it was back to school once again. I was now promoted into standard two – class 2A and my teacher for the next year would be Mr Emlyn Williams. I had instructions from brother Gwyn to concentrate more on my school work and refrain from spending too much time running around with the boys but, I'm afraid I followed my own decisions in my own way. Gwyn could never understand that my make up was so different from his own and I received a cuff around the ears so often when it developed into an argument.

My sister Edna decided to leave school at the end of that school year, and she began work at Dan Thomas' grocery stores in the Gilfach area, the co-op store, the Gwalia bakery and grocery store, and Dan Thomas, the family grocer. Those old fashioned shops were usually set out with a counter down each side, the left side was always referred to as the wet side, and the right, the dry side. The meaning of these terms referred to the products that were purchased at the particular counter. Behind the wet counter were all the goods such as butter, cheeses, margarine, bacon and hams, cooking fats, dripping etc., and the dry side contained all the packaged and canned goods, bottles, fruit, vegetables and everything other than dairy products. Edna commenced on the dry counter and she had to be fully experienced and thorough before even attempting to serve on the wet side.

There were two brothers, both local identities, Edwin and Daniel; Edwin operated a drapery store and Dan the grocery. Dan's daughter was a close friend of sister Edna, and I suppose it was this influence that made her take on the job.

The Carter family from Beech Cottage, next door, moved to Vere Street near the Gilfach Girls School and new neighbours moved in, Mr and Mrs Charles Teague. Charlie Teague was one of the signalmen who controlled all the trains from a signal box near the New Bridge, and operated the remote control levers for all the systems of points on the railway sidings shunting the full and empty wagons to their various lines to be hauled away.

My father also gave up playing football and cricket for the local team as age was catching up with him. I continued to do my weekly job for my Uncle Dai and, as often as we could, my friend Billy Crane and I would take on the unloading of one of the rail wagons on the slag tips. This was a 12 imperial ton fully loaded wagon, and we had the hard task of shovelling out the contents through a drop door at the side. It would take us eight hours to unload the wagon and it was gruelling work for two young boys. We were paid two shillings and nine pence for the completed job. The contractor was paid three shillings and sixpence per wagon so he let each one for cheap labour, making ninepence profit on each wagon and there were always far more offers to do the job than wagons available. I wonder what a child of eight and a half, and nine years in this modern age, would do, or how they would cope if they had to work so hard to shovel out heavy slag for eight hours in order to obtain the miserable sum of one shilling and fourpence halfpenny, in modern terms about 10p.

As the winter came on and the old year of 1927 was beginning to draw nearer its end, we continued to take part in all our favourite pastimes and games. My father and all the other parents were all boys at heart, and they knew what tough times children had to put up with, and some of them often came along to join us and take part. Electric street lighting was gradually replacing the old standard hand-lit gas lighters and, as long as a parent was taking part in our activities I was allowed, just like all the other boys, to stay out until 10 o'clock. This enabled us to take part in our team games such as 'Dicky show the light', 'Kick the tin', and 'Fox and Hounds', games that modern children would know nothing about in any way.

In November of that year too we experienced a terrible storm; it lasted almost three days; the winds were so powerful much damage was done around the neighbourhood. Hundreds of slates were blown off around the village, trees were blown down and windows blown inwards. Our greatest fear was the massive oak tree outside Oak Cottage; many rotted branches came down but, fortunately, it was a northerly wind blowing them on to the road. One branch was blown down from the big beech tree, and it shattered a glass lean-to near the back door, and smashed in the roof of our garden shed and workshop. When all the damage was assessed and the repairs were underway around the village, the local council decided that the oak tree was too dangerous and voted in favour of the tree being cut down and taken away. George Gummer (Snr) was given the dangerous task of cutting it down; it could fall in one direction only because of the cottages, Garland's sheds, and all the telephone and electrical standards in the vicinity. The tree was one of the biggest oaks I had ever seen; it had a girth diameter of a littler under six feet. There were no chainsaws or mechanical saws in those days, it had to be removed with a big cross saw, hand saws and axes. I was so sad to see it go; each autumn I could gather and pick up at least ten full metal buckets of acorns, and those acorns were valuable to me and my friend Billy Crane. We could trade with old Mathews at the Gwerthonor Canol farm, one full bucket and receive in return 15 apples. Acorns were a natural food for the Welsh pigs and finest fattening food of all, and our oak tree produced the biggest acorns in the district. It took George Gummer and his team three days to finally fell our oak tree. It was taken down one third at a time, from the top downwards, and ropes were used to allow it to fall in the correct area. Garland's shire horses pulled the three sections across the road and down to the railway lines where a big railway breakdown crane lifted the timber on the rail wagons to transport them to the saw mill. It was estimated that the oak tree was 800 years old, and I wonder now what home is adorned with furniture made from the beautiful timber, and what stories it could tell way back to the invaders of the valley. It was the end of another piece of history of Gwerthonor and the end of a landmark that had been around for so long.

The new year of 1928 was the beginning of the big Depression of the 1930s which affected the economics of the whole world. Everything was controlled by the big English companies, markets for all the products were getting less, workers were being stood down and dismissed everywhere, and the dole queues were getting longer each week. Our area perhaps was a little more fortunate, the steelworks, the blast furnaces and iron works were still producing steel to keep the country going and they needed coke used in the smelting process.

The Bargoed and Britannia collieries produced the finest grade of Welsh bituminous steam coal, and they were working full time. Britannia colliery coal was used for producing coke only. It was all passed through big crushers and carried by conveyors into a huge concrete silo. At the base of the silo, it was loaded through hand-operated shutes into the aerial buckets which travelled along the steel ropeways, along the river, to the Bargoed coke ovens. The coal gas was extracted and piped into gasometers, and the local tar also run off into big vats for the extraction of the by-products, and for making and maintaining roads. The big clinker coke brought out when the ovens were cooled was railed away to the steel works. Coal tar was plentiful and available at any time if we needed it. It was used on the roofs of all the outbuildings and sheds, and we simply spread it over everything with a soft sweeping brush, threw some sand over it to harden, and it would last for ever. We always referred to a road being tarred as Macadamed. This was a process from the Scottish engineer who first used the coal tar to make superb roads and runways. Two types of surfacing, using the coal tar, was used in our area. At the local Macadam works, two-inch stones or metal were tipped down an incline and sprayed with tar as they rolled into a big dump at the bottom. These heavily tarred stones were laid anything up to six inches in depth over the road foundations and rolled and consolidated by the old steam roller. The smaller half-inch sprayed metal stones were then laid over the top about three inches in thickness and again rolled. The whole surface was then sprayed with a fine cover of coal tar, with sand and gravel thrown over it and broomed, or brushed for a complete cover and once again rolled to make a perfect road. What a contrast to nowadays when bitumen from oil is used for a road surface, which breaks up in a short time and costs millions of pounds. We always had superb roads then, and the only gravel roads we experienced were the country and farm lanes and the lanes at the rear of all the terraced homes. The roads were sprayed regularly each year with tar from an ancient tar engine pulled along by a sturdy shire horse; the fresh tar was covered with sand and rolled once more by the old steam roller.

The tar engine, the name by which it was commonly called, was an innovative affair and it worked well. It consisted of a big boiler on four big iron wheels, with a hoist above to lift the steel drums of tar above the opening at the top, so that it would run into the boiler for the required capacity. Beneath the boiler was the firebox, complete with a big steel front door to feed in the coal, similar to the stoking of a railway engine. The tar was brought to the boil, and by means of a hand pump at the side, identical to a village water pump, passed through a long flexible tube to a spray nozzle at the end. The tar was sprayed manually over the roads by a tar workman, and with a few words of command to the faithful old horse, it moved along the road. Other workmen following shovelled sand over the wet tar, with the steam roller following to complete the job and with Davy Bennett also supervising as it all went along.

My father worked at the Britannia mine in the occupation of a repairer. He carried out all the repair work in and around the underground galleries and roadways, and fitted the steel horseshoe rings that held up and supported the roofs along the main workings. He had a regular job which was the important thing, right through the

Depression years, and although things were so tough, we got by far better than the unfortunate ones. One of the men who loaded the aerial buckets from the silo shute was Tom Carter and any information we required was supplied by him as we shouted our requests across the river at his job on the other side. Tom's job was very strenuous; he had to pull down a big steel handle to open the guillotine slide to allow the coal to pour out into the bucket. A big spring was compressed in this operation so that the slide would shoot back when the handle was released, to stop the flow of coal. Tom had to pull down on that handle until a full imperial ton had filled the bucket, and he had to repeat that operation hundreds of times in an eight-hour shift. We regularly hitched rides on those buckets by hanging from the handle below in order to get across the river, but we checked with Tom first that the line would not halt. We did not wish to be suspended 30 feet above the river if the machine stopped.

In February of that year of 1928 I heard a human voice speaking from a wireless set for the first time. It was one of the wonderful and important times of my youth. Uncle Dai had obtained a three-valve wireless set. The high-tension power for this set was obtained from the mains electricity supply, but the lower tension power came from a six volt accumulator, which was the term given to it in those early days. It was simply a two-cell lead acid battery, which gave sufficient power for about two weeks and then recharged. It had no loud speakers as we know them today but just a couple of pairs of headphones so two people only could listen to anything that came over the air.

I was given the task of climbing a big sycamore tree, situated in the field at the rear of the house, in order to attach the long aerial wire. The aerial must have been at least 100 yards long. Up on the roof of the house the next job was to fix the other end to the chimney, with another insulated lead down over the roof and through the front window to the wireless set. It would not operate without an earth so a thick earth wire came out through the window and was attached to a piece of pipe driven down into the soil in the front garden. All the neighbours from around the vicinity came in, one after the other, to hear this new wonderful magic sound. They put on a pair of the headphones, full of excitement and exclamations just to hear a crackle and the sound of a human voice coming from the set. Everyone was amazed and thrilled with the wireless set. It was so wonderful and, just by turning a knob on the old antiquated condensor, it was possible to adjust the sound to cut out the crackle and the static which was so bad in those early days. The sound often faded, making it necessary to readjust and retune with the condensor knob. The wireless set, soon to be called radio, would have a great effect on our lives in the years ahead. No longer would we have to depend on the old gramophone and the piano rolls for entertainment in our own homes. It was going to be another two years before we could afford our own wireless set at Oak Cottage.

I was progressing well at school and, in March of that year, I became a member of the junior school football team. We returned to school each day when the afternoon school session was finished and, as the evenings grew longer, for training and preparation for the annual Rhymney Valley school sports at the end of June. It was springtime. The March winds had blown themselves out, the spring showers had transformed the gloom of winter into a picture of green beauty. Everything was lush. The leaves were bursting out of the buds, the fields and hillsides were a carpet of spring flowers, and the masses of bluebells were beginning to transform the yellow and white into a sea of blue as they turned on their annual show. It was the beginning also of the bird-nesting season in the woods and fields, and along the mountain sides. As young boys appreciating all the wonders of nature, we knew every type of bird, the kinds of nests they built, their usual locations, and all the different colours and sizes of the eggs. We spent many hours searching the hedgerows, trees and banks, for different birds' nests and their contents, and each one we found we took great care of. We did not take any eggs, or rob any nest and it was our greatest endeavour to prevent anyone from causing destruction to those nests.

As one grows up there is always a bully or a stand-over ruffian who tries to do everything that is wrong and cause trouble, so it was inevitable that we would clash with this type in our daily lives and be involved in the trouble. Two of these bullies were brothers, Leslie and David Small, the sons of the licencee of the Halfway Inn, situated a short distance off the Pengam Square and very near to the home of our other antagonist Noah Thomas.

One of our regular pastimes at this time of the year was to catch the wild wood pigeons. The wood pigeon was much bigger than the common pigeon and it was greatly sought after by everyone to cook and serve as delicious pigeon pie. It tastes somewhat like chicken, a little darker in colour and it was tender just like a breast of a turkey. The pigeon nested at the top of the tallest trees and they often took over the used twig nests of the rook. They were always out of reach of even the most daring boys amongst us climbing the big trees, so

80

we had to devise a method of our own in order to catch them. Guns, catapults, and shanghais were illegal and forbidden so we had to overcome the problem in our own way. The days were getting longer, and about one hour before dusk, and before the pigeons settled into their roosts for the night, we would make our way across the fields, carefully avoiding the areas where any antagonist such as Noah Thomas might be slinking around, cross the Green Meadow and up to the top end of the 'jungle' carrying our missiles.

The top area of our woods we called the 'jungle' was a mass of huge oaks, ash and tall fir trees where the pigeons roosted for the night. Our missiles were different from the usual stones and rocks thrown at the birds in order to knock them over and capture them. Sometime beforehand we would cut many straight willow, holly, yew or hazelnut canes approximately two feet in length. The thicker end of each cane was sharpened to a fine point and an inch or so below the point, it was bound with a length of copper wire, to add a little more weight. At the other end, the thinner end, two cross cut splits were made at right angles to each other, and two cigarette cards, one cut half way at the centre, were forced into the splits to make each half card face twelve, three, six and nine o'clock to make a flight. A piece of string slightly longer than the cane was now used to propel the missile. A knot was made at one end and looped around the cane below the flight, the string was taken over the knot to anchor it at the flight end, pulled tightly and looped around the index finger of the throwing hand which held the missile around the copper wire. The dart was now ready to be thrown. It was deadly accurate and it was possible to propel it as far as 200 yards and more. Some scraps of bread and crumbs were now scattered in an open area near the trees, and down would come the pigeons ready to take the bait. Whilst they were busy with the bait, our darts would be aimed together at someone's command, from some distance away. We rarely missed, and bagged at least two or three birds with each aim.

On one particular occasion, the Small brothers arrived on the scene throwing stones and scaring away the birds. We were so annoyed we let fly our missiles at them and one of the darts penetrated the calf of the leg of Leslie Small. There were howls of pain and blood every-where. There was a skirmish between David, the older boy and some of my friends and blows were exchanged, but we managed to stop the flow of blood and tied up the bad wound with a handkerchief and off home they went with Leslie howling in pain. It was reported to Noah Thomas, by Small senior and Leslie was treated by the doctor incurring lots of stitches and a sore leg for a long period.

The next day there was an identity parade when we were lined up at school before Garnet and Gaffer, with stupid Noah Thomas in attendance grilling everyone. Eight boys in all, including myself, were picked out by the Small brothers. There was no evidence to show who hurled the missile, so we kept to our story that it was an accident in the process of one of our games. Mr Small, the father did not wish to take it any further, as he was thinking of himself and the loss of his custom, so he left it in the hands of the Gaffer. As a result we all received ten heavy cuts with the cane, five on each hand, and we thanked our lucky stars that Trefor Cadogan Jones was no longer in charge, otherwise we would not have been able to sit down for a week with sore backsides. The Small brothers still continued in their bullying ways but it quietened them down. We had taught them a lesson and our punishment was worthwhile.

Perhaps it was all a strange coincidence because at the end of April, the old Gaffer, T C Jones, died from a heart attack. He was digging in his garden in Gwerthonor Road, had a seizure and died instantly. There were no tears shed by any boy at Gilfach School, a few remarks and unkind parting shots, but little sympathy from anyone. In our youthful eyes another tyrant had departed, a cruel individual, who believed the cane, and the birch, were the answer, the cure, for all incidents and problems concerning children. A person who would never accept any explanation or excuse, a child should be seen, heavily punished, and never heard.

My father attended the old Gaffer's funeral, because my mother insisted that he should go as a resident of Gwerthonor Road, and as a mark of respect, but Fred Crane, the Crane brother's father at 2 Gwerthonor Road, refused to attend, he had experienced too many clashes with T C Jones involving his children over the years.

From memory now, the magnificent old hearse used by Fred Davies-Black, the undertaker was used for the last time at the Gaffer's funeral. There were so many deaths and suicides, caused by the depressed and tough conditions of the period that the business of Fred Davies-Black had increased by leaps and bounds and he had obtained a motor hearse – a modern one of course for the period – in place of the antique hearse. The old hearse was locked up in the shed for a long time, and then it was disposed of, and I have so often wondered what happened to that wonderful, magnificent old vehicle. Another chapter had ended in connection with our district Gwerthonor. The translation of the word *gwerthonor* from the Old Welsh language is interpreted as 'worthy of praise'. With all the majestic woods, glades and meadows, the rolling hills and moors, the sunken farm lanes with mossy banks covered with sweet-smelling violets, the green valley with all the stone cottages perched on the sides, as if a puff of wind would blow them all over, and even the polluting slag tips, indiscriminately scattered everywhere by absent companies and their landlords, and the spoils of industry oiling, and blackening, the fast-flowing river, the huge oaks, ash and beech, the red chestnut mixed with the red and white hawthorn across the floral fields and all mixed up with the sounds of song echoing across the valley, by what better name could it ever be known?

In June of that year Aubrey Carter, Tom Carter's older brother, came to see me with the proposition to take on the job, each weekend, of delivering groceries and goods from the local co-op grocery store. Aubrey was the senior assistant at the store, who worked and controlled the wet side of the establishment. I consulted my parents and they did not object, in fact, they agreed in every way, as money was so scarce that even the smallest amount was a help. On the third weekend of that month I started the job. The hours were 5 p.m. on Friday evening until 10 p.m., and on Saturdays 8 a.m. till 8.30 p.m. with a half hour for lunch on Saturday, and the full pay, two shillings and sixpence – one half-crown.

Competition between the grocery stores was very keen. Everyone had to eat but there was not very much money to go around under the difficult conditions, so every incentive was made to get the custom. We constructed in my own time a large wooden box from the timber of the packing boxes in which the goods arrived into the store, and fitted it onto the grocery hand truck. The previous boy was often still going until midnight, trying to get things completed, carrying small amounts in cardboard containers. I was aware of this as the reason he left, so I was making sure that less returns to the store could be made by carrying a big load, and finishing on time. Everything was sold in brown paper bags and all the items were usually delivered as a special incentive to keep the business of the customer. It was quite a strenuous job pulling and pushing that hand truck all around the district, up the back lanes of the cottages, and even around the farms, to deliver all the buyers' goods. Harry Mathews, the grandson of old Mathews at Gwerthonor Canol farm, served on the dry side of the store, so of course, he was a special customer, and I hated pulling that truck, with its heavy load of corn, and meal, and groceries, up through the rough tracks, through the manure and the mess, to the whitewashed farm-house at least twice each weekend. On the Saturday morning, I packed and weighed, on an ancient cast-iron grain scales, 5, 10 and 14 pounds of potatoes in their respective paper bags, and brought them into the store for sale and delivery. All the white and demerara sugar came in big 100-weight sack bags. This had to be packed and weighed into one and two pound bags also. All the maize, corn, oats, wheat and barley had to be weighed and packed into paper bags in the same way. It kept me busy for the whole morning, because the quantities had to be a sufficient supply for the whole week, and during the afternoon and evening once again I was pushing and pulling my loads around the district. I had to give up my special Saturday afternoon treat with the boys, the penny rush pictures, and the big bag of cut apples from Brobyn's fruit shop. I had to put off my stick-cutting job for Uncle Dai also until Monday evening, and this too sadly prevented me from seeing the silent Western serials that I had followed so keenly.

I gave my mother two shillings but retained sixpence, adding another sixpence to it from my stick cutting, and my weekly threep-enny bit from Granny, so I was still rich, with the total sum of one shilling and threepence each week. I continued to do this grocery job up until a few weeks before my eleventh birthday. A new manager took over the store at that time and reduced my earnings to one shilling and elevenpence. I refused to carry on and my father sup-ported me; slave labour he called it; 17 strenuous hours work for less than one and a halfpenny per hour. Other boys took on the job for that sum; none of them lasted more than two weeks. This manager had the upper hand, take it or leave it and there was always some other stupid person to take it on.

My birthday soon arrived on 26th July. I was now nine years of age. it was also the end of the school year, the last of the term's examinations were finished and, as always, we looked forward eagerly to the whole month of August, the summer school holidays. I achieved second position once again in the order of merit in my class examin-ations and I received more credit from my brother Gwyn, now approaching his seventeenth year. Trevor, the youngest member of our family, was three years old, little Toots was six years of age, Edna sixteen years, and Joyce about to become a teenager of thirteen years. We were all growing up in the most difficult economic and depressed times of our lives, but we were a happy family and we helped each other in every possible way.

I had applied to go to the St Athan boys camp for one week during

August and I had been accepted with another schoolmate, David Ridge, from Vere Street. This camp was situated along the coast about ten miles from Cardiff. It was organised by the Miners' Welfare Association in order to give 1,000 boys an active holiday during the school holidays each year, that is 250 per week for the month of August. Everything was provided and the fares paid, plus a bonus of two shillings and sixpence to spend. All we had to supply were running shoes, a pair of shorts and a sports singlet.

All the shops of the district had an early closing day during the week, that is from twelve noon, usually on Thursday, and then they stayed open until 8.30 p.m. or 10 p.m. on Saturday. It was the annual event of the Bargoed Carnival and they closed all day on this Saturday for the event and kept open on the Thursday. My week at the St Athan camp coincided with this event, so I worked on the Thursday and Friday evenings, and I was free to travel to the camp on Saturday, to return the next Friday afternoon without interfering with my weekend occupation. We caught the train from Pengam Station at 7 a.m. on the Saturday morning to travel into Cardiff. A special train was there waiting to take us all along the coast to St Athan. The camp was a huge complex, with big timber dormitories each accommodating 40 boys, with 20 beds down each side and an adult leader at one end to control and organise everything.

There was a big gymnasium, games rooms, and a huge cook house, and dining room to supply us with all our meals. It was all set in the centre of all kinds of playing fields, for our daily activities. I had a wonderful time, the weather was excellent and it was sad to see it end and travel home once more. Unknown to us in a few years' time it was to be taken over by the government, to become one of the biggest air bases in the country, for all the activities of the fighter and bomber aircraft of the Second World War.

The new year of 1929 brought us deeper into the big Depression. This was the year of the big crash on Wall Street in America, and unemployment there approached between 12 and 20 million. Tom Guntrip, who was to become the husband of my sister Edna, had 15 grocery and general stores throughout London's East End and south London. It was in this year also, trade being so bad, that he was forced into liquidation and lost everything. This was the trend everywhere, belts were tightened even more and South Wales began to be classed, like many of the industrial areas of England, as a depressed area and poverty increased everywhere.

My brother Gwyn was a little more fortunate. He had won various

85

bursaries and scholarships and commenced at Cardiff University in March of that year. My sister Edna gave up the grocery trade as they could no longer afford to employ her. She left home to take up a nursing career at Winson Green in Birmingham. Joyce left school also and worked as a daily help and companion for the Price family. Moses, the male member of the Price family became a sick man and the three sisters continued to teach at the local school. I reached my tenth birthday and continued to deliver the groceries and pack and weigh the dry goods at the local co-op store. It became essential and important now to keep the custom of everyone possible with the small amount of money that was circulating around, but it was to be the last nine months of work in this job for me. My sister Joan, the youngest member of the family, was born on the 26th September of that year, 1929. My father was in regular employment but I can still recall his weekly salary was just two pounds seven shillings and sixpence per week. Somehow we seemed to get by.

The year of 1930 approached, one of the periods in my life I wish to forget, and I have no desire to write about. The politicians in Westminster, with so much needed for so many essential things, spent thousands of pounds building a big new unemployment exchange at the junction of Gilfach and Bargoed. People and families were evicted from their homes, a common daily occurrence as they failed to pay the rents. It was a full-time job trying to help and assist the unfortunate ones, finding temporary homes in churches, halls and huts, for the homeless, and obtaining food for the hungry. All the children in a position to do so, took small items of food to school each day so that the teachers could distribute the proceeds to the hungry. There was anger and frustration everywhere. More English police were drafted into the Valleys and visiting politicians were howled down and stoned under police protection. They had no intention of improving anything. It was a period in our lives we would never forget or forgive.

Each year in July the eleven plus examinations were held to enter a secondary or grammar school. It was necessary to attain the age of eleven years before 30th June in order to qualify. My birthday was in July, so I was not eligible that year. I would have to wait another year until July 1931. I had full praise for our Glamorgan county education system: everything was free, all our books, exercise books, pens, pencils, paper, drawing materials, everything that was needed was supplied. The only cost for any parent for a pupil in a secondary or grammar school during my time was one shilling and fourpence sports fees per term, to cover travelling expenses for teams etc., and to provide a light tea for any visiting team competing against the school. This too was often waived for anyone who simply could not afford to pay it, so our education was absolutely free, and any bureaucrat who attempted to suggest any kind of payment was soon out of office.

It was in July of that year also I won the county essay for the junior age, and the ten-guinea prize for my entry entitled the 'Age of Steam'. It was at that time also in another writing competition with the weekly boys' books *Wizard* and *Rover*, I won five pounds, a football and a commemorative medal.

I was glad to see the end of that year of 1930 hoping that perhaps the year ahead would improve and conditions would be much better.

In the January of 1931 I became captain of the Gilfach boys' football team. It was to be the final season for soccer football in all the schools of the Rhymney Valley, as they would all be changing to rugby for the next winter season. Rugby was the most popular football code throughout South Wales, so we had to fall in line with the others.

In July with all the boys of my age I sat the eleven plus exams and I passed quite well. From memory now I obtained the twenty-fifth position in the order of merit for the whole county of Glamorgan, so I did very well. All the boys who were successful in our district had their names placed in a hat, and picked out in a draw for either Lewis's Grammar School or Bargoed Secondary Grammar School. I was drawn for Bargoed School which I thought would be a big advantage for me in many ways but, unfortunately, things would go wrong, because of the power and jurisdiction given to the Gaffer – the headmaster.

The school had recently been extended and big trades and manual rooms had been added. This suited me as it was my ambition and dream to become a civil engineer. I had many long discussions with my Uncle Dai – David John Davies. He was anxious and keen for me to follow in his footsteps to become a mining engineer, and even at my young age he would ensure that I would be able to attend the Treforest School of Mines for one evening each week. When I obtained my Matriculation in a few years' time, there would be a place for me immediately to go on to and reach that goal. All his help and knowledge, and all his books would be available to me, but I turned it down. Under no circumstances would I go down a mine.

My father was neutral about it. He was a man who would never compel anyone to do something they did not voluntarily wish to do. This was a trait in my father's character that I admired very much.

With my own family, and with everything in life, it was something I have tried to copy.

My uncle and I, having been so close in everything, from that time onwards began to drift apart. There was always a cold greeting when we came face to face and he never inquired how I was progressing, or asked about anything I did or made. I accepted it that way and perhaps it was one of the biggest mistakes I ever made but I was adamant I would never go down a mine.

The first year in Bargoed School was difficult and trying, as discipline was so harsh. Corporal punishment was still the rule, just like at every other school and any sentence or detention was carried out on a Saturday morning. A duty teacher was detailed to supervise recipients of detentions from all classes of the school from 9 a.m. until 12 noon each Saturday morning. Blows across the face and head were a common occurrence simply for failing to answer a question or just a few brief seconds of inattention.

Learning was instilled into everyone with the bamboo stick. It was allowable and there was little we could do about it.

Every subject during the daily lessons incurred homework, so it took at least two hours' work each evening to complete it. Failure to complete it meant attendance before the headmaster – big-barrelled bully, Joseph John Davies. If it was wrong in any way we were caned, and if it was correct and well done, we received no praise at all. This was simply the procedure that was expected. One of the greatest soul destroyers of that first year in Form Two, was Mr Leo Mathews, the mathematics master. When he came into the room there was deathly silence. If any boy moved, or fidgeted, he was clouted across the head. If anyone failed to understand one of his explanations to a problem, or answered wrongly, he was called out from his desk and slashed across the side of the face. Mathews did not believe in hurting his own hand on a hard head. If anyone tried to defend himself with a raised arm, he was hit on the other side also.

We all hated this master, and dreaded the maths lessons of arithmetic, algebra, geometry, and trigonometry. Fear made everyone learn and excel, there were never any low marks in a terminal examination. I suffered along with all my form mates for three years with his teaching, until the end of 1934, when he left to take a senior appointment at Howard Gardens Grammar School in Cardiff. How strange life can be! We met again 11 years later in 1945, in north west Germany. My tank squadron liberated him from a German Stalag prison camp and when he remembered and recognised me, he broke down, and tears rolled down his face.

I worked too hard that first year and, unfortunately, it was to be the downfall of my ambition in life. It was my intention to go on and sit the City and Guilds examinations, which surpassed the apprentice system and to obtain a first-class certificate with credits and distinctions. This complicated examination was a ticket to any senior job in any trade or occupation in the whole country. In September 1932, the beginning of the second year, I was placed in Form 3A, the academic class without any option or choice. It involved all the dry subjects including French and Latin. My manual trades subjects had come to an end and from that time onwards my interest in school work faded away. I was compelled to ingest useless Latin for two periods each day, ten periods per week for the next four years, studying grammar and the literary translations from Virgil. Frustrated and almost heartbroken I appealed to my father for help. On two occasions my father made special visits to the Gaffer – J J Davies and on the second appointment voices were raised, but Davies still refused to transfer me out of that form. He tried to convince my father that I would be far better off staying in that class and it would benefit me much more in the years ahead. His word was law in that school and what he said or ordered had to be carried out. I was determined to go my way and I gave up every Thursday evening to go to night school at the Bargoed Technical School, from 6 p.m. till 9 p.m., to try to catch up with my loss. With all this extra study I had to get up each Friday morning at 5 a.m., when my father began his day to go to work, in order to complete the homework from Thursday's daily lessons. How well I remember my dislike and hate for that useless Latin language. It was so strong that in July 1936 at the Matriculation examinations I took off into the woods, and spent all day lying in the sunshine on the mountainside, rather than sit the examination. It involved the whole day, three hours in the morning for the general and grammar exam, and three hours in the afternoon for the translation from Virgil and the other ancient writings. I confessed to my parents when the results were published at the end of August but they said nothing. They were on my side and sorry about it all.

I was 13 years old now, a teenager, and somehow everything seemed to be going wrong. All my keenness and eagerness at school was not the same. All my hopes and dreams of what I had wished for and hoped to do were shattered. My dear old dad tried to encourage me and urged me to stick at it and do my best. My brother Gwyn gave me no encouragement at all. With his disposition he believed everything was correct and in order, and I should put my heart and soul into those subjects that were so uninteresting to me, so I carried on, but it was all at a very low key.

Dear old Granny died in that year of 1932. There was only one of the Davies' name now remaining, David John Davies her son, my Uncle Dai and his only daughter Mair. When Mair married the name would come to an end. Once again it was a very big funeral for Granny. All the relations and offspring of the Webb family came from the surrounding valleys, and the majority of the population of Gilfach and Gwerthonor areas all paid their homage to this great lady. It was the modern motor hearse for the occasion with a long procession from the Gilfach Calvinistic Presbyterian Chapel to the Pengam Cemetery so that she could be united with her husband, that wonderful man, my grandfather. The hourly blast from the Britannia Mine hooter was silenced for one rare occasion, at the request of her son, my Uncle Dai, so that the wonderful massed singing of the marching column would not be interrupted. The deeply moving sounds of the long column echoed and reverberated through the hills and across the valley. I had grown quite tall at this stage of my life, and my mother insisted that I wear a bowler hat. For the first time in my life, I was a 13-year-old boy marching with the mourners behind the hearse with a black bowler hat perched upon my tousled head.

During the early months of 1933 two of my old schoolfriends, boys from the Gwerthonor area, were killed in mine accidents. Herbert (Bert) Davies a cousin of the Crane brothers, and the son of the eldest son of old Tard Davies from the Gilfach level, was crushed to death in a big underground earth fall in the Bargoed colliery. Just one week later, Glyn Stucky, one of the Stucky brothers, who lived next door to Granny in Maes-y-craig Street was killed in a similar accident. My old friend Tom Carter, also, lost a leg in another accident at the Bedwas mine in the Sirhowy Valley. I felt so sorry for Tom, as he had done so much for me in my younger years. He had given up the job at the big coal site, filling the aerial ropeway buckets, and had married and moved away to his wife's area in the small town of Bedwas, where he obtained work at the Bedwas colliery. A tragic accident severed his left leg at the thigh. It was all such a sad affair for Tom, a brilliant footballer, and sportsman, and brought to an end his involvement in these active pastimes. These accidents made me more determined than ever never to go down a coal mine. Although I was born and bred in this environment, I have never descended into a deep coal mine.

90

The beginning of the worrying years of my youth was approaching. On the European scene the dictators, Mussolini and Hitler, were filling the newspapers daily with their antics and the fear of war was once again on everyone's mind. It was just 14 years or so since the end of the last terrible mess in Europe, and everyone was still feeling the effects. The memories and condolences were still vivid after many losses in that great slaughter.

I was approaching my fourteenth birthday and about to begin my third year in Bargoed School. I was making sure now that I simply kept an average position in the middle reaches of merit in each terminal examination. I had learned my lesson after I was compelled to study subjects that were useless to me and to be denied the career I wished to embark upon. I became a member of the school rugby team that winter, and I thoroughly enjoyed the trips through the valleys to play against the various schools in our part of the county. If it was an away match we usually travelled on the old Brecon and Merthyr railway from Bargoed station, winding and twisting up through the valley in those warm, steam-heated, comfortable carriages to the familiar old towns, and the local grammar schools called Tredegar, Brynmawr, Brecon, Cyfather and Merthyr. At other times down the valley to Caerphilly and across into the Sirhowy Valley to Maes-y-Cymmer and all the various schools in Cardiff. Our greatest rival of all was of course the other local school, Lewis's Grammar School at Pengam. So life went on for me in the same old way, as I eagerly awaited the end of each week of lessons for the Saturday sport and a break from it all.

In October of that year 1933 Hitler withdrew Germany from the League of Nations and denounced the end of the Versaille's Treaty. He immediately reintroduced military service for the whole German nation. Sadly once again it was the beginning of the rapid rise of German and Prussian militarism and it was frightening for everyone. The League of Nations was just a farcical affair. It was weak and had no power to do anything. The diehard politicians were still living in their imperial way of thinking at the turn of the century and did nothing. It was the start of madman Hitler's militarism and the domination of the whole of Europe.

In January of the year 1934, Hitler began his huge deceit of the Western Powers. He signed a 30-year non-aggression pact with the leader of Poland, a ploy to give himself time to re-arm and build up his armies and military equipment. The outlook was sick to me. I was nearing my fifteenth birthday and shortly before that time Hitler's thugs assassinated President Dollfuss of Austria. War seemed inevitable now, but how far away was it all to be? All my hopes and dreams of a successful career were beginning to fade away. I believed that I was born at the wrong time.

Into the new year of 1935 and the middle of January, once again France gave in to Hitler's demands and returned the Saar region to Germany. France had gained control of it after the Versailles Treaty and now once again, it became part of Hitler's military empire. All the weak-kneed nations were appeasing this madman and giving in to his demands.

Our old antagonist Noah Thomas retired in March of that year. He had dishonestly deceived and crookedly served the community and the police force for 40 years. He was a sick man now and we knew his retirement was a farce, as he would still be roaming around, despite his disabilities, and causing innocent people trouble with his pimping and tale carrying. However, he had been given a long innings and his days were soon to come to an end. As the year slipped by, in October the other despot, Mussolini, having slaughtered so many people in his conquests of the North African states of Libya and Tunisia, invaded Abyssinia and Eritrea. It was going to be a shocking affair, resorting once again to the rise of the dreaded mustard gas and other chemical weapons.

It was to be my last six months at Bargoed School as the year of 1935 ended and we turned into 1936, and I would sit the Central Welsh Board Senior Certificate and London Matriculation exam at the end of the school year in July. My brother Gwyn had left Cardiff University and had taken up a position in Glasgow, Scotland. He was still studying to obtain his Master's Degree. In January I was chosen for the Welsh Schoolboys Rugby team in the position of wing forward and I played against Ireland and Scotland, both matches at the Cardiff Arms Park international rugby ground. We won the first match and the other was tied, and I had achieved one of my ambitions in life to play for my country.

It was in the month of April of that year 1936, the man who had been such a thorn in our side, and the enemy of every boy in the whole neighbourhood for so long, succumbed to the inevitable and passed away. Noah John Thomas had come to the end of his days.

It was the custom to attend and pay homage at the burial of every local inhabitant irrespective of their position, creed or character. On this occasion, the only time I ever saw it happen, everyone stayed away, and there were murmurs of condemnation everywhere. Each boy who had grown up in the area could remember a blow across the

92

head or a kick up the rear end. The lies, the deceit and slyness and all the unnecessary troubles caused by him still brought anger to their minds and hearts. There was an investigation and inquiry after his burial, as some person or persons unknown had draped his grave with masses of ivy and the little blue flower of the deadly nightshade. This was a terrible insult according to Welsh superstition. I was the only person who knew the ones who had committed the terrible insult, and I have kept the secret all my life. The culprits were dead and buried a long time ago, the two Crane brothers – Fred and Bill, the close friends of my boyhood.

It was then also that the international troubles in Europe developed towards a conflict. Hitler's troops marched into and occupied the Rhineland which had been under the control and jurisdiction of France since the end of the First World War.

Spring turned into summer of that year 1936 and at the beginning of July, I sat the Matric examinations. Twelve three-hour examinations were for me dispersed over a period of three weeks. I never bothered to study or revise because if all the knowledge in my head did not see me through, it did not matter any more. I had formed the belief in my mind that war was inevitable and if we survived it would certainly be most extraordinary. In the middle of those examinations on 13th July 1936, the Spanish Civil War broke out, with the rise of another military dictator, General Franco. It was going to be a wonderful practice campaign in dive-bombing and aerial bombardment for the Fascist forces of Mussolini and Hitler, a taste of what was in store for us all.

I celebrated my seventeenth birthday on the 26th of that month, the day the school broke up for the end of the year and the summer recess. There were 26 boys in that A Form including myself, and I shook hands with each one that afternoon as we left the school. Twenty-one of them had just a few years to live. They died between 1939 and 1945. There were five survivors of that form when the war ended in 1945 and for some strange reason I was one of them. I walked home that afternoon with two friends, John Selwyn Thomas and Glyn Aubrey Mathews. We had together been members of the school rugby team. John lived just a hundred yards away from dear old Granny's home in Maes-y-craig Street. Glyn lived at Tir-y-beth and was visiting his grandmother in Gilfach on his way home. I remember that afternoon so vividly, as it was hot and sunny and a thunderstorm was threatening. We discussed the worrying state of affairs with the antics of the madman Hitler, and joked about it all. Glyn died, shot down over the German Ruhr as a rear gunner in a Lancaster bomber in 1942. John went down with the battleship *The Prince of Wales*, of all names, off Singapore after the Japs entered the war in 1941.

I had a holiday break now until the exam results came out in the third week of August. I passed the examinations quite well with four credits and a couple of passes and I confessed to my parents that I had dodged the Latin examination, but they said little about it.

4

Commencing Work and the Death of My Brother

I obtained my first job at the end of that month, starting in the offices of the Powell-Dyffryn Company as a pay clerk, from 9 a.m. till 6 p.m. each day and from 9 a.m. till 12 noon on the Saturday. It was an easy job and the pay was poor. I disliked being penned up each day at an office desk so I gave it up after three weeks.

At the beginning of October I was offered a job by Evan Hughes, a friend of my brother Gwyn. He was the head of the lamp and battery section at the Penallta Mine. This mine had been one of the biggest productive mines in South Wales, having begun operations after the First World War and at that period employed nearly 2,000 men. It is still working 70 years later. Every underground employee was given a round disk a little larger than a penny with a number stamped upon it and referred to as a 'check'. At the start of each shift, morning, afternoon or night, this check was handed in and a lamp issued with the corresponding number stamped on it. The check was reissued when the lamp was returned at the end of the shift. This involved a great deal of recording. At the start of each shift a register was made and each check recorded in numerical order to record each man who had descended the mine. Every six-volt rechargeable battery cell was correspondingly numbered to the electric lamp, and every record was kept of the date it entered service, any repairs, when it was due for washing out the cells, the plates replacement, a complete record of the life of the battery. The heavy electric lamps were locked with a deadlock within the screw-on base and they could be opened on a magnetic unlocking base only, which released the deadbolt and allowed the lamp base to be screwed off. All the head cap lamps with a lead running to the belt-held battery were also sealed with a magnetic locking device, and similarly the oil safety lamps were locked in the same way. The premises were lined with long battery charging systems, all in banks with cups and copper electrodes to contact the terminals, and as each bank was filled the required charging power was set on a big ammeter on each board. The power was supplied by electric generators converting the mains alternating current to direct current and, as the load increased, it was necessary to start an extra generator. Every lamp had to be tested at the end of each shift, examined for any faults, or damage, topped up if necessary, cleaned, and the battery recharged. Each oil lamp was dismantled, the sealing asbestos washers changed, the safety gauze carefully examined and cleaned on a revolving brush machine, and the base refilled with colza oil. It was relighted on an electric spark box through an insulated terminal in preparation for the next shift. There were about 30 men employed in this section and my main task, after I knew the running of things, was to do the book work and the records. I started on the day shift, catering for about 1,200 men, from 6 a.m. till 2 p.m. each day including Sunday, Saturdays until 1 p.m. I did not have much time any more for recreation but I still continued my one night per week at school, and each Saturday I finished in time in order to get home and go to Cardiff or Newport to see the football teams play in the English Soccer League.

After some six months or so and into 1937 I went relieving to the Britannia and Bargoed Mines; there was always someone absent, or they became shorthanded or overworked.

In June of that year the European situation got worse. Lord Halifax, the foreign minister, another old Tory diehard, rushed to Berlin, almost begging Hitler to change his threats and antics, and appealing to him to keep the peace. The big appeasement of Hitler and his Fascist regime began.

In November we received a sudden tragic blow. It was the evening of the sixteenth day of the month, a dirty, cold foggy night. At approximately 6.30 p.m., there was a knock at the front door. My mother answered the door to a uniformed police officer from the Bargoed police station. He was invited inside, as poor mother realised something was wrong. Sadly he broke the news to us that Gwyn had died that morning, tragically killed in an accident. It was just one day after his 26th birthday. There was a complete silence.

For some time, the only sound was the tick of the old clock hanging on the wall. Everyone was stunned with the news. The police officer apologised for his sad visit and explained further than an inquest would be held, and then Gwyn's body would be transported by train to Pengam Station. He also said he would inform us later of its pending arrival, and suggested to my father that he make the necessary burial arrangements the next day.

It seemed to me such a sad waste of human life. All the learning and the studies he had undertaken, and the devotion he had given to his books and manuscripts throughout his life. All for nothing but a sad end with no reward.

On 20th November 1937 Gwyn was buried in the shadow of the Western Wall of the old Gelligaer Norman Church. All the old pupils and schoolmates from Lewis's Grammar School, and the local residents from Gilfach and the Gwerthonor area, paid their last tribute to him. The Gilfach Boys School closed at 2.30 p.m. so that the teachers who had known him so well could attend the funeral. It had been just a few days beforehand that we had received a letter from him telling us that he was looking forward to being home for Christmas.

It was to be a sad Christmas for us all that year. Joyce and Edna came home from Birmingham to be with us, but the tragedy hit my parents very hard. My father even gave up his job to seek something elsewhere in the New Year. I had to accept it sadly with the gloomy thoughts that perhaps it was my turn next. I was approaching my nineteenth year and things were very bad with the prospect of another war. The Spanish Civil War was causing so much bloodshed and so many casualties, and the atrocities were increasing. Hitler's dive-bombers and war planes massacred the Spanish town of Guernica, one of the most shocking events of that period.

At the beginning of March, Hitler threatened President Schuschnigg of Austria and gave him an ultimatum, and then on the twelfth day of that month, his troops and military might marched in and occupied Austria and incorporated that country under the Nazi Reich.

My father now became curator of the Gilfach bowling greens, the tennis courts and the children's playground which had been constructed on the site of Grandfather's old quarry. My sister Toots left Hengoed Girls Grammar School and began work at Loveday's drapery and store on the Pengam Square. Trevor was to sit the eleven plus examination that year and sister Joan was just eight years old.

In May of that year 1938, I commenced the afternoon shift, continuous shift work every day. On Saturdays the work ended at 8 p.m. and started once more at 4 p.m. till 10.30 p.m. on Sunday. I was receiving double time for the weekend work, and my aim was to obtain more money. I gave up the evening classes and it gave me a little more time each morning to concentrate on my books, without the temptation of going out in the evening. I bought myself a bicycle so that I could travel backwards and forwards each afternoon and night, and I fell foul of the law over one of their stupid rules. My bike was well lit with a red front and rear light, but the rule stated that the lower end of the rear mudguard must be painted white. I was booked and reported about 11 p.m. on a dark wet June night, and consequently fined three pounds for such a trivial offence. Once again it was just prejudice. The magistrate on the bench was Morrison the JP from Gwerthonor Road, the man I refused to salute and 'touch my cap to', as I grew up through my schooldays.

In July I sat the City and Guilds examination, which involved two days of theory and three days of practical tests, so I excused myself from work for five days. The written examination was conducted in Cardiff and the practical at a building site there also and on two other factory premises. I passed with flying colours, and I obtained my first class certificate, but I had gloomy thoughts about it all. Was it going to be any good to me? The situation was bad and it appeared that war was now inevitable.

Life went on in the same old way. The year of 1938 was drawing to a close, and Christmas 1938 was going to be the last family reunion. Gwyn was now absent and it was to be the last time that we would all be united together at Oak Cottage for the final days of the old year.

Part Two

War and the Traumatic tears
1939–1946

5

The Outbreak of War

It was midwinter, half way through the month of January, and it had been, and was to continue to be a mild winter, but with incessant miserable rain. I became a member of the old – wrongly named – 'Nazi club', that had taken over our old premises at the rear of Walters' store in Gwerthonor Place, where we sought refuge from Noah Thomas, and had now moved to the roller-skating hall next to the Gwerthonor Hotel. I spent many of those cold wet mornings there, playing snooker or billiards, with the boys, before work each afternoon. My father had taken over the Gelligaer welfare grounds as curator, and I often spent some mornings there also, helping out a little.

On 16th March Hitler's troops invaded Czechoslovakia and occupied and subdued that nation under Nazi rule. On 25th March, the Spanish Civil War came to an end, Franco and his Fascist forces had finally broken the Spanish people with over one million casualties. Hitler and Mussolini had achieved all the experience and practice their troops and war planes required for the shocking deeds to come.

The Westminster parliament introduced the Militia Bill, under which all male citizens attaining the age of 20 years were conscripted and compelled to do military service – and my twentieth birthday was just four months away. All passports of citizens between the ages of 18 and 40 years were cancelled and void, and no male person of that age was allowed to leave the country. It was our turn now to experience compulsory militarism also.

On 20th June I had to register for military service, one month before my twentieth birthday, and on 28th June I was given a railway voucher to Newport and instructed to attend a medical examination at the drill hall outside Newport railway station. I lost a day's pay attending that examination with no compensation in lieu, and I had no option or choice of any unit or regiment. I was simply told to follow military instructions. It appeared that from now on I was under military orders, and soon to be just an individual with an alloted number, a conscript with no rights at all. There was no such thing as the luxury of paid holidays for an employee in any job or industry during those times. If anyone wanted a break or a holiday they forfeited their wages. I took an unpaid holiday for two weeks during August and I spent much of it helping my father at the bowling greens and the welfare grounds at Gelligaer.

At that time also there was all the publicity of the weak diehard Tory politician Neville Chamberlain rushing to appease Hitler, and returning waving a piece of paper muttering, 'Peace in our time.'

It was a bright Sunday morning, 3rd September 1939, and a day I will always remember. I was cleaning my bicycle in the backyard and getting things ready for my afternoon's work when my mother came out to tell me that there was a special announcement on the radio at 11 o'clock. The day before, Hitler had invaded Poland and he had been given an ultimatum by the French and British governments to immediately withdraw his forces within 24 hours, otherwise the assistance pact with Poland would be honoured. The 24 hours had expired and I guessed what it was all about. We heard the solemn announcement by Chamberlain that we were in a 'state of war' with Hitler and the German nation. There was complete silence, not a comment or remark from any member of the family. I had my lunch, and with all the worrying thoughts on my mind, I said nothing, jumped on my bike and rode off to work in the usual way. The next morning, Monday, 4th September, the postman delivered to me the orders for my call-up. With no option, I was instructed to report for military service at the Guards Military barracks and depot at Caterham in Surrey, before midnight on Thursday, 7th September 1939, and with those instructions there was a one-way railway ticket voucher. I went off to work as usual that Monday afternoon and informed them of the situation. I was to become a private soldier on the disgusting pay of two shillings per day. I informed them that I was finishing the next day and would collect my pay and all that was due to me on the Wednesday.

The following morning at 9 a.m. I received a military telegram cancelling the order and to await further instructions. They had certainly muddled me around, so once again I had to give another explanation at work and produce the telegram hoping that I could continue with the job. It appeared that with the huge influx of reserves and territorial army volunteers and members they had no room at that stage for any more until the expeditionary forces had been worked out and shipped to northern France.

I continued in my job, not knowing when I would depart, until the end of the second week in November 1939. It was then I received the final instructions but this time they did allow me to spend Christmas at home, and report for service on 5th January 1940. I gave up my job once again at the end of November to have a month's break until Christmas and my final departure for military service.

The month of December 1939 and the closing week of that year was to bring us the beginning of one of the worst winters in my lifetime. Heavy snow began to fall and a huge freeze up began. All transport came to a halt, and telegraph poles and wires came down with the tremendous weight of ice and frozen snow. Trains were snowed up and abandoned in huge drifts throughout the country and we had to dig ourselves out to the road from Oak Cottage. The snow had drifted and piled up to the roofline of all the cottages, and all the homes facing east. It was an unusual holiday for me, as nearly all my time was taken up shovelling snow and clearing pathways daily along the footpaths to the village shops. For almost a week I piggy-backed my ten-year-old sister Joan to the local girls' school, picking my way through the huge drifts and carrying a shovel for emergencies. It was all such a bad omen for the first three months or so of war and I felt sorry for all those soldiers shivering in the forward areas of northern France. It was certainly a white Christmas to close the year of 1939 and, for me, it was to be the last festive season with the family, around a huge blazing fire.

It arrived, the morning of 5th January 1940, and it was a bitterly cold, grey morning, with clumps of snow everywhere. Slush and melting snow was pushed up into heaps and piles on the side of the roads and footpaths. The cold north wind was icy and bleak to meet me as I was about to make my departure into the unknown and uncertain future. I ignored the advice of my mother to wear an overcoat, as it would be just one more article of clothing to pack up and dispatch home when I reached my destination. It was about 6.30 a.m. and I said my goodbyes to all the other members of the family, and my father came along with me to pick up two other boys, Albert Turner, an old Gilfach schoolmate and Bert Higgs from Bargoed. Along with their parents we made our way to Bargoed railway station to travel to Newport to catch the 8.45 a.m. express train to London.

We said our last goodbyes as we boarded the warm comfortable carriage of the Brecon and Merthyr railway, and we were waved away as the shining tank engine pulled out of the station, hissing and puffing in the cold icy air. I stood up at the window with a feeling of sadness as the train puffed along through the Bargoed colliery sidings, clanking across the points as it passed the Britannia stick woods along the river, with the Charity Woods, now bare of leaves and flowers stretching a long way on the other side. The engine driver blew the whistle as we passed the familiar stockpiles of Norwegian pine props, and into the Britannia sidings, re-living the many times we released the logs to roll down to the river. Through the gaps in the trees I could get a passing glance of Oak Cottage across the valley and I wondered then – was this to be the last time for me to see it all? The train puffed on, stopping at Pengam(mon) station and then on through the valleys to Newport. This journey was only the second occasion I had left the border of South Wales, and perhaps it would be the last.

We boarded the London train and shortly after midday we arrived at Paddington Station. The small ticket pinned to our lapels gave away our identity, and we were helped and assisted in every way. The country was at war, and the aloofness and coldness of strangers seemed to have gone. Our payment for a cup of tea and a snack was turned down, it was on the house. We boarded a double-decker bus next to take us across London to Waterloo Station, and people stepped aside to let us get on. Once again the payment of our fare was not accepted by the conductor. At Waterloo we went into a Lyons Corner House restaurant; once again we did not pay. We had never received such VIP treatment in all our lives. We boarded yet another train at Waterloo to take us to our destination and approximately 4 p.m. on a cold icy afternoon with piles of snow slush everywhere, we arrived in Caterham railway station.

6

First World War Parade-ground Training for a Modern Military Machine

I walked up the long hill from the railway station, through the town of Caterham, along with scores of other boys the same age and conscript group as myself, to the entrance of the Guards Depot. I passed through the archway at the main gate, and my civilian life came to an end for a long time. I was now an army recruit and addressed as one. I would not become classed as a guardsman until I passed out in 13 weeks' time. The shouting and abuse began five yards inside that gate, and every movement I made now off the barrack square and parade ground, except on a Saturday and Sunday afternoon would be in double time. I was given a number 2735385, and allotted and detailed to a squad – Sergeant Starr's Squad of 45 recruits. We were housed in a first-floor barrack room with access by a stone stairway from the ground. At the top of the stairway were the ablutions, wash basins and toilets, with a barrack room on the left and right, with rows of iron beds down each side and a coal fireplace grate at the extreme end. A – so-called – trained soldier was in charge of each barrack room, and he was responsible for everything not done to disciplinary orders and rules. Each recruit had an iron bed, three biscuit mattresses that fitted the nineteenth-century iron slats when placed end to end, two grey army blankets, and a straw-filled pillow. There were no such things as sheets, we simply slept between the fold of one blanket and placed the other on top. For any extra warmth we used the greatcoat. The temperature outside in January was well below freezing point. A cupboard at the bedside had to contain various pieces of kit only, set out in the required pattern as per the disciplinary rules. On its top sat the two soldiers' webbing packs, small and larger,

105

fitted with pieces of cardboard to keep them perfectly square. The greatcoat was a heavy blue peacetime coat with brass buttons, folded in strict regimental fashion with the belt buttoned around the front making it appear like a body, hanging at the side of the bed. The uniform also was the First World War tunic with brass buttons to the neck, with a webbing belt around the waist and the old fashioned puttees bound around the legs to the knee, with black boots, a steel tip around the heel and 30 regulation rules of iron shoe studs on each sole.

The second day of my life as a recruit began at 6 a.m. with reveille and if anyone was not out of bed by five minutes after six they were tipped out and all their kit and equipment scattered over them. Every parade and assembly was now governed by the call of the bugle, and that day we received the various inoculations and a vaccination, and a farcical swearing in. Everyone was assembled, the oath was read out and everyone answered in unison the word 'yes'. On that day too I was issued with the remainder of my kit, and a 1902 Lee-Enfield rifle with bayonet and scabbard. I received an issue of brown paper and string also to pack up my civilian clothes and shoes into a parcel to dispatch them home through the parcel post. I had to pay the postage of course.

Day number three, my toy soldier training began in earnest. Reveille was blown at 6 a.m., and we were then allowed 45 minutes to wash, shave and dress, make up the bed regulation fashion, have kit neatly laid out and folded on that bed, and be on parade – breakfast parade – at 6.45 a.m. We had to be neatly dressed, in pressed uniform with all brass buttons and badges highly polished, and showing one particular article or piece of equipment for inspection, as per daily orders issued the night before. If anything was not up to standard or failed to pass the inspection by some young facetious officer, the squad sergeant reported it and the individual was marched in by a drill sergeant at the daily company memoranda before the company commander. The charge was read out by the drill sergeant and the person was asked if he had anything to say. The stupid disciplinary rules now compelled the individual to say to the officer, 'I thank you sir for leave to speak' before anything else was said. Failure to do this meant arrest and in double time off to the guardroom. This 'thanking to speak' riled me all through my army life in this regiment. A private soldier was the lowest form of life to a blue-blooded effeminate Guards officer, and the poor private was treated as such. The punishment at Memoranda was usually an extra hour's drill parade, wearing a 56-pound pack, on a Saturday or Sunday afternoon. At 7 a.m. it was breakfast in the mess hall, and between 7.30 and 8 a.m. the barrack room floor was 'bumped', the term used for cleaning. A swivel-handled heavy floor polisher was used until you could see your own reflection in the shine. Every broom handle was scrubbed, the wash house was scrubbed, all hand basins and toilets cleaned, the taps polished and all toilet wooden seats scrubbed white. The metal coal box was burnished with a burnishing chain, and the whole barrack room made presentable for the daily inspection. The first drill parade on the barrack square was at 8.15 a.m., after another inspection by a young officer in training, and 9.15 a.m. a break for five minutes before the next drill parade until 10.15 a.m. At this time, we were given a mug of hot cocoa, then one hour's physical training, followed by a hot shower and then a compulsory two minutes under the cold shower with the temperature below freezing. If anyone failed to stay under for the full two minutes, he received an extra two minutes to add to his discomfort. Dinner was at 12.30 for one hour then back on drill parade at 1.45 p.m. Two more hours' drill in the afternoon until 4 p.m. and then tea at 4.30 p.m. the last meal of the day. Six was the daily, compulsory shining parade. With a ground sheet spread out on the bed we laboured away shining, cleaning everything and applying blanco to all the webbed equipment. No one was allowed to talk or smoke for two hours until 8 p.m. At 8 p.m. all fingernails and toenails were inspected for cleanliness. From 8.15 to 8.30 p.m. it was compulsory rifle exercises, holding the rifle with one hand at arm's length for five-minute periods until one's arm ached with pain. Then there was bolt action for fifteen minutes, which was the make believe of unloading and reloading the rifle. From 8.30 p.m. till lights out at 10 p.m. the time was our own, sometimes it was possible to get a cup of tea at the canteen, or write a letter, or simply fall into bed at the end of a weary day.

This life and routine continued daily except on Sundays. At 10 a.m. there was a full parade on the barrack square to be marched into Caterham for a compulsory church parade. Any agnostics or non-believers, who confirmed their beliefs, spent the morning from 8 a.m. till 1 p.m. in the cookhouse labouring with all the dirty chores. At the end of the second week of my service, the politicians decided, after a public outcry, to raise the pay of a private soldier to three shillings and sixpence per day. I alloted ten shillings of my weekly pay to my mother, and she deposited that sum for me in the local bank under the name of my young sister Joan in case anything happened to me. The paymaster retained from each man three shillings and sixpence in credit so my weekly pay was the 'huge' sum of eleven shillings. From this sum we had to provide all our cleaning and toilet materials, polish, blanco, newspapers, etc., any canteen articles, cups of tea, cake, postage and writing materials, and if one was fortunate to be allowed out of barracks on a weekend, the admission fee to the cinema. If anyone was a smoker the little remaining did not go very far.

After three weeks of this monotonous drill training it was compulsory for the squad to pass a test in order to be allowed to go outside the barracks after 1 p.m. on a Saturday and Sunday until midnight. My first outing came after one month. I went to the pictures on a Saturday evening in Caterham with two other fellow recruits, Partridge and Nichols.

After a period of six weeks with the same old routine of drill, I had one hour's session with my squad, on the 30-yard indoor rifle range. I fired 10 rounds at a target with a .22 rifle, and this was to be the only firing practice I would receive before coming face to face with the German army. It was more important to our imperial masters to be able to salute and drill correctly, rather than to be proficient with the rifle and target practice to confront the enemy in the war that lay ahead. During the first week of April 1940, our recruit training was supposedly completed and we were transported to Colchester barracks in Essex to become part of No. 3 company of the training battalion.

My life was a little easier now but we still went through the routine of the breakfast parade at 6.45 a.m. each day, showing some highly polished article or piece of equipment, and then three hours of drill until midday on the barrack square. Another practice drill at 1.45 in the afternoon, followed then by weapon training until 4.30 p.m. This consisted of assembling and taking apart the Bren machine-gun and going through the make believe of practice firing, also through the routine of rectifying stoppages, assembling and mounting its anti-aircraft stand, filling magazines with dummy cartridges, and bayonet practice. On an average of two days each week, I was detailed of fatigue duties, and cookhouse chores, fire piquet and 24 hours of sentry duty on the main gate each fortnight. I was now considered to be a trained soldier. I had never been on a field rifle range, and I had never fired a .303 rifle or a Bren machine-gun! I had never received any field training, but thank heavens, for my own youth training in the hills and woods of South Wales and Gwerthonor as I grew up would help me far more in dire circumstances than any army training I had received up to that period. To our imperial masters and brass hats we could salute and march properly, so we were proficient soldiers.

It was the spring of 1940 and the last week of April of that year, when activity on the Western Front in northern France began to increase, and it appeared that the phoney war, as the press referred to it, was about to come to an end. The generals, commanders, and politicians were still believing in the mentality and system of trench warfare of the First World War, but they were in for a shock. They did not know what Hitler had in store. We had poor, miserable equipment, untrained conscripts, and out-dated weapons, no modern tanks or guns. It was pathetic and we would suffer through these tragic mistakes.

It was a beautiful sunny afternoon of that week. We had been issued with two suits of the new battledress, and were wearing our full webbing equipment, gas cape etc. Carrying a khaki greatcoat and a full kitbag we were bundled into army trucks to be transported to the Tower of London, to join and become part of the newly formed 2nd Battalion Welsh Guards. I sat on one of the wooden fabricated benches in the rear of the truck as it was driven through the county of Essex and Epping Forest. Everything was lush and green, and the trees were in full leaf once again. It was a perfect day for a country picnic. I looked down at my rifle as it caught the gleam of the sun reflecting in the highly polished surface of the wooden butt, and it passed through my thoughts of all the monotonous hours of continuous work and spit and polish that I had spent on its surface. My thoughts turned to anxiety and concern as I wondered if the darn thing would fire correctly and straight. I knew the procedures and rules, but what was the feeling when the trigger was pressed? I was a soldier; I had never fired my own weapon and it filled me with disgust. We arrived at the cobbled yard of the Tower and assembled and paraded to be sorted out in the unit. I became a member of No. 5 Section, No. 8 Platoon of No. 3 Company of the 2nd Battalion. I watched a pair of black ravens in the yard as I climbed the centuries-old stone steps to the barrack room. The walls were stark and cold behind the rows of iron beds arranged down each side. These beds, too, must have been almost as old by the appearance of them, still kept immaculate with black paint, with their thin basket-weave iron slats to support the familiar biscuit mattresses. It was an uncomfortable night for me and I was glad it was for one night only. At least, just like the many unfortunate individuals over the centuries before me, I can say that I spent an unpleasant night in the Tower of London although it was nothing to be proud of.

The next morning we were assembled on parade after breakfast. All our kitbags and greatcoats were loaded into an army truck and, in battledress and full equipment, we were marched as a complete battalion behind a drum and fife band through the streets of London to Waterloo Railway Station to board a special train to take us to Camberley in Surrey.

We arrived at Camberley about noon and once again we were marched through the town and for a further two miles to Old Dean Common. An encampment had been set up on the common with scores of army bell tents. The only structural buildings were the wash houses, toilets and the cookhouse. The mess hall was a big marquee tent, with wooden tables and benches. Each company was set out on different locations on the big common, and every platoon was allotted a bell tent for each section of eight men. Each man slept on a straw palliasse around the circular tent with feet towards the central pole. It was very uncomfortable with all our kit and equipment, and so crowded with eight occupants and with the circular tent walls just eighteen inches high, before they tapered to the central pole seven feet tall. I was part of No. 5 Section, and I knew the other members except for Corporal Randall, the section leader. We were all conscripts except Randall. All the other members of No. 8 Platoon I knew also from the early days, but many of the NCOs, sergeants and corporals I had never seen before, so we were all a fairly unfamiliar bunch. Randall, our section leader, was an awkward six-feet-three-inch fellow; he spoke with a lisp but something else more prominent for me to remember were his huge feet. He wore size 14s in army boots. The huge feet protruded and stuck out below the length of our army blanket and beyond the central tent pole, taking up the space of the man opposite much to his inconvenience. For the next two days it rained, everything was wet, and the tent was soaked. Each time one touched or bumped one's head against the canvas, the water came through, making it very miserable and unpleasant. We had to run through the mud and rain, covered with a groundsheet, to all our meals, to the wash-houses and toilets and to parades in a big marquee tent, then try to keep our clothes and kit dry covered with the saturated groundsheet. The groundsheet was also used beneath the straw palliasse at night to protect it from the damp ground.

It was 10th May 1940, and much to our relief the sun was shining brightly. It was a beautiful spring day and it was announced at long

110

last that we were to be granted seven days' embarkation leave. It was a big boost for me, as I had been a soldier for four months and one week, and during that time the only breaks I had were visits to the cinema on two occasions, once at Caterham, and once at Colchester. There was now a serious doubt in my mind, as in the early hours of 10th May, Hitler's airborne troops and parachutists invaded Holland and Belgium. They seized the Meuse and Rhine bridges and Moerdyk, Dordrecht and Rotterdam, and the French army and British expeditionary forces moved into Belgium. However, on the morning of the 11th there was a special train allocated to us at Camberley station to take the majority of the battalion to South Wales.

We boarded the train for Cardiff and the Welsh coast at 9 a.m. The other members of the battalion were to find their own way to various parts of England and North Wales. At last I thought we were on our way home but sadly it was not to be. On the outskirts of the town of Reading in Berkshire the train was stopped and suddenly a troop of military police appeared, racing along the length of the train locking the carriage doors. We all realised what was happening. Many men jumped through the windows and made off, despite the warnings from a loud hailer. The train was put in reverse and pushed all the way to Camberley Station. Once again we were marched back to Old Dean Common camp and lined up on parade and sorted out. Two companies, No. 1 and No. 3 were detailed for immediate urgent embarkation. Both companies were approximately three-quarters strength now, with the leave absentees and missing individuals who had jumped the train. I was one of the unlucky No. 3 Company. I had written to my parents telling them I would be home on the afternoon of the eleventh; now I would not arrive and they would be alarmed. We were given a hot meal and a haversack ration to carry in our kit. It consisted of two slices of bread, with a piece of meat to form a sandwich. We were then warned we would depart at 3.30 p.m. for Dover, to be shipped to Holland for a landing at Hoek van Holland – the Hook of Holland at the mouth of the River Meuse. The purpose of this landing, approximately 16 miles from Rotterdam and 15 miles south of the capital city – The Hague – was to bring out the Dutch government, the queen and the Dutch gold, if the German parachutists did not get there first. With all the confusion and haste preparing for our departure, I managed to write just five lines of a letter to my parents telling them of my destination, wishing them all well, and sending my last goodbye, because I never expected to return. I gave the letter to the padre, with one and a half pence for the postage as I climbed into the army truck that afternoon on the way to Dover for our crossing of the North Sea.

7

The Hook of Holland, and the Disaster at Boulogne 11–24 May 1940

It was a cool, cloudy evening as the small convoy of trucks drove through the English countryside with its load of approximately 160 men. There were three utility, 15-hundredweight trucks transporting boxes of small arms ammunition, a petrol blowtorch cooking-flame thrower, various dixies and supplies, a couple of company cooks, cans of petrol and extra supplies of fresh water. Each section had a Bren machine-gun with an un-assembled anti-aircraft stand. Each man carried three Bren magazines in webbing pouches, a full waterbottle, a ration of army hard-tack biscuits, and a cotton bandolier containing 50 rounds of .303 rifle ammunition. En route, we were joined by a further two companies of Irish Guards and our small detachment was under the command of Captain Heber-Percy. We arrived at the port of Dover as darkness was falling and we filed slowly on to the destroyer HMS *Whitshed*. The Irish boarded another destroyer HMS *Wild Swan*. Thank goodness we were not given the task of loading the supplies. They were slung in nets on to the decks of the destroyers, and we had to find the most comfortable position possible on the crowded ship. For the cold crossing we were wearing our full complement of kit over a greatcoat. I took off my pack and rolled army blanket, found a spot out of the biting wind behind a bulwark on the rear deck and lay down to face the cold journey across the North Sea.

The destroyer hugged the coastline around the Thames Estuary probably cruising a fixed course to avoid the minefields. In the semi-darkness we passed many sunken ships with their masts sticking out of the water, then it was out on to the North Sea on our way to the coast of Holland. Patches of clouds moved away to show the blackness

113

of the sea as the speeding destroyer zig-zagged along its course. All we could hear was the noise of the engines and the swish of the waves pounding against the hull. Just after midnight we obtained a big mug of hot cocoa from the ship's cooks, and our haversack ration, the meat sandwich, was now put to good use and washed down with the tingling hot cocoa. In the early hours, as the ship approached the coast of Holland, a red glow filled the sky. It was the fires from the first massed bombing of a western city in this Second World War.

The city of Rotterdam was being attacked by Nazi bombers, the first dastardly attack against the civilian population, and we were to learn that some 30,000 people were killed or injured, and all the central district of Rotterdam was destroyed. It was to be the first taste of the devastating bombing that lay ahead, the destruction, casualties, deaths and shocking injuries from fires and incendiaries.

In the pre-dawn darkness the destroyer moved in past the long jetty protruding out into the sea, and slowly manoeuvred into an anchorage at the side of the wharf. A gangplank was swung against the ship and No. 1 Company disembarked to their detailed positions in the gloom. As I believed was going to happen, my platoon was detailed to do the hard work and unload all our supplies and ammunition. We laboured with that cargo, all our kit removed, but with the rifle slung over our shoulders at the rear and the bandolier of .303 rounds tied around our waists. It was an unpleasant task climbing over those loose timbers, railway tracks, sleepers, and all kinds of objects to form a dump on some waste ground about 50 yards away. It was the first light of that dawning day, and it gave me the opportunity to get some idea of our location. The ship was tied up amongst all kinds of small vessels. Some distance along the wharf, where the long jetty stretched into the sea, ran the railway track and there were a number of fixed cranes for loading and unloading cargoes. The area was a big marshalling yard with railway tracks and wagons everywhere and a big turntable in the centre making it so easy to turn around locomotives and wagons and rolling stock etc. There were dumps of coal, timber, and steel everywhere, and farther along the vacant ground, a roofed enclosure had been built with lots of tables and benches. Scraps of rye bread were scattered all over the tables, as if troops or wharf workers had left in haste. The main road which swept around in a curve beyond this structure, was the highway to Rotterdam going inland along the river. In the opposite direction it turned along the coast northwards to the city of The Hague, with the small town and residential area of The Hook on the other side.

Near the coastal curve of the road stood the old Hook of Holland stone lighthouse with its revolving light high above the flat land and pointing out to sea. Many deep trenches had been constructed in the area by the Dutch. They were almost ten feet deep and shored up with heavy timbers and I presumed they were air raid shelters for residents. Recently there must have been heavy rain as many of them were ankle deep in water. Trudging along the road were many refugees, women, children and old men, pushing and pulling all kinds of carts, prams and contraptions on wheels loaded with their belongings, fleeing, I presumed from the Rotterdam area, in a northerly direction along the coast.

It was almost 11 a.m. that morning before we completed the exhausting task of unloading those supplies. We then took up our positions all around that area digging slit trenches and setting up the Bren guns on their anti-aircraft stands because we believed a Nazi parachute drop was imminent. The Nazis had captured and blocked the water escape routes from central Rotterdam and The Hook was now the only escape port in the area. The remainder of that day was fairly quiet. We made a few patrols along the route to Rotterdam for some five to six miles, and could hear the distant gun fire, but there were no incidents as far as we were concerned. That evening, until dark, the Dutch VIPs, officials and transports were secretly arriving, smuggled on to a Dutch gunboat and escorted out to sea. Boxes and crates of Dutch secretive matter, and the contents of the Dutch treasury, gold bars and valuables, were loaded and shipped out of port. Just after midnight we occupied the air-raid trenches, and there would be no sleep for us for the second successive night with the many sentries posted around the area, the expectation of the Nazi parachute drop, and the moving in of any fifth column. The uncomfortable and wet conditions in the trenches also kept us wide awake.

I did two hours' sentry duty that night from midnight to 2 a.m. with a fellow named Lewis. He had been very seasick coming over, and with the hard work all day unloading the supplies, he still wasn't feeling very well. We were on the roadside north of the lighthouse, about 30 yards apart, when he told me he was feeling ill. Unknown to me in the darkness, however, he sat down and was drowsing as the patrol came around, with Heber-Percy, inspecting the various posts. There was an awful row about it and he was threatened to be shot for sleeping at his post. A field inquiry was to be held at daylight and I gave evidence of my version of the circumstances. Lewis was placed under open arrest but the events of the coming day would put him out of trouble and soften Heber-Percy with his disciplinary action. We managed to get a mug of hot tea that morning, with some bully beef and army hard-tack biscuits. It was approaching 9 a.m., the sky was blue and clear, and the sun was quite warm, and from the distance we heard the sound of aircraft for the first time. Out of the east came the first wave of Nazi high-wing black Stukas, the dive-bombers. It was the first time any of our men had seen this plane. We had heard a great deal about it in Poland and other places, and it was our turn now to come up against it. There would be many, many more occasions as the war progressed.

The planes flew out over the sea and wheeled to come in out of the sun, then the destroyers opened fire as they moved away from the wharf backwards and forwards in the river to avoid being a sitting target. All the rapid Bofors guns were firing and it was like hell let loose. The Stukas broke formation and peeled off one after the other in a vertical dive over our positions and the ships. The noise of the screaming engines was frightening, as they pulled out of the dive about 500 feet up and released Hitler's notorious morale-breaking, screaming bombs. Huge explosions erupted all around us. I was deep down in the Dutch air-raid trenches at that time, debris was flying everywhere and the heat took away one's breath as it sucked the air into the centre of the explosions. As they pulled out of the dive and flew away, five Messerschmitt fighters dived down from above, machine-gunning the road and buildings in the area, cutting down several of the refugees fleeing along the road. After two runs across the area they turned back to the east, and we dashed around looking for casualties. All our unit were all right. There were near misses to the destroyers but they were unharmed, one small ship was on fire, three civilians were killed, and six wounded. We carried them to the lighthouse which was now being used as a first-aid post. This was only the first raid, and there would be many hours of it yet to come. It seemed obvious now that the Nazis knew what was going on and they were determined to destroy the ships and the port, and wipe us out.

Heber-Percy gave an order that we were to stand up and take action with the Brens against the next wave of planes. It would be sheer suicide, as we had no tracer bullets to direct the fire. It was just firing blind, and we all knew that when those screaming bombs began to fall, everyone would be diving for cover in terror from those spirit-breaking wails and screams, and the searing heat and blast as the hot air sucked at one's lungs making one gasp and gulp for air.

We heard a drone of planes in the sky 30 minutes later – another raid and this time I counted 12 Stukas. Out of the sun once again they dived, two more ships were ablaze, the destroyers' guns must have been red hot and again they were missed. There was a near miss to our ammunition and supplies dump, we were ordered to it and to carry it to the trenches. It was a thankless task but Nazi planes were about to help us and blow it to kingdom come.

It was shortly after midday and once again overhead was another mass of black Stukas. I reached a count of 22 and there were more. I was in the open and with Lewis. We jumped down into the side of the railway turntable to try to take cover in one of the safety manholes in the sides of the depressed circular area. We were side by side on our knees, the top was so low. The destroyers' guns were firing again, and the first bombs began to scream down and explode. The heat was intense as we held our breath in terror to prevent the awful suction, with such explosions, tearing at our lungs. Another bomb exploded on the perimeter of the turntable 30 yards to our left. I can still recall now the blast of sucking hot air. We were holding our breath with both hands over our noses and faces when I felt a terrible shocking wrench from my waist to my neck. I was sucked, along with Lewis, out of that manhole and hurled across the rails of the turntable on to all kinds of debris, boxes, cartons and coal. Then two open wagons landed upside down right over the top of me; I was trapped underneath. I was to learn that Lewis was wrenched and blown sideways from me and a wagon wheel crushed his leg, but he was alive. It was an hour or more before I was released. They axed through the side of the timber wagon to get me out. I felt awful, that terrible wrench must have injured something in my chest and stomach, and I would suffer from it for the rest of my life. HMS *Whitshed* had been hit and there were many casualties so we were ordered to embark immediately and get away from the place.

I was relieved to get aboard the destroyer once again as she moved past the jetty to the open sea, hoping we would get clear before the next raid. As the afternoon turned to evening, I was seasick with the roll, speed and zig-zag course of the ship, and I vomited blood from the trouble in my stomach. I went to the lee-side of the ship's funnel out of the wind, where the decking was quite warm from the boiler's heat, and I lay down and opened my jacket to allow my chest to receive this warmth from the deck. On two occasions before darkness there were alarms for 'action stations' to the ship's crew and depth charges were fired over the side. The thought of submarines and torpedoes gave me a scare. I had had quite enough for that day! The destroyer raced on through the night and entered Dover harbour about 2 a.m. the following morning. This was the third night without any sleep, and tired and exhausted, we filed down the gangplank and were escorted into a building where we were given hot tea and sandwiches. I was told to check in at the casualty clearing station, and I received a brief check over from an army medical officer. It certainly was brief, I had no visible cuts or wounds, so he simply told me I was all right and to report sick when I reached my destination. We were then ordered into army trucks for the journey back to Old Dean Common at Camberley. We arrived at Camberley in daylight for breakfast, after which our kit was inspected for any missing items which then were replaced. A hot shower followed and we were allowed to return to our respective bell tents to rest and sleep for the remainder of the day. The next morning, 14th May 1940, I reported sick and joined the sick parade. I was still in pain internally and feeling ill. It was typical army sick parade, where you are considered a skiver, even if you are almost out on your feet, so I expected no sympathy or assistance.

I was checked over once again by the medical officer having explained all the circumstances and I was cheerfully told that everything would be normal in a couple of days. So I was given Attend B, which meant being excused from all parades, to do light duties for three days. The light duties were fatigues, cookhouse chores once again and I was sick of it all. For three days I laboured around the common. I managed to write a few lines home to my parents telling them briefly what had happened, and to expect anything as the situation in France and Belgium was serious and Holland had now capitulated to the Nazi invaders.

On the morning of the 17th I had to report and join the sick parade once again. My three days had expired and I was nowhere like being fit and well. On this occasion it was back to M and D (Medicine and Duties) and back on to the parade ground once again, with the news that we were to carry out a three-day military exercise on the downs and moors around Camberley, on the afternoon of 18th May.

The news from France was serious and worrying, as the expeditionary forces and the French army had moved into Belgium when the Nazis invaded that country, and now the German army had broken through the Ardennes into France and our forces were in danger of being trapped. We still departed on the military stunt to suit the brass hats playing soldiers, moving their pins on maps and boards, with miles of imaginary battles in the woods, and the heathlands of that area. We were wearing our full kit and the task of carrying Bren guns and heavy Boyes anti-tank rifles for miles was tiresome. Trying to obtain some sleep with just a greatcoat and a groundsheet for two miserable nights with such heavy dew made it very unpleasant, and then on the morning of the 21st, we marched ten miles back to Old Dean Common camp. Everyone was tired and exhausted and we were given a hot meal that morning much earlier than usual at 12 noon. We were assembled in the big mess tent for that meal and they broke the news to us that we were to be shipped to France that afternoon. The German army had smashed through the French defences and they were heading, with their armoured forces, for the Channel ports to encircle and trap the whole British army. Our mission was to be a débâcle and a disaster – they referred to it as a 'disaster and the magnificence'. It was to be another of the awful mistakes, ordered by the old diehard, First World War, incompetent military commanders. No questions were asked, no inquiry ordered. It was all swept under the carpet.

In 1948, with a little more authority as a police officer, and still angry about the awful mess at Boulogne, I visited the Department of Documents at the Imperial War Museum. My visit was to find out the story from the official records. The staff were helpful, but I was made more angry by the fact that so many recorded incidents were incorrect according to my own experience.

I am now going to give an outline of those records and then relate what really happened to my platoon and myself. The only person to whom I have told my story in full was my father on a hot, late night in June 1940, as he sat in Grandfather's old armchair and I relaxed on the couch, with my feet up, in the living room at Oak Cottage. He reported the matter to the local member of parliament – Morgan Jones – who said that it would be unpatriotic to do anything about it.

The persons responsible still flouted their medals and the whole affair was hushed up. We were an abandoned, under-strength platoon, with no radio, or means of communication with anyone, no orders, no instructions and almost every man was a 'green' conscript. I had never fired a 303 rifle. There were no maps, no medical kit, no food, no transport, no mortars and no grenades (a missile that I had never seen). We had a miserable amount of fifty .303 rounds per man, 3 Bren machine-guns with one box of ammunition and one useless Boyes anti-tank rifle. We were thrown in like lambs to be slaughtered, to hold back the mighty and formidable 2nd Panzer Division of Hitler's elite Nazi Army.

I was the only man from that platoon – No. 8 Platoon – to escape and to make my way back to the port of Boulogne and return across the Channel.

Many years later I read some of the details from Nazi General Guderian's reports, translated from German, in *Erinnerlingen Eines Soldaten*, written in Nuremberg Prison, an Order of the day, 10th May 1940 and Top Secret. The awesome amount of armour listed and bearing down towards us was:

523 Panzer 1 tanks
955 Panzer 2 tanks
349 Panzer 3 tanks
278 Panzer 4 tanks
106 Czech T35 tanks
238 Czech T38 tanks
96 small armoured command vehicles chassis 1
391 large armoured command vehicles chassis 2
A Total of 2,936 Tanks and armoured vehicles

The amount of weapons carried by that force was:

4,407 machine-guns
955 20mm guns
349 37mm guns
334 37mm guns mark 2
278 75mm guns

According to General Guderian's reports on 17th May 1940, the overwhelming Nazi Panzers became unstoppable, the administration of the British GHQ was evacuated to Boulogne. The situation was so serious, Lord Gort issued an order for the immediate evacuation of all 'useless mouths', the sick, wounded, pay corps, chaplains, etc., in the Boulogne area. The responsibility and the defence of the port was given to his Adjutant-General, Sir Douglas Browning.

On the 20th May, General Rommel's armour bypassed Arras, captured Amiens, and obtained a deep bridgehead across the Somme. The 2nd Panzer Division captured Abbeville, and reached the coast at Noyelles. The advance was so fast, Nazi Field Marshal Von Kleist with no orders, the whole of 21st May was a general halt awaiting further orders. On that same night, Guderian received orders to attack and capture the Channel ports, the 10th Panzer on Dunkirk, the 1st Panzer on Calais and the 2nd Panzer on Boulogne. The advance started at dawn the 22nd May, with the 2nd Panzer moving up the coast to Boulogne.

This Nazi Panzer Division soon encountered the French 21st Infantry Division under General Lanquetot. It was a shocking disaster, the French were wiped out and consequently more troops and artillery were caught on a train heading for the front. Two other battalions heading for Boulogne were destroyed; the other two battalions were destroyed by the 1st Panzer on the way to Calais.

A heavy air-raid on the 19th destroyed the Hotel Imperial, Sir Douglas Brownrigg's HQ, killing many staff officers. The HQ was quickly moved to Wimmereux, three miles north of the port of Boulogne to organise the defence of the port. Various allied survivors trickled into the port, Pioneers, remnants of the 36th Infantry Brigade, and stragglers from the Durham Light Infantry.

The defence of Boulogne was all anti-aircraft, two troops of the 2nd Heavy Anti-Aircraft Regiment, two troops of the 58th Light Anti-Aircraft Regiment, one search-light Battery, plus a detachment of RAF Balloon Command, which was ordered to return to the UK on 21st May, which has never been explained (I can interject at this point and say – like so many other things that have never been explained).

A plea for help and reinforcements was sent urgently to the War Office by Brownrigg, and a small detachment of Royal Marines arrived on the 21st to help with the evacuation of civilians and non-combatants.

At that time the 20th Guards Brigade, consisting of the 2nd Irish Guards and the 2nd Welsh Guards were under canvas at Camberley. According to official records, they received embarkation orders on the morning of 21st May, one hour after returning from a gruelling night exercise (this is incorrect – it was two nights and three days.) These two units together with the Brigade Anti-Tank Company, and a battery of the 69th Anti-Tank Regiment embarked at Dover on the night of 21st May in two small ships and the destroyer HMS *Whitshed*. Neither of the Guard's battalions had maps, wirelesses, mortars or grenades. Brigadier Fox-Pitt had been ordered by General Dill that he was responsible for the defence of Boulogne, but I do not think that he had any idea of the situation over there.

I would like to comment on a few things at this point: my unit, or the battalion, to which they referred, consisted of three companies

121

only, number 1, number 3, and HQ company. Number 2 company did not go and each company was not full strength, each about 20 men short, due to the absentees from the leave train. The ships began to arrive at Boulogne at 0630 hours (the correct time was 5.45 a.m. in darkness) on 22nd May.

The troops disembarked, forcing their way through the refugees and panic-stricken civilians crowding the quay. Brigadier Fox-Pitt decided to position the Irish Guards along an area two miles to the south. The Welsh were given the task of blocking and defending the main access roads from the west and the south – a formidable assignment as all the roads passed hilly terrain, which even a division would have difficulty to defend.

The Nazi 2nd Panzer division pushed on, and at 1500 hours on the 22nd, the leading elements were in sight of Boulogne. The situation was extremely perilous, no unit had any idea what was happening elsewhere. Dispatch riders were sent out to try and contact Brigadier Fox-Pitt, but failed to find him. It was then reported all units had deduced heavy fighting was going on in the Welsh sector, reporting that they had been subjected to heavy shellfire and probing from reconnaissance groups. Again, I interject: there was no contact and no communication between any unit; they would have no idea what was going on.

At 0100 hours on the 23rd, the Panzers had encircled the town, Brownrigg evacuated his HQ and sailed for England on the destroyer *Verity*, unable to inform Fox-Pitt of his departure owing to a breakdown in communications. My comment – any excuse is better than none.

At dawn, Fox-Pitt deduced the Welsh and Irish were alone; GHQ had gone, with no hope of reinforcements. To bolster his defences, he placed 800 Pioneers to the left of the Welsh. I escaped along this flank, I never saw one Pioneer. To me this appeared to be make believe.

The Nazis completed the encirclement of Boulogne and, an hour after sunrise, they attacked in force. This fell initially on the Welsh, whose outposts on Mont Lambert were heavily attacked by enemy tanks, although one Welsh platoon was cut off, the line held. I was the only man to return from that platoon, the attack came ten minutes after first light and it is nonsense to state that the line still held.

By midday, the Irish strength was two and a half companies, as they withdrew into the port. The Welsh withdrew also, street by street. At 1500 hours they were told to prepare for evacuation as streams of shellfire poured in from the heights of Mont Lambert. The destroyers

Vimey, Keith, Whitshed, Vimiera, Wild Swan, Venomous, Venetzia and *Windsor*, with the French destroyers *Cyclone, Orage* and *Frondeur*, bombarded the enemy.

At 1830 hours, the Stukas appeared overhead with their vicious dive-bombing attacks, the *Orage* was set on fire, the *Frondeur* was hit and out of action. The commanders of both the *Vimey* and *Keith*, were killed, and the battle for the harbour began as German tanks moved on to the wharfs.

At 9 p.m. the *Wild Swan* and *Venomous*, with the low tide low down in the harbour, blasted the enemy with their Bofors guns and 4.7s as the last troops jumped from the wharfs.

I am now going to relate the happenings, the incidents and the story of my escape and journey back to Boulogne harbour from our position on Mont Lambert and the main Boulogne–Calais road:

I left the mess tent that early afternoon, 21st May 1940, and made my way back to the bell tent. Corporal Randall was there with some of the other members who made up the section, John Partridge, Nicholas, Lewis and Roberts. We took everything out of the tent and packed all our surplus articles in the kit bag and the big pack. Our kit which we were to carry consisted of the small pack, webbing equipment with two bren gun machine pouches, gas mask and gas cape, waterbottle and greatcoat. Inside my small pack I placed my mess tin, clean and washed after the midday meal, a groundsheet, hold-all containing some needles, cotton thread, a safety pin, a packet of bachelor buttons, my shaving kit, toothbrush and toothpaste, a tablet of soap, a writing pad and envelopes, a cleaning duster, a small tin of Brasso – of all things – a shoe brush and an army towel. The reason for the bachelor buttons was that we wore old fashioned army braces hooked on to trouser buttons; there was a stupid rule that a trouser belt was not allowed to be worn, the bachelor button was a press-stud type and avoided the tedious sewing on of buttons with needle and thread.

We carried our kit bags and big pack to the company store and collected an entrenching tool, which was buckled to the side straps from the webbing belt on the opposite side to the waterbottle. This tool was just like a child's super sand spade with a short thick handle, the whole tool with blade and handle being about two feet long. One cotton bandolier of .303 ammunition – 50 rounds per man, and two bren magazines each man, 24 magazines for the section and a box of ammunition to fill the mags with some in reserve. The total magazine complement was approximately 760 rounds. There were 2,000 rounds in the box, and this also had to be carried. We also obtained a Boyes anti-tank rifle with three magazines each loaded with five rounds of .5 inch cartridges. I checked my field dressing in the right-hand fob pocket of my trousers and cut the few cotton stitches sewn over the top of the pocket. I then quickly scribbled five lines of a letter to my parents giving my destination, wishing them all well and hoping that they would hear from me again. I gave it to the padre once again with one and a half pence for postage with the hope that it would reach its destination.

The bugle call echoed across the common to fall in line, to be inspected and checked. Every waterbottle was filled and all equipment in order. It was approximately 3 p.m. and we boarded the army trucks once again for the journey to Dover harbour, just seven and a half days since I was there on my return from Holland, and I was still feeling unwell.

The journey to Dover was uneventful, as everyone was quiet and subdued with the tension and apprehension of what lay ahead and it gave me time to think and ponder about it all. I was responsible for the Boyes anti-tank rifle, which was housed in a long wooden box almost eight feet long with rope handles and this was the way we had to carry it with a man at each end. We boarded the faithful old destroyer HMS *Whitshed* once again, this time all bunched together with the platoon trying to make ourselves as comfortable as possible. The battalion as they referred to it was No. 1 Company, No. 3 Company Battalion, HQ Company. No. 2 Company did not go and my platoon was below strength, about 35 men in all under the command of a lieutenant, the platoon officer. My section No. 5 consisted of seven men with Randall as the section leader. It was a cold night crossing the English Channel, with a biting wind and a choppy sea. I felt a little squirmy and hoped it would pass away when we got ashore. There was almost a clear sky with patches of cloud moving quickly with the breeze. The stars looked down on to the cold cruel sea, with a whitewash behind us as the destroyer steamed towards its destination, the port of Boulogne.

About 5.30 a.m. we could pick out the buildings and structures of the French port in the half light as the ship slowed down to enter the harbour and carefully manoeuvred against the quay. There were muffled voices all around the dock area and the rail head, in the early morning gloom, and it appeared to be crowded with people carrying all their bits and pieces, bags and packages. There were no lights or lighted areas anywhere, as it was of course, a total blackout to give nothing away to any German aircraft. No. 7 Platoon led the way off the ship, each section in single file. Then it was our turn, my section No. 5 with Randall in front, taking the first stint of carrying the bren on his shoulder. Partridge was behind me supporting the rear end of the anti-tank rifle box by the rope handles, with his left hand, his rifle over his right shoulder. I had the front handle in my right hand, with my rifle slung over my left shoulder, making it the easiest way to carry it along. At intervals we would change hands, and after a period pass it on to two other members, to give us a break. On the quay we had to push our way through the crowds, all fleeing the war, clamouring and hoping perhaps to get on the ship to take them away. The time was a little after 5.45 a.m., and it would be daylight soon in about half or three-quarters of an hour as we tramped along the cobblestoned road on the left and away from the dock area. I had no idea of the direction we were taking. We had been told nothing, simply followed the person up ahead past the buildings, shops and houses, just like a lot of sheep. The platoon officer was in front of Randall, at the rear of No. 3 section of No. 7 Platoon, and led up the front by 2nd Lieutenant Hughes and Platoon Sergeant-Major M'Nair. It was the crack of dawn and first light of the day, and we now started to climb uphill along rows of terraced houses, their front doors opening on to the footpath. The streets were deserted, we never saw a soul, and whether or not the homes were occupied we did not know. Grumbling began amongst the men ahead and behind me, all were asking each other, 'Where are we going? How far are we going?' We were completely ignorant of all that lay ahead. We believed that we were going just a short distance, as there were no maps, no medical kit, no compass, no radio for communication, no transport of any kind, and we had no extra supplies of ammunition, just the bare amounts we carried. We left the built-up area behind and the countryside became hilly as we marched along a secondary road with hedges and trees along each side. The scene was familiar – hawthorn hedges with the white blossom reaching the dirty brown stage as the petals dropped. There were lots of red hawthorn also with a carpet of fallen flowers beneath each bush, and the trees were just like our own too. Oaks and beeches and ash, with elderberry and holly. In the open spaces blackberries grew everywhere, with clumps of gorse and thistles.

I tried to pick out certain objects, and landmarks in my mind, perhaps with a great deal of doubt, we might come back this way. We passed a few small farms along the roadway but everything seemed deserted. There were chickens around and old roosters making their early morning crow, but animals were very few and far between. It was a very heavy wet dewy morning, signs of a fine day and the grass along the roadside was wet so we walked on the roadway to avoid the wetness of the long grass stalks. The sun was shining now, it was going to be a warm sultry day as we climbed another hill with a small, two-storey farmhouse a few yards off the roadside surrounded by trees and a hawthorn hedge and here we saw our first inhabitant as a man came to the gate to see us pass by. Two small children were at the closed upstairs window looking out, giving a little friendly wave as we passed by.

At least, I thought, these folks have not fled. Perhaps they had nothing to flee for, that small whitewashed cottage being possibly all they possessed. One thing that remains vivid in my mind was a huge horse chestnut tree up over the bank opposite the cottage, its white flower clusters brown and falling to prepare for the big crop of conkers. Thoughts ran through my mind of the times at home that I had climbed those same trees for my bag of conkers.

Very soon we came to a T junction, the road turned off to the left and our route continued on. At the junction on the roadside was a small crucifix statue, so common throughout France, and the stone step at the front of the statue was covered with an old offering of dead flowers. A few yards away was a signpost with a single arm, old and rotting, covered with moss and lichen, the pointed end broken away, but we could still make out the faint lettering and the name Mont Lambert, as it pointed our way along the road. At first I thought it must be the name of a village or place, but to my knowledge of French, *Mont* usually translated as a mountain peak or high ground, and I realised we were heading for a mountain top – Mont Lambert. We had a five-minute halt at this stage; we removed our kit and took off the greatcoats, as it was getting warm and uncomfortable. I took just a mouthful of water from my waterbottle with a doubt in my mind as to where we could obtain more when the bottle was empty. We must have covered about 5 or 6 miles by this time, and the terrain was still rising. The countryside became rolling downs, with many dips and hollows, small valleys and ravines, covered with spreading gorse and blackberry, and dispersed with some trees and flat areas fenced into fields with tall lush grass running to seed after the rich spring growth. No. 9 Platoon now went off to the right probably to their allotted position. We continued on for another quarter of a mile and then No. 7 Platoon turned off to our left. We continued straight ahead to the highest ground which I presumed was Mont

126

Lambert. As the road reached the high point, a cutting had been constructed which again I presumed had been made to avoid a hump-back over the rise. This cutting made a bend to the left for about a distance of 40 yards, and then flattened out to a bank on the left side about three feet high. There was a road junction at that point, our road meeting the main highway from Boulogne to Calais, and this was to be our position, an awesome task to try and hold back the German army. At that time we did not know that our opponents would be the mighty 2nd Panzer division of Hitler's unstoppable armoured blitzkreig. We were all at three points of a triangle. No. 7 and 9 Platoons at the two base points and my platoon, No. 8, at the apex point on the junction of the main highway.

Along with Partridge I was ordered to dig in about two feet below the top of the cutting, which gave us a view down the road to the right, and it appeared this road had another T junction some 500 yards away, behind one of the downs, which led back to the port of Boul-ogne. I protested about my position, because as I stood up I was exposed to the skyline, and the other side of the cutting was a little lower. My protests at first were ignored; so I commenced digging quickly to get down below the surface. After a lot of hard work between Partridge and myself, the platoon officer decided that I was correct, and we were moved along the cutting about 20 yards, where our view was not so good, but at least we would now be concealed from the open skyline. I proceeded to cut a swathe through the grass ahead using a bayonet as a slasher in order to get an unobstructed view. We dug into that cutting with the entrenching tool to a depth of three feet. We then placed all the cut grass at the bottom of the slit trench and Partridge and myself could now kneel and look over the top of the cutting. I carried the Boyes anti-tank rifle up to the trench leaving its wooden box on the road. We had ten rounds of .5 inch cartridges in two magazines, and a rifle each with 50 rounds of .303 in a cotton bandolier tied around our waists. As I have said before, Partridge and I were in the scandalous position of never having experi-enced firing either of them, and we were expected to carry out the ridiculous and awesome task of stopping the German army! The remainder of the platoon had dug in the top of the bank along the road in twos and threes, 10 to 15 yards apart for a length of about 150 yards. Randall and two men, Nicholas and Roberts, were in the nearest slit trench to us with the section Bren gun. We handed over the spare magazines we carried and in all they were capable of firing and disposing of the lot in five to ten minutes, so just like condemned men we were awaiting execution from the massed armour and enormous firepower of the German army.

It was approximately 1 p.m. and the big Humber military car pulled up into the cutting and the driver unloaded a dixie of tea, some loaves of bread and a container of baked beans and mashed potatoes. At last, we received something to eat to appease our hunger and a big mug of hot tea to wash it all down. It was a warm afternoon and about 3 p.m. two French officers, or what appeared to be French officers, came up the road on horseback. One of them was mounted on a scruffy, boney, miserable-looking horse. They both looked all around, scrutinising our positions, and then rode off across the downs in the opposite direction, away from Boulogne. No one challenged them or asked their business or identity in any way, and the platoon officer even saluted them. I thought to myself and even complained to Partridge that we must be under the command of an officer and NCO of 'Fred Carno's Army'. Not one person asked these so-called French officers for their credentials, and I was convinced, and I have been all my life, that those two officers were part of the notorious '5th Column', which the German army sent ahead of them all over Europe. From the pinpoint shelling and mortar fire that was to come, it was obvious they had leaked all our positions.

About 6 p.m. that evening we experienced the first screaming, long-distance shells, which must have been the big Nazi 150mm guns by the shell-holes they made in the surrounding countryside. Maybe they were unaware of our positions, or perhaps they were simply bombarding the high ground. It would be a great asset to them to flatten the port area of Boulogne. Partridge and I dug deeper in our slit trench. We went down another foot, and it was hard going with rocks and earth, but we tipped it over the side and let it run down the slope of the cutting on to the road. Our fears were increasing, the night was approaching, shelling would increase even more, and then as the German range decreased, the dreaded mortars would be used containing the steel balls and pieces of metal and every kind of projectile that would tear and rip into human flesh. As darkness began to fall across the landscape we were alone in that small hole in the ground. We could see nothing, and could only peer into the darkness, hoping the enemy was not there as the frightening and monotonous 'crump' of the bursting shells reflected a glow from the flashes on the shining foresight of the rifle as it rested on top of the trench. The dew began to settle as the time moved slowly on into the cool and clammy atmosphere of that May night. The luxury of sleep was a long way off, as too many thoughts filled our minds. We had to remain alert and ready because very soon the dawn would arrive. One half-hour before the first light is always the worst time of the soldier's life, the time when all human functions are at their lowest ebb, the time when every attack begins, the time when so many men are due to die, never again see the sun rise.

It was almost 3 a.m., when we received a visit from the platoon officer accompanied by Sergeant Green telling us that one man must remain alert at all times, and we were to 'stand to' at 5.30 a.m. It was impossible to sleep anyhow, so we just took turns sitting on the bottom of the slit trench, while the other kept straining his eyes in the darkness and gloom wondering what was going to happen. The hour of 5.30 a.m. arrived, and Randall and Sergeant Green rushed along the road ensuring that each man was alert and prepared. A few minutes later there was a lull, and the shelling stopped temporarily. It appeared to be like the calm before the storm. The concentration and the anxiety increased with the half-light and, as expected, the rapid fire of the spandau machine-guns began again, and the streaking red tracer bullets whined and whistled across the countryside, thudding into banks, mounds and bushes. There must have been four machine-guns out there, whether they were tanks, armoured cars or infantrymen we did not know. Suddenly I saw a glimpse of the enemy for the first time, a motorcycle combination – a motorcycle and sidecar – sneaking behind one of the downs about 1,000 yards away, with a machine-gun mounted on the front of the sidecar. The platoon along the road was firing now and, there must have been other units, the probing reconnaissance troops of the division or army group behind. The firing stopped, while obviously pulled back to report the resistance ahead. As is the usual practice, the whole area had to be 'softened up' before the attack began, so we were in for a deluge of massed shelling and mortaring and perhaps too, aircraft bombing in support of the ground troops. It was shortly after 7.30 a.m., and the same Humber car raced up the road and into the cutting. The driver skidded around to face the direction to get away back to the remainder of the company behind us, and quickly hoisted out of the rear, two dixies, one of tea and the other must have been baked beans, along with three loaves of bread. He dumped them all on the roadside behind and to our left and raced off once again with screaming tyres. This was to be our breakfast, but we would never have the pleasure of tasting it or satisfying our hunger. Who was going to collect it and distribute it around with the Germans a short distance away?

At almost 8 a.m. the first mortars began to rain down on our position. Green and inexperienced, we were in range of these dreadful weapons and, as I was to learn later in the war, one of them was the fiendish Nebelwefer rocket mortar, nicknamed by the troops in later years as the 'Sobbing Sisters'. This weapon I must admit I feared more than anything throughout the war. It instilled in me many times fright and terror as it was one of Hitler's morale and spirit-breaking weapons. It affected me more at night, cowered down in slit trenches in the darkness, hoping that one would not drop on my own particular spot. There were three versions of this weapon, 5, 10 and 20–barrelled mortars fired electrically. The five barrel was used by the infantry and pulled along on two wheels, the others were mounted on wheels also and generally pulled along by a half-track vehicle. The projectile, unlike the shell had no trajectory, it simply whirled and twisted through the air, with the most hideous, fiendish scream and wail, something between the screaming of an hysterical child and a howling dog, the frightening cry of the banshee or a dying hound. Some exploded 20 or 30 feet in the air, others when they hit the ground, and many rolled along the ground smoking and then exploding. They contained all kinds of jagged steel, metal balls, and even pieces of shattered glass ripping and tearing through the air to cut and maim an intended victim. They caused shocking wounds and many civilians in Belgium and Holland died of terror as they rained down from above.

We were awaiting a heavy attack now and I sighted the Boyes anti-tank rifle down the road, cocked, with a round in the breach. I tried the shoulder rest once again, the leather buffer curved slightly around the shoulder joint but I was still apprehensive about it, its range, its capability and its reaction when it was fired. All these things were passing through my mind as another salvo of mortars began to sob, wail and scream through the air. We both ducked and crouched down in that small hole as they exploded all around us. One of them landed in the road cutting and blew our intended breakfast to pieces. There were baked beans plastered all over the road and up the banks of the cutting, so now our hunger would increase, adding to our discomfort and fear. Firing intensified now and German tracer bullets whistled above. The infantry moved up and two armoured cars came briefly into view. I opened fire with the anti-tank rifle, and with nerves and fear I snatched the trigger. The shoulder buffer was not tightly anchored against my shoulder and it gave me an awful kick, so I do not know what happened to that first shot, but I learned a lot. The whole platoon was now firing and both myself and Partridge resorted to the rifle. I fired for the first time, ten rapid shots. The enemy must have realised their opposition was a little stronger than they anticipated and there was another short lull.

The time must have moved on to approximately 9.45 a.m. and the Humber car came racing up the road and screamed around in the cutting to make a get away once again. The driver this time signalled and beckoned to the platoon officer in a trench some 50 yards down the road. Ducking and weaving he ran up the road to the vehicle, a few words were said, he hurriedly piled into the car, and it raced off back towards Boulogne. 'My god,' I said to Partridge. 'Be prepared, it looks like every man for himself!' A few minutes later, three Czech TNT tanks began advancing towards us, one on the road, the others abreast coming up over the downs, firing their guns and machine-guns, aiming at the fresh mounds of earth dug out from the slit trenches by the rest of the platoon along the road. I opened fire once again with the anti-tank rifle. Each shot was a hit but it bounced off the armour with a shower of sparks. I emptied the magazine, not bothering to replace it, and I tossed it behind me down the cutting in disgust, as it was totally useless. The platoon's Bren guns were hitting the tanks to no avail and with all the small-arms rifle fire the tanks stopped and hurriedly took cover behind the downs. I wondered why, at that time, as we were helpless against them and I was to learn years later the reason for it all and experience it personally. When a tank is peppered with hundreds of rounds of small-arms fire it sets up a hailstorm inside the turret, flakes of metal, paint and chips and anything loose flies everywhere like missiles; the noise is frightening to the crew, who expect something heavier to hit them. I assume that they pulled back for this reason.

However, realising how hopeless it was, with just 35 men and abandoned by the officer in charge, Sergeant 'Nitzy' Green jumped out of his slit trench and dashed up the road. He was almost on his hands and knees making himself as small a target as possible, waving his hands beckoning us all to get out as best we could. Sadly he raised himself up too high and the tracer bullets almost cut him in half from the chest up and he died instantly. With a terrific hail of fire, three armoured cars joined the tanks in a fresh advance up the road over the banks towards our positions. The situation was frightening and absolutely hopeless now and it appeared that we would all be wiped out. Partridge and I were in the best position up on the cutting, and out of the direct hail of bullets. The tanks came lumbering on using their guns on the slit trenches, and it would be suicide now to try to get away.

The first tank with its engines roaring sped up the road and mounted the bank over the top opening of Randall's trench. It skidded and slewed the tracks right over the top of the trench. There were three men in that slit trench, now probably buried alive. The tank rolled and jerked back to the road. Dumbfounded I saw Randall struggle out of the trench on to the road, one arm raised above his head in surrender, with dirt and soil spilling off him like rain water. At that precise moment, three Nazi infantry men jumped off the rear of one of the armoured cars. The leading brute with his left hand forward on the barrel of his rifle, and his right hand on the small of the butt brought it around with an awful swipe and crashed the butt into the side of Randall's face. Pole-axed, Randall dropped like a stone to the road and Partridge in a half whisper said 'Oh my god, what a way to die.' The next second I was out of that trench scampering and rolling down the cutting to the road, with Partridge behind me. We dashed across the road to the left for some 20 yards and slithered down the road drain incline into a small ravine, up over the bank on the other side and down into the hollow below amongst the gorse and blackberries. The firing had stopped, the platoon was overrun, and they must have been all dead, wounded or captured by this time. Sadly Randall was never heard of again. He must have died in cold blood on that road.

8

My Escape

Hidden amongst the gorse and blackberries, we were in a quandary as to what to do. At least, I thought, the tanks would not go down that ravine and up over the other side. They had achieved their objective. All the high ground on Mont Lambert and the road down towards Boulogne, from the positions we held, was wide open to them now with all their armour.

I suggested to Partridge that we keep going cautiously across the country and down the inclines keeping to the undergrowth cover and away from any buildings. It seemed to me that as soon as their artillery and heavy guns were brought forward they would blast any building that afforded any shelter or cover. We kept going over another incline and down the other side towards a small farmhouse and some sheds, and what appeared to have been a poultry run. As we approached the place cautiously intending to bypass it, and veer more to our left in the direction of the port, someone spotted us and waved and beckoned us with one hand. It was, to our surprise, a fellow named George Davis from No. 7 Platoon. There was blood all over his face and he must have been wounded. When we reached him we discovered he had been hit in the rear of the left shoulder at the top of the arm by a tracer bullet; he could not see the bad wound but could only attempt to swab it with his right hand to try and stop the bleeding. He was quite hysterical, cursing and swearing, issuing oaths and exclamations alleging that Platoon Sergeant-Major M'Nair had run away with the majority of the platoon leaving him and 2nd Lieutenant Hughes to their fate. I asked him where the officer was and he pointed to a chicken shed a short distance away. We hurriedly helped Davis back to the shed and to our horror there was Lt. Hughes lying on the ground in a shocking state, he had a terrible wound in the head, an awful tear in the side of the neck, and a gaping wound in his chest. It was obvious we could do nothing for him, and he was still bleeding profusely. It amazed me that he had lived so long but he was sinking fast. He then muttered with difficulty a few indecipherable words and died. In situations like this one cannot be sure about one's own feelings whether it is rising anger, and bitterness, or just pity for everything that had happened. Hughes' head was resting on his rolled gas cape, and I took his wallet from the blood-soaked jacket and stuffed it into one of my empty Bren gun pouches. I was still optimistic of returning to report it, then I turned him on his side, removed the gas cape, unrolled it, and spread it over him.

Meanwhile Partridge had ripped away Davis' shirt from around the wound. The bullet had torn through the fleshy part of the shoulder without entering the body. We used both our field dressings to pull the gash together and tie it up tightly to stop any further loss of blood. We did quite a good repair job considering the unfortunate circumstances that confronted us. The enemy began firing mortars around us once again and we had to make a quick decision on which direction we should go. As I had predicted, every building that offered shelter or a cover would be mortared or shelled. There was some difficulty with Davis at that time, he was so bitter and angry that he wanted to go in the direction No. 7 Platoon had 'run away' to use his words. I told them both that I was going in the same direction as before to try and make my way back to port across the ridges and the downs using any undergrowth as cover and to follow the direction the smoke was rising in the distant sky from the fires caused by the shelling of Boulogne. I did not intend to hang around and argue and set off leaving them to make their own decisions. Davis, in his determined state, went off his way and Partridge again followed me. As the mortars began to increase, we broke into a slow run to try and get away from the area. I was beginning to feel the strain now. In the last four nights I had obtained a total of about five hours sleep. I was weary, tired and hungry and the distance back to safety – if there was such a thing – was about seven miles. When one is in strange unfamiliar countryside with no idea of direction, it is very difficult, and it appeared that we were going in a semicircle; then as we came over one ridge we could see the road, once more twisting down in the direction of the port. Some small-arms fire was whistling past which we assumed was coming from our own forces around Boulogne. There was no sign of any German activity at that particular point on the road that was visible to us from below the ridge, and we carefully moved on but we were soon experiencing mortar fire once again so the Germans were not very far away. We carefully and stealthily made our way through the patches of gorse, undergrowth and the few trees when the road was visible, and we walked upright behind every ridge that blocked the view of the road.

I wondered what time of the day could it be? Was it late morning or early afternoon? I was feeling so hungry, worn out and tired, but I still remembered the wise old recipes of dear old Granny and her health-giving nature's food. I snapped off some young new running shoots from the blackberry, with the soft, green tender stalks and soft thorns, pulled down the skin and ate them. It was soft and sweet and juicy, almost melting in the mouth. I had both food and drink with each bite. This is where I have always felt guilty because we hesitated there and I moved off once again almost five yards in front of Partridge. A salvo of 'Sobbing Sisters'came over and one of them dropped behind Partridge, smoking as it hit the ground and started to roll forward. I shouted a warning to him, 'Down' and dived to the ground as it exploded, but Partridge was too late. Those shocking steel and jagged missiles caught him in the back, in the neck and backs of the legs. As I hit the ground, I also felt a pain in the back of my left heel, where a piece of metal had cut the back of my left boot, raising the leather just like lifting orange peel off the fruit with a thumbnail. My heel was bleeding and my sock became staturated with blood. My main concern now was John Partridge and, worried and scared, I looked at him lying on the ground. I pulled off his gas mask, his gas cape and webbing, and his jacket and shirt. He was in a shocking mess. He was gasping for breath and bleeding badly, almost in panic, what could I do? I was so helpless, I had nothing. I made a pad out of the shirt, ripped the tapes off the gas cape and tried to tie it around his back to stem the bleeding. I pulled him to his feet, lifted him on to my shoulder with a fireman's lift and struggled along to try to get away from that area in case another rocket salvo came over. How far I carried him I do not know. I shall never know, but absolutely exhausted, I had to put him down. Then I tried turning him on his stomach on my opened gas cape and pulled him along, but that too was hopeless. I gave it up, totally exhausted. I then sneaked a view at the end of the ridge and I could see beyond the road, some 600 or 700 yards away, two Nazi soldiers setting up their machine-gun covering the road ahead. I was in the frame of mind now that nothing mattered any more. I was angry and hurt; revenge filled my mind more than anything, and I wanted to get those Nazi gunners at any cost. I had two rounds remaining, one in the breech of the rifle and one left in the magazine. I pushed the rifle through the grass beneath the gorse and a clump of blackberries and set my sight on the German's head lying beneath the Mauser machine-gun. I held my breath and actually took the first pressure (which is absolutely necessary) on the trigger of my rifle. At that precise moment I was one hundredth of a second from firing the shot and a strange omen happened, I hesitated as a yapping, hysterical and frightened small dog came bouncing up the road almost mad with frenzy from the gun fire and explosions. The German gunners opened fire and cut the dog almost in two, but it wasn't the machine-gun as I would have thought, but a total of four with tracer bullets splashing all over the road. At that same time also John Partridge gave a choking cough, tried to say something and died. I pulled back my rifle, but if I had fired, every German gun and fire power would have been concentrated on my position. I supported my head and covered my eyes with both hands. It is impossible now to describe that awful feeling of frustration and hopelessness, where my spirits and morale had reached the lowest point of helplessness and despair of my whole life. I just wanted to give up and lie down and die. After some time I reached the point and decision that I must walk out with my hands in the air and surrender, but then again it raced through my mind that I had seen the brutal execution of Randall as he surrendered, and now the target practice on the dog. What hope would there be for me? I too could be cut down like the dog. Once again I was in a quandary. Now the half-tracks were moving into the area of the machine-gunners, towing the batteries of guns, setting them up to bombard the areas ahead. I could hear the orders being shouted by the Nazi officers and I witnessed one officer along with his Feltwebel (sergeant) set up and sight the range finder for the artillery, and fire the first salvo, then listen on his radio from some observation post and bark further orders to raise or lower the gun sights for the next salvoes.

I was in a desperate situation now. Ahead of me and slightly down the hill was an open fenced field about 150 yards across to the next ridge and undergrowth cover. The field was about 20 inches high with lush grass dotted with the tall field dog daisy and the red poppy, probably kept for hay. I had to cross that field if I was to get away, yet it was in full sight of the German gunners along the road, some 700 yards away. I considered once again walking out to give myself up and I decided what did it matter any more? It was all over for me anyway, so I would attempt to cross the field with one desperate effort to get clear of the Nazi's. I wiped John's blood off my gas cape in the bracken and grass and pushed my webbing equipment around the belt to my sides. I tossed Lt. Hughes' wallet into the bushes, as I did not want to be caught with an officer's wallet in my possession. I cut off the hood of the cape with the bayonet, pushed it over the top of my steel helmet, tucking in the surplus and clamped it on my head. I brought it forward as far as possible over my forehead and tightened the chin strap over my chin under the bottom lip. Then, I put on the gas cape and fastened all the press studs down the front. The gas cape was a type of oilskin plasticised material and coloured grass green, so I hoped it would camouflage me across that open field. I looked ahead for a landmark and a guide. The only object of prominence for me to see lying on my stomach was the corner post situated diagonally across that field.

I waited for the next deafening gun salvo when they all turn to the rear for the flash, covering their ears to dull the boom, then I dived across quickly on to my stomach below the bottom fence wire. I could raise my head to a limit of about six inches, just enough to see the corner post through the grass down the slight incline. I turned slightly on to my left side so that I could bend my right knee and dig in my right heel to push me forward. I could not use my left heel, as the injury was still too sore, so it meant covering the whole distance on my left side only. I stretched both arms forward pushing the rifle ahead with my right hand as far as possible pointing in the direction of the corner post to guide me. I grabbed a clump of lower grass with my left hand and pulled, as I pushed with my right heel till I moved up to the rifle and then repeated the difficult procedure and crawled as my right leg straightened. This meant I moved forward about one foot with each effort. I had 150 yards to travel and at the distance of one foot with each movement that meant at least 450 pulls and pushes to a safe cover across the other side. I could not raise my stomach off the ground without the danger of being seen by German field glasses. I have relived that crawl many, many times during my lifetime. It sapped every last bit of energy out of me, and how many times I stopped and lay still with sheer exhaustion I do not know. How long it took me I do not know either, because after I passed the half way area I was often seized with cramps in my leg and left arm. With the guns firing, explosions, and small arms fire whistling over me from our own forces it was an unforgettable nightmare. By the time I eventually reached the corner post I must have lost half a stone with perspiration from the strenuous effort, and heat, enclosed in that gas cape. At least I had made it to the corner and under the bottom fence wire to reach the cover of undulating ground once again!

I discarded the gas cape quickly. All the studs up the front had torn off, the material also was torn, and ripped, rubbing along the rough ground as I crawled. I had to massage my aching left arm and leg to bring back the circulation, then I lay on my back to rest for some time as I gazed up at the sky wondering and worrying again what lay ahead. I started off once again absolutely exhausted but determination made me push on. Then suddenly, as I made my way up a hollow, I saw the big horse chestnut tree opposite the white-washed farm cottage where the children had waved from the window. It cheered me up, as I realised I was going in the right direction. I must have travelled in a semicircle and I would almost be making my way back in the wrong direction from where I had come had I not spotted that tree. I climbed up the side of the hollow skirting the cottage, dashed across the road, up the bank on the other side and into the field behind the bushes. I scrutinised the farm cottage carefully, where everything seemed deserted, and I assumed that the occupants had fled. It must have been into evening and it was now cloudy, and I was sure that darkness was not far away, so I tried to move along a little bit faster. It was a big effort, but I kept going. The area ahead we had come through previously in early morning darkness, so my doubts started to return. I saw no one, and no sign of life or movement anywhere. The first row of terraced homes suddenly came into sight and I racked my brains to try and remember if we had passed by them. I still carefully kept off the road and took no chances, but I kept it in view from every bit of available cover. The house I had seen must have been at the extreme end of the Boulogne area before the open country-side. The houses all ran downhill on one side of the cobbled road with a narrow footpath, and each front door entered on to this footpath.

I approached the rear of these houses, with its untidy lane and rubbish scattered everywhere. I tried the backyard door of the first house at the top of the hill. It opened and I cautiously went inside. There was an outside toilet, with a wooden seat and a bucket, and flies, and a small garden fenced with netting wire to the adjoining house. I could look down right across each back area to the bottom of the street. I tried the back door by pressing the thumb lift catch and again it opened, then I released the safety catch on my rifle and I went inside to the kitchen cum living room. It was untidy and unclean, with a table and chairs and a cooking stove. A door entered into a short passage to the front door, stairs up, and a front room on the right, which must have been the best room, complete with fireplace. One particular thing that struck me, and in later years in Europe, especially Belgium, was the rear vision mirror screwed to the outside of the top of the window on the footpath. It gave me a view down the hill along the footpath to the extreme end and everything appeared deserted. I climbed the stairs to the bedrooms, one at the rear and two at the front connected by a narrow landing. I went to the left front bedroom and looked out of the window across the countryside. The guns were flashing and hurling shells into the port, tracer bullets screaming into the built-up areas and buildings over to my right. I could see the Nazi tanks and armoured cars moving around and firing ahead towards the port also, and German ground troops behind the tanks and I just hoped they would not start shooting and shelling my present refuge. I sat on the unmade, untidy and not too clean bed, unbuckled my webbing gaiter and removed my left boot and sock. I had a half-inch fleshy cut at the side of the heel that had bled a great deal saturating the sock. With apologies to the occupants of that house, I squeezed the blood out of my sock on to the floor, I ripped off a piece of the not too clean sheet and wiped out my boot, then I found the cleanest part available, ripped off another small piece, wrapped it around my ankle and heel, and replaced my sock and boot. The surplus pieces of that sheet I stuffed into my Bren gun pouch, in case I had to surrender. I now had a white flag in my possession, then I quickly left the premises by the same back entrance. It was now dusk and I tried to figure out British time. The clock had been advanced two hours making double summer time, and it would be daylight in mid June up until almost midnight, so I assumed at the end of May it must be after 9 p.m. In order to beat the darkness I had to hurry. It had been the longest day of my life. I came into the residential area proper now, always carefully moving along the rear as the explosions and bullets were getting nearer.

I saw no inhabitant or soldier anywhere, as everything had been abandoned and deserted, and I slowly reached the port area as darkness began to come on. Many buildings were on fire and damaged, lighting up the area but I kept going and reached the end of the cobblestoned street, from where I could see the wharf. I was among various shops now, the glass was shattered everywhere and I had no trouble entering one of them to try and get a view of the way ahead. That particular building was a big perfumery store with thousands of bottles and boxes of scent and perfume lining the shelves and glass cases. I climbed the stairway to the first floor and looked across the big open area to the dock buildings. I could see the railway station at the end of the wharf. There was a big Red Cross ambulance and hospital train near the wharf, the shelling was awful and if there were any wounded aboard that train they would certainly be getting a bad time.

I could pick out the British steel helmet on various fleeting figures and my spirits rose. In the dock area there were two ships, both destroyers with their superstructure low down in the water, both firing their heavy forward guns and multiple-barrelled Bofors guns over the top of the train against the enemy on the higher ground. I ran down the stairway and two shells burst outside the building shaking scores of bottles in a shower off the shelves. I picked up one single-boxed perfume bottle, the price tag on which read 1,750 francs. I had no idea of the exchange value of the franc, but it seemed an enormous price to me, so I stuffed it into my Bren gun pouch, burst out through the damaged door and ran as fast as I possibly could across the open area to the wharfside buildings and docks. The destroyer was moving backwards with the momentum of the guns and then steaming forward a little each time near the wharf to enable the troops to jump down from the dockside on to the deck. Everything was desperate now as it steamed in reverse to get away. It was about five yards from the dockside, I went back a little and using the last of my strength, I ran, jumped and just cleared the distance to the ship. There was cursing and swearing, because I had landed on a number of people in the darkness, but it did not matter to me. I was on that ship, so I crawled and dragged myself to a clear space at the stern behind a companionway crowded with troops and people down below. I lay down on that deck in a crouch as the ship still fired salvo after salvo of the big 4.7 inch guns, blasting everything in front of it as it slowly turned to head to sea. Nazi shells were bursting everywhere, as the tanks had reached the wharf. I closed my eyes and covered my ears, out on my feet, totally and completely drained with exhaustion. I went out like a light into a deep sleep. I was stepped on and disturbed all that time we were at sea, but thank god I had made it! With just seconds to spare. I was among the Irish on board the *Wild Swan* and safely on my way back to Dover.

9

The Aftermath and My First Leave

The destroyer steamed into Dover harbour in the darkness and slowly manoeuvred into a berth at the wharfside. There were ambulances, and all kinds of military trucks and officials waiting on the wharf. We slowly filed off the ship, and saw lines of tables covered with sandwiches and biscuits and urns of hot tea. These were manned by the women's volunteer service in their blue uniforms, attending to everyone. There was also a special train waiting to carry us all away once again. I was in an awful mess. My battledress was dirty and badly bloodstained from John Partridge; they took one look at me and helped me to the casualty clearing station. I was attended by medical officers and orderlies and I quickly explained it was not my blood, but requested that they look at my heel. I removed my boot and the bloodsoaked piece of sheet around my ankle. They treated it with antiseptic and bandaged it telling me 'I would live' and to report sick when I reached my destination. I boarded the train to find some of the remainder of No. 3 Company there. We were all taken once again back to Colchester, ushered into trucks at the station and driven back to the training battalion barracks.

It was almost midday when we arrived at Colchester on 24th May 1940. We were given a hot meal and temporarily sorted out into various barrack-room huts. The remainder of the battalion had moved from Camberley and it would take more time to sort out who was present, and all the ones missing. My kit bag was in the company store, with all kinds of other things, so I had another battledress, a clean shirt, underwear, socks and boots and I slept for the rest of that day and night.

It appeared that the majority of No. 7 Platoon with platoon Sergeant-Major M'Nair, whom Davis had complained about so bitterly for running away, had been evacuated in the early afternoon of the 23rd. Two-thirds of No. 9 Platoon, the greater part of No. 1 Company and all HQ Company had returned safely also. The whole of No. 8 Platoon, except for me, were missing as I expected, all killed or captured. The remnants of the battalion under Major Windsor Lewis surrendered on 26th May. Major Lewis escaped and returned to Britain six months later having made his way across France and Spain to Portugal. George Davis did not return. He became a prisoner of war.

I reported sick the following morning with my heel problem and was given seven days Attend B and a pair of new boots. It was back to the old routine of dirty, greasy, cookhouse chores and spud peeling once again and I was sick of it all. It meant that I was fit enough to do all the dirty fatigues but not allowed outside the barrack gates and I was desperate to get in touch with my parents. Not knowing what had happened, they would be frantic, as hundreds of boats and every type of craft were crossing the English Channel in a desperate attempt to rescue and evacuate the remnants of the British expeditionary forces on the beaches and coastline of the French mainland. That afternoon there was a farcical 15-minute investigation with the battalion paraded on the barrack square because of the accusations and rumours about PSM M'Nair and the early evacuation of his No. 7 Platoon. It was obvious no one could speak up, as the victims were all missing, and all I knew was hearsay from Davis, which appeared to be true. I could say nothing, as there was no one to corroborate my statements and even so, anything from a lowly guardsman would not be believed. There were no questions asked, and no inquiry about any other incident that happened. I could see quite plainly they wanted to hush it up quickly and forget the whole débâcle. The situation made me feel bitter and angry; it stuck in my gut never to go away.

That evening I succeeded in sneaking out from the rear of the barracks and reaching a phone box, I got through to Bargoed Post Office, just one minute before they closed at 6 p.m. They put me through to Gilfach Post Office run by Miss Biddy Harris and my cousin Mair, Uncle Dai's daughter, her assistant. I asked her briefly to pass on a message to my mother that I was safe and well and my address was as before at Colchester Barracks, and I would write as soon as possible. I heard later that Mair ran all the way to Oak Cottage to tell them the news, and my mother wrote back that evening. I received the letter a day and a half later. In that particular letter she enclosed the address of her sister – my Aunt Ethel – at the married quarters of the RAF base some ten miles from Colchester, and urged me to go there when possible. At least, she wrote, it would be a break, a welcome cup of tea, and a place to get away from it all for a short time.

That evening I wrote a long letter in reply telling them what had happened, and I made up a small parcel with the perfume I had carried in my Bren gun pouch from Boulogne and temporarily forgotten. I sent it to my young sister Joan and she kept that perfume unopened and on display on her dressing-table until she died in 1986. I wonder now after 50 years, what has happened to that sealed 1,750 franc, packaged bottle of expensive perfume with its sad story of long ago, and its lace ribbons adorned around its neck. In 1985, when I paid her a visit, I asked her why she had never used it and she replied, 'It was a bottle of too many memories, I have to treasure and keep always.' The following Saturday, after being assigned Medicine and Duty once again, shortly after midday I set out to visit Aunt Ethel. There was no transport on those country roads outside Colchester so I walked the whole distance through the Essex countryside until I reached the air base and found the officers' married quarters area. The entrance was controlled by RAF police, and I had to state and explain my business. Being just a lowly private soldier wishing to enter the officers' quarters compound, I was not allowed beyond the controlled barrier. A corporal was dispatched to contact Mrs Ethel Herrick the wife of Squadron-Leader Robert Herrick, with my name, rank, etc. for permission to see her. About ten minutes later the corporal returned with the message that Mrs Herrick was indisposed and unable to see me! I felt so disappointed, frustrated and angry. Snobbery and class had come into it again, it just wasn't done for a lowly private soldier to be entertained by a squadron-leader's wife! I tramped all the way back to Colchester tired and miserable and I swore that I would have nothing to do with Mrs Herrick for the rest of my life. I have kept to my word, never to forget!

The news from the south and east coasts was frightening. The gallant efforts of hundreds of people who manned every type of craft, big and small, evacuating the men from the French beaches to Dunkirk was magnificent. Thousands were rescued and brought back to safety under appalling conditions and constant aerial bombardment, cheating death and captivity from the Nazi hordes.

I now approached the Company Quartermaster, CQMS Williams, for leave and, as he knew what had happened, being a member of Company Headquarters, and he was sympathetic about it all, the application went through with all the usual red tape. In early June 1940 I was at last granted my first seven days' leave. It was a difficult journey home for the first time, as everything was so disorganised. There were servicemen everywhere trying to make their way home or to some detailed destination in groups and squads. Again and again passing through London I was stopped and delayed by military police checking everyone and inspecting all passes and transport vouchers. I reached Paddington Station and finally boarded the express for South Wales. I had to stand for the entire journey, the whole train and all the corridors were absolutely jam packed with passengers. I was stopped and checked again at Cardiff Station and it was necessary for me to walk from the Central Station through a Cardiff district to Queen Street railway station in order to catch another train up the Rhymney Valley to my home. My shoulder flash revealed the identity of my regiment and so many times once more I was stopped by anxious individuals seeking news of various people. It appeared that No. 1 Battalion of the regiment had received a bad time also, retreating from the French town of Arras and many were still missing. I was unable to help them and it was a relief for me when I finally boarded the train to take me up the Rhymney Valley to Pengam Station.

It was a warm sunny Tuesday afternoon, and I felt relaxed and excited as I left the train at Pengam Station carrying my full complement of kit, including a big kit bag. I walked up very familiar territory known as the Black Path, bypassing the Pengam Square and the Grammar School hill, leading to Gwerthoner Road. The first person I saw was Stan Davies the co-op store baker's roundsman, with his bread cart and his faithful old horse, Mary. With a warm handshake and excitement he helped me stuff my equipment into the rear of the bread cart, and with a few words to the old horse, we were trotting along at the fastest speed along Gwerthonor Road to Oak Cottage. Stan pulled up at the front gate, jumped out and banged on the front door, offloaded my kit, turned the horse and cart around, and with a few words of encouragement went on his way back to finish his bread deliveries.

My mother was surprised and glad to see me, but there was no one else at home, so the kettle was soon boiling for a welcome cup of tea in a comfortable chair. I took off my army boots and for the first time for five long months I could sit down and relax once more. Joan arrived home from school with a warm greeting, and then she went to inform Uncle Dai and my Aunt May, and in a short time it was all around the neighbourhood with everyone coming to see me. Mrs Morgan from the corner shop in Vere Street raced down with 50 Players cigarettes as a present and welcome home, and all this activity went on until early evening. That night I sat up till the early hours of the morning as I told my father the details of what had taken place, and he was angry and disgusted. The next day, as I have said previously, he went along to speak to Morgan Jones, the local member of parliament, but it was all hushed up.

It was amazing how news travelled. Sergeant Mitzy Green's sister-in-law, who lived in the Bargoed area, contacted Mrs Green by phone suggesting that I might provide some information regarding her notification that he was missing, so I went missing also from early morning for the next two days up on the mountainside lying in the sunshine. So many people from all over the area came to see me and my mother seeking information about missing sons and husbands. It was sad and depressing and all I could say to them all was I could not help them. I did make a special journey to Pontllanfraith to see John Partridge's parents and sadly related the truth and the unfortunate incidents that happened causing his death. They too had been informed that he was missing, and even after my trouble to tell them everything, his mother would not accept it, still believing he was all right and he would turn up again. I regretted afterwards that I had made the special effort to visit them. How difficult it was and how depressing, when someone was told the truth yet she had misgivings about believing it; yet when I prevaricated and said I did not know and could not help, people believed me. When I eventually saw Mrs Green, I said I could not help, that I was in a different area, and she accepted it for years until the end of the war, hoping falsely that her husband was alive. I have always wondered what would have happened if I had told the truth.

My leave had come to an end and once again I made the train journey all the way back to Colchester.

10

The Battle of Britain and the Wimbledon Line for the Final Defence of London June 1940–42

I began my long dreary journey back to Colchester in an overcrowded train to London and another train to my destination, to face up to the usual drudgery, drill parades and the same old routine.

It was 10th June 1940 and we were informed that the battalion had orders to pack up once again and move south, nearer to the coast, the Goodwood Park racecourse, outside Chichester in Sussex.

I was a member of a new No. 8 Platoon now and there were many new faces from the training battalion adding to the few original members who had fortunately missed the draft to Boulogne by travelling independently from the leave train at Camberley. Once again we packed our kit and boarded army trucks for the journey to Goodwood Park. It was unpleasant, rough, and most uncomfortable. At our destination, our quarters now were the racing stables and buildings on the vast expanse of green downs along the racetrack. The conditions were primitive with just a few outdoor cold water taps and temporary bucket toilets, with a straw palliasse laid out on a groundsheet to rest and sleep. We were back to the routine of living by, and answering, the various calls on the bugle with monotonous drill parades each morning and afternoon on a flat area of grasslands. I was feeling unwell. I had developed a cold, my stomach was causing me discomfort again, and I was suffering from feverish hot spells. I endured it all for two days, but I was getting worse. It was a bright sunny morning of 15th June, my throat had become inflamed and I felt too sick to even shave, so I struggled down to the sick parade at 7.30 a.m., to form up on parade before the Drill Sergeant-Major. The usual stupid standing to attention to be inspected was carried out and I was reprimanded and booked for being improperly shaved. I can still remember giving my name and number to be entered and booked on this charge, then I must have passed out and collapsed. The next thing I remembered was waking up in a hospital bed at Goodwood Park Military Hospital with a temperature of 103 – I was sick, very sick!

They diagnosed severe inflammation of the breathing tubes and acute tonsilitis. The hospital was actually Goodwood House, a wonderful old mansion commandeered and converted into a military hospital for the duration of the War. I spent three weeks in that hospital until I recovered and was classed as fit once again. It was a wonderfully restful three weeks, with every care and attention given, and I did not relish being posted back to my unit once again.

At the end of June and the beginning of the month of July 1940, I received instructions and my posting back to the 2nd Battalion at Byfleet in Surrey. The battalion had moved from Goodwood Park racecourse to the town of Byfleet, and the various companies were billeted in private houses throughout the district, commandeered and taken over by the military. I was given a railway voucher from Chichester railway station, and I had to find my own way to Byfleet. I went to London and caught a train on the Southern Railway, as it was known at that time, to Byfleet. I arrived just after midday, then asking directions I walked up through Byfleet until I found No. 3 Company Headquarters. The three platoons were out on a military exercise but the same old faces were there – Company Sergeant-Major Edwards, PSM M'Nair, who appeared to be a little more subdued now after Boulogne accusations, and CQMS Williams. I was detailed back to No. 8 Platoon and sent along the main road to a house called 'Redstacks'. This house backed onto the Byfleet golf course, three floors with bare wooden floors, with palliasses and kit arranged neatly along each wall. I collected my kit from the company store with a palliasse of straw, and found a vacant space on the second floor with my old section, wondering how long this would be my future resting place.

In Europe now, France had capitulated and was already divided into the occupied and unoccupied zones. The greater part of the British Expeditionary Forces had been successfully evacuated, but we had nothing left, all the equipment, guns, and munitions had been lost. The Nazis now had full control of the whole European coastline from Norway to Spain. They had all the airfields and ports, and from this time onwards we were in for a terrible time.

It was back to the old routine once again, more drill parades, route marches, and military exercises. I settled in with all the new faces, and we soon got to know each other. Our platoon was to be commanded by a new platoon officer Lieutenant Pelham. In July the Messerschmitt fighter and Nazi bomber attacks began, and at first the airfields became the main targets. We were only a short distance from Farnborough airfield, the big aircraft factory at Weybridge and the site of the old motor racing track at Brooklands so we could expect many attacks. It all began in mid July ten days before my 21st birthday, one of July's beautiful sunny days at around 10 a.m. we were on parade as usual drilling on the Byfleet golf course. Fifteen Messerschmitt fighter aircraft began their low level machine-gunning, swooping over the barrage balloons around the Weybridge area, across the village of Byfleet as low as 500 feet with cannons and machine-guns raking everything in their path. The whole battalion broke ranks and dived for cover into the bushes, bunkers and trees, and fortunately no one was hit or injured, and an air battle commenced above us as the Spitfires and Hurricane fighters attacked the Nazi planes, chasing them back to the English Channel.

Once more, on 27th July, the day after my 21st birthday, we were attacked, and a number of civilians were injured but again we had no casualties. The commanding officer now began to be more cautious and we paraded at company and platoon strength for the remainder of the summer in order to disperse quickly and take cover. The air battles over southern England now intensified, and in our area of a number of square miles we rushed daily to crashed aircraft to rescue any of our own airmen and to round up any Nazis who had bailed out from their crippled aircraft. It became a daily lottery until the end of September counting the number of kills of downed Nazi planes, and sadly too, many of our own pilots. It was a regular awesome sight to see the massed formations of Nazi bombers with groups of Messerschmitt fighters high above escorting them. They were ready to peel off to attack, our own aircraft climbing to deal with the bomber fleet as they made their way to south and south-west London, with all the anti-aircraft guns pounding away, making hundreds of black puffs as they exploded in the air.

By the beginning of October, Hitler realised he could not wipe out the British airfields, although so much damage was done and hundreds of aircraft destroyed on both sides. I can recall from memory being on the alert all day around 24th September when 324 German aircraft were reported shot down in that 24-hour day, and our losses also were enormous. If we could believe the military authorities, 197 of our own aircraft were shot out of the skies.

As the daylight hours grew shorter towards the end of 1940, the massed night bombing began. Ordinary time had been advanced two hours during the summer time to increase the evening daylight span, and it was to continue throughout the winter ahead and for the remainder of the war. It had been strange to experience the sun shining at eleven o'clock at night but it was a big advantage and we soon got used to it as the years went on.

Our worries now as the year of 1940 was drawing to a close were the responsibility of rescuing people from the rubble and the bombed areas, and the enormous fires caused by Hitler's oil bombs and incendiaries, and an even greater worry was the feared invasion of Nazi forces across the English Channel and the North Sea. Every signpost and every name of every locality, town, or village was removed throughout the whole country. There were to be no clues as to the name or identity of any place to remain. All signs on billboards, shops, factories and premises including post offices, were painted out, nothing would remain to give any clue to his whereabouts. All our travels and movements anywhere as troops were worked out on map references. The church bells and school bells everywhere were to be silenced, and to be rung as an alarm only in every locality, for a suspected drop of Nazi parachute troops, or airborne intruders, and we were ordered to carry loaded arms day and night, on or off duty. By Christmas 1940 the danger of invasion increased, and we had very little in the way of arms and munitions, the greater part having been lost to the Nazi forces in Europe and, until supplies were built up and manufactured, things were desperate. We now became a mobile force, each platoon was allotted a commandeered civilian bus or coach, with a civilian driver so that we could be rushed to any area day or night, if an invasion alarm was given. If we took part in military exercise route march, or parade, the coach was always waiting near at hand for an emergency.

At all vulnerable points along main roads, high points, and important locations, concrete pillboxes were quickly built, all recorded and mapped for us to know immediately any defensive position in case they were needed. Concrete tank obstacles and traps were built and co-ordinated with wide trenches in defensive lines all over southern England from the coastline and our last defensive positions that we were to hold as a battalion was a line known to us as the 'Wimbledon Line' for the final outer defence of London.

We continuously carried out manoeuvres for two and three days and nights almost each week exercising all this area and knowing our correct positions if it became necessary to occupy this last line of defence. Early 1941, the months of winter were most unpleasant, but the danger was so great no one could be complacent. All day long we were on duty or on exercises and then, at night as the Nazi bombing began, we rushed from place to place searching for the injured and buried survivors, and helping to douse and put out incendiaries and fires. Many miniature, temporary, artificial pools were constructed in all the built-up areas so that ample supplies of water were ready and available to tackle an emergency. Our hours of sleep seemed to get less each week and we were often totally exhausted.

In January of the new year 1941, I was granted my second seven days' leave. I had been a soldier for just over one year and this was only my second break away from it all. As the winter turned into spring our losses of arms and ammunition began to improve. The armament factories were going flat out and we began receiving the imported gangster-type short-range Tommy guns from America. It was a deadly, close-range weapon with snub-nosed bullets, a weapon we needed badly with the danger of Nazi airborne troops landing anywhere. Another addition also was the introduction and supply of the Sten gun, which could be produced quickly and cheaply. During the spring of that year 1941 with so much foot slogging, exercises and route marches, my heel began to give me trouble. The rear of the ankle became inflamed and swollen, and a considerable lump developed on the heel making it very sore and causing difficulty in getting my boot on and off. The date was 7th May, almost one year since I was hit during the sad affair with John Partridge, and I hobbled down to sick parade at Company Headquarters. PSM M'Nair who was taking the parade, had always avoided contact with me because it had become known to him, through the grapevine, about my incident with 2nd Lieutenant Hughes. He passed me by at the inspection without comment, apprehending another unfortunate individual, so I was relieved when we were all taken by army truck to battalion headquarters to see the medical officer. The medical officer took one look at my foot and ordered me on to the battalion ambulance, and I was taken immediately to Botley Park Military Hospital at Chertsey in the county of Surrey. My heel was examined and X-rayed at the hospital, and I was put into bed in a casualty ward and operated upon the next morning. I did not know very much about it until I came to, late in the afternoon on 8th May. The surgeon had cut off the big callous lump and removed a tiny piece of metal a little bigger than a pin head that had lodged against the heel bone. It was sewn up and I spent the next three weeks in bed. I had carried that piece of mortar splinter in my foot for almost one year despite all the miles of marching, and I was very thankful it had not been any bigger.

Botley Park was another private mansion turned into a military hospital, with wonderful extensive gardens and grounds, so my stay there was enjoyable and restful until I was posted back to Byfleet in June. On my return back to the unit and my platoon at Byfleet I reported sick once more and was given Attend C for one month and excused everything. I wore a pair of gym shoes for the whole time. I spent the long days alone keeping the house Redstacks clean, neat and tidy, hiding myself away on the sunny days at the bottom of the garden adjoining the golf course, or up in the top attic rooms of the house.

The situation of the nation was very grim. There had been enormous losses of shipping caused by the Nazi U-boats, the bombing had been devastating and Hitler's hordes were poised to strike and invade across the English Channel from the occupied countries. The break suddenly came and Hitler made the greatest mistake of all. On 22nd June 1941, one day ahead of Napoleon's disastrous invasion of Russia, Hitler turned his forces east and invaded Soviet Russia. The effect on our situation was almost immediate as the loss of shipping had been so bad, and it would have been devastating and perhaps the end for us all if he had succeeded in crossing the Channel. It would give us more time now to re-equip and re-arm to a greater preparedness because we did not know that at the end of the year Japan would strike in the Pacific and the United States would enter the war.

My foot improved slowly and six weeks had passed by. I did nothing and I was getting tired of it because I was not allowed out of billets, so I made myself fit and returned to duties in order to get my leave in July. It was so good to go home once again but the journey was so slow. With an overcrowded train and the sounding of air-raid warnings across the country, it slowed to a walking pace to avoid being a fast-moving target for the enemy planes guided by the straight railway tracks. When I reached Cardiff and I began to walk across to the Queen Street Railway Station, the air-raid warning sounded again and two Nazi bombers escorted by three Messerschmitt fighters attacked the docks. I was 100 yards away from the station in a back street and I had my rifle and all my equipment which was compulsory in case of an emergency recall. I fired from the shoulder five shots from my rifle at one of the low-flying fighter planes before they made their getaway.

On my return to Byfleet, we received orders to vacate our billet Redstacks and move to another billet down a side road off the main Byfleet to Woking Road and we occupied this place until September.

The advance into Russia by Hitler's eastern armies was so great and devastating that it appeared to have no effect on movement of the masses of troops and equipment in northern France and the Channel coast, and the military were still concerned and worried about an attack across the Channel and North Sea. One of their worries was also the vulnerability of the ports of Liverpool, Birkenhead and Manchester from any airborne drop on the island of Anglesey and southern Ireland. There were only small detachments of troops on Anglesey around the port and Irish ferry at Holyhead, and there was no airfield and no opposition on the whole island if an emergency happened with the ports, which were so vital for the imports of food and materials, just a few miles away along the North Wales Coast. My company – No. 3 Company – was now ordered to pack up and move to North Wales to garrison the whole island of Anglesey and we would be replaced at Byfleet with a holding company from the training battalion. Other things were happening also – Company Sergeant-Major Edwards was sent back to the training depot along with Platoon Sergeant-Major M'Nair much to our relief. The rank of Platoon Sergeant-Major was abolished in the British army and I believe that M'Nair was the last person to hold that rank. Our new Company Sergeant-Major was now promoted to Quartermaster Sergeant Williams and I approved of him. He knew of my capabilities and standing in the Company and he was also a regular rugby and soccer player in the company and battalion team just like myself. He knew all that had happened and anyone could talk to him without rebuff and he would listen to all the grumps and grievances.

We were transported to London in our civilian bus with all our company equipment in army trucks and entrained in two carriages hitched to the rear of the Holyhead express. We travelled through the English Midlands and along the North Wales Coast to Bangor, across the Menai Strait over the famous Menai Bridge to that wonderful tongue-twisting longest-named railway station in the world – Llanfair pwllgwyllgogerychwyrndrobwillantysiliogogogoch, or the shorter version, Llanfair P G. In normal times the name begins at one end of the station and ends on the extreme end of the station. At that time it had been removed, like all other names throughout the country. We left the train at the station and boarded army trucks which carried us along the coast road to the small town of Beaumaris, then inland for a further two miles to a huge country mansion called Henllys. We occupied one first floor wing of this beautiful old house, the remainder having been sealed off containing all the dust-cloth-covered furniture, fittings and treasures from the house. Our residential quarters were bare wooden floors with the usual palliasse and straw-filled pillow. There was no heating of any kind and with the approaching winter it would be a cold time for us all. Our cookhouse and mess room became one of the converted outhouse stables, but at least we were away from the battalion and much of the usual red tape.

As the short November days with all the mists and rain began, we had to rely on the radar information over the telephone for any approaching enemy aircraft. One platoon was on duty around the clock and when any messages came through we were out on the vast expanses of coastal flat sandy areas, or in the hilly interior, or along the north coast from Red Wharf Bay to Bull Bay and Holyhead Bay, skirting the villages of Moelfre, Amlwch and Tregele. Many of those long nights were bitterly cold as we heard the Nazi bombers, with their familiar missing-beat droning engines, fly across after their bombing missions in Lancashire and make their flight down the Irish Sea, and back to occupied France.

Christmas 1941 was a white Christmas with a thick mantle of snow, but it was a pleasant day and we received quite an enjoyable Christmas dinner. Our main recreation when free of duties was football. Each platoon formed a team and we spent many hours on the coastal playing field at Beaumaris. I spent three weekends, at different times at the home of Norman Evans, one of my section mates. His father was one of the Irish Sea ferry captains operating between Holyhead and Dublin, so it made quite a break.

December 1941, just prior to Christmas, brought us the news that the Japs had attacked Pearl Harbor. America entered the war, we were no longer alone, and the year of 1942 was to bring many changes to me and the rest of the battalion. Our planes were now getting the upper hand of the Nazi air force, the danger of invasion diminished and in February once again we packed our kit to return to Byfleet to rejoin the remainder of the battalion. It was a short stay at Byfleet before we were on the move again, this time to Hendon in north London. We were billeted in vacated civilian houses just a short distance from central Hendon. A straw palliasse on the bare boards became our accommodation but the warmer spring days were with us in early 1942. The nights were hectic with the Nazi bombing raids as we rushed all over the city pulling out survivors from flattened burning buildings and helped to douse masses of falling incendiary fire bombs. Our free time was so much better now with plenty of cinemas to break the long monotony and the unpleasant rescue operations. I received another leave from Hendon and I was glad to get home for a short break away from bombing and the long nights. Our stay at Hendon soon came to an end, and reorganisation began with the initial preparations, and intense training, for the second front – the invasion of Nazi-occupied Europe.

11

The Formation of the 2nd Armoured Reconnaissance Battalion and the Guards Armoured Division 1942

It was just like starting all over again but the military commanders had to have one more big ceremony before their toy infantry soldiers were turned into radio operators, tank gunners and armoured vehicle drivers, a complete turn around from their infantry companies. We were collected and taken by army truck to the big parade ground at Hendon Police College for a three-hour session of ceremonial drill. When it all ended we were paraded and informed that the next day we were to move to Codford in Wiltshire to be trained for a new formation of the British army, a tank battalion to be equipped, when they came off the production lines, with the new modern, fast, powerful, heavily armed Cromwell tanks, the striking reconnaissance unit of a Guards Armoured Division.

Once again we packed and loaded our kit for the journey to Codford and the Salisbury Plain training area. Codford was a miserable, isolated village with a few scattered cottages, a couple of shops, a post office and a small one-man police station. The camps, one at each end of the village were not completed, there was mud everywhere, and we were detailed daily to do the labouring duties for the pioneer troops erecting the Nissen corrugated huts and the wooden buildings, making paths into the camp sites and trying to landscape and improve the general area. After a week or so we were sorted out, our No. 3 Company now became No. 3 Squadron, and each platoon became a 'Troop', No. 7, 8, 9 and HQ Troop. The Bren machine-gun and the useless Boyes anti-tank rifle were no longer a part of our equipment.

155

We still retained our rifle for drill purposes, but we were issued with a Smith and Wesson .38 pistol. I was glad to see the last of the Boyes anti-tank rifle, I had carried it with aching arms for so many miles, hating it, because I knew how useless it was. To begin with we received a few old Crusader tanks which had put up such a poor performance in the Western Desert of North Africa. Its armament was the old two-pounder anti-tank gun and the Bren machine-gun. It had been out-ranged and out-gunned by the Nazi tanks everywhere in North Africa, but it would help us with driver training and tactics around the areas of our camp. Many newcomers joined us, men chosen from the 1st Infantry Battalion and the Training Battalion.

Our old commanding officer of No. 3 Company had escaped from Europe, and he now became Colonel Windsor Lewis, the new commanding officer of the battalion. He was a harsh disciplinarian, a small, cynical individual who, wearing a civilian cap, would pass as a farm labourer. He used a walking stick because of a limp and a shortened leg resulting from a First World War wound. He was uncivil at all times to the men under his command, his disciplinary punishments at his daily memoranda parades were extreme and, to describe him truthfully, to a private soldier he was most unpleasant.

It was at this time that I received a jolt caused, I believe, by Colonel Lewis investigating the men of his new command. Sergeant-Major Williams – now Squadron Sergeant-Major – sent for me one morning and told me in the usual army fashion that I would be transferred to the 1st Infantry Battalion if I continued to be, using his own words, 'A b. idiot and refuse promotion.' He emphasised, in army language, that I would be peeling spuds and digging trenches for the rest of the war, when I was needed for more important things, and he would allow me three hours only to think it over and then report my decision to him immediately, at the midday meal. I thought it over and with all the NCOs ordering me around, and copping all the dirty work, because I was head of the list with my name beginning with the letter 'A', I accepted, and that same afternoon I was up before Colonel Lewis, given a dressing down and then promoted to the rank of corporal. I had to change my attitude now, with all the experiences and the blood and guts of the bombing and its many victims, and my hidden anger from the débâcle of northern France. We had to win that awful war, and I would be a part of it for a long time, so whatever I did, I had to make it as easy as possible. The next week I was on my way with Norman Evans, George Clark, two old section mates, and three newcomers, to Colchester for a three weeks' drill instructors course at the Training Battalion. On my return, as the days of autumn and the first taste of the wet winter ahead was with us, we settled down to serious training, procedures and Morse, engine courses on our new tank motor and all other heavy vehicles. We obtained a simulator, a complete moving and tipping turret equivalent to a fast-moving tank over uneven ground for sighting the telescope sight and firing by a system of lights at a moving target.

Our living quarters were the half-round corrugated iron Nissen huts with a concrete floor and a door and window at each end. There were ten camp stretcher-type plywood beds down each side with a palliasse and pillow and the issue of two grey army blankets. In the centre of each hut was a small, round cast-iron stove, with its cast-iron flue going up through the roof. Every evening, when duties had ended we were allowed to collect a ration of one bucket of coke per hut from the locked-up dump behind the quartermaster's store. This ration gave us enough warmth for the evening. We were isolated but we did have a camp NAAFI canteen open until 9.30 p.m., with a half-size billiard table and tennis table with some benches and small tables for anyone to play cards. This was to be our training and daily life through the winter months of 1942 into 1943. We were allowed one weekend pass per month, and if anyone could afford it, they could travel home and return between 4 p.m. on Friday and midnight on Sunday. Apart from my leave I managed to get away three times to make it home and return. It was necessary to catch the 5 p.m. train from the tiny Codford railway station to Bath or Bristol, another train to Cardiff, and for me another train up the Rhymney Valley to home. Owing to the air raids it was a slow journey in the old steam engines. The lighting was so poor, just one small globe behind the blacked-out windows. The Fireman could only replenish the engine firebox under cover to avoid the huge glow into the night sky, such a give-away to an enemy bomber high above. I used to arrive at Cardiff in the early hours of Saturday morning to catch the 6 a.m. train up the Rhymney Valley. I would start my return journey at midday on Sunday and then normally arrive at Codford about 11.30 p.m., so it gave me just 24 hours at home, but it was worth it all.

Our newly arrived Cromwell tanks were formidable machines, fast-moving monsters, almost travelling time bombs, fully loaded with petrol, arms, and ammunition, vehicles in which we would soon have to eat, sleep and live, and for many also to die. It was 36 imperial tons of steel and armour plate, powered by a massive 300 horse-power modified Spitfire meteor, Rolls-Royce engine. On flat country it could

157

reach 50 miles per hour and crawl at a walking pace. The armaments consisted of either a 75mm or 90mm gun; two .3 inch Besa heavy machine-guns; one turret mounted and synchronised with the gun, the other in the front co-driver's compartment; one twin Vickers turret-mounted machine-gun; one two-inch mortar in the turret head capable of firing high explosives; black or coloured smoke for screening, or phosphorus fire bombs. We also carried two Sten guns, one rifle, one very light pistol with white, red, and green signal cartridges, and each of the five members of the crew carried a .38 Smith and Wesson pistol. Around the revolving turret were racks of high explosive shells, armour-piercing shells, and armour-piercing heat shells, HE grenades, phosphorus grenades, mortar bombs, boxes of Besa belt red tracer ammunition, .38 ammunition and .303 rounds. Each tank carried a powerful radio with an auxiliary petrol generator to keep the batteries fully charged. A tank helmet and headphones were worn by all the crew at all times for the intercom system, because it was impossible to hear anything above the noise of the tank engine. Each tank had a frequency link to the rest of the troop, and the troop leader was radio linked to the squadron. The squadron commander had a further frequency link to the battalion which in turn was linked to the corps and divisional commands. The turret had two hatches at the top, and each man had a revolving periscope which could be raised or lowered. The traverse of the turret was operated by a manual handle or hydraulic power by moving a handle left or right. The gunner had a foot operated rising and lowering seat as his eye engaged the flexible rubber eyepiece on the telescopic sight, the firing could be done with the foot or hand for either gun or the machine-gun as the gunner's shoulder controlled the elevation of the gun mounting. The steering was operated by left and right breaking sticks or handles, the gear lever was operated through a gate with an entry for each stage of the gears, and between the driver's knees was a big binnacle illuminated compass. Consequently, we had to have much intensive training to be skilled perfectionists in every position in the tank, and rectify, at record speed any stoppages with the machine-guns, besides evacuation drill, diving headlong to the ground from the top of the 12-feet high turret, without injury.

In February 1943 we loaded the tanks on railway transporters and we were entrained to the battle tank ranges at Castle Martin in south west Wales for one week for gunnery practice on moving targets under shocking conditions at full speed, using live shells and ammunition. As far as I was concerned the Cromwell proved its worth to me, and we had a formidable weapon. The cold wet drudgery of infantry foot slogging was over and the Nazi armies were in for an unexpected onslaught. On my return from Castle Martin I was sent to Paton, to the British army poison gases research centre, situated in southern England, for a three-week course. I obtained exceptionally high marks, and to my amazement I also received a credit and a high commendation from Colonel Windsor Lewis, and from that time onwards I became the Squadron Poison Gas NCO.

In May 1943, once again, I was sent to Nottingham for a two-week course at the Rolls-Royce tank engine establishment. I was given a trade insignia and an increase in pay, and I became a Gunner Mechanic first class.

As the spring days turned into summer of that year of 1943, Britain became a concentration of arms, men and equipment. Thousands of American troops became established, and dominated everywhere. Hundreds of flying fortresses took off daily in massed formations to pound the German and occupied cities of Europe. At night it was the roar of the fleets of RAF bombers on their missions across the English Channel and the North Sea. We still received retaliation bombing from the Nazi air force, and the ports of South Wales were hit badly. Newport, Cardiff and Swansea were bombed and letters from my mother revealed the sad fate of many families and people known to us.

In June, I became involved in an accident and was hospitalised once again. It happened in the early evening of 25th June 1943 and I had already obtained a weekend pass to go home that evening. We were conducting an exercise on the Downs, recovering a disabled tank from a bog with a big Scammel tank transporter. I was on board that transporter when the pulling chain snapped, sending us out of control down the hill to be pitched headlong into ten feet of water. Five of us were submerged, but we managed to get out. There was an icy north wind blowing, and in full battledress and a tank suit, we were soaked to the skin, cold, wet and miserable for six hours before we reached camp and a change of clothing. I had an unpleasant night catching a chill and the next day on the Saturday three of us were sent to hospital. I was detained with a high temperature and an almost fatal dose of pneumonia. I spent three weeks in bed at the West Suffolk Military General Hospital, with big doses of M and B drugs, the treatment used before the discovery of antibiotics and virus drugs.

Then I was transferred to Brent Leigh Hall convalescent hospital in Lavenham in Suffolk. After a wonderful two weeks' rest at this

159

establishment, I was sent to a military convalescent and recovery barracks on the outskirts of the rural town of Bedford on the banks of the beautiful Avon river. It was an easy time for me at those barracks, I was put in charge of a barrack room, and given the daily orders by the regimental sergeant-major to control and detail the men to all kinds of fatigues and duties around the barracks. We had two drill parades per week, but they were not very grand with a mixture of men from all different army regiments throughout southern England. I remained at those barracks for six weeks until I was posted once again. I had been away from my battalion for eleven weeks, almost three months, during which time it had packed up and moved to a camp three miles outside the town of Thetford, for further training on the flat lands of Norfolk, supposedly a replica of the terrain of Holland.

I was given a rail voucher to Thetford on 8th September 1943, to find my own way to the battalion encampment. I soon settled in again amongst my troop mates, and my commander, or troop leader as we referred to him, became Lieutenant Rex Whistler, the son of the world-famous artist Rex Whistler. Lieutenant Whistler wasn't the type cut out to be a soldier, but I suppose wealth bought him the commission in this regiment, just like all the others. He was entirely different from all the other officers, quiet and inoffensive in every way, and he spent much time with his own paintbrush and pot of paint, during our maintenance sessions, painting the name and adding that expert touch around the vehicles of his troop of four tanks.

Our stay at Thetford was short and as soon as autumn turned to winter, we were on the move once more to the isolation of the Pickering area of the wild, bleak Yorkshire Moors. The battalion was divided into two camps, as was the usual procedure, and our Nissen hut encampment was at the extreme end of the small country town of Pickering and north of Pickering Castle. This was to be our last battalion camp in Britain. I celebrated Christmas at that camp in Pickering on a cold snowy day and as the New Year of 1944 was with us, I had been a soldier for four long years. I was promoted now to the rank of sergeant and I received my last days' leave in residence in Britain as preparation for the invasion of Europe became more intense.

Hitler's tactics changed somewhat now. The bombing missions were less frequent with the losses of planes from the anti-aircraft defences and the night fighters, and we experienced for the first time the VI buzz bomb. This fiendish weapon was just like a small plane racing across the sky, belching flames from its noisy rocket motor. Suddenly without warning the motor would cut out and dive to earth with its huge load of explosives, causing havoc and devastation. Many were shot down but hundreds got through to their target area causing death and destruction.

The months of December through to March 1944 gave us a cold, wet winter and I was thankful, out on those bleak moors, that we were dry inside the steel of the Cromwell tanks, and not dug into slit trenches and holes with just a groundsheet to keep off the rain and snow. By the final week of April 1944, every man was an expert at his job. All our final training procedures and practices were made, the radio frequencies procedure, code words, and map training, with reference points along the advance centre lines, and every detail possible, and we began to waterproof all the battalion tanks, ready for our move to the coast of Southern England.

We were unofficially told now that, at a designated time and place, we would move as an invasion force into a coastal area of France, on the sea bed, as our final preparations would allow us to submerge to a maximum depth of 16 feet to reach the shore line with our engines running underwater. We had to be prepared to go into action immediately coming out of the sea and, by a system of cordite charges, to blow away the sealed waterproofing around the guns, the turret and the engine.

This all sounded awesome to us but we conscientiously and carefully began to waterproof and seal every rivet, every nut and every joint from the underbelly upwards. At the beginning of May 1944, the tanks were loaded on to flat rail transporters at Pickering railway station. We moved south and our journey ended at Brighton, the coastal resort on the south coast. We were billeted in some damaged houses towards the Hove area and as soon as we settled in, we began to test the waterproofing of the tank hulls. We used the numerous temporary fire storage pools and tanks around the area, built a ramp in and out, and settled each tank in the pool to the engine covers level.

We scrambled inside and all around to check for any sign of a leak, or to detect any suspicious spot and reseal it. The various odd pieces of equipment were now delivered to us to fit and arrange and to make completely waterproof the whole upper area of the vehicle.

The powerful exhaust system of the engine was emitted upwards between the rear vertical armour plate and a one foot space to another armour plate across the vehicle. Over this complete outlet we bolted and sealed one eight-feet high metal chimney, with a quick release wire cable attached to the top of the tank turret. When the tank was clear of the water, the cable would be released and the forward momentum of the tank would snap off the chimney to the rear. A tall intake breather was fitted for the engine and all the heavy steel engine covers sealed and waterproofed, allowing access to the fuel and oil intakes only, these would be sealed later. The turret was locked in the straight ahead position and the gun mounting locked also in a level plane. They were now sealed and waterproofed and inserted in the sealing and completely ringed around with special cordite charges with a detonator wired to the battery and a switch in the driver's compartment. The muzzle of the guns and the sight hole of the gun-sight were completed in the same way so that, when the switch was activated, the cordite exploded to blow away the seals and water-proofing, allowing the tank to go into action immediately when clear of the sea.

We carefully went through all our instructions and details now as the month of May ended and the June days of summer began. We faced an unknown worrying event ahead of us and our preparations were now matters of life and death. Southern England was just a mass of machines, arms and men. One could almost believe that the places would sink with so much weight, as every port, every harbour, was packed with all kinds of ships and transport, infantry landing craft, LCTs (landing craft tanks), liberty ships, tugs and warships. The huge armadas and the mass of men and equipment were poised to land on the shores of France. Our preparations were completed and each tank crew was issued with a seven-day food pack, which consisted of ample food in sealed cans for five men all packed in a large wooden box. The contents even contained a ration of 10 cigarettes per man, boiled sweets and energy chocolate, all kinds of canned foods and fruits, and even a roll of toilet paper. The box was tied securely on the engine covers, and immersion in sea water would not affect any of the contents. We bolted extra empty ammunition boxes along the track guards and on the rear of the turret, and containers of fresh water were tied on and all soakable articles, personal clothes, blankets, greatcoats and our precious petrol cooking stove were temporarily stowed inside the turret.

At five o'clock in the afternoon the orders came through for us to move. We set off in convoy later, under cover of darkness, travelling 50 miles along the coast to a huge security encampment just outside the port of Gosport at the head of the Solent and Southampton water, with Portsmouth harbour a few miles away. The greatest assembly of ships in history was already on their way across the channel. Thousands of planes were pounding the Nazi coastal defences and every type of warship from E-boats to men-of-war bombarded the French coast.

12

The Final Hours and the Normandy Landing at the Arromanche Bridgehead June 1944

Inside the Gosport encampment we were in exile from the outside world, there was total radio silence and we were not allowed contact with anyone. There were no phones or any outside communication, as security was extreme and all written letters were forbidden to be dispatched until we had moved. We refilled the fuel tanks, checked all the oils, the track tension and the hydraulic systems and examined carefully any likely trouble spots. The remaining open engine covers were sealed and waterproofed, the driver's entry and the right-hand turret hatch likewise, leaving the co-driver's and front gunner's entry and the left-hand turret hatch open only; we were prepared to move at five minutes' notice.

The American sea-borne landings to the right along the Normandy coastline had encountered an enormous task and for a long time it was very serious, they had such a difficult time. The Canadians and others in the centre had also received setbacks and enormous casualties. Our advance forces on the left found it a little easier and soon obtained a foothold and a small bridgehead, but greater difficulties lay ahead, as far as our own situation was concerned. We had to get a whole armoured division ashore, and my battalion, the reconnaissance battalion, was the first unit of the division to be landed.

We had one free evening in the canteen at that security encampment trying to obtain a little information of what was happening 40 miles away across the English Channel. We drank cups of tea, ate rock cakes and enjoyed glasses of beer. The following day would come, our turn to be ferried across the sea.

We had a hot midday meal on that day, the day did not matter any more to all of us, or the date either as it was just another anxious day. I was the duty sergeant and I had the task of collecting all written letters to hand over to the squadron clerk for dispatch later and distributing the incoming mail that had been received and addressed to any individual number, rank, unit, British Expeditionary Force. I was issued, for use in my troop, two syringes of morphine and two red labels with a tiny stub of pencil, with the words – day, date and time printed on them. I carefully taped them in their thin cellophane wrap around the inside calf of my left leg with sticking plaster strips, and each man was made aware that I carried them. Their purpose was that if any badly injured person was injected to relieve the awful pain, the day, date and time would be hurriedly written on the label and then tied to his identity disc around his neck to alert the medical aides.

I can recall now that in the next 12 months on five occasions I gave an injection of morphine to a badly injured colleague. Around the small of my back beneath my shirt I now tied an escape pack. This pack was a half-inch thick cellophane, six inches by five inches package, containing water purification tablets, a small compass, a bar of sustaining dark energy chocolate, a tiny knife and some bandages. The buttons of my battledress were black, regimental domed buttons which I had replaced by removing the ordinary four-holed buttons. The middle button had a secretive screw-on top, inside in the small interior I carried a tiny compass. I was dressed in a gaberdine-type tank suit with a tank fibre helmet and headphones. I also took with me an old battered Kodak box camera, complete with its loaded film of six snaps, and ten spare films, a total of 66 potential photographs if I was successful, all in a paper bag to stow inside the tank.

It was 4.30 p.m. and warm and sunny as we climbed on to our respective tanks and moved towards Gosport docks. The sea was fairly calm with the whole area full of ships and landing craft. Our destination was a big LST (landing ship tank) with its big drop door down resting on a low part of the quay, and one after the other, each troop moved across the entrance door into the belly of the craft, turned around and lined up behind each other along the high sides of the ship and down the centre nose to tail. By 6 p.m. the whole battalion of approximately 60 tanks were aboard the landing ships. All the supply vehicles, recovery vehicles, transporters and auxiliaries would come behind later with the hope that a portable mulberry harbour towed across the sea would be in place at the bridgehead to give them direct access to the shore.

There are four tides in each 24-hour period in Southampton water and our LST lifted its big drop exit door and manoeuvred out that evening on the tide. We could see nothing behind the sides of that ship as darkness closed around us, and it was fairly quiet except for the throb of the ship's engines, and the swish of the waves. Our destiny now was under the control of the ship's crew to get the vessel across those miles of water and drive it forward until its flat bottom hit the beach, irrespective of the depth of the water. We were now given a briefing of the proposed events that lay ahead, and the plans and orders that we had to carry out. We were told that it would be half-tide, that is half way out on the ebb. The time of landing would be 0400 hours (4 a.m.), the depth of water could not be accurate, but it would be between six and twelve feet deep, and the distance to the shoreline clearance would be approximately three-quarters of a mile. When the ship began its straight line push to the beach, we would be given the compass bearing over the radio to set on the binnacle compass. Each tank was given a number in numerical order to move, and a radio order to that particular number would be given to turn left or right at a 45 degree bearing to the compass for approximately 30 seconds when levelling out on the sea bed off the drop door and then each tank commander controlled the tank to turn to the beach to avoid any collisions in the water. The centre line of tanks in the ship would proceed straight ahead on the compass bearing. There would be three, spaced, small white concealed lights on the dry land under the control of a beach master and each tank commander headed for their respective light until they reached the shore. The whole beach area would be under shellfire from the Nazi guns and the possibility of enemy aircraft dropping flares to light up the area for air attacks could not be ruled out.

Midnight arrived, and it was the beginning of another day. We sat on the deck of that ship leaning back against the tank bogies, talking and trying to doze, but every man had too much on his mind and it was impossible to sleep. We were out on the open sea not knowing how many ships were in our particular armada, or how many warships were escorting and keeping watch over us. We could see a few stars up through the sides of the landing ship ignorant of what was going on around us in the darkness of the early day. Two-thirty a.m. – 0230 hours – and we were ordered to board the tanks, start up and run the engines for five minutes to warm them up in preparation to restart at 3.45 a.m. The drivers and front gunners remained in their compartments now and the three other members of each crew sealed and waterproofed the co-driver's hatch. The radios were tested and checked and each intercom to every member of the crew was given its final test. At 3.15 a.m. the turret crews slipped down inside through the last open hatch, it was locked on the inside and fellow supply transport members who travelled with us and would return with their vehicles on another landing, sealed the hatch above our heads.

We were now entombed and wondering what lay ahead. We had plenty of air from the engine breather but when the engine was started our supply would be the contents of the tank interior only, which would be sufficient to get us ashore. I shall always remember that morning. We had an interior turret light and we could speak to each other over the intercom but from what I recall now, very little was said; each man lived with his own thoughts, and I can remember vividly that sinking feeling in my stomach as we anxiously awaited what lay ahead. The time was 3.45 a.m., and the order came to start the engines. We were oblivious to everything now. We could hear nothing over the noise of the tank engine, except instructions in the headphones and our own intercom system. I assumed the landing ship was now on its straight run to the beach and as the seconds ticked away, dead on time at 4 a.m. we felt the jolt and our forward surge as the ship grounded on the sea bed. Through the periscope and through the blackness of the pre-dawn, I could see just a faint gleam from the starry sky and the big drop door silhouetted against the flash of gunfire as it fell open down on to the sea bed and then I heard the instructions for the first tank to move. There was a deathly silence and a brief respite as we heard the crackling radio tell us that the first tank had submerged to a little below the gun mounting approximately nine feet drop, the tide was on the ebb and about half out. It was a big relief to me to hear this, our turret hatches would be well above the water and we would have good periscope vision ahead; we were warned not to break the hatch seals in case of any holes or big depressions in the sea bed. My tank was number nine in the evacuation line and what a strange feeling of anxiety it was to feel the tank level off on the beach floor and crawl towards dry land in the darkness. Everything went well, and there were no mishaps. The beach area was under shellfire as expected and the sky constantly illuminated with the flashes of our own guns and the enemy's, all over the bridgehead. We were ordered not to fire the cordite charges

around the seals but to break open the hatches as soon as we reached
land and follow the directions of the military beach supervisors and
head inland about one quarter of a mile to a collecting and harbouring
area.

We reached the destination allotted to us without any trouble as the
first half light began to form on that pre-dawn day. It appeared to be,
as we expected, an orchard of cider apples which were to become
such a familiar sight in the weeks ahead. We worked furiously for the
next hour removing all the superstructure objects over the engine and
exhaust, and scraped and cleaned off as much of the goo sealing
and waterproofing as possible so that the turret, engine covers, the
gun and its mounting and all hatches were free and workable once
again. Then dispersing our vehicles amongst the apple trees facing
the bridgehead perimeter, we dug in, with shells still exploding in the
area around us. This task was much easier now, because we carried a
pick and two shovels on the rear of the tank, and as the days passed
by we were to learn by experience the preservation of our own safety
in the method we used to 'dig in'.

As daylight came we became familiar with our surroundings and
we tried to sort out our equipment and pack the clothing and blankets
etc. in the outside boxes so that the turret was free from obstructions,
and our movements were not impeded in any way. We had to be
patient now, prepared at any time to move forward until the division
with all its tanks, transports, supporting infantry and guns were safely
ashore, organised and ready. In the meantime the massed guns and
the forward troops were pounding the Nazi forces, who were pushing
forward with small gains each day. During this short lull it gave us
brief opportunities in small batches to go and examine all the captured
or destroyed Nazi armoured vehicles and guns. We checked over the
updated Czech tank, the Nazi Mark 4, the Panther and the giant Tiger.
The Nazi Tiger tank was to be our greatest worry. It was a lumbering
56 tons, with the armour plate on the front of the turret almost 12
inches thick, and it carried the formidable all-purpose gun, anti-aircraft, high-explosive and anti-tank, the mighty Nazi '88'. It was a
useful exercise for us to understand and check over the opponent's
armour. The French town of Bayeaux had been captured in the first
days, and I also had the opportunity to see the world-famous historic
Bayeaux Norman Tapestry, dating back to the Middle Ages, hanging
in the Bayeaux Norman Church. Incidentally, this was the first picture
snapped with my old camera, whether it would develop clearly I did
not know. I wondered also why Hitler had not stolen this priceless

object and taken it away with all his other loot. Meanwhile our location was under constant shellfire and we started to get casualties, so it taught us to take further precautions and dig in below the tank body. We would dig a trench about a foot deep, six feet long and six feet wide approximately, and run the tank over the top then pile the surplus soil against the track bogies. This trench gave us a clearance from the bottom of roughly 2 feet 6 inches, enough room for the five crew members with groundsheets on the earth floor and an escape out to the front and rear of the tank. The tank protected us from exploding overhead and ground missiles, a practice we continued until the end of the war.

Early July 1944 we pushed out to advance along the Bayeaux to Caen railway towards the city of Caen and the Orne River. It was a difficult task but we relieved the paratroops in this area and reached the railway bridge over the River Orne. At this time we were supported by the Coldstream infantry battalion and we consolidated the area. The main forces of the German army were pivoted around the city of Caen, including the elite Adolf Hitler's SS division, our opponents in the weeks ahead. To the south-west of this city along the Orne river, the terrain was marshy and difficult and a stumbling block for our push to Caen. Our efforts now were switched south towards Benny Bocage and Villers Bocage, more difficult terrain with sunken roads with high banks, just like the English countryside and more stiff opposition from the Nazi SS. We had the first experience of one tank being knocked out in this area. An HE shell hit the front of the turret and the explosion and force killed the front gunner in his compartment below; the tank was intact, the remainder of the crew bailed out, but we recovered the tank half an hour later. There was another sad blow also, Lieutenant Rex Whistler, the commander of No. 8 troop was killed, standing too high with his head out of the turret hatch, he was hit with machine-gun bullets and died instantly.

At night we were continuously attacked by Nazi aircraft dropping magnesium parachute flares, lighting up the whole area and then dropping anti-personnel bombs filled with all kinds of shocking missiles from steel balls to slivers of jagged metal. At this time our supplies of petrol were still carried in thin tin kerosene-type containers; many leaked badly and the bombs ripped through the dumps causing many fires and lighting the target area even more for the Nazi bombers.

The days moved on into the second week of July and our progress and advance around the bridgehead was slow, the Nazi resistance was so great. The military command now decided to wipe out the city of Caen, the main Nazi stronghold impeding our advance along the coast. I was to witness the greatest mass bombing of the time, over 1,000 bombers were to saturate the old city of Caen. It all began at night just after 11 p.m., when wave after wave of RAF fleets of Wellington and Lancaster bombers dropped their tons of high explosives on the old city and the Nazi positions. As dawn and first light arrived, massed formations of American B24 flying fortresses continued their onslaught. The dust began to drift our way – clouds of mortar dust from the old buildings of Caen. We coughed and spluttered and almost choked hour after hour, and it blotted out the sun, settled on everything, just like a giant dust storm. We breathed it, we swallowed it and sneezed it, and were going to taste it for days. Two-thirds of the city was demolished; how anyone could possibly live after such a high explosive saturation was unbelievable. However, the Nazis still held on. Our division artillery now pounded the area southwest and we moved forward in a massed tank attack. Every gun, every machine-gun barked and spluttered, the whole front was alight with thousands of red tracer bullets streaking across the downs. Many Nazis surrendered, and many died, and we advanced about two miles, but still failed to break through. It appeared that the bombing was not the success they anticipated, as so much rubble and devastation would be more of an impediment than a help to capture the city of Caen.

Life was becoming hectic now, as our day would begin by being alert and ready to stand to half an hour before first light, in preparation to resist any counter attack or to attack in advance, so we had to find our own methods to keep up with this routine. We carried a seven-day food pack and as soon as stand down came, one man would quickly operate the spirit stove for a hot drink. In the ration pack there were tins of ready mixed tea, sugar and powdered milk and as soon as the water was hot we had a hurried mug of tea. With the rations also were self-heating cans of beans, soups, and Irish stews etc. We simply struck the fusing strip, similar to the friction side of a matchbox, and the ingenious can would be heated in one minute by a system of phosphorus around the inner skin of the can. We had ample supplies of hard-tack biscuits and a can of butter, and our hurried breakfast was ready in minutes. In our own inventive way also we sweated an outlet tap to a clean, washed-out petrol tin, and filled it with drinking water. The tin was secured over the exhaust chamber of the engine, hot flames shot up from the powerful emissions of the exhaust caused by the unburnt fuel in the cylinders, and the water was hot at all times for a quick boil on the stove for tea, and for washing and shaving.

Confined to our steel turret from daylight to dusk, the days were long and hot. It was necessary to answer the call of nature by providing oneself with a suitable empty tin and to dispose of the contents overboard. As dusk came on, after a trying and tiresome day we would normally pull back and the supporting infantry would move up and dig in ahead of us to consolidate our gains, and prepare for the hours of darkness, of constant shelling and salvoes of mortars. An armoured vehicle is useless at night except for shelling an enemy position from a hull-down position or behind a ridge. Our duties never seemed to end. The supply vehicles would arrive so that we could immediately refuel. The Cromwell consumed about a gallon of petrol per mile, and it was so difficult to fill the tanks in the darkness from flimsy four-gallon tins, the spillage was so great until they copied the proficient German jerry can and introduced it hurriedly about two months later. The guns had to be cleaned and checked, munitions reloaded and packed, any maintenance to the tracks, engine and turret traverse undertaken and, of course, we had to dig in for our own protection. It usually took half an hour for the following day's planning and tactics and the squadron command briefing, all the map references, code words, and centre line of advance and attack. With all this there was normally two hours of sentry duty and radio watch, so last of all was a meal and if possible a wash. We would be lucky to complete all these tasks by midnight and perhaps obtain three hours sleep before stand to once again before dawn, and then it was almost impossible to sleep with the swarms of awful mosquitoes worrying us, the crescendo and thunder of our own artillery and the thud and explosions of enemy shells and mortars. Weariness was a problem, especially when we had to be alert and quick thinking all day long. We could never be complacent, our survival was too important.

Another serious problem now was the deadly sniper. We lost one man exposed to the skyline in moonlight out in the open. From that period onwards we had to be extra careful not to become a target from any building, high ground, or trees, and I can recall many times until the war ended, I brought down an inexperienced newcomer to our unit in a rugby tackle, who was hesitating and exposed to danger from a hidden sniper. Between June 1944 and May 1945 nine members of my battalion fell victims and died from the deadly accuracy of the Nazi sniper.

We were now moved 12 miles west along the bridgehead to advance towards the Normandy town of Caumont and the Vire River. The move was at night to prevent the Nazi intelligence obtaining information from their spotter aircraft and once again we were soon to learn that our opponents were the Adolf Hitler SS troops. In this attack No. 1 Squadron was the leading unit. A *Panzerschreck* (tank terror) – in our language, at Bazooka, knocked out one of the leading tanks and disabled another. This weapon was an 88mm stove-pipe weapon commonly called by the Nazi infantry *Openrohr* which I believed actually means 'stove-pipe'. The inner core of this missile, when hitting armour plate, penetrates the metal leaving a clean hole about one inch in diameter and explodes inside the tank. This fiendish weapon is fatal to the tank crew if it hits the turret or the front of the tank with a direct hit, so we did not know at that time what had happened to the crew. With the other disabled tank the crew baled out and escaped unharmed, and the Nazis captured it and must have towed it to the rear of their lines for examination, because this was the first Cromwell to fall into German hands.

The following day was 26th July 1944, my twenty-fifth birthday and another unforgettable day. Something I particularly remember was the first SS atrocity for us to experience personally. It was around mid-morning as we crept forward through a wooded area with fields and hedges, about two miles from the town of Caumont. There were orchards of cider apples everywhere, an area where they distilled and produced large quantities of the potent liquor Calvados, as well as cider. We suddenly came upon one of our colleagues, the driver of the lost tank on the previous day. He was a very popular and well liked member of our unit, with the name of Nicholson; he was well known through his expertise in singing the old hill billy songs. He was in an upright standing position against the trunk of a cider apple tree, with his head slumped forward on his chest and his arms hanging loosely in front of his body. To our horror we found that he had been pinned and nailed through his tank suit to the trunk of the tree with empty mauser machine-gun cartridge cases. They had been hammered home with some heavy object through his clothing into the tree trunk leaving him propped upright with his weight suspended in his nailed clothing.

His boots were missing and his feet were bare. We released him and lifted him down and checked him all over, but we found no wounds or injuries and no blood, it was a mystery to us as to what had caused his death and we could only presume that he died from the blast. There was bitterness and anger amongst all our squadron members and many of the angry militant extremists swore revenge. To me this was desperate total war and we could expect more of it. That evening after burying our troop mate we harboured for the night in the vicinity of a farmhouse, the occupants had fled; the place was undamaged but deserted. In one of the barn outhouses there were two big vats of cider, a common thing on all the Normandy farms, and concealed behind the vats we found a wooden box containing four four-litre stone bottles – demijohns of Calvados. I had never tasted it before and, because it was my birthday, a special occasion for me, I sampled it, one quarter of my enamel drinking mug. It must have been around 30 per cent proof alcohol and so strong my head was swimming immediately. It was commandeered by the troop officers and spirited away otherwise we would have all been out of action with that firewater. My 25th birthday had given me five wasted years of my life with nothing but war and I could only wonder how many more birthdays would I celebrate before it all came to an end?

The following day, 27th July, our push forward continued and we scattered and wiped out patches of stubborn infantry. On the outskirts of Caumont we confronted a fleeing German half-track vehicle trying to get away with a supply truck, and aboard the half-track were a number of infantry. The Cromwells' guns and Besa machine-guns made short work of both, and the truck was set on fire. The occupants of both vehicles were killed, except one Nazi from the half-track who ran forward with his hands up. We checked him over as we did every German prisoner, if the circumstances permitted, to find out if he was SS. We found his tattooed number – he was an SS trooper as expected. To our amazement we discovered he was wearing British army boots, which aroused our suspicions immediately. He was made to take them off and we discovered they were Nicholson's boots with his army number stamped on the uppers. The news flashed through the whole squadron. In the anger, bitterness and hatred of war, amongst the sunny groves and fields of that picturesque area of Normandy, on that July day in 1944, there were no questions asked, no judge or jury, no trial, the verdict was unanimous. That German SS storm trooper was executed.

We entered and captured Caumont the following day, after further skirmishes with the SS, and the infantry took over to consolidate the town area. The mulberry harbour was well in position now and men, supplies and equipment were pouring ashore. As a result, a big mobile laundry and hot showers were brought up and we enjoyed the luxury of the hot water, a change from our usual hurried daily ablutions with a cut down petrol tin. Every shirt, and complete underclothes and socks were passed in and exchanged for fresh laundered items powdered with DDT. We would now be able to get a complete change at least every 14 days or so, unless we were too far ahead in our advance against the enemy.

At the beginning of August 1944 the Americans broke out with General Patton's massed armour. Their opposition was not as difficult as ours against the SS. We started the slow progress into the Fleurs Valley and the town of Fleurs in western Normandy but we were gradually gaining the upper hand. We lost another tank and its crew as that offensive began, knocked out by the Nazi Tiger tank. My own tank hit a mine also and the track was blown off putting us out of action for nine hours. I had a lot of admiration for the pilots of the army support aircraft with their destructive rockets, two under each wing. When our advance was held up, the supporting artillery would fire yellow smoke shells on to a stubborn area to direct the planes to the target. Their daring attacks were so good to observe as they released and fired the rockets to wipe out the Nazi guns and vehicles, assisting our advance so much.

My squadron was now ordered to take the lead towards Fleurs. We entered the town and, to our surprise there was no opposition, the place was deserted, the population had fled. We were surprised by it all, as the aerial photographs and intelligence reports had told us it was a German stronghold, so we pushed on through the town into the rich agricultural valley. Then, without warning, we were attacked from the rear. It was around 10 a.m.; we were immediately ordered to halt and harbour to ring around a large field, each tank facing outwards to defend our position in a complete 360-degree circle. It appeared that we were caught unawares and surrounded. It was an all-day awesome battle and we were unable to make contact with the battalion, as the radios could pick up no signals because of the terrain.

It was an unpleasant eight hours. Every gun and machine-gun was hot with the enormous fire power we directed against the Nazis and our ammunition supplies depleted so much that there was danger of being overrun. Finally, about 6.30 that evening a squadron of Coldstream Sherman tanks broke through and began to attack us, until they realised and recognised our units. Before darkness fell the Germans were routed, but for us it was one of the most difficult and hardest days of the Normandy battles. We were now given a rest for two days to catch up with all our maintenance and make preparations for the actions ahead. From this time onwards our tactics would change and for all difficult situations in an advance each troop of tanks would carry a platoon of infantry riding on the engine covers. It would help them in their foot slogging and their dismounting and mopping up the enemy would help us.

13

From the Breakout from Normandy to the Liberation of Brussels

The summer of 1944 was drawing to a close, the days were still hot with clear blue cloudless skies and the daylight hours were gradually decreasing as the weeks went by. The Americans had advanced on our right, west of the Fleurs Valley. They had captured Avranches on the coast and then pushed on east to Alvecon and north to Argentian and our forces advanced south of Caen towards Falaise. The Nazi forces were caught in this pincer movement leaving just 20 miles to escape in a gap between Falaise and Argentian. This area was to become known to us as the Falaise Gap.

On the evening of 28th August 1944, our maintenance and preparations were complete, as we rested at the head of the Fleurs Valley in western Normandy. Our briefing that night was detailed and comprehensive. We studied the air photographs in detail, our code words were listed with all the map reference points ahead and our centre line of advance was directed right through the gap to Falaise to smash and rout the withdrawing Nazi forces.

At 15 minutes before first light on the morning of 29th August we started to move. The Cromwell tank was now about to make one of the fastest lightning advances in armoured warfare, to smash and rout the German forces for 300 miles, to reach the centre of Brussels at ten minutes to nine o'clock on the night of 3rd September 1944, exactly five years since the declaration of war. Five miles from Falaise the first signs of the battered German forces became evident, as the roads were littered with all kinds of smashed Nazi vehicles, burnt-out wrecks and hulks bombed and blown up by the terrific power of the RAF and the American air force. All these obstructions in our path

176

were smashed into with the full power of our tanks and pushed to the roadsides to let us through, and the softer lighter front fenders of the tank tracks became buckled and bent with the continuous bulldozing against the Nazi vehicles. At full speed through the town of Falaise with its crumbling shell-torn, damaged buildings along the route, we began catching up with the fleeing Nazi forces.

For five long years the brutal Nazi war machine had dominated Europe bringing death and destruction to so many innocent countries and their civilian populations. It was our turn now. There would be no more hesitating or retreats, and no mercy for any Nazi soldier overtaken with a weapon in his possession. It was a feeling of exhilaration as we raced on smashing into transports, troops carriers and supply vehicles. The defeated German troops were ignored and bypassed, to be rounded up by our forces behind. Any German seen with weapons was blasted and peppered with every gun in our possession. It surprised me to see so many horse-drawn transports with the German forces and we smashed into them in the same way. Fortunately, many of the animals were unharmed. The mess could be sorted out by the troops behind us, we were the spearhead unit and it was our task to race on. Northern France was wide open along with the route to the Belgian frontier.

That night we harboured in a small wood alongside a farmhouse about 35 miles from Lisieux and Thiberville and the important crossroads on the highway Rouen to Alençon. Our next objective was to smash the Nazi forces before they reached the River Seine. It was midnight before the squadron supply vehicle caught up with us. Tiredness and fatigue was our greatest problem. However, we had a big meal in the early hours not knowing when the next opportunity to eat would be.

Before dawn we were on the move again and I recall so well that uncertain feeling of butterflies in the stomach when one is the leading tank of a division and part of an army corps moving through enemy terrain and then the uplift and satisfaction as one flashes back the radio message announcing the code words of each objective reached and taken, as we pushed forward. By ten o'clock that morning we had liberated the town of Lisieux and by midday we reached the vital crossroads at Thiberville. Many Nazis surrendered but we ignored them and pushed on leaving them for the following troops to round up. We made our first contacts with the Marquis – the French resistance – here and two of them climbed on to the engine cover of my tank. Following their excited instructions we diverged off our centre line of advance to the wooded area north around the small town of Brionne. We bombarded and machine-gunned every piece of cover, satisfying the Frenchmen's instructions over 10–15 miles before rejoining the centre line of our advance to smash more vehicles off the road. By late afternoon we raced through the town of Evreux, and the junction of four highways, 20 miles from the River Seine approximately half way between Rouen and Paris, and we reached our objective and the river by nightfall. We harboured that night while the rush was on to bring up the engineers to quickly erect a Bailey bridge across the Seine near Vernon. The familiar names of towns known from the First World War and the horrific battles of that period were now becoming predominant each day.

At dawn on 31st August 1944 we crossed the River Seine over the hurriedly erected Bailey bridge for our next objectives: Les Thaliers across the main Paris to Rouen highway to Gisors and Auneuil and a further 25 miles to the city of Beauvais.

We halted and harboured once again as darkness came down that evening to proceed carefully by torchlight to attend to all our maintenance, gun cleaning, checking and restocking our fuel and ammunition supplies. It gave us some concern that night to hear rumours from the drivers of the supply vehicle that all petrol was being diverted to the Americans and General Bradley's forces, racing through France further south. As a precaution and breaking the safety rules we roped extra tins of petrol, as many as we could possibly carry on the rear tank engine covers. With all our usual tasks of digging in, a hurried meal and sentry duties I recall my tank crew managed to obtain two hours' sleep that night, a little was better than none at all! Included in our vigilance, the 30-minute briefing that night told us to make two vital objectives: the city of Beauvais and a further 75 miles to the city of Arras and its surrounding areas, and we were alerted also to the fact that armoured cars of the Household Cavalry were some miles away on our left flank.

It was the morning of 1st September 1944 as we reached the outskirts of Beauvais. It was just after 9.30 a.m. and hundreds of French citizens turned out to greet us and cheer us along our way. It was heartening to have this welcome telling us there were no Germans in the area. By 10 a.m. we reached the city centre and the public areas and gardens in front of the big public buildings. Trenches and air-raid dugouts had been constructed throughout the reserves and gardens. We halted here, arranged our tanks in a defensive position, posted sentries and men on the guns and the remainder of us occupied the trenches, whilst the squadron leader and troop leaders consulted the French officials and resistance leaders. This gave us the opportunity to have a break and quick brew-up of tea.

In the middle of war with all its problems and anxieties, laughter and mirth always seem very far away but on this occasion I had reason to laugh with little sympathy for the victim. As soon as the city was liberated by our presence the French began rounding up the collaborators and fraternisers with the hated 'Boches' (Germans). About 20 women, somewhere between the age of 18 and 40 years, were dragged along in front of the town hall. Each one was abused and maltreated and trussed to a chair in line, hands tied behind the chair, with their legs tied to the chair legs. Each one in turn was given the horse clipper treatment and their hair locks were ripped off, others followed behind with the razors until the whole assembly was completely bald. We watched all the procedures as each victim was dealt with. It was then that the funny incident began, at least it was funny and laughable to me, although not for the victim. Along the road wobbled a short fat French madame, almost as round as she was tall, along with a group of followers in support. The left hand of that portly lady supported in a balanced steady position, a bright blue chamber pot, with the right hand gripping the handle. She reached the last but one victim in the long row of chairs and carefully put down the pot and its contents on the ground by her side.

We were all intrigued, wondering what it was all about. With her hands now free, the large madame viciously slapped the collaborator across the face a number of times screaming abuse at her the whole time. She then picked up the pot and poured the rich brown lumpy contents over the unfortunate victim's head and screamed more abuse at her. Her task completed, swinging her empty pot by the handle in her right hand she wobbled and rolled off down the road with applause and cheers from her followers. It was so funny to me I had to laugh and I raced to my tank to get the old box camera. I was a little too slow. I took a picture of the line of victims but I only managed to obtain a rear view of the fat lady wobbling away down the road. Whenever the city of Beauvais is mentioned, or comes into a news item, it brings back that incident to me with a smile, as I remember that September day a long time ago.

With more detailed knowledge of the areas up to 20 miles in front of us obtained from the French officials, we pushed on towards our next objective, the city of Arras, the biggest town on our advance route since we left Normandy. About four miles beyond Beauvais we picked up two members of the Household Cavalry escorted by a number of French resistance members and some children. Their armoured car had been knocked out five miles north of Beauvais, near a place called Sangeons and they had escaped. They were so pleased to see us as they made their way to the rear to find their own unit; it was a warning to us that the Nazis were still hitting back. Information from the French authorities told us that the Nazis were fleeing from the city of Arras and we were ordered to increase speed to push forward the 70 odd miles to the city, and again, the route was littered with burnt-out, abandoned vehicles. The air force had certainly done their job. We carried a large, square, bright-orange canvas recognition signal to alert our planes and we were getting so far ahead of the divisional forces we now had to be ready to display it in an emergency. On two prominent high-ground positions along our route I can remember we sighted two big signal bonfires. The resistance were in control, and it relieved our anxiety that there were no Nazi forces to contend with. Our advance took us roughly half way between the towns of Amiens and St Quentin as we joined and raced along the Paris to Arras main highway. We did not enter the city but skirted the northern side. As we approached the built-up areas, scores of bare-footed Polish and Baltic workers streamed across the fields laughing, shouting and crying, to greet us, so we made a halt and a short break.

One middle-aged lady, crying bitterly and shouting a welcome in English, demonstrated in front of my tank making gestures and beckoning us to climb down and speak to her. I did just this, and she threw her arms around my neck as a welcome, saying, 'I am English I am English.' Between her sobs she told me that she had lived there since the end of the First World War after she had married a Frenchman. I realised her tears were of sadness, not of joy, when she explained that her husband had been arrested and taken away the day before. I had quite an interesting conversation with her and she was amazed that we were the advance units of the British forces, believing that we were still struggling to keep a foothold in Normandy. They had no news only Nazi propaganda and all radios had been confiscated and banned by the German occupational forces and the Gestapo. I gave her an eight-day-old *Sunday Express,* which my mother regularly sent to me, for her to catch up with the news and events. I wrote down her name and address but, unfortunately, it was lost with all my other personal belongings when my tank was destroyed just four days later on 4th September 1944.

Arras was to bring our first casualties since Normandy, however, not by the German force but by our own air force. The supply vehicles following in our wake were attacked by RAF Hurricane fighters, two of my squadron colleagues were killed and three injured. Sadly, I can say that more members of my battalion were killed by our own air force and the American air force than the German air force during the whole campaign. One of those boys was the driver of a petrol supply vehicle. He had always been the squadron sanitary man around the camps at home and responsible for emptying and replacing the toilet buckets, to put it more crudely in army language, he was the 'shit wallah' and he was known by the name of Shit Williams. It fell to me again to write to his parents but I could no longer tell the truth of what really happened. I must mention too that we were issued with what was referred to as a 'green envelope'. One per man each week, and of course all letters were censored by the squadron officers. The green envelope, however, was allowed to pass with a signed declaration on the rear side stating it was personal matters only and contained nothing that would assist the enemy. I managed to scrounge two or three each week so that the contents were not revealed to any officer who censored the mail.

Late afternoon and early morning of that day, we were continuously urged on by various French groups of Marquis to diverse to different areas where they claimed that numbers of Nazi troops were sighted taking cover and refuge. We had to oblige, bombard and shell patches of woodland and large areas of cover everywhere north of Arras towards the town of Lens. We overran and captured Vimy Ridge, one of the greatest slaughter battlegrounds of the First World War. On this occasion the French resistance had a signal fire burning and it was certainly a contrast to what had happened on that blood-soaked land 30 years previously. One incident affected my troop in an unusual way as we harboured when darkness came down. During our probes all over the place that early morning, we had traversed across an extensive field crop of onions, the tank tracks had pulped and picked them up crushing and juicing them in the tank driving sprockets. When we finally halted to carry out our usual tasks and duties at the end of each day, the onion fumes were so strong everyone was shedding tears and for the short rest period that night we were compelled to dig in well away from the tanks, and the detailed men on radio watch were almost crying for their whole stretch of duty.

The following day, 2nd September 1944, incidents were few. We covered almost 100 miles and liberated the whole area to the town of Lens and the big town of Douai, then halting for the night at a small village called Nouvelle St Vasse. We refuelled and restocked from the supply vehicles that night, and I had the luxury of three hours' sleep in the hay barn of a small roadside farmhouse, one of the few buildings in the area. It was at this place and during the extensive briefing that night, that our squadron leader informed us that the Corps Command had requested the War Ministry to relieve us and pull U8 back for a rest – Churchill's reply and official dispatch stated 'Keep them there till they drop', so if you are a soldier who cares? One was just a cog in the machine toiling until the teeth break and then what did it matter, there was always another to be rushed into its place! With the detailed briefing that night was the order to cross the Belgium frontier and blast and smash everything and anything obstructing our route to the Belgian capital, and to liberate and capture the city of Brussels. I had my doubts about it all that night. It seemed such an impossible and awesome task, with diversions left and right as always happens. Our planned route and centre line of advance to Brussels was 94 miles and how much of the German army awaited us in our path? They had to halt, fight and retaliate somewhere now!

My detail incurred the two hours before dawn for sentry duty and radio watch the next morning, the dawn of 3rd September 1944 and the anniversary almost to the hour of the outbreak of war five years previously, and now I write these lines 45 years on, almost to the day. I remember vividly that sentry early morning; I was feeling so tired, jaded and weary, and very uncertain. If I could only crawl away to curl up and sleep and just forget it all. I carried a small notebook in my pocket, which wasn't exactly a diary, but I jotted down notes, towns and routes, and incidents etc. and lots of information. It was forbidden of course by battalion orders, for security reasons if captured, and my entries were always made as I wrote a letter or during darkness with a small pencil torch. My entry in the early hours of that morning, because I was feeling so low, was just one line that I remember so well: 'Sept. 3rd I hope I shall see the sun rise tomorrow.' Sadly, the following day, I threw away that notebook when I lost everything and was in imminent danger of being captured. Nouvelle St Vasse – I shall always remember that small French village! At the crack of dawn we vacated that village with roaring Rolls-Royce engines, to pick up speed from its small boundary area towards Lille and the Belgium frontier. We skirted around Lille on the southern side without incident, then our route turned towards the Belgian frontier and the first Belgian city of Tournai as our goal. The time was 0630 hours, 6.30

a.m., and we dispersed and spread out to attack and seize a Nazi airfield ahead, not knowing what we were about to encounter.

Two Nazi aircraft had already taken off – two Messerschmitt fighters – and as we reached the perimeter of the airfield we observed two fighters, one Stuka, and a Donier bomber on the runway. Racing on to the aircraft we opened up with all our firepower. The Donier, loaded with bombs, blew up with a tremendous explosion destroying both fighters, leaving the Stuka intact and turning it sideways with the blast. I believe my tank travelled faster than it ever had done before as we stormed across the field and three of us abreast had the pleasure and satisfaction of smashing into the Stuka. We braced ourselves for the crash and it disintegrated like matchwood, a combined weight of approximately 115 imperial tons of steel slammed into it like a tornado smashing it to pieces. We swung around, our guns and machine-gun tracer raking all the hangars and buildings, setting them on fire. My reward for that early morning effort was 18 hens' eggs boiling in a big dixie on a wood fire – the Germans' breakfast – it was our spoils instead, and we ate the lot.

Our advance now was due west, regrouping after the successful attack on the German airfield and at approximately 7.40 a.m. we crossed the Belgian frontier. For my squadron and the battalion it was a remarkable achievement, as we were the first Allied troops to enter Belgium, and my tank, at that stage, was the third in line to cross over. In just six days we had advanced all the way from western Normandy and by 8 a.m. we entered the first Belgian town of Tournai. The population went mad, flags and bunting appeared like magic, every window and every building became draped with colour and Belgian flags, bunches of flowers and floral tributes were thrown on to our vehicles. The route was lined with hundreds of cheering citizens. The whole population had turned out in force and many of them in their excitement and happiness put themselves in danger trying to clamber on to our moving tanks in order to shake hands with us and move faster but the task was getting harder. We always expected to make slow progress against the Nazi army but we never dreamed that the celebrating citizens would almost halt us on our route.

Leaving behind the perimeter of Tournai, after such slow progress, we continued in an easterly direction through the countryside, our next objective the town of Leuze, 10 miles away. We entered Leuze at approximately 11 a.m. with the now familiar Belgian crowds almost hysterical with delight to greet us after years of Nazi rule. It was nearing the central district of this town that I saw a crowd of citizens surrounding and attacking a large warehouse-type building. The windows were heavily barred with a steel grid across the double-wood entrance doors. The windows had all been smashed behind the bars and now, old and young were standing on each other's shoulders to reach inside, removing packages and passing them down to people below. We moved our tank over towards the building and I asked in my best French what the packages contained. The reply was *le thé* – the Nazi tea storage depot. I did my unofficial good deed for the Belgium citizens. We quickly eased the tank against the steel grid and doors, pushed them in and moved off again with the tank column and a cheer from the people around. I hope they enjoyed the looted tea after years of drinking Nazi rationed Ersatz coffee.

Another 10 miles and by early afternoon on that day we entered and liberated the town of Ath, approximately 40 miles from the suburbs of Brussels. The huge crowds of Belgians lining the route seemed to be increasing and with so many people congregating on the road, our progress slowed down to a crawl. We did not wish to be involved in an accident or cause injuries by running people down, but there were many near misses. We could understand the enormous enthusiasm and fanatical excitement of the Belgian citizens being liberated from the Nazi rule, so we had to be tolerant and try to increase speed where it was humanly possible.

By early evening we were still 19 miles from the Brussels city suburbs and we received the most extraordinary order over the radio. We were ordered – if we failed to reach the city centre of Brussels by darkness – to switch on our headlights and push on as fast as possible to our objective! This amazing order had never been heard of before in a war operation. We did not even know if our lights were functioning correctly, as they had not been used since we were in Yorkshire, and in night driving we had always used the small, white concealed convoy light below the rear of the vehicle to follow the vehicle ahead. Dusk was beginning to come on as we reached the small town of Halle. We were nearing the Brussels suburb of Uccle (I believe now from memory that it was spelt this way), and we were just 6 miles from the city centre. This advance onwards would now be one of the most amazing journeys of my life. We hurriedly tuned the radio on to the BBC News Service – the up-to-date news given out was nearly three days behind our present position and the security clamp-down was ordered. No positions or locations of army units involved would be mentioned so as not to assist the Nazi intelligence of a detailed advance or detailed areas. Radio silence would now be enforced to

Front view of the three conjoined houses fronting Gwerthonor Road, Ash Cottage, Beach Cottage and Oak Cottage in 1975

Gelligaer Norman Church, 1102. Stone tiles recut by grandfather, 1890

The bridge opposite Oak
Cottage, 1927.

Welsh National Costume

Quarry Mawr east side, and the moorland approaches at the entrances outside, 1927.

Hengoed Viaduct, six-
teen giant arches across
the valley.

Britannia Colliery. The
derelict power house
from the bridge opposite
Oak Cottage.

My brother, Gwyn, 20 years old.
Myself, 13 years of age.

The north end of Bargoed
town, leading down to the
railway station, the Bargoed
Collieries and by-products
works.

Gwyn Alway BSc, 26 years
of age.

My brother, Trevor,
15 years old.

2735385. Recruit Ronald Alway.
February 7th 1940

Sgt Starr's Squad, Caterham
Barracks, Jan 1940. Alway, No 3 top
row. Partridge, No 6 front row.

Rotterdam, 12–13th May 1940. The first massed bombing of a western city.

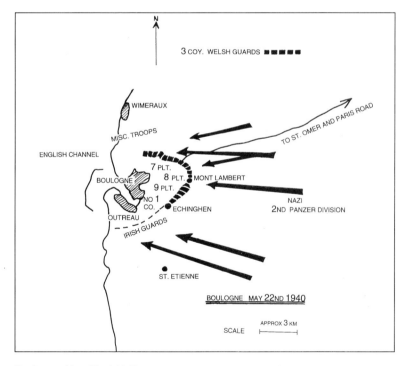

N

3 COY. WELSH GUARDS ■ ■ ■ ■ ■

WIMERAUX

MISC. TROOPS

TO ST. OMER AND PARIS ROAD

ENGLISH CHANNEL

7 PLT.

8 PLT.   MONT LAMBERT

BOULOGNE

9 PLT.

NO 1
CO.   ECHINGHEN

NAZI
2ND PANZER DIVISION

OUTREAU

IRISH GUARDS

ST. ETIENNE

BOULOGNE   MAY 22ND 1940

SCALE   APPROX 3 KM

Boulogne, May 22nd 1940.

The Czech TNT 38 tank of the Nazi 2nd Panza Division 1940.

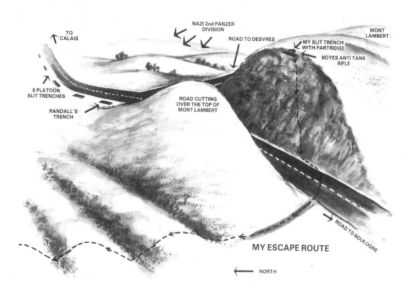

The cutting, Mount Lambert.

Sisters Joyce,
Toots, Joan,
myself, mother,
and Edna.

The Cromwell tank,
illustrated copy
from my tank log
book.

Invasion pamphlet
and warning to all
citizens.

Warning to every
British soldier.
Don't keep a
diary!!!

DON'T
keep a diary

Issued by the Ministry of Information *in co-operation with the War Office and the Ministry of Home Security.*

If the
INVADER
comes

WHAT TO DO — AND HOW TO DO IT

receive such orders you must ren
if you run away, you will be
you wi

No 8 Tank troop, Pickering, Yorkshire, September 1943. R. Alway, end-right, front row. Lieut Rex Whistler, No 4, front row.

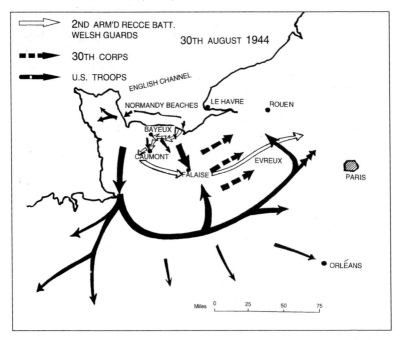

Batt route of advance at 30th August 1944.

Market Place, Beauvais. A 1932 postcard.

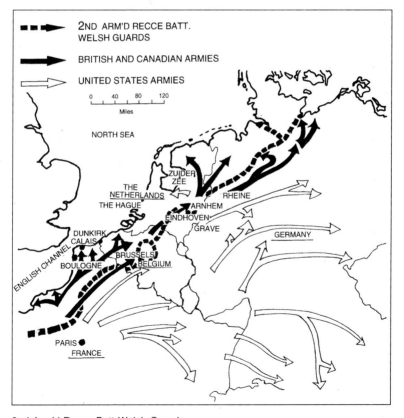

2nd Arm'd Recce Batt Welsh Guards.

Marie-Rose Vranks. Outside her school. Sent to my mother in October 1944.

The damage smashing Nazi vehicles. Snapped by a grateful Belgian citizen and endorsed 'Pour vous Monsieur toujours, n'oubliez pas et la! – et des boches!' (For you Monsieur always, never to forget it! – and the Boches! 22nd September 1944.

General Horrocks, C.O. 30th Corps. The entrance to Mechelen Town Hall, September 1944, with the Burgermaster of Mechelen unveiling the plaque commemorating the liberation of ten Belgian cities in two days. My head, right corner!

The Ardennes. A street in the city of
Namur. Xmas Day 1944. Ian Card, R.
Alway, M. Culot-Housiaux. Tom Canavan
and Wack Jones.

The Ardennes. Snow, Boxing Day.

Our wedding reception, Brisbane House, Brisbane Street, Launceston. January 7th 1950.

Joseph A. Alway. My father, age 70 years. 1953.

Bargoed Colliery during its heyday, 1938.

The 300 acre site of the Bargoed Colliery, coke ovens, by-products, and washeries, 1989. The World record production of steam coal hewn with the pick and shovel only, 1200 imperial tons, in 8 hours, was made at this site in the 1920s.

Number One Colliery, Penallta. One of the last mines to close in South Wales in 1991 after 86 years of production.

How green is my valley?!! North up the Rhymney Valley from Bargoed, 1989.

keep the Nazis guessing where we were and the main thrust of our movement and to avoid giving them any assistance as they regrouped after their rout from France.

There were unclear reports coming through that the rearguard of the Nazi forces were making desperate moves to get out of the city through the northern exit routes but we were continuously being held up by the surging excited population and were unable to move faster. We gradually made our way through the suburbs, where our vehicles were again festooned with floral tributes thrown by the citizens. My vehicle was the fiftieth in line as we approached the central area when tragedy struck. It appeared that not all those cheering citizens were Nazi haters but that they included supporters of the occupation regime. As we passed alongside those city buildings an enormous bunch of flowers adorned with ribbons and bunting was thrown from above from a high building. It landed on the engine covers of the tank immediately behind my vehicle. The radio operator of that tank, a squadron colleague by the name of Brian Jones, clambered hurriedly out of the turret to retrieve it. Riding on the vehicle were two young Belgian youths waving the national flag. Brian picked up the big floral gift to put it on the turret but it was primed with a deadly booby trap and exploded. He was decapitated and died instantly. The two Belgian youths were badly injured along with numbers of citizens at the side of the vehicle. It was a sad affair and impossible to trace its source. It delayed us again, holding up the whole tank column but we had to move on and, at exactly ten minutes to nine o'clock in the semi-darkness, we reached the Grande Place. At the site of this famous area in the capital city, the huge Palace de Justice was smouldering, with billows of smoke emitting from the impressive entrance at the top of the steps. It was an historic occasion and a wonderful achievement for me, my squadron and my battalion. We were the first Allied troops to reach central Brussels and to liberate the city after years of Nazi rule.

I clambered out of my tank and ran up the steps of the Palace de Justice with a drawn pistol at the ready. I pushed past a number of Belgian citizens, hurriedly padded my mouth and nose with my handkerchief and barged through the doors into the smoke-filled interior. Inside the Nazis had set fire to all the records and thousands of documents; the Belgian authorities had made a magnificent effort to prevent the building burning but masses of papers and documents were charred and black and still smouldering. I stirred a pile of charred documents with my boots as I coughed and spluttered in the smoke and it fell apart. In the centre some were intact. I picked them up quickly and got out of the building. Among those papers was an envelope and inside a propaganda postcard depicting an English girl welcoming the Nazi sailors sailing to England. I handed the papers over to Intelligence later, but I kept the postcard and I have retained it all my life. It is illustrated here with the translation, my souvenir of the night of 3rd September 1944, the Liberation of the City of Brussels.

Because We Are Travelling to England

Today we want to sing a little song
We want to drink the cool wine
And the glasses shall be clinked together
As it must be a separation
　Give me your hand
　Your white hand
　Live well! My treasure, live well!
　Because we are travelling to England.
Our flag is waving on our mast
It is announcing the might of our realm
As we don't want to suffer any more
The Englishman laughing about us,
　Give me your hand . . .
If the news comes that I have fallen
That I'm sleeping in the depth of the sea
Do not cry for me, my treasure! And think
That his blood has flowed for the Fatherland
　Give me your hand . . .

Our Squadron now halted around the cultivated verges of the Grande Place where we immediately dug slit trenches as a precautionary measure while the squadron leader consulted with the Belgian officials. We were urged to join in the celebrations and to proceed immediately to the Brussels Radio Station where arrangements had already been made for us to broadcast our announcement to the European population and for us to send personal messages to the folks back home. Permission now had to be obtained from the battalion and divisional commanders, but when the radio request was flashed back we were banned from making a broadcast. A radio broadcast could assist the Nazi Intelligence and alert the German air force for a retaliation and reprisal bombing with the fearsome V1 and V2 rockets, and assist the enemy by naming our regiment and battalion. I was very disappointed. It would have been a wonderful opportunity to send a message to my family not knowing when the next chance would be available to write a letter. However, urged on by the Belgians once more to wipe out any resistance in the city, we took on board, riding on the engine covers, members of the Belgian resistance as guides to direct us through the darkened streets to prominent Nazi establishments. Our objective as a priority was the Gestapo HQ and, as we moved one block away from the Grande Place, the streets became silent and deserted. It suggested immediately that the Nazi rearguards were still around. Our guides took us quickly to the Gestapo building and we opened up with everything we had possessed. Every window and door was raked with thousands of Besa machine-gun bullets, armour-piercing shells and our own speciality – the 90mm heat shells. We fired eight of these shells into different locations of the building, they penetrated through the massive stone masonry and exploded inside. Satisfied that we had silenced everything on the inside, we moved back to the Grande Place.

The supply vehicles were arriving as we returned. They had been escorted through the area for us to refuel and replenish our stock of ammunition and supplies as quickly as possible. It was well after midnight when our tasks of cleaning the guns and various mainten-ance duties were completed. My tour of sentry duty was from 1 a.m. to 3 a.m. On 4th September 1944, dawn was about 6.30 a.m. so we heated a few tins of food for a meal just after 3 a.m. At 3.20 a.m. that morning there remained just two and a half hours before standing to and our quick briefing before moving on. I climbed into the tank, tired and fatigued. I wrapped a blanket around me and curled around the circular base floor of the turret under the gun, with a small web-bing pack as a pillow. I closed my eyes and fell asleep oblivious to the whole scene and the world.

14

Another Escape

It was 4th September 1944, and I was disturbed and awakened from my hard uncomfortable resting place at almost 5.30 a.m. I had managed just two hours' sleep for the start of another long eventful day. It was still dark but hundreds of Belgian citizens were milling around. Sleep did not matter to them on such a special occasion as this when they were free of Nazi restrictions and the nightly curfew.

I remember well appreciating a mug of hot tea that morning with a tin of baked beans and hard-tack army biscuits, as we were hurriedly briefed for the day ahead. As the first glimmers of light appeared, we moved off. Our stay in the city of Brussels had come to an end. A photographer from the *Pictorial Belgian Weekly* was taking pictures to be published that day, the people were calling out and waving, and all clamouring to shake hands with us as we pulled away, to the north-west towards the town of Aalst. As soon as we reached the countryside our first battle began. A huge tree had been felled for a roadblock, and small arms fire began to hit our vehicles. The tree felled by the Nazis was no obstacle for the Cromwell, the tracks climbed right over the top and onwards giving us fleeting views of small numbers of Nazi troops. We made short work of them all with thousands of Besa bullets and high explosive shells. We unfortunately set fire to a big haystack but we could do nothing about it as we pushed on to enter and liberate the town of Aalst. As the morning progressed we turned north towards the city of Mechelen and, by noon with flags and decorations displayed everywhere and hundreds of cheering Belgians, we drove in and liberated the city.

Translating the code words on the radio messages, we learned that other units of the division had entered the seaport of Antwerp unopposed about 15 miles from our position. It was the first big port to be captured since Normandy and in a few weeks our massive supplies and equipment would be flown in and unloaded without restraint.

Leaving the city of Mechelen after our brief stay, we set our course for the big city of Louvain 32 miles away. It was late afternoon and into early evening when we reached the outskirts of Louvain and once again we drove into the city without any opposition, to be greeted with the displays of flags and decorations everywhere. Louvain was badly damaged and in a state of seige before it fell in the First World War. What a contrast now! It had long been repaired and rebuilt, then abandoned by the Nazis. It was a magnificent place with many beautiful old buildings and cobblestoned streets. Our time there was very short and we pushed straight on in a southerly direction to mop up the area along the Louvain to Brussels road. About a distance of approximately seven miles from Louvain, the villages and the populated areas became silent and deserted, the crowds that we had now become so familiar with were no longer there and our suspicions were aroused immediately. I was on edge, as the area and the terrain were completely unknown to us although we had our maps to guide us. On occasions like this one imagines all kinds of things, the unpleasant thoughts of an ambush, or a trap or other disastrous and deadly incidents. We had learned so much of the cunning of the SS and the German forces. At the army time of about 1900 hours, 7 p.m. that evening, the sun low in the western sky, with long shadows and hollows receding and lengthening in many places as we slowly moved along, we reached the perimeter of an area called Tervuren, ten miles from Louvain on the route back to the eastern suburbs of Brussels. The road divided into three cobblestoned streets to pass through the village; everything seemed deserted, there were no visible signs of any residents and the only noise was the sound of our tanks' engines, a giveaway to any enemy in the area.

We were ordered to halt and await further orders from the command, as we were a lone squadron with no other support. There was a pause now with some indecision as to how to proceed. Our maps indicated that the road went straight through the area and if each separate tank troop proceeded along each of the three roads they would be out of sight of each other because of the buildings. The roads were narrow and cobblestoned in the familiar Belgian way and if anything happened we would have difficulty in getting out. We would have to rely on the Cromwell's 'neutral turn' to spin around to get out in a hurry. This 'neutral turn' as we referred to it, was an innovated movement with the epicyclic gearing of the Cromwell. If the left steering stick was pulled whilst in the neutral gear, the right tank track would lock, while the left track continued to move, and with a little acceleration the tank would spin around to the right within its own length. Alternately with the right steering stick pulled, it would spin to the left. It was a quick and efficient way to get back out of a narrow area in an emergency and in a desperate hurry. However, the order came for us to move each of our three tank troops along a separate road (a tank troop consisted of four tanks), No. 7 troop to the left, No. 9 the centre and No. 8 the right, with HQ troop behind No. 7 troop along the left-hand road. My task was to head along the right-hand road, if anything perhaps, this was the most narrow of all three, and 100 yards ahead was another road at right angles, crossing over and intersecting all three entrance roads. We were ordered to proceed at a crawl with extreme caution and to be alert to the intercepting crossover road. I had a premonition – that sinking feeling that something was about to happen, and whether the attack would come from the left or the right was just a guess.

The next few minutes would be another period in my life that I will always remember vividly and clearly. We hurriedly checked the free run of the Besa machine-gun belt over the top of the gun, as it fed into the firing compartment, and a shell was already in the breach of the gun. My radio operator Robert Winston Owen Charles Bush had a second shell on his lap for a quick reload, with another Besa belt at the ready. The turret was traversed to the right for the gun to fire down the intersecting road. The gunner had raised his spring seat and had his shoulder pressed up the mount of the gun to lower the range to 200 yards, with his right eye pressed into the flexible rubber eye-piece of the telescopic sight, his left hand on the turret remote traverse handle, his right hand on the trigger for both the machine-gun and the gun. The front gunner reported everything ready. He could only fire ahead from the front of the tank within a radius of 75 degrees. I had the radio switch on to the intercom, as we checked again, for all the crew to hear and follow each order quickly. Tense and ready we edged slowly along the road to the intersection, out of view behind the line of homes and buildings along the route, then halted and reported our position. The troop leader relayed the information to the squadron leader. We were now ordered to ease the tank forward a few yards past the end of the building line until the driver could obtain a sighting through his turned periscope down the intersecting road and report any information. I conveyed that order to the driver and to report what he could sight down the road – his last words were, 'OK – out.' In those final tense seconds as we moved forward, my last two words inside that tank were also about to be spoken!

At that split second there was turmoil, as the inside of the turret became a giant hot hailstorm, the only possible way to describe it. An 88mm Nazi shell had ripped through the driving compartment between the front driving bogie and the track, through the divider, and killing both men, the driver and the front gunner, lodging in the two-inch mortar rack of phosphorus and smoke bombs which exploded into flames in a shower of fiery death on the gunner. The turret was a wall of flames in a second and those last two words I shouted into the mike were, 'Bale out'. Using my set as a springboard behind the gun and gasping for air in the heat I hurled myself through the hatch and rolled down on the engine covers. Bob Bush had already baled out through his hatch rolling and trying to douse the phosphorus flames on the legs of his tank suit, and the tank was still crawling forward. I did the fastest dive of my life over the back down to the road, dashed along for about ten yards and threw myself into a narrow entrance that led to the rear of that home. Bob Bush was behind me as the tank blew up in a mass of flames, with the blast hurling him on top of me. Meanwhile the remainder of the troop, witnessing what had happened, spun around and sped off with the rest of the squadron. We did not see them again that night and it was better to lose one than a lot more in that situation.

As we lay crouched in that small alleyway we could hear the tank hulk burning fiercely, the petrol tanks must have exploded and showered everything to add to the inferno. Every window in the vicinity had shattered. While the fire was so fierce we knew the Germans would not approach. Darkness was about half an hour away and this was the main reason I surmised, that the squadron raced off to avoid any further traps. In muffled exchanges we decided we had better lie 'dogo' until darkness came to our aid. Bob Bush's shins were blistered from the fiery phosphorus burning through his tank-suit trousers and his battledress trouser legs underneath. The high elevation of the gun in the turret had protected us both but the shower of flame had caught his legs standing on the base of the turret below the gun. It was just one of those things. Good fortune had helped both of us, but now we were in the next phase and in a hopeless position if the enemy decided to probe along the road. But yet again it seemed to me that they did not know if any of our unit was waiting to ambush and trap them also. Maybe, if it was just a small rearguard anti-tank detachment; they had claimed a prize and they might slink off quietly and quickly.

The period of time in that unhappy situation seemed like hours and hours, with the hopes and wishes that darkness would come quickly. Neither of us had the means of telling the time. I did have an army issue pocket watch for synchronising and checking our time and objectives reached but it was a cumbersome object to carry and I kept it on the ledge at the rear of the turret behind me, and of course it was now destroyed with everything else. The time dragged on, the last small explosions from that fiery grave ended and we heard the sound of a vehicle engine. To me it appeared to sound like the Nazi half-track, and I was sure it must be the towing vehicle of the German 88mm gun. Through the silence, as it was almost dusk, we could make out a few clanks and metal contacts. Our spirits rose a little, as we thought they must be dismantling the gun from its firing position to tow it and move away. At least that was our hope. We still lay low until the last sounds had receded and complete silence reigned once more. The whereabouts of the residents from around the area puzzled me. The Nazis had either ordered them all out or they had made themselves scarce for their own safety. Darkness gradually came down, the sky was clear with no clouds, the stars would soon be visible and we would have some vision for a restricted distance ahead. We would be able to see the silhouette of any building, tree or other obstruction in our path and we decided to move.

I removed the two syringes taped to my leg, crushed them with my boot and tossed them into some patches of grass ahead of us and we cautiously and silently worked our way back to the street keeping close to the building line. I reluctantly removed my notebook from my inside jacket pocket and quietly dropped it into the street drain. I did not wish to be captured with it in my possession; with all the information and incidents contained and recorded in its pages, I would have been shot. We reached the end of the road where we first entered the area and paused, undecided which way to go. I quickly unsnapped the fasteners on the front of my tank suit and unscrewed the top of the central button of my battledress jacket, one of the things I never at any time expected to do, and I tipped out the tiny compass. Bob Bush was in pain with his burnt and blistered legs, so we tore up his field dressing, and bound them roughly with the bandage to prevent the rub and irritation of his burnt trousers. We consulted the compass and made our direction due west towards the suburbs of Brussels, an estimated distance of six or seven miles.

We walked across what appeared to be an open cultivated area now, with a few trees and bushes. We climbed over fences and across ploughed land and gained more confidence under the cover of darkness. After some time we could make out ahead of us more buildings silhouetted against the starry sky and we moved towards them, perhaps to find out where we were situated and perhaps too, someone might be moving around so we pushed on with greater hopes. It was difficult in the darkness. We had no idea where we were as we came to a built-up residential area wondering whether to risk moving through the streets. We decided the risk was too great fronting the houses so we tried every possible way to get to the rear of the buildings but it was even darker there and we became more frustrated. We decided between us that perhaps it would be better to creep into a back entrance somewhere, find some kind of outbuilding and lie up for the night. Bob Bush found a back entrance and tried to open the door; in the eerie silence of the night it squeaked like a stuck pig as he pushed it inwards very slowly. We waited for a while in case of any alarm, then edged our way inside. At the end of the entrance path we saw a tiny chink of light no larger than a quarter of an inch, the extreme corner of a window where the black-out material minutely failed to cover completely over the wood frame. I crept up to it silently but I could see nothing because the inside obstruction appeared to have curled blocking all vision inside. We heard no movement or sound so whispering to each other as quietly as possible, should we risk tapping the window, or move around and knock at the back door? We hesitated, undecided, then I said I was going to risk it and knock on the door. I whispered to Bob that I believed we must be in a Walloon area and if they spoke or made any inquiry behind the closed door about the intruder, I would not have a clue what they would say, their language was Walloon, very similar to Dutch. If the occupants were Flemish they spoke French, and I could probably understand. We had already discovered in our short period in Belgium that the Flemish disliked the Walloon and there was much animosity between them.

Bob Bush remained concealed in the darkness, while I drew my .38 pistol from my belt holster and tapped the door with it three times and waited. The interval seemed like hours and there was no answer, so I tapped again a little harder. I heard a movement inside and then a male voice in French.

'Who is it?' I replied, '*Parlez vous anglais, monsieur?*' The answer, '*Non, pourquoi?*' (No, why?) Then, in my best French, I said, '*Je suis un soldat anglais. Voulez-vous aider moi?*' (I am an English soldier. Will you help me?) The door opened and into that dark interior I said, '*Boches ici?*' The man hurriedly replied, '*Non, non monsieur entrez, s'il vous plait.'* Bob Bush appeared and we both went in and quickly closed the door.

We were to learn that the man was Monsieur Charles Vranks who had a market garden and a small shop in the town of Jodoigne about six or seven miles away. He had come with his wife Madame Vranks, and their 14-year-old daughter Marie-Rose to care for a sick sister. The girl Marie-Rose was learning English at school and this helped us a great deal, as they knew more than we did of all the areas now liberated by the Allied troops. Their own town was still occupied by the Boches when they had left three days before. They even told us that the infamous Nazi concentration camp at Breendonk, west of Brussels, had been liberated and many people set free – the start of opening up the awful disclosures of what was to come from these camps in the months ahead. Breendonk was a detention and transportation centre for the more notorious camps inside Germany and Poland. They had been listening to a quiet transmission of radio news when they heard my first knock, but had scurried away to a hiding place before coming to the door fearful that it was the Nazi knock.

Madame Vranks examined Bush's legs and bathed them carefully with a solution of brine, cold water with a little dissolved salt, then using my field dressing, cut off the bandage and lightly bound the burns to keep the air out. I still had the escape pack tied around the small of my back, so we used the extra bandages around his legs. I gave the large slab of energy chocolate to Madame Vranks. It wasn't the usual delicious chocolate, but I guessed they had not tasted any for many years. They told us too that there were no Nazi troops in the vicinity and it was early morning of that day that they had seen a few small groups moving away from the area in a hurry. Monsieur Vranks knew every detail of the district having lived there all his life, and he offered to guide us back to the outskirts of Brussels, or until we contacted any other troops of our division. He could also knock up many people that he knew along the route in case of a doubt and they would know what was going on. We were aware too by that time there would be hundreds of transports, auxiliary units, and artillery moving up under the cover of darkness. We accepted his offer gratefully and at about 1 a.m. Belgian time we set off, Marie-Rose and her father in front; we followed a few yards behind with drawn pistols.

We trudged through that Belgian locality tired and weary in the early hours of that morning 5th September 1944, for a distance I could only estimate of about three miles, then we heard the sound of a motor vehicle, which became clearer and more audible with every dozen yards. We soon came upon a big convoy of 25-pounder guns, some of the division's artillery had halted along the road and there were Belgian citizens everywhere. The Vranks family had guided us and helped us so much and brought us through safely. I jotted down their address in Jodoigne, shook hands with them both with our grateful thanks. I sent that address to my mother the next day when I wrote a letter home. She corresponded with Marie-Rose for some time, which assisted her with her English. After the war, in later years, she became a nun and then suffered a horrible end in the massacres of the Belgian Congo with the Mau Mau type of killings and uprisings for independence. The gunners of that unit took us to their battery commander to whom we gave an outline of what had occurred and he ordered the escorting military police to provide a jeep to take us back to our battalion.

Under the star-studded sky about two hours before the dawn of that day we were dropped off at battalion HQ. The squadron was some miles away, harboured on sandy ground adjacent to woods and plantation pines for a rest and a break and to bring everything up to full preparedness once again. We obtained a refreshing hot mug of tea from the cooks with biscuits and bully beef to appease our hunger. Bob Bush's legs were treated and dressed by the medical orderlies and then we were driven to the squadron location north of Brussels. The area was a quiet secluded place and, except for the tank troop on sentry duty and radio watch, everyone was fast asleep in the trenches beneath their individual tanks. The troop leader was surprised to see us as we were all considered dead in the conflagration of the tank but everything would be put before the squadron-leader at daybreak. In the meantime I scrounged a blanket and a groundsheet, crawled into a hole in the sandy soil and fell asleep. It had been nine long days and nights since we began the push from western Normandy, a total of approximately 216 hours, the total amount of sleep and rest I had obtained during that period was about 22½ hours, so when my head rested on the hard sandy ground I went out like a light. I could count my blessings now – it was the second escape for me from the Nazi army since 1940.

It was after midday that I was aroused by one of the troop with a mug of hot tea, as they had allowed me to sleep undisturbed. I soon obtained my kit bag from the squadron stores supply vehicle and cleaned myself up for the squadron Memoranda which was still carried on, even in the middle of a war. I was commended for getting away and returning so quickly with Robert Bush; so that we now had time to obtain a reserve tank from the Battalion to re-organise our unit. I soon obtained a writing pad, as there were many spares around carried by the boys and the offers were numerous; I had to write a letter home after such a long interval. I began to count my personal losses: my old camera had gone with about 50 undeveloped war photos, which was a magnificent record of incidents, actions and details along the routes, along with all the remaining films; two beautiful French ladies' wristwatches and an engraved French silver railway pocket watch I had confiscated from the loot contained in a disguarded Nazi SS prisoners' pack; all my personal kit, although fortunately I had plenty of spares in my kit bag; my precious notebook with so much information and details of everything since we left southern England; eight special Welsh cakes, the last of a parcel sent by my mother and made by my Auntie May, the sandwich variety with a thin slice of Caerphilly cheese between the two layers and laced with winberry jam; a tin of boiled sweets hoarded from my rations in the seven-day food pack with about 500 cigarettes; five-star bottles of French cognac which I had traded for 20 cigarettes in Beauvais; souvenirs and odds and ends, which I had collected along the way, but at least I was still alive and in one piece so I had no reason to complain.

It was a restful, uneventful few days for me at that particular location. We had the luxury once more of the army mobile showers and a complete change and replacement of shirts, socks and underclothing. It gave the following army units and organisations time to move up into Belgium to consolidate and occupy the liberated areas. A start could be made also by the engineers to repair and fix up the smashed and badly damaged railway systems to the Channel ports, which were being captured one by one with thousands of Nazi prisoners to be rounded up. Another vital phase of the war was the occupation and destruction of Hitler's V2 rocket emplacements to end the bombardment of London and southern England from the coast.

The season was turning into autumn, the weather was changing and we began to experience heavy rains as we prepared to move into northern Belgium to tackle the next difficult obstacle – the Albert Canal.

It was 10th September, north of the city of Louvain when the German army began to put up strong resistance and continuous counter attack. The fighting became very fierce and for a few days we experienced difficult and serious times. We lost two tanks, and their crews, from No. 9 troop in one afternoon's desperate fighting. In a tremendous counter attack towards dusk by fanatical SS units, we came very close to being overrun, until a battalion of Irish Guards Sherman tanks were rushed forward to our assistance and to repel the Nazi forces. However, we reached the town of Diest and the road to Tessederlo just four miles from the Albert Canal. The task of the supporting division infantry was to assault the crossing and, in the pouring rain and the early hours of 15th September, we made the crossing over a Bailey bridge hurriedly erected during the night, and pushed on to the small town of Beringen.

We harboured that night a few miles south of the small populated area of Leopoldsburg. Harbour, by the way, I can mention once again, was the term we used in all our radio transmissions to halt and assemble for the hours of darkness. We refuelled that night, replenished our ammunition and supplies, completed our maintenance and took on board a new seven-day pack of rations, not knowing the difficulties and the long distances and experiences that lay ahead over the next few days. Our briefing told us that the next objective was the town and surrounding area of Hechtel about 12 miles from the Dutch border.

The following morning, we advanced as a squadron along the unfamiliar route. We had made a halt in line along a straight piece of road with the tank engines switched off, when we suddenly received one of the biggest frights of the campaign. It was around 11 o'clock in the morning and we had made a quick brew of tea. All through the war we had always heard the exaggerated rumours and Nazi propaganda about Hitler's secret weapons but now we were alarmed as it looked as though we were about to be attacked by one of them. We knew that he possessed an airplane that could fly without propellers but at that time little or nothing more. Across the sky, faster than anything we had ever seen before, with a fiendish whistle and a fanatical scream, streaked a black airplane. It looped on to its back, climbed vertically to gain height and looped again to come whistling and screaming down towards us in seconds, releasing two bombs, which fortunately missed and exploded 50 yards behind our column. Unknown to us then, this was the first military jet aircraft to fly and attack in a war operation. Hitler had beaten us to it again! And we were to become the first military target for the first jet fighter, on that historic day, 16th September 1944 in northern Belgium.

Following that alarming incident, just an hour later our advance turned east, towards the town of Hechtel, which was to become one of our biggest and most successful battles of the campaign against the Nazi army. Five miles from Hechtel we suddenly came under shellfire, and there was trouble ahead. It would appear that the German forces were about to put up a fierce resistance having to defend the Reich itself now, the frontier being just 30 miles away. The open country before the built-up area of the town was flat and undulating with German infantry dug in all over the area. The squadron dispersed along a wide front approaching the town to attack with every weapon we possessed. For an hour or so, it was hell. We overran dugouts and slit trenches everywhere occupied by the Nazi infantry, many of them were crushed as the Cromwell tracks churned into the soft sand. Perhaps for me it was retribution, as my thoughts flashed back four and a half years to what had happened to my own section mates on Mont Lambert, outside Boulogne. But it was war, kill or be killed, and we pushed on to attack the town, as buildings and roofs crumbled with the devastating power of our guns and fires began to erupt everywhere. Many Germans surrendered, sullen and frightened. They were no longer the defiant, arrogant, jackbooted thugs we had known for so long. The town was soon subdued and captured, for us to discover once again one more brutal criminal act. Inside the lower floor of the town hall, where the SS and Gestapo had done their dirty work, some 40 young Belgian and Dutch youths aged between 17 and 22 years had been arrested and detained. Each one had been shot in the leg with a single bullet to disable him and prevent him from taking part in any military resistance and support with the Allied forces. The instigators, SS and the vile Gestapo, had fled back towards their own border, while the ordinary German soldier, the *Wehrmacht*, had been left to defend the area and face the consequences.

It added and instilled more bitterness and hatred amongst our own colleagues towards the cowardly SS and the Gestapo. Sadly, too, we had casualties in the Hechtel battle, one of them being a member of my own troop, another Jones, was killed. Once again it happened that his frame was too high in the turret and his head was out of the hatch. A high explosive missile hit the tank top and he was killed instantly.

Late that same afternoon we moved north-east for about ten miles and entered the populated district and village by the name of Pietre. The people were frightened but the burgermaster (mayor) of the area came along to welcome us, because he could speak fluent English. He gave us much valuable information and told us that there were no more German troops in the surrounding area, the road east to the town of Bree was undefended and the road ahead to Roermond on the Holland-Germany border was wide open to Munchen Gladbach, Düsseldorf, the River Rhine and the Ruhr. The big bridge at the junction of the River Meuse and the Albert Canal on the highway from Maastricht north to the Dutch city of Eindoven was also undefended. All this information was made known to the squadron leader and given in haste to the battalion and divisional commands. At this point we had come farther east towards the German frontier than any other British troops. Not one item of this information was acted upon by the High Command.

However, as darkness was coming down and we harboured for the night, we were informed that 20,000 parachutists and airborne troops were taking off from British airfields in a vast air armada. Included in this huge air strike were 14,000 giant gliders towed in twos and threes by Halifax, Lancaster and American bombers, all filled with airborne troops and equipment. The 101 first and 82 American airborne divisions were to drop between the Dutch cities of Eindoven and Nijmegen in central Holland to seize all the canal bridges and the River Meuse bridge at Grave, 11 miles south of Nijmegen on the lower Rhine. The British 1st Airborne Division would drop beyond the Upper Rhine at Arnhem. It became another awesome military order for us too: we had to immediately rejoin the centre line of our advance north of Hechtel, race into Holland to link up with the Americans holding the bridges, smash our way forward to seize the massive, high road bridge over the Lower Rhine at Nijmegen and then push along the highway elevated above the flat land between the upper and the lower Rhine, to link up with our own airborne troops across the huge road bridge over the Rhine at Arnhem. It appeared that this arduous onslaught was to fall to us to take the lead and head the divisional advance once again. In all these military operations, when things go well and correct, the generals and Brass Hats get enormous praise and publicity, but when things go wrong, very little is said and criticism is practically nil. Unfortunately, the lower ranks and the soldiers, who bear the brunt of the casualties, injuries and deaths, have to put up with it all, with guts and determination. I have often wondered what would have happened if the débâcle of Arnhem had not been carried out and the information given by us had been acted upon to attack the Ruhr instead.

So it all happened. Fifteen minutes before first light that next day, 17th September 1944, we moved north towards the Dutch border 12 miles away and, again, were the first Allied ground troops into Holland. The faithful Cromwell tank became the first vehicle to cross over and we increased speed towards the first important Dutch town of Valkensward. Just south of Valkensward we crossed the Dommel River bridge. There was no sight of any American airborne troops and we still had another 12 miles to the city of Eindhoven.

Towards noon we reached the city and halted briefly, to give the opportunity for a quick brew up of tea. I traded two cigarettes with a clog-wearing, middle-aged Dutchman for a one-guilder note as a souvenir. We got a passing glimpse of the huge Phillips electrical works, which would no longer be making equipment for Adolph Hitler, and had our first meeting with small numbers of American parachutists as we once again crossed over the Dommel River to the flat country of Holland. The roads now became elevated, like causeways over the dead flat landscape, and we were silhouetted targets standing out against the skyline until we reached St Oedenrode with more Americans and another bridge over the Dommel River. Nine miles on was Wilhelmina Canal, another vital bridge and the town of Veghel. This bridge once more was defended by a group of American airborne troops and with broad smiles they cheerfully waved us through. A short distance ahead there was an elevated crossroads, an intersection of our route and a road running parallel with the canal and the town of Veghel. We were now approximately 25 miles from the city of Nijmegen, and at that stage the two biggest towns on the advance route in front of us were Uden and then, roughly at the half-way mark, the town of Grave and the all important bridge across the River Meuse. The River Meuse, now in Dutch territory, became the River Maas, and reports informed us that it had been taken intact, without opposition, by the American parachutists who were waiting for our link-up.

We raced on, entered Grave and crossed the bridge with just ten miles to the perimeter of Nijmegen. It was evening now, and we had covered about eight of those ten miles when there was a sudden order to halt. The Coldstream and Grenadier Shermans would move up, press forward to take and enter Nijmegen, and our instructions were to pull back along the route to consolidate, hold and defend the bridges. Our lines of supply and communications were long and vulnerable, the greater part of the British 2nd Army was still many miles behind us in northern France and entering Belgium.

That night was unpleasant, dirty and wet, with heavy rain. We were getting reports and information that the British paratroop division were in trouble, the greater part of which had been dropped north of Arnhem and the Upper Rhine. The Intelligence reports to the high command had either been wrong or ignored, as there were three Nazi army divisions north of the Rhine and the unfortunate paratroops

200

were in for a shocking time, with no armoured vehicles to support them. The river was behind them, and heavy fighting was still going on for the huge Arnhem bridge. Arnhem was still 11 to 12 miles north of Nijmegen road bridge, and at 11.30 p.m. that night the vital bridge had not been captured. It was undamaged and intact, and our whole armoured division were still on the south side of the Lower Rhine. We heard reports too that a young Dutch patriot had secretly risked his life to crawl along the girders beneath that huge road bridge. He defused the explosives planted there by the Nazis and cut the detonating cables to the charges and the Nazi groups on the north side were unable to explode the set charges to bring down the bridge. However, in the heavy rain there was fierce fighting that night and one of the Coldstream Shermans commanded by a troop sergeant succeeded in crossing the bridge in the darkness after midnight. He was awarded the DCM, and at daylight our forces were consolidated on the other side.

In the meantime that morning we advanced from our bridge crossings defence and entered Nijmegen to attempt to cross the high railway bridge 100 yards downstream from the road bridge. It was a double-track railway bridge, and whoever the aircraft pilot might have been, whether he was German, British or American, he did a very accurate feat of bombing. Almost in the centre of that bridge, ten to twenty yards apart were two big bomb holes, through the left-hand tracks and right through the bridge. The bombs or explosive missiles, or whatever they might have been, had passed clean through the bridge and probably exploded below the high span nearer the flowing water, because the bridge was still usable, at least we believed this. When we hurriedly checked the bridge before attempting to cross, the maximum distance between the bomb holes and the parapet edges of the bridge along the right-hand railway tracks was just seven feet, so any mistakes or bad judgement would send a tank hurtling through the bomb hole or over the edge of the bridge, with a drop of sixty feet to the river below, and certain death. We desperately ripped up lengths of railway track with chains behind the powerful Cromwell and then struggled and strained to manhandle them just a few feet with each strenuous effort to run them along the edge of the bomb holes to give us a little extra width as a precautionary measure.

How well I remember that crossing now! It was an incident in my life I could never forget, crawling slowly along, high above the lower Rhine River, exposed to the sky, and a target from miles away across the flat lands, unable to see the tank tracks from the turret and peering anxiously and precariously down through the bomb holes on one side and the brink of the parapet edge on the other hesitatingly, almost whispering instructions to the driver through the intercom, our lives depending on his accuracy and skill.

Incidentally, a few miles east of Nijmegen, the River Rhine divides into two rivers about 11 miles apart, the lower Rhine is the Dutch River Waal, which flows into the sea near the estuary of the River Meuse or Maas. The upper Rhine, which the Dutch name the Lek, flows through from Arnhem and then Rotterdam, with its mouth at the Hook of Holland so familiar to me from four years previously when I was blown up. The huge port Europort, now the biggest port in Europe and the busiest probably in the world, begins at the Hook.

In 1975, when I sailed up this river to Rotterdam, the old jetty and the lighthouse had gone, instead there were giant wharfs and docks so different from those days in May a long time ago.

However we crossed the bridge without mishap and reached the northern bank safely to halt for a short time amongst huge glass greenhouses containing vines. The area would immediately become a very dangerous location if the Nazi shells fell around, with the vast area of glass everywhere. There was one main highway north and this road too was raised above the flat land like a long causeway, and for miles the flat agricultural land each side was saturated and heavy with the torrential rain. Every vehicle moving along this road was outlined against the sky and of course the long expanse of this highway was the target of the Nazi artillery. Our danger now, moving down the embankment off this highway on to the saturated land, was of bellying and getting hopelessly bogged. The weight of the tank would make the tracks churn uselessly as the full weight of the vehicle bellied on the ground making it immovable, and the recovery vehicles were miles away south of Nijmegen. We pushed along that elevated highway to within a half-mile of the town of Elst, approximately five miles from the Arnhem bridge. The task was hopeless, the conditions and the weather were appalling. The road had to have free access for supplies and moving vehicles forward and for recovering the wounded and casualties suffered by the paratroops. We pulled back a mile, but our movements were hampered by the boggy conditions as we moved off, and east of the highway to dig in, to hold the area. Our location from then onwards was under constant fire, and we would be unmercifully bombed, shelled and mortared day and night. We had one small advantage from the conditions: the heavy wet soil dampened down the explosions, as the missiles became embedded in

202

the soft earth. That first night was hell and to add to our troubles we were bombed after midnight by German aircraft.

The dawning day of 19th September held more problems for all of us and was a sad day for me personally. We had three days' rations remaining, fuel was low and stocks of ammunition down. The radio told us that the German forces had attacked in force from the perimeter of the German border in South Holland and cut across our vital supply lines, so we were now isolated and cut off. That day also, although the weather was a little brighter for our aircraft, we were angry and appalled to watch our own planes dropping containers and supplies by parachute, and to see them all drifting and landing on the German positions. More problems too! Nazi frogmen came down the river floating explosives under the cover of darkness, to attempt to demolish the Nijmegen bridge, but vigilance and alertness nabbed them in the nick of time as they tried to blow it up. They were to make two more attempts but without success, as every ripple and every bubble each side of the Nijmegen was blasted with heavy fire. That night it rained again and, as darkness was coming down with the low clouds and gloom, the bombardment increased. We were then experiencing the awful fiendish wails and screaming howls of the 'Sobbing Sisters' the Nebelwefer mortar, that awful weapon and its missiles that had always been a nightmare to me ever since my experiences in 1940.

I was doing a tour of sentry duty with my troop and was walking towards one of the troop tanks situated behind a farm shed grown over with a climbing plant, with a few scattered bushes around. With all the fiendish wails, the exploding and whining shells, and the crescendo of booms, it was impossible to hear the resounding bump and plop as a mortar hit the soft wet earth. As I have said before, some of them roll along the ground smoking before they explode. It happened again! I had reached the tank but, unknown to me, one of those deadly missiles had rolled towards the sloping underfront of the vehicle and exploded. I was partly shielded by the protruding track but a fragment of that awful missile travelled under the sloping track and ripped across the side of my left thigh tearing away a piece of flesh; two other tiny pieces ripped the inside calf of the same leg and I went down in agony and pain.

I quickly obtained assistance from the troop members, clambered into the tank and closed down the hatches to use the turret light to render first aid. The shrapnel had undercut the skin for a length of two and a half inches and ripped away a piece of flesh with the top skin and flesh left overhanging the gash. We pressed it down into the wound, padded it with a field dressing and bound the thigh tightly and securely and then I quickly bandaged my bleeding calf. My tank suit trouser leg and my battledress trouser leg beneath were sliced through and needed repairing or replacing. I was fortunate, it could have been far worse and my luck was still holding true!

I was in the unhappy situation of not being able to obtain medical treatment as our unit was isolated and cut off. Day after day and night after night we held our defensive position, hoping that each dawning day would bring low clouds and misty rain to keep away the Nazi planes and again for the second time we watched another aircraft drop of supplies fall on the German lines. I took it as easy as possible and my leg improved and then, on about 25th or 26th September, I cannot recall the exact date, the last airborne troops across the upper Rhine capitulated. Out of the whole division less than 2,500 men escaped back across the river, the majority of them wounded. Another débâcle and a shocking mistake by the generals and military planners. Another week went by under shocking conditions, the Nazis were driven back farther south, putting our lines of supply back to normal and, after two and a half weeks we were relieved at last. For the greater part of that time we had lived on army biscuits, tea and Dutch potatoes we dug out of the wet soil.

There was mud, thick, wet mud on everything, our clothes, boots and vehicles were caked with it as we slowly moved back to Nijmegen. It was the first time I could get a good view of the huge battle-scarred bridge as we crossed to the southern side. In such a short time we had come so far from western Normandy, across France, Belgium and Holland, but sadly we failed in our efforts to aid and rescue the unfortunate men of the Airborne Division.

On examination by the battalion medical officer, my wound had closed and the overhanging skin and flesh had knitted very well, so I was refused to be relieved and leave the troop. I was ordered to continue duties in the usual way but this decision was going to affect me for the rest of my life.

In 1979 my leg was classified '6–14 per cent disability indeterminate duration', combined assessment, and I was granted the miserable sum of just over two thousand Australian dollars and medical attention for that particular injury only. My other injuries and problems were disallowed on appeals. This was my miserable and disgusting reward and gratitude from a nation and its diehard Tory politicians and bureaucrats, after forfeiting six and a half years of the best young years of my life as a military conscript and fulfilling all that I did towards the defeat of the Nazi forces.

15

Winter 1944 and the Advance Across the Rhine

The rains came continuously now, with overcast skies above and mud below, as we commenced another push south-east of Nijmegen. We crossed the German border for the first time just north of the small town of Kleve but once again deep mud stopped the advance. Our armoured vehicles were getting bellied and bogged and the recovery vehicles were operating full time to drag us out, so the thrust forward was abandoned. Infantry units had to be brought up to occupy and consolidate the captured areas. The town of Kleve was just five miles from the River Rhine, and north of the Ruhr.

The weather was appalling each day, winter was ahead, and for the time being all operations switched to defence. More infantry units took over and we pulled back into Belgium, east of Brussels, to be billeted in a small school. For a short period we received regular meals prepared by the squadron cooks and, apart from the usual sentry duties at night, it was a chance to get more rest. The month of November brought snow for the first time as we worked on our vehicles, cleaning the weapons, general maintenance, changing links of damaged tracks, and straightening and taking buckles out of front and rear fenders.

In early December we moved north into the Walloon area of Belgium and for a week my tank crew was billeted with an aged Belgian couple. We used the floor of their main room to sleep on at night. Each Belgian home appeared to use a large, cast-iron pot-bellied stove for heating, the flue usually fitted to extend right across the room before its exit through the wall, for extra warmth. Wood, coal and all heating fuel were in desperately short supply and almost unobtainable, so during our movements into the surrounding countryside with our vehicles, we loaded up old fence posts, tree branches and stumps, and anything burnable that we could find, in order to provide some warmth for the old couple.

In the second week of December 1944, as the closing days of that year were approaching, we received orders to move east to the coal mining town of Sittard. Once again it was at night to prevent any air observation of our tank movements to any particular sector. German observation and spotter aircraft were always on the alert to pick out any massed movement of armour or troops, to provide their intelligence with even the scantiest information. It was a terrible night, blowing a gale with torrential rain, and as black as ink making visibility almost nil, and we had just a tiny concealed white light to follow beneath the rear of the vehicle ahead.

It was during the early hours of the morning, almost 2 a.m., when a most extraordinary incident happened. Something one could never believe possible in war. We crossed the River Meuse, so our radio information code informed us, although we could not see a thing in the inky blackness and driving rain. The area was north of the town of Maastricht and there, a slice of Belgian territory juts out like a sore thumb, about 20 square miles of it, towards the German town of Aachen, with the Nazi border to the south and east and the Dutch border on the north. We were moving north towards Amstemrade, about two miles from the German border, at a normal convoy speed, ushered by the battalion motorcycle RPs, with No. 1 Squadron ahead followed by our own squadron in the appalling conditions. We could occasionally get a blurred outline of a motorcyclist through the driving rain but we could hear nothing because of the tank engine, just the radio orders and static in our headphones, and our own internal conversations through the intercom. We must have travelled four or five miles after crossing the Meuse River through those terrible, wet, unpleasant, bleak conditions when the column halted abruptly as there were explosions up ahead. Our leading tank, totally ignorant of everything, suddenly discovered we were travelling behind a convoy of Nazi vehicles retreating to the German border. There was chaos and alarm up front. We must have been following behind them for some distance, unknowingly escorted by a Nazi motorcyclist. However, the leading tank, finding itself in such an awkward dilemma, fired through the supply vehicle in front of it and stopped dead. No one could leave the road as visibility was practically nil, so we simply remained stationary and helpless for half an hour, and the Nazi convoy got away unharmed. There were no further incidents after that unusual encounter but it slowed our movement to a crawl and in the gloom, mist and heavy rain we entered Sittard shortly after daybreak. It had been a most unusual night, but strange things happen in war and there are exceptions to every rule and every plan.

Sittard was a big Dutch coal-producing area and of course the main occupation for its inhabitants was coal mining, so we now enjoyed the luxury of using the pit head baths in between times, when the miners were below ground. Our duties and tasks were to hold a defensive line across the German border half a mile north of Sittard with a tank squadron in the forward position and a tour of three days and nights. One troop at a time for 24 hours was in the frontal area in amongst gardens and houses of the border village looking across a large expanse of No Man's Land. The front ahead was open heathland heavily mined and interwoven with trip wires, which when disturbed would fire upwards a magnesium flare to floodlight the expanse with brilliant light during the hours of darkness, an alert to warn us of any Nazi patrol.

The remainder of the squadron occupied a small village hall across the Dutch side, all in reserve and on the alert. A long wide ditch was the obstacle along the border, the access was across a small bridge which carried the road into Nazi territory. In Sittard itself, my tank crew were billeted each night on the floor of the front room of a mining family named Van Rongen. The Van Rongens had three children under 14 years and, as a reward for the use of their home, we looted and confiscated three bicycles from various houses across the frontier and gave them to the children, who were thrilled.

It was 14th December and it had started to snow again, becoming cold, miserable, and unpleasant. The Dutch population appeared to be all devout Catholics in that locality and I was surprised by some of the ridiculous practices they obediently carried out. On each Sunday morning the Catholic priest would parade from his residence to church for mass. His long white train, as he marched along in all his finery, headgear and robes was held up by two small choirboys, while ahead of him marched another small boy ringing a silver bell. When the ringing bell was heard the residents would come out of their homes, and go down on their knees, irrespective whether it was mud, slime or snow, until the priest had passed. All bystanders did the same ritual, dressed in their best clothes, down in the mud or water they would kneel until the procession had passed by, and think nothing of having soaked or stained their clothing.

On the morning of 17th December, working on our vehicles in a Sittard street, to prepare for our tour of duty across the border, we were suddenly attacked by three German aircraft. Two of them swooped down to machine-gun our position as we dived for cover, the other dropped its complement of bombs on the town. Fortunately, it was a narrow escape and no one was hit and no damage was done, but then the news was alarming. The previous night, 16th December, under cover of a thick, dense fog, the Nazis had started a huge winter offensive into the Ardennes on the American front and had taken them by surprise. Three Nazi armies, the 5th, 6th and the Panzer 7th army, with the 14th infantry division, and the 10th Panzer Division, had begun an all-out assault to reach the River Meuse and to smash their way across Belgium to the sea. Ahead of the assault they dropped hundreds of paratroops, almost to the suburbs of Paris, to attempt to sabotage bridges and important military objectives.

We could understand the situation, as it was only a few days to Christmas. The Americans, as we had discovered on so many occasions, were relaxing and taking it easy at that time of the year, when the Nazis struck. It was snowing heavily and bitterly cold and they made startling inroads into the American lines, deep into Belgium causing enormous casualties in the appalling conditions. The ensuing battles were enormous and bloody, and there was an immediate emergency. All the Allied forces north of the River Meuse – American, British, and Canadian, were all placed under British command. On 24th December, Christmas Eve, as the situation was desperate, we were ordered to move south to hold the line of the River Meuse. Through the cold biting wind, the falling snow and the blackness of the night of Christmas Eve and the early hours of Christmas Day, we were driving south to the Belgian city of Namur, where the vital highway crosses the Meuse Bridge to Brussels, Antwerp and the North Sea, a long journey of almost 90 miles from the border town of Sittard. We reached the Belgian city of Namur as daylight was breaking on Christmas morning and we halted in one of the city thoroughfares, a short distance from the bridge across the River Meuse.

Across the river was American ground, and under American command, and the outcome of the heavy fighting going on there in Ardennes controlled our future movements and orders, and our involvement in the fierce battles. If the Americans failed to stop the Nazi push towards the Meuse, we would be ordered forward to support them. In the semi-darkness of that Christmas morning, the air was biting cold, light snowflakes were fluttering in the cold breeze, and piles of snow had been pushed up on to the footpaths by all the military traffic moving through the night to cross the river ahead. We had to wait and as the light increased we were told to prepare some food for a meal and make a hot drink. There were many comments of relief from the rank and file. Our hot water container was working well. The new one had been utilised after the loss of the other in Belgium previously. The long drive from Sittard had produced plenty of exhaust flames beneath the tin making it almost at boiling point. So on that early morning of Christmas day 1944, with our spirit stove on the footpath, we prepared our banquet of hot tea, a tin of heated sausages and hard-tack, buttered biscuits, with more biscuits spread with marmalade and jam for dessert. In the cold and frosty air the menu was excellent and our hunger was satisfied.

We waited anxiously for hours. The Nazis were still pressing forward according to the scanty radio information released to us, and our thoughts were with those American boys suffering and dying on that cold Christmas morning. Huge reinforcements were being rushed forward to stem the Nazi push and we hoped it would be successful, then perhaps our intervention would not be required. Furthermore, it would hurt the integrity and pride of the US command and the American troops, if British armour had to intervene.

With all the problems of that cold Christmas period, one person was jubilant and very happy. I am referring to an important official of the Belgium province of Brabant, a Monsieur Culot-Housiaux. This Belgian patriot, a member of the resistance, was arrested on 2nd September by the vile Gestapo and taken to the Gestapo headquarters in Brussels for interrogation. As a result he was sentenced to be executed by a firing squad on 3rd September and detained in the Brussels HQ to await his fate. In the panic of destroying everything and fleeing Brussels that day, his execution did not take place and he escaped in the late afternoon just before we entered Brussels and bombarded the same Gestapo HQ that night. He remembered our divisional insignia flash on the arm of our squadron members – the shield with the ever-open eye – and he also recognised our Cromwell tanks. He lived in the Rue de Coppin, in Namur, just a short distance away, and he rushed around to greet us and shake hands with his rescuers. It was a special Christmas day for him, as he had not expected to live to see it. He brought his wife later to take a photograph as a memento and thanks, so Ian Card and Tom Canavan and I posed with him on the cold Christmas morning. He removed two bottles of 1920 rare seven-star cognac from the secret hiding place behind the fireplace in his home and presented them to us as a Christmas present.

A few hours later we heated our Christmas dinner on the footpath of that Namur street a short distance from the Meuse River bridge. Five miles away the fierce battles of the Bulge were intensifying in the Ardennes' snow. I still remember tossing a coin with Tom Canavan to decide whether it would be a can of stewed steak and vegetable or Irish stew. My choice of stewed steak won the toss and M Culot-Housiaux joined us with a toast, and a glass of his aged cognac. Our share, to celebrate Christmas Day, was half an enamel mug of that special cognac for all the crew; it gave warmth and cheer to us all as the snowflakes fluttered around us on that special day.

Christmas night was bitterly cold, as we still awaited orders, with one troop on alert, radio and sentry duty for a tour of each two hours through the night and into Boxing Day. Once again throughout Boxing Day and night we anxiously waited, anticipating a move forward at a few minutes' notice. That order never came, much to our great relief. The American troops had stemmed the Nazi onslaught and they were on the offensive pushing them back. Consequently, our long, cold wait was in vain, but thank goodness was the unanimous comment as we left Namur and moved up into Holland.

The new year of 1945 arrived and Hitler's last desperate massed attack to break through had failed. The Nazi armies' attempt to reach the River Meuse in 48 hours had also failed, as had the attempt to smash their way across Belgium to Antwerp and the Channel ports. They suffered enormous losses. It was estimated they lost 250,000 men, casualties and prisoners of war; 600 tanks and guns and more than 1,500 aircraft. American losses were heavy too, and casualties exceeded 60,000 men.

Hitler was now scraping the bottom of the barrel, with enormous losses on the eastern front and the ravages of the terrible Russian winter, and it was the beginning of the end as we began our preparations to cross the Rhine to finish that awful miserable long war. From the end of the first week of January and into February, the worst period of winter, the war became static as far as we were concerned. The weather was so bad, it seemed to rain or snow everyday, and the long nights were terribly cold and unpleasant. We were most grateful to occupy a Dutch barn, often sharing the premises with the owner's cows, all kept under cover at night. The engineers were working flat out building airfields and roads, with huge earth-moving machines and bulldozers turning the flat areas into airfields and covering the runways with steel mesh to allow aircraft to land, and bring them forward almost up to the front line for the final onslaughts ahead. The short daylight hours were often monotonous, but gave us a little more

211

time to catch up with our correspondence and a few recreational slides on the frozen waterways.

During the second week of February 1945 our operations began once more. We started attacking the area of Venraij in eastern Holland, successfully crossing into Reich territory and the town of Kevelaer. Then supported by our own First Infantry battalion we captured, after heavy fighting, the town of Xanten just a few miles from the main obstacle, the River Rhine.

On 14th February, the Canadians attacked east of Nijmegen, our old battleground, and captured Kleve, and they too reached the River Rhine ten miles or so north of our position. The build up now commenced with men, guns and armour for the big offensive to cross the Rhine.

Hitler's military forces were getting more and more hard pressed each day. On 31st January, the Russians smashed their way forward, reaching the lower Oder River just 40 miles from Berlin. More units and fresh drafts of troops were rushed to the Eastern Front on Hitler's orders, to try to stem the Russian armies crossing the River Oder. This relieved the enormous pressure and decreased the opposition for us to contend with in order to cross the Rhine in the west.

Meanwhile from numerous airfields in Britain, the airborne troops and parachutists were preparing for their massed drop across the Rhine to form a bridgehead for us to attempt to cross.

At the beginning of March 1945, the Russian forces swarmed across the River Oder, and on the night of the 23rd, the American 7th and the British 6th airborne divisions dropped out of the skies in a huge air armada across the Rhine. After an enormous artillery bombardment all night long across the river, the engineers commenced the task of bridging the Rhine with a pontoon Bailey bridge. The location and area was the German town of Rees on the eastern bank of the river, approximately halfway between Kleve and Xanten. We moved up that morning, 24th March, leading the armoured division across that hurriedly-constructed pontoon floating bridge – Hitler's last formidable barrier of the Nazi Reich.

16

The Final Defeat of Hitler's Forces and the End of the European War

We crossed the unstable pontoon bridge that morning, as the current flowing north strained the anchor cables on each bank and the floating pontoons sunk lower with the weight of our vehicles. There were no incidents, our squadron crossed safely, and we pushed on through the German town of Rees and turned north towards the town of Emmerich.

The terrible devastation of war was now becoming more evident with each mile, as Hitler's folly had cost the German nation dearly. Buildings and structures everywhere were just rubble, smashed and pulverised by the overwhelming Allied air power and our massed shelling. White flags of sheets, tablecloths and scraps of materials fluttered from any half-standing structure affording a kind of shelter to the hysterical and frightened German civilians. We added to the mess, any type of masonry or building structure showing any sign of hostility and no white flag was blasted as we moved along.

We appeared to cross and recross the Holland–Germany border a number of times until we entered the big Dutch town of Enschede, forty miles north of the Rhine crossing point. Resistance now began to increase stubbornly, with the German army still fighting fiercely. Our own supporting first battalion infantry took the brunt of the battles and the familiar names began to appear of Welsh towns, given to routes and roads, occupied and taken over by our forces.

The rainy and windy days of March were coming to an end. Intense concentration all day long from daylight to dusk, and very little sleep was getting me down, and at night I became edgy with the German shelling and intense mortar fire. It was the morning of the first day of April, and we had experienced an unpleasant night of intense shelling in an area of poor sandy heathland, with concentrations of

213

pine trees, about the only thing that would grow there. The shells had ripped into the trees scattering the shrapnel and debris everywhere and puncturing many of our storage bins. I was glad to get moving instead of being a sitting target, as we approached the region between the Vecht and the Ems rivers. A number of Germans had surrendered and I was sorting them out when Squadron Sergeant-Major Williams raced up in a jeep to tell me to get my things and get out quickly. I was going home, and I had been granted leave from the front. I thought at first it must be a joke, as it was April Fool's day and early morning, but thank goodness it was true! I was getting out for a well deserved break. My last leave had been one year and three months previously from Yorkshire. What a wonderful surprise and relief it was! My spirits soared. I grabbed my pack and kit and almost jumped into that jeep to take me back about five miles to battalion HQ.

At battalion headquarters everything was ready. My leave pass and papers were there and I was informed I could change any money, that is French, Belgian, or Dutch currency, and the new currency German marks that had been quickly printed and introduced by the Allies to defeat the Black market, at the staging camp at Calais on the English Channel coast. I had not drawn any pay since May 1944 and there was a credit entry in my soldier's pay book that I could draw from, also at Calais, in English pounds.

I had a few French and Belgian francs, proceeds of a few exchanges for cigarettes, one Dutch guilder and 20 American dollars, proceeds of a secret sale of a German Luger pistol to an American soldier. The Luger I had confiscated from a Nazi 55 lieutenant on the outskirts of Beauvais, kicking myself for not retaining more of them instead of tossing them away, they were in such demand from the American troops. I also had two one pound notes, two half-crowns and a shilling coin I carried in my pocket, the residue of my last pay in England, so I was rich!

An army truck now conveyed me and a number of fellow men from the other squadrons of the battalion, back to the Dutch town of Enschede. More fortunate members from the other units of the division and the 30th Corps joined us to travel south west to Holland to a railhead where the rehabilitated and repaired railway had reached. Pulled by a British locomotive and made up of a train of old wooden slat hard-seat continental carriages, we began a slow journey through Belgium and France to Calais. I sat on those hard wooden seats for ten hours through the night as the train slowly and monotonously steamed towards Calais, leaving me with a sore backside when we reached our destination.

However, it was worth it all. I changed my currency, withdrew thirty pounds of my pay, and was given a civilian food ration card for seven days. I spent the night at the transit camp, crossed the Channel in the dark, early hours of that next day to reach Dover in daylight, when my seven days' leave began. There was a special reserved train for London and on my arrival I just made it across the city to Paddington Station to catch the 9 a.m. express to South Wales. Just like all passenger trains in wartime it was jam packed and I travelled the whole distance to Cardiff sitting on my pack in the train corridor. There were now no deafening roaring tank engines, no gunfire, no whining and bursting shells, and for me and it was wonderful watching the peaceful tranquil countryside slip by as the train sped on. It was April and springtime, the most beautiful season of the year. I arrived in Cardiff at midday and I raced across the back streets to Queen Street Station to catch the train up the Rhymney Valley and home. During my years of absence my three sisters Joyce, Edna and Toots had all been married and left home and I had been unable to attend any of the weddings. Edna now lived in London.

No one at home even knew that I was on my way home. They would all get a big surprise. I removed my army boots as the train steamed away on the last stage of my long journey, and I put on my civilian shoes from my pack. What a relief it was too! I had suffered the tightness of those boots almost continuously night and day without being able to take them off for the whole of the past year. I watched all the old familiar places pass by as I looked out of the carriage window and I had the compartment all to myself as the train entered the long tunnel and then the stop at Caerphilly station. The old castle was still there with the sun glistening on the waters of the moat, as it was likely to be hundreds of years after I had passed on.

Hengoed soon appeared with the mighty stone viaduct across the valley bringing back memories of Grandfather and his gnarled hands, worn by the constant heavy toil of cutting those huge carved stones. Pengam station next, time for me to get out, with a grunt and a scowl from Mr Mullet the ticket collector, as I produced my military pass, I made my way up to the black path passing the old familiar Haunted House where I had so often raced past in fear as a small boy, through the Welsh swing kissing gates, on to Gwerthonor Road, at the top of the Grammar School Hill. It was early afternoon, there was no one around and the road was deserted and quiet. I reached Oak Cottage and went around to the rear, opened the back door and called out, 'Anyone at home?' My mother was ironing on the kitchen table with the old flat iron, and she almost dropped it with surprise as she looked up and saw me. Poor old Mum! There was a trace of tears in her eyes as she greeted me and she said, 'I thought I would never see you again, are you all right?' The coal fire in the big grate was burning brightly as usual, with the big cast-iron kettle singing on the hob, and within minutes the magic, reviving cup of tea was made and sitting steaming hot on the table with slices of the Welsh batch loaf and delicious Caerphilly cheese. What a luxury it was for me, I had not seen any bread, let alone taste it, since I left Gosport for Normandy in June 1944.

I sat in the old armchair – Grandfather's old chair – put my feet up and relaxed. Joan, my sister, would come home from Hengoed Girls' Grammar School on the 4.30 p.m. train. Then I decided to go and see my father at the Gelligaer bowling and recreation area, where he was the curator, and I wondered about my bicycle. I had not seen it for such a long time, and it would be such a change to ride the bike once again, but my hopes were dashed. My mother informed me that the bike had been stolen. Trevor had used it to ride to work and it had been taken from the parking area where he usually left it. My mother did not like to tell me in her letters, hoping it would be recovered, but sadly it was never seen again. I blessed the thief who stole it in anger and hoped he would fall off and break his neck!

However, the family soon came home, very surprised to see me, so we all enjoyed a long talk. My mother then insisted that I go along to see my Aunty May so I carried out her instructions. Joyce was now living at Cefn Forest, up the long hill from Britannia Colliery, the hill my father always referred to as Hill 60. It had such a steep gradient to the top of the other side of the Valley, and by the time one reached the top, one would be a thousand feet above sea level and worn out, was the explanation he always gave.

Toots, my other sister, was living at Penpedaerheol, commonly called Penpeter, because it was such a mouthful. This place was a small village nestling above the picturesque 'Green Meadow' and my old haunts as a boy, the familiar woods we called the 'jungle', on the outskirts of Gelligaer from which the local council and the parish obtained its name. Here stands the old Norman Church, where my parents were married and my brother Gwyn was buried. I would put off those two visits until the following day. Being accustomed to so little rest and sleep, I stayed up till 3 a.m. that night talking to my father before the big warm coal fire. Even then I could not sleep, everything was so quiet, and the bed was too soft, after laying my head on the hard earth for so long, and I was up again as usual at daylight.

The second day of my leave I did walk up Dad's Hill 60 to see Joyce and her husband Bill. Bill, like so many others connected with the coal industry, was in a reserved occupation and not liable for military service. Then I went along to see Toots, whose husband was absent in the air force and stationed in southern England. I went on to help my father, doing a few odd jobs for him around the area, and then we called into the Plough Inn to meet and talk to some of the locals, getting all the advice in the world on how to bring the war to an end. For the next four days, I took things easy and, between the frequent showers of rain, I walked across the mountains and the moors just to see the old places once again. It was springtime and the lush countryside was beginning to put on its wonderful show.

The time was short and passed by so quickly. Early on the seventh day I said all my goodbyes once more to depart to Cardiff to catch the 9 a.m. express train to London and to see my sister Edna on my way back to Dover. I arrived at Paddington station just after midday, caught the tube to Hyde Park Corner, walked through the park to Westbourne Grove in west London, and found sister Edna's address. The house was owned by a Jewish baker and the four floors were let in flats. Edna and her husband, Tom, occupied the lower floor, and they had a caretaker arrangement with the owner. Edna did some of the cleaning of the access areas and Tom worked at an aircraft factory in west London but I had to leave that evening to catch a train from Waterloo station to Dover to cross the Channel on the midnight military ferry. The bombing had ceased at that time thank goodness. Hitler was almost brought to his knees and the VI and V2 rockets fired from inside Germany were out of range. I had a meal with them both when Tom arrived home, and caught up with all the news and told them what had happened to me. They came with me by bus to Waterloo station to see me off on the 8.15 p.m. train to Dover, so my leave had come to an end. It was back to war!

It was a cold, uneventful journey across the English Channel back to the transit camp at Calais. This was my fourth crossing to the European mainland across the North Sea and the English Channel in five long years and I hoped good fortune would hold out for me, and this journey would be the last.

On arrival at the transit camp, we were issued with a couple of army

217

blankets and a stretcher-type bed, with instructions that breakfast was at 6 a.m. and we were to move on at 6.45 a.m. Once again it was the long, slow, cold journey sitting on the continental wooden slat seats in unheated, poor carriages, up through France, Belgium and Holland until we arrived at the dismounting area in the early hours of the next day. We received a hot drink and a meal and were then ushered into service corps vehicles east across the Rhine pontoon bridge, to the corp headquarters then on to the division areas to our own battalion HQ. One of our own supply vehicles took me forward to my squadron and about 10 a.m. I joined up with my troop, back to my tank once again.

During my absence the battalion had advanced about 20 miles and the greater part of the time had been taken up with big artillery bombardments softening up the areas ahead. I had been relieved for the period of my absence by another colleague. I took over and he was glad to get out of it, so I was back in familiar surroundings with my crew once again.

It was a cool bright sunny morning as we pushed forward, on 15th April 1945. Our opposition was getting weaker, and we were alarmed by the number of young boys, members of the Hitler Youth, who rushed into the line to oppose us and to halt our advance. It was a sad, unpleasant affair concentrating all our enormous fire power against these young inexperienced youths; some of them maybe were young fanatics but the majority were just driven and bullied forward to their fate by their brutal Nazi officers. So many of them we captured were terrified, and in tears, and glad to be out of it. That same afternoon as the storm clouds gathered for a huge downpour of rain, we smashed into the town of Lingen. The damage was enormous; one of the biggest structural shell-torn buildings was the Lingen Hotel which was on fire. In this area too we came upon and experienced for the first time one of Hitler's autobahns adjoining the main autobahn, north-east of Bremen.

Night after night we were shelled as we harboured for the hours of darkness and although pushing forward each day we never seemed to catch up and overrun this artillery. Our greatest hazard appeared to be the danger from land-mines, cunningly and cleverly buried in the road which sadly caused the death of five of my troop colleagues, including Bob Bush. We were engaging a small number of stubborn Nazi defenders, when Bob Bush's vehicle hit a mine at the verge of the road, but it wasn't just one mine, it had been cunningly wired to a string of five others along the road. They all exploded beneath the tank belly turning it into a roaring inferno in seconds. The crew had no hope of an escape and died in the awful conflagration. This became one of the most unpleasant and disturbing incidents of my life during the war years and I shall always remember it. Afterwards, I climbed into the cooled-down, derelict hulk of that Cromwell and lifted out the blackened, powdery, skeleton frames of the three crew members in its turret for burial, carefully laying each one to rest in a hurried grave by the roadside as darkness came down that night. I tried many times later to write to Bob's parents but I gave it up, I could not, and just did not know how to express it in a truthful way.

I did not write any more letters of condolence, because I had had enough and today as I write these lines, I know that his parents are long passed away, but should I have told them how he died? Would it have increased their sorrow or would it have been more truthful and merciful than the cold yellow telegram simply saying in black print that he was 'Killed in Action'? It is an answer that I shall never know. The death of Bob Bush hurt me deeply, as he had been such a jovial happy-go-lucky and troopmate for so long, and escape together six months previously made that friendship even closer.

The following day, 24th April, another troopmate, Stan McIntyre, died in a foolish accident, tampering with a jammed round in the breach of a confiscated Luger pistol. The remaining original members of my squadron were getting very few.

On the morning of 25th April we stormed into a place called Ahlhorn and then turned east to the small town of Wildeshausen. Both places were undamaged with every building flying a white sheet of tablecloth and there was no opposition. Everything was quiet and subdued. There were no Nazi swastikas any more – they had all mysteriously disappeared. Near this area we crossed the Hunte River unhindered and drove on to the main autobahn to Bremen about 25 miles ahead. Bremen, like so many other important German cities had been pulverised many times by the RAF and American Fortresses and, as we neared the southern areas, the evidence of the massed bombings was clear and vivid with the rubble and the mess of smashed buildings. We did not enter the city as the damage was so terrible, but skirted the southern side and pushed on. Our role as the reconnaissance spearhead of the armoured division was to press on and leave the mopping up and the occupation areas to the units behind us, so our next vital objective and prize was the city of Hamburg, about 62 miles further north. The opposition was scattered and light; middle-aged men and Hitler youths, drafted from auxilliary units into fighting defence forces for the last stand, surrendered; also many women auxiliary aides, so almost unruffled we reached Eldorf and the outskirts of Sittensen, on the Oste River, on the afternoon of 27th April.

That evening we harboured as a troop only, about two miles ahead of the squadron, on a patch of undulating ground dotted with a few trees and a single farmhouse about 600 yards behind us. We had already searched the house, occupied by four elderly Germans. We carried out our usual duties, preparations, and maintenance, dug in as normal and made ourselves a meal, and each tank in the troop detailed for a two-hour roster stretch of sentry duty and radio watch. It was a night threatened by rain, with heavy low black clouds making the atmosphere as dark as ink, visibility was practically nil and there was no moon.

My crew had already completed a two-hour tour of sentry and radio watch, there were no incidents, and everything was silent and still. The time was just after midnight and we were trying to settle down for a few hours, in our tomb below the belly of our tank. I was suddenly disturbed and alerted by a member of the crew on watch crawling in to report there was an unusual scratching sound emitting through the gloom some distance away in front of us, and should he awaken and alert the troop leader? We all cautiously crawled out, with pistols drawn, to listen and investigate the sounds. I had the Sten gun which I always kept by my side at night. It was dark but I too picked up the slight noise out of the gloom, which sounded to me as if someone was dragging or pulling some object intermittently along the ground. It was impossible to estimate the distance from its source, so I ordered the sentry to immediately alert the troop leader. Within minutes the troop leader was with us and gave whispered orders to alert every man to stand-to quickly and each gunner to climb silently on to the vehicles, to man the Vickers machine-guns mounted on the turrets and to await a command to open fire. Suddenly out in the darkness we heard what appeared to be an American-accented muffled voice call out the words, 'Any GIs there? Please help me.'

The first reaction and thought that rushes to every man's mind was that it could be a trap or a cunning trick. There was hesitation, and then the troop leader called out, 'Halt! Whoever goes there, call out the last three letters of the alphabet!' In the tense atmosphere I expected the order to fire but it was certainly quick thinking by our troop officer who whispered to me, 'It's not a Kraut, hold your fire it's a Yank!' Thank heavens I hope he is correct, I thought, as we went forward and stumbled across a man on the ground who muttered,

'Help me, bud, I'm wounded!' To our amazement as we pulled him forward and had a quick look with a pencil torch, we discovered that he was a Canadian corporal, an escaped prisoner of war, who had been shot with one bullet in the back of the left thigh and another bullet in the right foot. We eased him down hurriedly into the trench beneath my tank to check his wounds by torchlight, and to find a few answers as to who he might be, and how he came there, because we were the most northerly advanced Allied troops in that part of north-west Germany.

We made our newcomer as comfortable as possible, tied up his bad injuries as best we could until assistance came at daylight, and gave him some food, cigarettes and a stiff drink of a half a mug of French cognac. He told us that he had escaped from a Stalag POW camp, much to our surprise, about two miles away from our present position. The nervy and edgy Nazi guards had fired at him in his escape and assumed he had been killed. He lay in agony until darkness, then he had dragged himself and crawled the whole distance, with hopes of what scanty information he had, of meeting up with what he believed to be American troops. The information was promptly radioed to the squadron and we discovered that the command knew all the time of the Stalag POW camp in the area. I asked about the order given to call out the last three letters of the alphabet. The explanation in reply was if it was a Kraut, he would pronounce the last English letter in our way as Zed but the Americans always use Zee. I gave him full marks for his quick thinking.

The next thing I received was an order to accompany the troop leader through the pitch blackness of the night on a compass bearing to a map reference of the location of the POW camp, to try to rec-onnoitre the area, to get all the information possible about the guards and, if possible contact the inmates behind the wire and then to radio the information promptly back to the squadron commander. As a soldier I was familiar with all kinds of patrols, but this was one thing I had never done before. By pencil torchlight beneath the tank we set out the detailed military map carefully and accurately, adjusting it to comply with the points of the compass and set our bearing to the exact point of the reference point given to us. I removed my tank suit, and slipped two extra Sten magazines into the inside pocket of my battledress jacket, and pulled a balaclava over my head.

The troop leader gave his orders to Sergeant Evans to take over, keep the Canadian comfortable till assistance at first light, and arranged a password for our return. I still remember that password, much in common with what had just happened, it was 'Zeider Zee'. Armed with all the detailed information we could get from the Canadian and only the illuminated face of the compass and the needle to guide us, we set out into the unknown, and the blackness of the night. I followed in single file about two feet behind, visibility was almost nil and many times we had to move to the left or the right to pass obstructions, such as clumps of trees, hedges and buildings and then pick up the direction bearing again to get on course. Underfoot it was difficult, too, with broken ground, potholes, mounds and fences. We had travelled for approximately three-quarters of an hour. It was 0120 hours and the visibility improved, so we could only assume that the moon had risen behind the heavy black clouds, giving just enough light for us to pick out objects much further ahead and to help us move more quickly. More buildings confronted us – they must have been the village – and from our instructions the camp was approximately a quarter of a mile beyond, with the terrain rising slightly higher, so we were on the right track.

After another five minutes or so walking silently forward, we moved and diverged to our right to avoid a farm and its building which we had also been told to look out for. When we skirted this obstacle and picked up the bearing once more the country was flat and open, there appeared to be no background but we could make out the huge fenced area of the camp with just blurred outlines of the inside buildings. There were no lights or signs of any perimeter searchlights anywhere, as I was expecting. As we got closer we picked out one of the watch towers on the outside perimeter double fences, which also was in darkness and unmanned, and the lieutenant remarked to me that the guards must have known our forces were in the vicinity, for it seemed as if they had fled. We made our way around the perimeter, some distance away from the outer fence and hidden in the darkness, until we found the big, double high-wire gates, two sets of them in the outer and inner boundary fences. They were all closed tightly and appeared to be unprotected by any Nazi personnel. Our next task was to move along the boundary to find the nearest building to the perimeter fence. We discovered the outline of one we estimated was about the distance of half a football field away, and this would have to be our target. I did not realise how difficult it was to find and locate suitable rocks and stones, stirring around with my boot in the darkness, it must have taken ten minutes or so to locate half a dozen sizeable stones. I removed my jacket and let fly with a throwable piece of rock over the top of the high wires at the outlined building. It was such a big target I had to hit it somewhere. We heard the 'clunk' of the rock hitting the target, so I aimed a second and a third stone all on target. It was amusing to me then to pick up the sound of the muffled voices of some of the occupants, and I guess I would not like to repeat what was being said by those inmates or the remarks, probably very uncomplimentary, as the stones hit their sleeping quarters at 1.30 a.m. The officer went up to the wire and I threw more stones until we heard a door open so the pencil torch was flashed repeatedly hoping someone would see it and come forward to investigate. I threw more stones and the sounds of the muffled voices increased, so at last someone must have seen the torch signal. I picked up the Sten gun and waited back in the darkness. Two shadowy figures appeared silently at the inner wire fence and the lieutenant called out in low tones across the gap between the two fences. I heard him inquire if they were British prisoners of war and what was the situation inside the camp. He identified himself and mentioned my rank and name, and instructed them to convey a message to the person in command to the effect that leading units of his battalion would arrive at dawn just after first light. The inmates believed all the German guards had fled, more figures arrived at the wire and there was a buzz of excitement as the news spread. I was told afterwards that the commander of that section was a captain of a sunken merchant ship, Captain Evans, who came, much to my surprise, from Cardiff and that the men were merchant seamen kept apart from the military and airmen.

They were instructed to keep their heads down and take shelter in case the Germans mortared the area in retaliation. The lieutenant wished them well and we made our way back to the troop quickly with the improved visibility, on the opposite return compass bearing, gave the password as we approached, and rejoined our colleagues safely. The information was radioed back to the squadron and the battalion, and then on to the brigade and divisional command for the wheels to start turning for assistance and arrangement of transport for all those POWs.

Half an hour before dawn we were standing-to ready to move forward as the squadron arrived. We reached the road and, as daylight came, we passed and detoured around a number of road blocks prepared for resistance but they had all been abandoned and we entered the village and soon reached the open gates of the camp and the excited prisoners of war.

I shook hands with so many men that morning – soldiers, airmen, and merchant seamen a real mixture – and even met up with one of our lost troopmates in Belgium, Ian Card; they were all free now and anxious to be repatriated and on their way home. I had a long talk with a merchant seaman named Ellis whose home was in Hengoed, although I did not know him. I asked him to call my parents to give them some reassurance and news. I tied up a few things into a small package, including a couple of wristwatches from my gatherings and confiscations along the way. He made a special visit bearing the news to my mother, who was excited and thrilled, and delivered the package to her safely. I received this news in a letter just two weeks later.

Another extraordinary incident occurred that morning also, taking me back to my schooldays. As I mingled amongst all those happy and excited men exchanging greetings and thanks for their liberation after four and five years in captivity, I saw one face which looked familiar, and pondered where I had seen it before. With exclamation and surprise I said to myself, 'No – it can't possibly be!' I stared again, that person was dressed in his air-force clothing and I walked across to him, offered my hand to him and I said, 'You can go home now Mr Mathews, it's all over for you.' He looked at me and took my outstretched hand and, as he shook my hand, he said quietly, 'How do you know my name?' I said, 'How could I ever forget it? I can still feel those blows across my head from you when you were trying to force into me trigonometry and algebra in Bargoed School in 1931.'

He released my hand and stepped back with a surprised exclamation, 'No!' I said, 'I was the schoolboy you annoyed so much by always addressing me as "Aalway", instead of "Allway".' He put his hand to his brow and broke down with emotion. He said, 'I remember you now, I am so sorry.' I felt humiliated and embarrassed with what had happened and I said, 'All is forgiven, I understand, I have seen and witnessed so many others give way to their feelings in different situations in this war and I have reached that point so many times myself.' He recovered and apologised and told me he had been shot down during a raid against Bremerhaven in 1943, he had bailed out injured and sustained a broken leg when landing, so he became a prisoner of war. I tried to cheer him up with the reassurance that he would soon get home. He gave me his address in the Ely suburb of Cardiff and made me promise that I would pay him a visit when I returned. I spoke to him for 15 minutes, all the time that could be spared, told him what had happened and our progress through from Normandy, and also the fate of some of my schoolmates. He remembered them all. I wished him well; our halt with those happy men had come to an end as transports began to arrive to evacuate them back to Holland. We had orders too. We had to push on to our next objective.

It was 29th April 1945 and we were moving along the Bremen to the Hamburg autobahn 25 miles south-west of the southern suburbs of Hamburg. We were getting reports that the Russians had encircled Berlin and that street fighting there was desperate and bloody, as Hitler made his last stand and American advanced units had contacted the Russians on the lower regions of the Elbe.

Our progress was cautious and steady and, on the last day of April and into the first day of May, we entered the southern areas of the city of Hamburg. The mess was shocking as the city had been turned into rubble by the massive Allied air raids, and thousands of civilians had perished in the devastation and the enormous fires. We were now just about 30 miles from the Baltic Sea. To enter the city proper would have been slow and time wasting, and once again we left this task to the units behind. Our centre line of advance turned north-west towards Buxtehude and the rich, fertile country along the valley of the Elbe estuary to the North Sea. On 2nd May we entered the town of Stade.

These were the final days of the war and there appeared to be no more serious opposition. We commandeered houses and buildings for our accommodation, ordering the German occupants out. It was the end of digging-in and the cold hard earth. The country was rich rolling downs with big homes and Nazi hunting lodges. I pushed my way into one of them a few miles beyond Stade and souvenired a beautiful old ornamental German pipe, which incidentally was left at Oak Cottage and still on display 40 years later.

On 4th May 1945, between the town of Stade and Assel on the banks of the Elbe estuary, I fired my last shots in anger at that Second World War! At that point the river was easily two miles wide, if not more, and along the opposite northern side a ship was moving downstream towards the mouth. We elevated the gun to its maximum range and fired five shells at this ship, but the distance was too great, it was out of our range. The shells fell short into the water harmlessly. I kept the brass shell case from the final shot with the intention of taking it back home but, sadly, it disappeared through the efforts of a light-fingered thief near the city of Bonn in the winter of 1945.

It was early morning of 5th May and our vigilance was easing. We relaxed a little with all the precautionary methods of war and were expecting at any time what we had hoped and had waited for for years, the ceasefire and the end. Our position on the evening of that date was 35 miles from the German port of Cuxhaven, our final objective at the mouth of the Elbe estuary, so at dawn the next morning we moved on once more. Hitler was finished and General Jodle had begun the surrender negotiations to take effect at 2141 hours on 7th May 1945. As we advanced and pushed on we began to think more of our own preservation. We kept off the roads, bounding along the green countryside in case of mines. It was the wrong time to get blown up! We occupied a German farmhouse that night, and everyone was calm but excited, just waiting for it all to end. By 11 a.m. on the morning of the 8th, we were two miles outside the port of Cuxhaven and we halted. The war had officially ended but it was still going on for us, as there was trouble in the port area, where one of the Nazi naval ships would not surrender.

We waited an hour and then slowly moved into Cuxhaven heading for the docks. The Germans had surrendered their arms and there were various stacks of rifles and dumps of pistols to meet us along the way. The defiant Nazis aboard the ship still did not hoist the surrender signal, moving slowly backwards and forwards in the water. We surrounded the dock area ready for the order to blast it from all directions. Our patience was wearing thin and we were getting edgy when they finally gave up but, with the stupid traditional rules of navel warfare, we were forbidden to board that ship to round up those last defiant Nazis. Only navy personnel with the rules of salvage and surrender were allowed to carry this out. At least this is what we were told, so it angered me and all my troopmates.

All over Europe the celebrations of victory were in progress. We quickly drove away to occupy and take over the Nazi barracks to make ourselves comfortable and to await the outcome of it all. There was new hope then, and for me, the war in Europe officially ended at 1350 hours on the afternoon of 8th May 1945.

17

The Allied Occupation and My Last Year of Military Service

On that night 8th May 1945, a curfew was ordered. No German citizen was allowed on the streets or in the open after 8 p.m. otherwise they risked arrest. A non-fraternisation order was also issued and we were not allowed to speak to any German national or have any contact with them at all, except in the course of duty. There were other problems, too, as food was desperately scarce for the population and the hundreds of thousands of displaced persons, many of them transported to work under Hitler's rule and many of them traitors and volunteers working for the Nazi regime. Everything was in a shocking mess and those days of occupation at Cuxhaven were hectic.

Many of the east European nationals had to be rounded up and directed into a displacement camp and in the unprotected areas, bands of them began to attack and molest German homes, for revenge, loot and reward. We were compelled to enforce the rules of law and on some of our patrols we fired over their heads to subdue them. There were problems also with the demarkation line between the Russians and the Allies, along the line of the Elbe River. It was understandable to us, as they had struck deeply across the Elbe in many places, and had naturally occupied the areas. There were all kinds of uncertainties amongst us. There was the fear of the antagonistic militarism of Churchill, and his belief that we should turn against the Russians, or perhaps, an order to pack up for a move to the east against the Japs, so everyone was confused.

However, things settled down a little, and soon we were ordered to move south to pass in and hand over our armoured vehicles, to resort back to a Guards Infantry Regiment once more. The time had come for us to part with the faithful Cromwell and our days as a tank unit had come to an end. We drove in convoy some 30 miles south. Colonel

Windsor Lewis stood in a jeep at the roadside taking his last salute from his armoured-tank battalion. We reached an assembly area to vacate the tanks for the last time, everyone sorting out their bits and pieces and various keepsakes and treasures from the ammunition boxes and stowing containers, clefts and crannies inside the vehicle.

My last effort was to conceal the last fired empty shellcase inside my greatcoat; I cut into the faded paint on the turret roof my name and address, the date and the motto of my old school – *Tu'ar Goleuni* – Towards the Light – and I said goodbye to that faithful vehicle for the last time. Our transport now became the squadron army trucks and we were taken to a small country village astride the main Hamburg railway line to the south. There was a small siding at the railway station, which appeared to be an important junction in the transport communication system of the Nazi railway. It was our duty to take over this area with one troop on a 24-hour roster of guard duty. Our mess hall became the ground floor of the commandeered café hotel on the village square. A number of houses were also taken over, the occupants were ordered out for us to use as billets. The long hot summer of 1945 was approaching and our daily life became easy, relaxing and enjoyable. We were five miles away from the remainder of the battalion and we were getting a well deserved rest after nearly six years of war. By the middle of June 1945, we were back to the usual daily army routine, but if we were free of duties, our tasks ended at 3 p.m., so we made good use of a swimming hole in the stream flowing at the bottom of the village and enjoyed the warm lazy days of summer.

It was reassuring that the Japanese War was approaching the end and we would not be required to take part in the Far East engagements; so everyone was thinking and hoping that the days of demobilisation and the return to civilian life were getting nearer. The Allied military government was set and now in full control and the occupation zones of the Allies were sorted out.

At the beginning of July we packed up once again to move to a British occupation zone in the Ruhr, the terrible devastated area all around the city of Cologne. We crossed the Rhine once more over the pontoon bridge at Rees moving south on the west side of the river until we came to the damaged outskirts of the devastated city on the west bank. The massive road bridge across the river was a sorry sight, blown up and smashed through its centre, it bowed its wide road into the water, with twisted girders, rails and bituminous road remnants causing white ripples in the flow of the river. Alongside, the military

228

pontoon bridge, the only access to the city, stretched across the water, dwarfed by the massive broken structure by its side. We crossed over the unstable floating pontoons supporting the narrow bridge, straining the anchor cables, and dipping slightly with the weight of each vehicle. Cologne was now a sea of rubble, broken and smashed buildings with a centre clearance made for moving traffic along the streets. In the midst of it all, about a quarter of a mile from the river, standing out like a sentinel above the devastated city, was the cathedral and, although badly damaged, it appeared to me to be the only building standing, and identifiable as its original structure. What a shocking mess! However could they rebuild and replace it all? Casualties, too, from the years of bombing must have been enormous.

We drove on through the city, where thousands of Germans still existed, living in cellars, broken smashed remnants of houses and shelters erected from bricks and rubble of what was once their houses. We reached the autobahn north to drive on to our destination, the area known as Mannheim, the same name as the Germany city of Mannheim. We took over an undamaged German barracks, well fitted out and comfortable, and this was our temporary accommodation in order to supervise an attached Nazi prisoner of war camp and a huge Russian displaced persons camp. The German army prisoners were confined in their own camp behind high barbed-wire enclosures, which had been Allied prisoner camps just a short time previously when Hitler reigned supreme. They were gradually being sorted out and allowed to return to their German homes. We controlled the gates of these camps and kept law and order.

All the internal workings and day-to-day routine in the Russians' camp was controlled by their own officials and they, too, were gradually sorted out with batches being repatriated back to the Soviet Union. I had my suspicions that some of these groups being taken away were volunteers working for the Nazis, by the way they were closely guarded and kept apart from everyone as they departed, and I guessed there was disciplinary punishment awaiting them when they reached the Soviet Zone.

I saw many displaced persons' camps and gained much knowledge about the East European inmates in that last year of occupation; it was always the Russians who were the most disciplined and organised. In that particular camp at Mannheim, every morning at 6 a.m., every able-bodied individual, male and female, was assembled in a long column of fours in military order to march and jogtrot about five miles across the countryside. As they marched they sang Russian songs in the massed chorus which echoed against the hills in the silence of the early morning. It reminded me of the custom back home.

It was our duty also to scrutinise them in and out of the gates in case anything they carried was looted or stolen, or being smuggled out for sale on the black market, or smuggled in from proceeds of looting isolated properties. Many Germans were moving along the main roads and autobahns, riding bicycles and carrying all their possessions, endeavouring to return to their original homes. They often fell prey to marauding Poles and Baltic nationals, and so often we went out in pairs and threes voluntarily to try to apprehend these terrorists. There were murders and mysterious deaths occurring daily but there was little we could do about it; there was no civil police administration at that time.

The days went by and it became 26th July 1945, another birthday for me – my 26th – but, just another uneventful ordinary day, with heavy showers of rain. The wasted years of my life were getting longer. The following day the radio reports from the BBC informed us that an ultimatum had been given to the Japs to surrender and lay down their arms or otherwise face the consequences. The ultimatum was rejected and of course one week later they regretted it. About this time we were given an order to move from the Mannheim area, away from all its problems, into the scattered residential town of Bergisch Gladbach five miles east of Cologne. We were billeted there in two three-storeyed houses opposite the burgermaster's office and the town hall, across the square in the centre of the town. There was no visible damage in this small town and we appeared to be in the better class residential area, away from the industries and the heavy bombing. My accommodation with my troop was on the second and third floors of the building, the ground floor of which had been a stationery and paper shop. By this time everyone, including myself, had gained possession of a German-army mattress, illegally or otherwise, and it made sleeping much more comfortable than on the bare floorboards.

Once gain we were separated from the battalion, which made things a lot easier. Except for a few parades with the squadron a great deal of our time was spent in Cologne itself, on humanitarian exercises, trying to get some organisation in the city, searching through miles of destruction trying to sort out the children, the sick and infirm. Food was desperately short but we somehow managed to get them a little to eat, until their own German civilian organisations were set up to take over under the control of the Allied military Government.

It was on 6th August 1945 that we heard the news, towards the end

230

of a beautiful summer's day, that in consequence of the Japs refusing to surrender and lay down their arms, the first atomic bomb was dropped on Hiroshima. Sadly, we no longer had the powerful tank radios to pick up the news broadcasts from London and the BBC, but one enterprising member of my troop produced a Nazi valve wireless set, scrounged on the black market in Cologne in exchange for some of his hoarded cigarettes. He successfully got it in working order from the mains supply in our billet, and three days later, 9th August, we heard the announcement that Russia had declared war on Japan. It appeared to be a little too late, because that night also was broadcast the news that the second atom bomb had been dropped on Nagasaki, with all its terrible destruction, appalling casualties and radiation sickness.

On the day previously, it was pleasing to hear, too, that the United States, the UK, Russia, France and other nations signed a London agreement to include a charter for an international tribunal to set in motion the trial of the Nazi war criminals.

On 12th August, I was included in a party of twelve sergeants to visit the terrible extermination camp at Belsen. We travelled up through Ruhr then east to Hanover. The Belsen site was approximately 20 miles north of Hanover, and about 40 miles south east of Bremen. It was an unforgettable experience, as the awful rotting smell of death still lingered everywhere. Nazi and SS prisoners of war were still digging and cleaning up the massed graves and I did not envy any of those officials and British troops directing operations there. I was glad to get away from the place. It made me very thankful that we had pushed north-east towards Bremen and not east, or it might have been our task to enter and overrun that shocking Nazi concentration and extermination camp. On our return journey I saw the mess and destruction of Solingen, Düsseldorf, Wuppertal and Dortmund and the awful results of what war can do to cities and their civilian populations. Wuppertal was the biggest interest to me because its public transport system had been the monorail, with transport cars suspended above the roadway, but the majority of it, just like all the buildings, was broken, with cars still hanging precariously from the smashed rails all over the place. We arrived back at Bergisch Gladbach before darkness that night. It had been a long and eventful day with scenes never to be forgotten.

Two days later, we were warned that we were to make another move to a German army barracks about a mile north of Bergisch Gladbach, on top of a hill overlooking the surrounding area, to be all together once more as a battalion. This barracks was partly damaged by Allied bombing but there was enough room for us all. It was excellent accommodation and comfortable and of course it suited the command, the RSM and the drill sergeant-majors, because it had a huge barrack square.

The 14th August 1945 was an exciting day for me and for millions around the world, with the wonderful announcement that the Japs had unconditionally surrendered and the Second World War had finally come to an end . . .

In London the wheels were put in motion in the Coalition Government to prepare for the hundreds of thousands of servicemen to return in an orderly fashion back to civilian life. Ernest Bevin brought out his age and service points system for the demobilisation. To me it was unfair, most points were allotted for age, and the much older married men with far less service took preference over my group.

I became the squadron education sergeant with two assistants, and all ranks of the squadron received two hours' instruction each day of either Maths, everyday affairs and English. I taught the English lessons, chiefly all the rudiments and correct procedures of grammar, spelling, punctuation, letter writing etc. We also started a battalion newspaper with the support of Major Parish, the squadron commander, a troop lieutenant as editor, and myself as his understudy. The purpose of this was to publish all kinds of news and the plans of members of the battalion due for discharge, news from home towns, interesting letters, comments, jokes and news in the battalion. We could get it printed for next to nothing by a local German printer and the small price would cover all expenses. We produced just two weekly editions before we ran foul of diehard Colonel Windsor Lewis, the commanding officer. He stopped it immediately, and reprimanded everyone concerned, as it was contrary to all good order and discipline! That was the end of our newspaper.

August turned into September, autumn and winter lay ahead, and our recreational time turned to football. Below the barracks there was an excellent football field lined and marked, complete with goalposts, so we commenced our inter-squadron games. We formed a battalion team, and our relations with the German population were improving, as the non-fraternisation rule and curfew were both abolished and we opposed local German teams quite often.

At the beginning of October, we had a wonderful trip to the Grand Duchy of Luxembourg. One of the senior officers had some connection with the grand duke, now in full control of his state, and a football match was arranged with the Luxembourg state team. We were housed and entertained in the barracks of the guard attached to the Caserne-Royal, the duke's palace. It was very amusing to me and all my colleagues to see everyone in uniform – soldiers of all ranks and the police – salute us each time they passed by. On one occasion they turned out the whole guard for a general salute just for me and a party of four members of my troop. We had never before experienced such VIP treatment.

At the beginning of October we were on the move again as a complete battalion, north to the Baltic Sea and the port of Lubeck. The demarkation line between the Allied administration and the Russians had been agreed upon and the area east of this line was to be Russian occupied territory which later was to become part of the East German Republic. The Russians occupied Lubeck and we were to take over as they withdrew east across the harbour boundary. The demarkation line extended along the east side of Lubeck harbour entrance, south along the east side of the big lake, Ratse Burger See south again, and along the east side of another lake, the Sohaal See, east of the Lubeck–Elbe Kanal to the eastern side of the town of Lauenburg, then south-east along the Elbe River. As we drove into Lubeck, the Russians were in full control and there was a huge portrait of Stalin displayed at the crossroads in the centre of the city. The greatest number of Russians we saw at our first glimpse were sailors, and each one removed his cap in allegiance and saluted the portrait of Stalin every time they passed by. Lubeck was a beautiful city with extensive parks and waterways. The docks area was damaged, as were some of the big residential five- and six-storeyed apartments, caused either by Russian bombs or their artillery, I guessed.

We occupied a number of these damaged apartment buildings, a troop in each house for billets in a residential area, and we used our German mattresses to sleep on the floorboards of the empty rooms. Many newcomers had joined us, young inexperienced members sent out from the training battalion in Britain to bring us up to full strength, to replace so many of our original squadron losses and members who would be released in the weeks ahead. Our purpose in Lubeck appeared to me to be just a show of strength as an occupational force as the Russians moved across the demarkation line. The Brass Hats were trying to make sure that we had no contact with them, which of course was impossible with our daily duties. We had been filled with so much propaganda about them, which we all discovered was not true. I was keen and anxious to see some of their units and equipment, and to discover how they kept those thousands of vehicles, tanks and guns going which had smashed the Nazis all the way back to their own frontier at 40 degrees below zero in the Russian winter.

I was relieved of all squadron parade duties and took over as caterer in the sergeants' mess. I took charge of the bar and the catering, with the responsibility for the takings at the bar and for ensuring that the cook's duties were undertaken promptly and efficiently. In between times, I had the opportunity to visit many places in Northern Germany that previously I had known only as names on maps and news reports. I went as far as Ellensburg on the Denmark frontier and visited Kiel and the famous canal that flows from the Baltic Sea to the mouth of the Elbe near Cuxhaven. Kiel had been the target of so many air attacks throughout the war, with its pens and waterways holding, and building of Nazi U-boats. There was terrible damage and destruction there caused by the RAF air attacks.

During this period also, while the commanding officer, Colonel Windsor Lewis was away in Bonn in connection with military planning and affairs, we received an invitation from the Russians across Lubeck Harbour to visit them, be entertained and to tour the area towards the Baltic port of Rostock, and on to the Polish frontier where many of their battles had taken place. It sounded great to me and an opportunity to learn more about the Soviet Army. We were sure Windsor Lewis would refuse, whether or not it would be an insult to the Russians. In his absence, thankfully, our own squadron leader gave consent, so five sergeants and three corporals were granted a pass for two days to accept the invitation.

At 8 a.m. the following day, a Saturday, we crossed the line to be met by a Russian lieutenant and four Red Army soldiers. We carried the small webbing backpack, a webbing belt with the holstered side arm and .38 pistol, with an attached water bottle full of our own treated water. One member of the Russian party could speak fairly good English, so at least we would have an interpreter even if it was a poor one.

In our packs we carried some rations, a few tins of Spam, some stewed steak, a tin of Ideal evaporated milk, our prepared drinking mixture of tea, sugar and powdered milk, a ration of bread and army biscuits and a tin of butter. We went on board a medium German petrol-driven bus. The Russians appeared to have plenty of petrol and this bus was the first I had seen powered by petrol. All the public transport and trucks we had seen on the Allied side were powered by a charcoal burner fitted to the rear of the vehicle. We drove east for a distance of about 20 miles through an attractive small town called Grevesmuhlen. There were a few scattered, burnt-out German vehicles along the roadside but this was the only damage we sighted as we went on to the port of Wismar on the Baltic Sea.

I was interested in what was going on everywhere, jotting down a few notes in my pocket book. Our interpreter did not know very much about the area, but he did his best in halting English to answer our questions. There appeared to be Russian soldiers everywhere and I could pick out the different races, the Caucasian, the Mongol and the blonde North Russian nationals all mixing together harmoniously. There was a great deal of damage in Wismar in the area of our stay, and many of the very old, antiquated but picturesque buildings were smashed and destroyed by Soviet bombers and their heavy guns, so our interpreter explained to us in his best hesitating English. We were taken to a German school which they had turned into their headquarters and barracks. The entrance once again was adorned with a huge portrait of Stalin. There were German workers, old and young, and prisoners of war everywhere doing all the work of cleaning up with shovels and carts, supervised by Soviet soldiers.

On our side of the border we were allowing them to return to their homes but not so with the Russians. We were told very strongly that they had to work to pay for all the war crimes and damage and to compensate for everything they had done. All the cleaning, kitchen duties, waitressing and washing at this Russian headquarters was carried out with compulsory labour by German women. I expected, from all the information that had always been conveyed to us, to find the Russian soldiers slovenly, poorly clad, and poorly armed. This was not so, however. They were well disciplined, their uniforms were rough and coarse, but their repeater rifles were in advance of our Lee Enfield single shot rifles, and they all appeared to be wearing fur-lined jackboots. Many of them were down at heel, and this was understandable too, as they had come a long, long way from Eastern Russia, through rain, mud, and snow, and appalling conditions. With my understanding of war and under all the shocking conditions these Russian soldiers had experienced, I could not criticise the Red Army troops that I had seen.

We left Wismar to be taken north-east along the main route a few miles inland from the Baltic Sea, through a number of small towns all damaged by Russian guns. The most interesting I recall now from that journey was a place called Neubokow; I remember copying the name from the railway station sign. There were more burnt out Nazi vehicles

pushed off the roadside but no heavy military guns or armour anywhere and late in the afternoon of that interesting Saturday we drove
into the Baltic port of Rostock. The central area of Rostock and the
docks area was devastated and our interpreter kept emphasising it
was caused by the air power of the Red Army air force and the Russian
guns. Evidently it was a bloody battleground before the Russians
overran the city but I had never heard any news item saying that
Allied air power had attacked it. After our touring inspection we were
taken to a damaged German barracks, occupied of course by the Red
Army.

Again we were greeted with a huge portrait of Stalin at the main
entrance and smaller ones across the front of the guard buildings
inside the barricade and then escorted to the mess hall for a meal. I
was intrigued, as were my colleagues, as to what was going to take
place inside. It must have been known that we were coming, as there
was a special table at the front of the hall. I did not know everything
about Soviet officer ranks, but it seemed to me that the main rank
was lieutenant and everything higher appeared to be a general. They
all had red collar tabs and red epaulettes with rows of medal ribbons
splashed across the chest like fruit salad. However, there were three
lieutenants at our table, something unheard of in the British army.
How could anyone imagine even the lowest rank of an English officer
and gentlemen eating and dining in a mess hall with the rank and
file and the lowly private in the British army? By Gad, sir, it's just not
done!

There was a short speech to welcome us which, of course, we did
not understand, then came the first item on the menu – soup. It was
well presented in china bowls but what it was made from I have no
idea; there were pieces of green vegetable leaves floating in it which
I could only presume were cabbage, anyhow it was quite good and
tasty. The main meal was fish served in a white-coloured sauce, with
slices of very coarse rye bread. There was plenty of it if anyone wanted
more and they did tell us the name of it, but I had no idea what it
meant. We produced our tin of butter at our table and it was greatly
appreciated. We were offered green tea to drink, no milk and no sugar,
but through out interpreter we politely asked if we could drink our
own tea and hot water was produced immediately. The Russians
sampled it with grimaces, and whatever they said, perhaps it was
better that we did not understand. The inevitable vodka supplies were
then brought in, a portrait of Stalin was produced at the head of the
table, and we drank toast after toast to him, as various speeches

were made, which we did not understand. We simply followed the procedure like sheep and clapped when everyone else clapped and applauded. They then brought in an orchestra and groups of Russian soldiers in a choir to sing Russian songs. I enjoyed some of it but it went on for too long and it was enough for our group.

Excusing ourselves from the table, we strolled around the barracks with the interpreter and a group of interested soldiers, and everyone seemed proud and pleased to show us in detail all the different arms and equipment. I thought they might have been secretive but this was not so, we were allowed to clamber over and examine everything. There were numerous tanks, guns, artillery and Soviet-army vehicles in neat rows in one big compound and scores of captured Nazi vehicles being worked upon and repaired by Russian soldiers. My interest was with the main Russian offensive armoured vehicle, the T34 Tank. I was surprised when I clambered over it, as there was no emphasis at all on the finish of this vehicle, and the comfort was nil. But I suppose what did it matter? It had done the job of crushing the Nazi forces and they had lost thousands of them. They were simple, and required quick training to handle and as long as the crew had enough practice with the gun and machine-guns and the reliable efficient diesel motor kept going, they were a formidable weapon. On the one that I examined I found that the welded plates were rough, as if done in a big hurry; a person could get cut badly on some of the protruding beaded welds. The tracks were very wide, almost two feet, double in width of the Cromwell which I assumed would assist stability and traction in the ice and the snows of Russia. It weighed about 26 imperial tons and had a speed of about 22 miles per hour. The diesel engine, I was told, was very good, and developed between 350 and 400 horsepower and the domed turret carried a 76mm gun, although I had seen one with an 85mm gun. Many of the guns were mounted on this T34 chassis, or towed by this tank, and many were manhandled and pulled along by manpower. I saw no animals and no horse transport; I guessed they used them but we saw none. I did see one JS Tank – the Joseph Stalin was a huge lumbering weapon but was being worked upon, so I was unable to get a good look at it. It was the answer to the Nazi Tiger Tank, which weighed around 52 tons and carried an awesome 122mm gun which outranged the formidable Nazi 88. Our interpreter could not, or perhaps did not want to, tell us any more about it. The time seemed to fly but it had been a most interesting and knowledgeable evening and that night they found us a bed in the barracks on German army mattresses.

I did not know how they normally got the Russian soldier out of bed at reveille in the Red Army but here they went around with a big hand bell, accompanied by banging and shouting in the Russian language. This was our rude awakening on the Sunday morning. We ate our breakfast from our own rations and then we were taken through the rich green countryside through Ribnitz and on to the port of Stralsund, opposite the Baltic island of Rugen. Ribnitz was damaged, and it made me wonder if any big town in the whole of Germany had escaped without damage.

Stralsund was a large town almost surrounded by water with a big causeway stretching across to the tourist holiday and fishing island of Rugen. The Russians informed us there was a terrible battle to overrun Stralsund and we saw the awful devastating mess as a result, plus the Soviet bombing and heavy guns, with masts of sunken ships protruding up through the water all along the coastline of the island. Hundreds of German prisoners and workers were in forced labour there cleaning up the damage and the dangerous buildings, supervised by armed Russian soldiers. I would have greatly appreciated a visit across that shell-torn causeway to see this island but time was short and the distances too great, we were still 100 miles from the Polish border, so we had to turn back to start our return journey. We arrived back at Lubeck that evening to cross back into our area. We shook hands with our Russian hosts and thanked them for their hospitality, and a wonderful sightseeing tour. To me personally it was something I would always remember – two full days of my life with the Red Army!

In November 1945 as the year once more was approaching its end, we packed up again to move south to the barracks outside Bergisch Gladbach; our tour of duty on the Baltic coast had come to an end. On the 18th of that month I joined a party of NCOs in a group for a visit to Berlin. The trial had already begun of 24 top Nazi war criminals and we had the opportunity for a half-day's observation and hearing of the trial; it gave me the chance to see those butchers in person. Twelve of them were sentenced to be hanged, including Borman, Hitler's deputy, although he had escaped and was absent. Three of them got life sentences, eleven received from 10 to 20 years' imprisonment and three were acquitted. For all the misery, destruction and bloodshed of that awful European conflict, justice would be done.

The dreary miserable days of November passed by, during which I went to the educational classes. The release demobilisation groups began to operate. The senior married members of the battalion in their

238

forties, who were still with us having been recalled from the reserve after years in civilian life, began to be released. Squadron Sergeant Major Williams, a police sergeant in North Wales, was one of them. Other members, who had no home or next of kin to return to, having lost them all through bombing or having been orphaned in their younger days, signed on and remained to complete their 21 years of service. Just the thought of this almost frightened me. I had had enough, I wanted to get out. In my own mind and calculations of the discharge routines, I had estimated that I had about four months more to do until the announcement of my group's releases – the days and weeks would not pass quickly enough.

Christmas 1945 was another white German Christmas with a heavy mantle of snow. It was a quiet, uneventful, easy day. The late December days were short and the nights were bitterly cold and dark. Electricity was desperately short and had not come back to the street lights with all the damage and the mess. We did have an excellent and cheerful Christmas dinner in the mess, despite all the shortages and rations, but we all looked forward to better things in the New Year.

In the middle of an icy cold January of the new year 1946, we moved on this time to a barracks on the outskirts of the city of Bonn, which had become the headquarters of the Allied military government.

I went searching on the black market for a sizeable suitcase, which I obtained illegally of course, for a few packets of cigarettes. At least, I had something useful now to pack and carry all the goods and chattels I had gathered along the way, without them being damaged in a canvas kit bag.

As each demobilisation group fell due we would congregate at the main gates on a Monday morning, awaiting each colleague marching out from his final appearance at Colonel Windsor Lewis's Memoranda, shaking hands and saying goodbye as he boarded the army vehicle to be taken across the Rhine on the journey home. The faces of the battalion members were changing each week. At the time we left Yorkshire two years previously, I knew every man personally and his name, but now there were so many new faces I was lost. The QMS – Quarter Master Sergeant Jones – became the squadron sergeant-major. I was offered promotion with the rank of QMS; all I had to do was sign on – to complete 12 years' service, but it was not for me; I refused.

At the end of February, I took over the sergeants' mess catering job again to be free from orderly sergeants' duties and guard duties in the squadron, and to be away from all parades and drills. It was the countdown for me, I had about eight weeks to go before my number came up.

In the first weeks of March I took advantage of my two last visiting and touring trips in the German Reich. The first was a wonderful tour down the Rhine Valley, along its west bank and along the Moselle. The other was a visit to the two dams destroyed by the RAF dambusters and the bouncing bombs. Both had been hurriedly rebuilt by Hitler after the enormous flow of released water had caused so much damage and loss of life. In my absence a miserable thief removed my shellcase from beneath my bed and with it my precious souvenir of the last shot fired in anger in 1945. All my endless inquiries and interrogations in the squadron failed to find the culprit and my prize.

On 3rd April 1946 I was ordered to attend a medical examination with the other members of my release group on a special parade with the battalion and medical officer. This was again a typical farcical army examination, lasting by my wristwatch a total of seven minutes. The army form W3149, a declaration showing the person signing was perfectly fit and well had already been filled out, and I was told to sign it which, unfortunately, I did in order to get it over with, without thinking of the consequences and I have regretted it all my life.

On 29th April, I was brought up before the squadron commander at his daily Memoranda yet again, to be asked and cajoled to sign on for extra service, and I refused. My group was due to be released on the next Monday, 2nd May 1946 – May Day.

On my last weekend of service with a British Army Guards regiment, the last day of April and the first day of May, a Saturday and Sunday, I collected and gathered all my things together. I handed in my kit leaving me with my personal possessions only, a full suitcase of all my souvenirs and collections, an army kit bag with my greatcoat stuffed inside, a few spare socks and shirts etc., and a civilian suit length of a tweed material that I had obtained on the black market.

On Monday morning at exactly 10 a.m., I was marched in to Colonel Windsor Lewis for the last time. Except for the short period he was absent, in his escape from Europe, I had been under his iron disciplinary command since April 1940, six long miserable years. With the glory of the regiment and the battalion still ringing in my ears, I was dismissed and marched out without even a thank you or a handshake. I boarded the army truck with my belongings and waves and good-byes from the few remaining long-serving colleagues of my squadron to begin my last journey to the Rhine crossing at Cologne – Homeward bound!

I examined my documents as the truck drove on. My release leave with full pay began on 2nd May and expired on the 8th July 1946; I could draw this in fortnightly instalments from the post office. My accrued pay and all my dues were credited in my army pay book to be drawn at Calais, where I could change all my currency into sterling.

At the changeover and checkpoint on the French border I was stopped by the military police. I was to be searched personally, and my kit bag and suitcase ransacked for any illegal carrying of pistols or arms. I objected angrily and decided to hit back. I exercised my authority. I refused to be searched by a lance corporal and demanded it be carried out by a senior sergeant.

They found nothing, of course. I had experienced and had enough of guns and these unimportant upstarts, who had never seen the front line, angered me and I told them so. I was cleared through the transit camp at Calais and I crossed the English Channel overnight arriving at Dover in the early hours of the morning. We were entrained to London quickly and then the whole trainload of released men were put on to another train to Manchester, to an army fitting-out civilian clothes depot. I spent an hour inside that clothes depot. I chose a tweed suit, a shirt, tie, socks, a pair of shoes, a trilby hat and a waterproof trench coat. I spoke sympathetically to one of the private soldier attendants, and he packed it all carefully for me in a large oblong cardboard box. I gave him a half-crown for his trouble. I found my way to Manchester railway station to catch a train to South Wales. I changed trains at Shrewsbury in Shropshire and went on to Cardiff where I arrived at 2.30 p.m. I wasted no time getting across to Queen Street Station to catch the train up the Valley and home. The train steamed leisurely up the valley past all the old familiar sights and places; the compartment was empty, I was the only passenger.

Once again I took off my army boots and gaiters never again to wear them, and I put on my faithful 10-year-old civilian shoes. They had travelled with me everywhere undamaged, tucked away in my kit bag and stowed away in the company, and later the squadron, stores truck. I sat back on the seat to try to sum it all up. In June 1939 under compulsion I had to register for military service, when my release leave ended on the 8th July 1946, it would be seven years and one month, the best young years of my life wasted by war. I had grown up and was approaching 27 years of age. What did the future hold? I had never had a romance and I had never had a girlfriend! I felt uneasy and uncertain. I left the train at Pengam Station, kit bag on my shoulder, the heavy case in my right hand, and the box balancing under my arm, along Gwerthonor Road to Oak Cottage. What a wonderful feeling it was to be back home.

18

1946 and Life as a Civilian

It was Tuesday afternoon, May 1946, when I walked through the front gate of Oak Cottage, along the side lane we had always called 'the gulley' to the back kitchen door. The door was wide open and, as I walked in, Mrs Stan Davies the neighbour from Ash Cottage, was there with my mother enjoying an afternoon cup of tea. I dumped my case, kit bag and cardboard box in the corner and I sat down to join them with a fresh cup of tea, and for the following half-hour I related some of the things that had happened and my journey home. When Mrs Davies left, the first thing I did of course was to get out of my army uniform for the last time. The last occasion I had worn civilian clothes was just after Christmas 1939, almost six and a half years before, and my clothes tucked away in the bedroom still fitted me well. What a strange feeling it was to walk around once more free and relaxed and not wearing khaki uniform, no army boots, and with a comfortable open-necked shirt. I sorted out my kit bag and my suitcase with all my souvenirs and spoils of war. I had an article for everyone, something I had confiscated or commandeered on my way up to the Baltic Sea. It had become a regular habit for me, on many occasions to quickly jump out of the tank turret and throw German packs and containers on to the tank rear. These had been hurriedly abandoned by retreating Nazis or prisoners of war, and especially Nazi SS officers or NCOs, and my crew and I always found a few spare minutes to tip them out and to share the spoils.

That evening with my parents, Joan, Trevor, Toots, Joyce and husband Bill, excusing the absence of Edna and her husband and Toots' husband, we had a special celebration and a beautiful supper, with one of my father's prime cockerels, to welcome me home. I would receive my weekly army pay now for the next two months or so, and after my absence for so long it was time I did nothing and had a long holiday. I was offered my old position at work but although there was nothing else available in the area except the coal mines and all their auxiliary works, that was not for me. I wandered around the whole district: everything was still all owned and operated by the Powell-Dyffryn companies. The majestic and beautiful Charity Woods and the old garden and allotments along the Rhymney River, from the old sewer outlets to the bridge at Pengam, and the site of the cordial and lemonade bottling works of Thomas and Evans had all gone, covered over with millions of tons of slag and waste, a gigantic tip, even over the top of our wonderful Mutton Tump. The fast-flowing river tumbled along blacker than ever, thick with tar, oil sludge and sewerage.

The Aber Bargoed tip behind the Bargoed Colliery, fed with the incessant overflowing slag of the aerial ropeway buckets, had expanded farther and higher, a huge ugly landmark for miles, north and south of the Valley. I thought to myself that surely this exploitation and pollution by powerful private companies for profit must cease and they must be compelled to bury the stuff in the miles of headings and inroads underground. It was going to change but it would take disasters and a long time to stop them polluting and desecrating those lush green valleys of South Wales. The transfer from war conditions to peace and progress was about to begin. The Tory bureaucrats were out of office and all the coal mines, after years and years of exploitation and oppression, would be nationalised and taken away from them. The railways too would follow in the same way.

On 20th May, I took out the suit length of material from my belongings, wrapped it in a sheet of brown paper, and off I went in the hope of finding a tailor to measure me and to do the job of making it into a smart double-breasted civilian suit. It was excellent quality German fabric and I felt quite pleased that it cost me just 100 Players cigarettes on the black market in the German Ruhr. I had looked around all the shops, everything was difficult to obtain. The material on sale was all utility-grade wartime production, and expensive, and I would have to surrender the greater part of my rationed clothing coupons to buy anything. I found a Jewish tailor in the High Street in Bargoed and he agreed to measure and fit me out with a suit made from the material for five pounds, and no questions asked. It satisfied me; I had the army issue suit and a good German suit, so I was pleased my wardrobe was complete.

The month of June that year was warm with long summer days and I helped my father a few days each week pushing the heavy roller and the lawnmower over the greens. The rolling was getting a

244

little strenuous for him, and he was glad of my assistance. I enjoyed it too and it helped to keep me fit.

The long lazy days of summer moved along, and I went down to Cardiff a number of times to meet up with some of my old army troopmates. Some of them had not found a job or else they were in no hurry. One of them, 'Smokey' Lloyd, had gone back to the Cardiff steel ropes factory where he was a foreman. I was offered a position there but it did not suit me, so I declined. I found Mr Mathews' address in the Ely district, and I spent a whole enjoyable evening there, we had so much to talk about. He was a changed person entirely from those early days of the 1930s, or perhaps maybe I had grown up.

I went back to my old school to check over and examine the departed list of my former schoolmates and I felt fortunate that my name was not among them. I had to go along to visit John Selwyn Thomas' parents the next day. That same day too I went on to see Glyn Mathews' parents living at Tir-y-beth, those last two schoolmates I shook hands with leaving school in July 1936.

In August of that year I decided to go to the Ministry of Labour rehabilitation courses school at the Treforest Trading Centre outside Caerphilly for six months, picking up the threads of making bull-nosed staircases, all types of joinery and cabinet making. Two of the other boys with whom I had grown up, Bill Crane, went back to plastering and Haydon Edwards to bricklaying. The proposition was that we become partners, and form a building and joinery business, if we could get established and find a suitable site and headquarters.

In September and October, I played a few games for Caerphilly United in the Welsh league. I could have gone on to greater things with professional soccer football but I had the hidden feeling that my leg would not stand up to it with continuous strenuous activity, and the best young years of my life had gone, so I excused myself from it.

The winter of 1946 was cold and bleak and Christmas of that year was the last for me at Oak Cottage and in South Wales. The youngest member of our family, Joan, had left Hengoed Girls Grammar School and travelled into Cardiff each day to work, a job she conscientiously followed, until she became one of the chiefs, and worked there for 41 years until she died in 1988. Trevor, my brother, was working as a fitter and turner in the engineering workshop at the Bargoed Colliery works. We were the only three at home with my parents, so it was a quiet old-fashioned Christmas with a huge coal fire blazing in the huge grate and snow one foot deep covering the countryside.

The old year turned into 1947, goods and commodities were in short supply, and we were still rationed for almost everything but it was gradually improving. In the middle of that first month of January, the wintery weather was appalling. Once again we were snowed in and I had to dig out through the snow that had drifted up to the front roof line at Oak Cottage. On two consecutive days, dressed in Wellington rubber boots, a heavy overcoat, with my big rubberised trench coat over the top, and my old army balaclava with a cap pulled over it, I trudged through the driving blizzard to find sister Joan at Pengam Station hoping the train had got through. The train did push through to Bargoed Station but could go no farther. Walking behind me trying to keep in step, with her arms around my waist from the rear, to shelter behind my back from the icy driving blizzard, we slowly stumbled through the bitterly cold howling storm along Gwerthonor Road.

Half an hour later after a hot drink I went back again all the way to Penpeter to help my father get home in the same way. The next day Joan insisted on going to work. It had stopped snowing during the night and I escorted her to the station, hoping the train would not run. By mid afternoon the blizzard started again with even more intensity. With a plough in front of the train, it managed to get through again, and for me it was another expedition through the icy blizzard to get my sister home. My father did not even attempt to go, common sense prevailed, with the whole area under two feet of snow. I have always vividly remembered those two days, and Joan often brought it up in many of her letters. They were the worst conditions I have ever experienced in my life.

At the end of January, our business plans did not work out the way I had expected, as the two other proposed partners started working around the district independently as the rebuilding industry started its upturn.

Consequently, I packed my case, took the early train with Joan into Cardiff to catch the 9 a.m. express to London to visit my sister Edna, to look around and find out what prospects there were for me in that city. Edna and her husband Tom had moved to the Notting Hill district, and I soon found my way from Paddington Station. There was plenty of work with all the vast rebuilding programmes as there was such a mess everywhere resulting from the Nazi bombing. The difficulty was accommodation. Everywhere I went, I found nothing. It appeared to me that all the flats, liveable apartments, and undamaged inhabitable premises, in the North and East End were all occupied by immigrant Jews from Europe, displaced persons, refugees and every European nationality. It amazed me where all those so-called down-trodden unfortunates had obtained all their wealth to take over so many places, and it made me angry. From my recollection now it must have been the afternoon of the second day in February. I was walking along Oxford Street, occasionally stopping, looking into shop windows, and watching the crowds of pedestrians surging past me, when suddenly someone tapped me on the shoulder from behind and caught hold of my arm. To my surprise it was Richard Davies from my old battalion. It was a nice surprise, we had a great deal to talk about, and so many things to discuss. In the course of our conversation I inquired where he was living and what he was doing in Oxford Street at that time of the day. He did not disclose then what he was doing, he simply told me he was on his way back to his 'digs', just a few hundred yards away, and he invited me to go along with him for a cup of tea and something to eat, and he would tell me more. We turned down Dean Street, into the crowded areas of Soho, until we came to a place called Trenchard House and then he told me he was a member of the police force. I realised that the premises were the new modern West End Section house, and single men's quarters of the Metropolitan Police. It was an impressive multi-storeyed residential quarters with all up-to-date facilities, and a big canteen like a restaurant on the ground floor.

We had a meal there and then took the lift to his quarters on the fifth floor. Each man had a private room just like a hotel with all facilities. Charladies did all the work – cleaning, polishing, making the beds, changing the linen etc. It was all provided free of charge to single men and married officers were paid an allowance where they lived. Everyone had to pay for their food, which was available 24 hours around the clock and was responsible for their own washing, with all amenities provided in the basement. I was impressed and as I had already told him that I was looking for a job, he encouraged me to join up. He explained to me the procedure, that he had to pass the second class civil service examination, then he would sit the first class later to qualify for a higher rate of pay. He told me also, with my qualifications, I would be exempt from sitting both the second and first class exams, and all I had to do was pass the medical examination, and answer a few probing questions before a security tribunal. I would then be accepted to go either to the Hendon Police College or the Peel House School in Westminster. He persuaded me to go with him, there and then, to the West End Central Station to fill in a detailed application form. I thought it over and finally agreed. He took me along, introduced me to the inspector at the desk, and I filled out and completed the details on the form. I shook hands with him and he said, 'I shall see you and meet up with you again in a few months, all the best!' I thanked him, then made my way back to Notting Hill to Edna's place wondering if I had done the right thing but, I thought, I had only made an application to join, and I could still turn it down. I received more encouragement from both Edna and her husband and the next day I caught the train back to South Wales.

On arriving home that evening, I told my parents what had happened and that I had made an application to join the London Police Force. There was nothing left for me in South Wales after our building business arrangements had fallen through. They were both sadly disappointed that once again I was leaving the district and this time permanently. I tried to soften the blow by explaining I would travel back as often as I could, for weekends and holidays. Things were made worse by the fact that my brother Trefor was leaving also to go into an engineering centre with the P & O shipping lines to become a ship's engineer.

On 28th February I received a rail travel voucher and instructions to be at Peel House in Westminster at 3 p.m. on 2nd March for a medical examination and interviews, and to bring pyjamas etc. to stay overnight, with all my references, certificates, army documents and release papers and, if necessary, to be prepared to sit either of the civil service examinations on the next day.

Early morning of that day 2nd March I went to Cardiff once more, all prepared to catch the express train to London. I boarded the Underground to Victoria, following the route supplied to me. I walked along Vauxhall Bridge Road towards the river until I found my turn off and my destination, Peel House. Others were arriving, about 20 to 40 in all and I soon got to know some of them as we congregated in the canteen for a cup of tea. Approaching 3 p.m., I was the first to be called, in alphabetical order, my name beginning with the letter 'A', for the medical examination which lasted half an hour, then a further ten minutes or so on strength tests of the arms and fingers, and lifting maximum allotted weights. I had no problems, I passed the medical; then I was taken to another waiting room for the interview before a tribunal and examining board. I went in before the panel of five men all dressed in civilian clothes. They appeared to me to be high-ranking officers of the police administration. I was told to relax and sit down whilst they examined all my credentials. I had a glowing army release certificate and reference of my service, courses, achievements and all my duties as an army instructor. I had the senior educational certificate of the Central Welsh Board and the London Matriculation and they were impressed. I was asked a few personal questions and various things that I had done in my regiment and finally if I had ever been brought before a court for any crime or offence. I told them yes, on one occasion, for riding a bicycle without a white reflector plate, and that was the one and only offence, which brought a few smiles around the panel. I was sent out for about five minutes and then recalled. They congratulated me, informing me that I had been accepted. I could go home to await instructions to return in about three weeks, when the training course began. I was exempt from sitting any examinations and I would be eligible for a special increment of pay after completing five years' service.

I walked back toward Victoria, caught up in the surge of the rush hour and the thousands of people moving down Victoria Street, Buckingham Palace Road, Grosvenor Place, and all the intercepting streets from Pimlico. I did not realise then that just one year or so hence, I would be living and working in that area. I was pushed and jostled to reach the Underground tube, then on to Notting Hill. I stayed the night at Edna's place, and the next morning caught the express at Paddington for my return journey home. I arrived home safely and reported to my folks what had happened, and that I would be departing in about three weeks. That three weeks of my life was to be my last period in South Wales. I still assisted my father often when he needed me, but I had to make the most of it, to make a nostalgic journey around all the old haunts and places. I went on a couple of trips on the old Brecon and Merthyr railway route, and I feel pleased now 43 years on that I did, to recall those memorable journeys because, in 1962, almost 100 years after it was built and opened for traffic in 1863, it was destroyed by a Tory administration under British Rail for not paying its way. They ripped up all the rail tracks, pulled down the many steel-arched bridges to sell them for scrap, along with all the old magnificent steel and brass locomotives, destroyed all the small arched stone bridges and tunnels and sold some of the land that carried the railway tracks, disposing of the wonderful railway carriages as junk. One monument they would not destroy, although they tried, was the high Bargoed Stone Viaduct which carried both the Great Western Railway and the Brecon and Merthyr over the roadways, the Rhymney River and the cleft of the valley after leaving Bargoed railway station to divide into separate rail tracks up each side of the valley. This viaduct with all its grandeur will remain, I hope, immemorial with many of its massive carved stones cut by that super craftsman, my grandfather.

I boarded the train at the lower end of my father's Hill 60, down the stone steps where the road bridge crosses the railtrack on to the old Pengam (mon) station and the sidings to the Pengam 'house coal' colliery, gradually being dismantled and cleared away. The train steamed away through the Britannia sidings, past the overhead conveyor bridge to the concrete silo feeding the aerial ropeway buckets, and then the piles of pine pit props; our wonderful Charity Woods across the river had gone, replaced by a new gigantic slag tip. It was sad, I could not see the river below or the huge steel compressed-air pipeline that fed the collieries works, snaking alongside. It was there, so often, along with the Crane Brothers, we had cried out with excitement as we discovered the nest of the rare yellow hammer in the glades of the hawthorn and hazel, or the stone chat along the rocky outcrops. The stick woods were still there on the Britannia village side, as the train swept into a big curve past the Gwalad-y-Waun farm where we had so often raided the pear orchard under cover of the evening mist. With clouds of smoke and steam we entered the stone tunnel, known to us as the 50-yard tunnel, then out into the Bargoed Colliery sidings to cross the river, into Bargoed Station, to begin the climb up the valley.

I am so glad that I made that journey, before it was all destroyed to reminisce and remember that route from a long time ago. In 1986, almost 40 years later on a return visit to that area, an enterprising private company, realising the potential of the old railway route, purchased some of the rail-bed track, rebuilt many bridges to turn it into a narrow gauge railway for a number of miles calling it the Brecon Mountain Railway, adding it to the exciting famous small trains of Wales. This railway runs into the magnificent Brecon Beacons National Park, the first two miles of which were open at that time taking passengers to the destination of Pontsticill on the shores of the Tal Fechan reservoir. Work was still going on to extend the line to Torpantau where it would pass through the old stone tunnel completed in 1861, the highest tunnel in the British Isles, 1,313 feet above sea level.

The company building their own rolling stocks had to use the bogies from the South African Railways, a locomotive from the East German Railways, one from South Africa, and another from the old slate quarries of North Wales. What a sad state of affairs it has all been, when one realises that the first railway in the world, began on part of

250

that rail-bed track, constructed by my ancestors between 1802 and 1804 – approaching 200 years ago.

However, I continued with that last nostalgic journey to Brecon and then to Merthyr-Tidfyl. I then took the Great Western to Cardiff and up the Rhymney Valley to Pengam and home.

On or about 20th March of that year 1947, I received the instructions to report to Peel House in Westminster by 4 p.m. on the 30th March, and a rail travel voucher to Paddington Station.

Another stage of my life was about to begin.

that rail-bed track, constructed by my ancestors between 1802 and 1804 — approaching 200 years ago.

However I continued with that last nostalgic journey to Brecon and then to Merthyr-Tydvil. I then took the Great Western to Cardiff and up the Rhymney Valley to Pengam and home.

On or about 20th March of that year 1942, I received the instructions to report to Peel House in Westminster by 4 p.m. on the 30th March, and a rail travel voucher to Paddington Station.

Another stage of my life was about to begin.

Part Three

Life as a Central London Police Officer

19

I Become London Bobby PC 175A

The second last day of that month was a typical March day turning towards the middle of spring. The strong blustery wind, carrying a little cold misty rain, rustled the budding branches of the huge beech tree and the ash at the rear of Oak Cottage. Many of the old beech nuts swirled around our gully on the north side of home, as I set out for Pengam station carrying my suitcase, in the company of my sister Joan, to catch the early train to Cardiff. I still received the scowl and a grunt from old Mr Mullett as he issued me a ticket in return for my rail travel voucher; he asked no questions so I said nothing but 'Thank you', as I left the ticket window.

I said goodbye to Joan as she turned off to the rear of Queen Street to her work in Cardiff, and I continued on to the station known at that time as Cardiff General, for my train, the South Wales to Paddington Express. The train was dead on time and I found myself a seat to settle down with a newspaper, the *Daily Herald* for the next three hours until I reached my destination. After the train left Newport and entered the Severn Tunnel, I began to ponder and think – the future was so unknown, what did it all hold for me? Many things had happened to me before under compulsion, but this was all being done now of my own free will. It was a challenge for me and I had to meet it in my own way.

When I left the train at Paddington I had some spare time so I went on to Notting Hill to see Edna and I guessed too I would be welcomed with a meal and a cup of tea. I spent about an hour there, then continued on to Victoria and along Vauxhall Bridge Road to Peel House. I reported in about 3.30 p.m. with all my particulars etc., received my allotted accommodation quarters for the night, deposited my suitcase and belongings and was instructed to assemble with all the other newcomers in a large meeting room at four o'clock for a lecture explaining all the procedures of the training courses. I got acquainted with three other members, by the names of John Collar, an ex-Coldstreamer, Bill Bullock from Gloucester and another Welshman John Davies from Camarthen. It turned out all three of us had surnames beginning with A, B, and C and we were to become members of the same instructional school.

The following morning with a total of about 60 recruits we were divided into two training schools and our school members were taken by coach to Hendon, which was to be our training base for the months ahead. I knew the Hendon area from my short period there during the war years. The facilities and buildings were so much better than the old buildings compacted into that congested area in Westminster. That day was taken up with all the necessary arrangements to begin our training. We would be paid the full rate of a police constable but we had to pay for our own food or provide it ourselves and be responsible for our own washing. The hours would be from 9 a.m. to 5 p.m. with a break of one hour for lunch. At the end of that first day all individuals were sorted out for accommodation as there was limited space for everyone. I was transported with four others to Paddington, to occupy the Section House quarters above the old Paddington police station. Many years later this place was pulled down and a modern up-to-date building replaced it. There was a canteen there on the first floor for breakfast, or any other meals, day or night; we were above this area, with access by a stairway, and we would be taken by police transport to and from Hendon each day.

Our living quarters there were not luxurious but quite comfortable for the period we had to reside in them. There was a long room partitioned into cubicles approximately 12 feet by 6 feet, with a single bed, table and wardrobe, and access from a passage along one side. It was lockable and secure, we all had separate keys, and it was kept clean, tidy and liveable by the charwomen employed there. The beds were made daily and the linen changed twice weekly. Each Saturday and Sunday were free for us to go home, if it was possible, or to go to wherever we wished, but every weekday evening we were expected to revise and learn the day's tuition, for a weekly written examination each Friday. Our main text book was the Policeman's Bible, known as the Black Book. This book was a thick volume of Police law, remedies, procedures and hundreds of acts and regulations, divided into different sections for all types of misdemeanours and crimes, and it was essential to learn almost all of them off by heart, and word perfect.

During the month of April it was just like going back to school all over again sitting at desks in lecture rooms, going through all the interpretations and explanations of the Black Book with the instructor, interspersed with periods in the gymnasium for physical training and the elementary procedures of jujitsu and unarmed combat.

A great deal of it was familiar to me from my army training and it assisted the instructor to perfect many of the others with practical exercises and help from many of the ex-army members. It became necessary to learn so much word perfect, to interpret correctly so many acts, rules and regulations, all the details of traffic regulations, practical procedures and compiling evidence. The hours of each day seemed long, much of it interesting, some of it monotonous and dry, but everything had to be learned to have complete knowledge, to make decisions in so many situations.

On Saturday afternoon and evenings, I usually made my way into central London or south of the river, wandering through the markets, viewing the bomb-damaged areas and browsing through the second-hand shops and stalls. These excursions went by quickly and on Sunday I would often spend the day with my sister Edna, her husband Tom and young Brian their small son. During May our daily schooling gave us many days on traffic observations around the city, in the public galleries of magistrates courts, to observe the sittings and hearings, and at the Old Bailey criminal court, to follow through a big trial.

Throughout the month of June our detailed instruction continued and I can recall now one of those days filled with anxiety and concern leading up to one of my greatest tests that I was to experience with traffic control. It was a very wet sultry afternoon, a Friday, during the second week of that month in 1947. Along with John Collar, I was taken to Hammersmith Broadway in west London, for a thirty-minute test, an incident in my life I always remember. There were no modern flyovers in the road systems as we know them today, but there were traffic lights operating under a time delay, with actuating rubber road pads set in the roads at each intersection. The main Great West Road, carrying the enormous build up of traffic into London ended here to divert in all directions, as the Castelnau highway came over Hammersmith Bridge.

There were other roads intersecting there also, King Street, Broadway, Grove Street, Brook Street, Hammersmith Road, West Kensington Road and Fulham Palace Road, a total of nine roads. Two of them carried four lanes of traffic, two each way, and the other seven carried six lanes of traffic, three each way, a grand total of 50 lines of traffic crossing over, turning left and right and intersecting into all the other roads. The traffic lights were all switched off and it became a nightmare test for me to control and direct 50 intersecting lanes of traffic in the pouring rain, plus trying to control the thousands of surging impatient pedestrians crossing over the intersections through the enormous flow of traffic. I succeeded in carrying out that almost impossible task for 14 minutes, until I lost control, when the lights were immediately switched on. Collar lasted about nine minutes so my effort was the best performance of the whole squad. In normal circumstances there, when a breakdown or power failure occurred, it took four men to control the traffic at any time.

At the beginning of July I graduated from the Hendon School and I received my posting. Once again with Collar and Bullock, I was transferred and attached to Cannon Row Police Station in the Scotland Yard building of Whitehall, the headquarters of A Division. I was allotted a Number and became PC 175A. I moved out of Paddington and my residence for a short period was Trenchard House off Piccadilly, which was the regular quarters of C Division and when vacancies became available I would move to an A Division section house in Victoria. I caught up with Richard Davies once again when I settled in there, with a room allotted to me looking across the back of Piccadilly on the fifth floor. I was issued with two uniforms, one for everyday duties with two pairs of trousers, and a dress uniform for all ceremonial occasions. This uniform was the tunic style with silver buttons up the front to the closed neck, cuffed breastpockets, and cuffed side pockets, all with silver buttons, a black polished belt pulled in around the midriff, with a snap buckle, epaulettes with the silver divisional letter and the individual's number, straight trousers, black boots and the London police helmet. The helmet, despite the criticism of its ancient traditional appearance, was the most comfortable headgear I have ever worn. It was quite light, cool in summer, and warm in winter, and it shed the rain, so preventing it running down the neck. We were given a boot allowance, which was our own responsibility, and we could purchase boots from the police stores. They too were the closed type, no lace holes and no toe cap, making the boot upper fairly waterproof. I obtained a pair of goloshes also, which was the usual procedure, so that the rubber casing enclosed the boot to make it waterproof and to shed water off the oilskin waterproof trousers when standing for long hours on traffic duty in the pouring rain. At that time all uniforms were buttoned to the neck, the regulations had not been as yet introduced that allowed an open-topped tunic and a collar and tie.

The A Division police district was quite an extensive area controlled from three police stations, Cannon Row, the principal one off White-hall; Rochester Row near Victoria Station and Hyde Park Station in the middle of Hyde Park, and I was destined to do a tour of duty attached to all three.

The boundaries stretched from Charing Cross and Hungerford Bridge to Westminster, Lambeth and Vauxhall Bridges along the embankments of the river, along Vauxhall Bridge Road to Victoria and Hyde Park Corner, all of Hyde Park, St James's Park and Green Park. It included Trafalgar Square, Buckingham Palace, St James's Palace, all the Houses of Parliament, the Mall area and all the government areas of Whitehall and Downing Street. Many of the police officers at Cannon Row had permanent jobs attached to the Palace and the Houses of Parliament. In the months ahead I would be on duty in many unexpected places that very few people were privileged to see. Such places as the inside of 10 Downing Street, and its high-walled gardens, Buckingham Palace and many of the prominent government administration buildings.

On the first Monday of July 1947, my life as a duty police constable began. I was posted for a tour of one month's duty to a beat, one week 6 a.m. to 2 p.m. with alternate weeks 2 p.m. to 10 p.m.; that made it two weeks of what was referred to as 'early turn', and two weeks of 'late turn'. It was the routine to write one's name and number and room number on the call board of the section house, and the duty officer there would arouse you at the requested time. That first morning to try and arrange my routine I was awakened at 5 a.m. to get ready for my first day's duty, with a quick breakfast in the canteen, allowing 15 minutes to get to Cannon Row. Along with John Collar I set out that morning at 5.45 a.m., down through Piccadilly to Trafalgar Square and down Whitehall to Cannon Row. We discovered, that without any incidents or hold ups on the way, we could cover the distance in 10 minutes. On the return journey home, especially in the early afternoon, it did not pay to wear the uniform proper, despite not wearing the black and white 'on duty' armband, as we were stopped and held up by many people with queries, and other inci-dents, and it often took us an extra hour or one and a half hours to reach the section house. We were new and inexperienced but, after a few days we lived and learned, and from then onwards the helmet was left at the station, and we wore a civilian top coat to get backwards and forwards each day.

During that first week of being so 'green,' I remember well, I was accompanied by an experienced officer in order to learn the beat, with all the various diversions to contend with along the routes, to observe the various traffic snarls and to relieve the men on point duty for a short break and meal breaks. There were just two beats only, from Cannon Row, number one and two, the great part of its jurisdiction were all security areas, high-density traffic and normally low-crime areas.

That first beat duty for me covered the area from Birdcage Walk to the Palace, St James's Park, Constitution Hill to Hyde Park Corner, Green Park and the Mall and around Trafalgar Square and all the area on the right-hand side of Whitehall. The second beat was to cover the area from Trafalgar Square down Northumberland Avenue to the river, all the embankment to Westminster Bridge, to the top of Victoria Street and around the Houses of Parliament and Westminster Abbey.

The second week of duty for me was 2 p.m. till 10 p.m. and I was on my own for the first time, as there was a shortage of officers. I was told briefly about the various troublespots in the long summer evenings, and left to work it all out for myself.

We were briefed before leaving the station with all the information on the area, lists of stolen vehicles etc., checked to see if we carried the baton, whistle, notebook etc., given the relieving times, and the approximate time to leave the beat for the half-hour meal break. There were no radios; all over the metropolitan district of London, about a quarter of a mile apart, there were blue police telephone boxes complete with a blue light above, with direct communication to the nearest police station. Anyone could use this phone direct to the station, and this too was our main means of seeking assistance, or reporting anything urgently and obtaining all the emergency services. If the blue light was flashing anywhere it was necessary for the nearest officer to answer it promptly, as this was the only way for the station to contact the police in that area.

In the big crime areas outside the jurisdiction of Cannon Row it was a known practice of smash and grab gangs, burglars and other criminals to keep the patrolling officer of the area where the job was to be carried out under constant surveillance at night and to watch his movements. In consequence of this, as I was soon to learn when I moved on from Cannon Row, each patrolling officer on night duty was given two staggered ringing-in-times throughout the night, to ring from a police box, and these times, just like the meal time, changed each night to confuse the criminal. If one failed to ring in within one half hour each side of those allotted times, the alert would be raised, all the area and squad cars informed and an emergency declared that something was wrong, and a search began. The blue police box was to become a very important means of communication in my future night duty, for my own safety.

It was surprising how quickly it was possible to settle down and learn everything; in just two weeks, I knew the routes and destinations of every numbered double-decker bus that travelled through that district. I obtained a detailed direction manual and I could direct anyone to each and every one of the thousands of streets, any theatre, prominent building, museum, sportsground or exhibition building throughout the whole of London. I knew my police law, although inexperienced with dispensing it, and I had a St John's Ambulance first aid certificate and a life-saving certificate, so I felt confident in everything I did. Perhaps if anything, to begin with, in obeying the rules, I was too efficient; I recorded every detail and occurrence on my patch, it was all entered and recorded in the big occurrence book at the station by the station sergeant at the end of each shift. I got ticked off a number of times for entering too much unnecessary information so once again I had to learn by experience.

Every 48 hours the guard was changed at Buckingham Palace and I had to be present to control the crowds. At that time, until it was changed years later because of the spectator interference, the palace guard stood outside the main gates and patrolled the flagstone area along the front of the railings. My old regiment had returned from the occupation duties in Germany and I recognised some of my old colleagues who had stayed on, performing their duties there, and of course they recognised me with a hidden nod. Among the crowds of spectators there were always the sneak thieves and the pickpockets taking advantage of the careless tourists with open handbags, purses and wide open, unprotected coat pockets, so it was necessary to have one's eyes everywhere to assist the gate police. At that time also it was the gate police officer's duty, with his knowledge of all the important people and his briefing of whom might be visiting, to alert the guards of any approaching VIPs. The majority of people did not know the sequence of the guards on duty and how they operated in unison and with perfect timing but it was all familiar to me. During those years it was the old Lee Enfield rifle with a fixed bayonet standing at ease. With a quick side glance to his colleague the guard would know

what drill movement to make by a system of taps with the rifle butt
on the hard surface of the footpath: to slope arms, to salute, to patrol
or to present arms and then to carry it out after the known lapsed
time drill knowledge had expired, to complete the drill movement.
How they do it in modern times carrying the sloped rifle at the side
of the body I do not know but the sequence of taps must be the same;
times have changed.

The various complaints made by pedestrians and citizens all over
the district amazed me, and I can recall now just two of them pointed
out to me, in protest, as a 'green' police constable in my first two
weeks. That July was hot and sultry, and in the late afternoon when
it became the hottest and most uncomfortable time of the day, one
was expected to have four arms, two heads and an encyclopedia of
knowledge to comply with, and answer, all the queries of tourists and
passers-by, and it made me have the tendency to dismiss some petty
things in my own mind and do nothing about them. This I soon
discovered I could not do or neglect because there would be reper-
cussions. One irate individual, who appeared to me to be an ex-army
officer, and which I found was true when I recorded his name etc.,
bitterly complained that a slightly raised flagstone on one corner had
damaged his new patent leather black shoes as he kicked against it. I
had to record it all in my notebook even to the measured unevenness
of the raised half-inch rise, and that person added his signature to my
notes. When I passed in my notebook, it was the station sergeant's
responsibility to inform the Westminster Council to put it in order
quickly. I was told later that this eccentric complainant had even
phoned the Information Room at Scotland Yard to find out if I had
done my duty of reporting it and having it rectified, so nowadays I
just wonder how they get on with potholes and broken footpaths
everywhere. I was beginning to learn by experience why everything
had to be recorded in my notebook, otherwise I would be accused of
neglect of duty and fined. I discovered too that I had to possess the
patience of Job, and have kindness and care and every consideration
for all individuals, young and old, and it did not matter how frustrated
I became I dared not be impolite to anyone and risk being reported.
Such was a policeman's lot at that time. What a contrast nowadays!
Among those massed surging crowds one did not know with whom
one was dealing, and again and again a police officer's number would
be taken and a complaint made against him for the slightest thing, or
any rudeness. Yet again it was reassuring to read the daily letters
pinned to the noticeboard at the station with one's number on it,

sending thanks and appreciation for some simple advice or service. Those days I believe are gone, the London bobby of those times no longer exists.

It was still the middle of my second week of police service when a second incident occurred that I remember well. An elderly, powdered and painted, angry, and obviously well-to-do lady confronted me with all the troubles of the world connected with a bent nail, not the finger variety, but the rusty one, and she demanded I go along with her to rectify it. I was walking down Whitehall leaving Trafalgar Square near the Whitehall Theatre when I met her. Across the road there was an open souvenir shop and the proprietor, an accented Italian, had placed a length of canvas over the window to keep out the sun. The wind was causing trouble and making it flap so he had driven a nail through it about waist high into the side window frame and bent it over slightly. The lady had already engaged in an argument with the excited Italian, and he refused to do anything about it. The lady insisted it was dangerous to passers-by, so I obliged and ordered the shopkeeper to remove it. He did remove it reluctantly; I made an entry in my book and the lady thanked me and I went on my way. When I went off duty that night and handed in my notebook for the shift's incidents to be recorded in the station occurrence book, I was told the old girl had been there to express her thanks, and had put five pounds in the police funds charity box on the counter. I have often wished over the years that I could have recorded and listed the thousands of strange questions and all the funny, awkward incidents and happenings that were part of my life as a central London police officer.

On the Friday afternoon of that week, almost completing the first two weeks of duty, once again I became the victim of circumstances, the first of two incidents which would make me decide never to carry a wallet for the remainder of my life, and I have kept to it rigidly. It was approaching 5 p.m. and the start of the mad rush hour with hundreds of people en masse racing across the crossings at the intersection of Parliament Street and Bridge Street to bus stops and Westminster underground station, choking the footpaths across Westminster Bride, Great George Street and around Parliament Square from Victoria Street. There were no traffic lights allowed in that area due to a law that all members of Parliament took precedence over all traffic and pedestrians, and had to be given safe conduct at all times to cross to the Houses of Parliament. As a result there were two officers on duty controlling the traffic and pedestrians at the intersections of Parliament Street, Bridge Street and Great George Street, plus additional pedestrian crossings with the Belisha beacons flashing orange lights. I had just relieved the man who was controlling the crossing in conjunction with the pointsman at Parliament Street and Bridge Street for his meal break. In the enormous flow of traffic around Parliament Square, a heavy market lorry lost is front wheel and hit a No. 11 double-decker bus travelling by its side in the lines of traffic; the driver swerved to avoid it and another bus on its right hit the No. 11 turning it over on its side to crash on to the lorry. There was total chaos, I rushed to the blue police box a short distance away to get assistance and then ran to the toppled bus on top of the lorry. Both decks of the bus were crammed full of passengers and all of them had been thrown across to the underside. In the midst of all the blood and mess, I carried a middle-aged lady, unconscious and badly injured, on to the green lawn near the fountain on the north-west corner of the square. I removed my tunic rolled it and placed it under her head for support. Half an hour later when things were almost back to normal and all the casualties had been taken away I went across to recover my tunic and my notebook to make a few notes.

Sadly I had been bitten again! My wallet, which I had completely forgotten in the emergency and left in my pocket, was missing, with all the contents and nine one-pound notes, a lot of money at that time. Sadly too it was to happen again in an emergency. I would lose another wallet and ten pounds, but I would learn my lesson never to carry a wallet again.

Towards the end of the third week with another spell of day duty and traffic relieving in Parliament Street, and the intersection of Marlborough Gate and Pall Mall to the Mall, I had another birthday. I was 28 years old, and that evening I went across the city to Shepherd's Bush to my sister Edna's new address for a birthday tea, complete with candles for the benefit of young Brian, my nephew.

At the end of the month I was notified to move out of Trenchard House to take up residence at Ambrosden House situated in Ambrosden Avenue a short distance from Victoria Station. A police van was provided to move all our belongings and John Collar and Bullock and me and bring us into the A Division area. We did not have all the new modern facilities at this section house, as it was one of the older buildings in that part of the city, but it was homely and comfortable, and there were just 30 of us in the whole building. The ground floor was a recreation area, the canteen and the office and quarters of the resident section house sergeant. The first floor was a dining room area with facilities we could use if we wanted to cook our own meals. The second and third floors were private individual rooms which were our living quarters with an ablution area of baths, showers, and washing facilities. It was all serviced by the daily charladies and centrally heated so it was quite convenient to dry any washing on the steam radiators in one's own room. It was a good area with easy access to the main bus routes in Victoria Street, the tube station, Victoria Palace Theatre and cinemas and it was also much more convenient to get to Cannon Row without all the congestion and hold ups of Piccadilly.

To start the month of August I was posted to number two beat, alternate weeks of early, and late turn. With no other details of the area and the route, I was on my own to work it all out myself owing to the shortage of police officers to fulfil every duty, and all the security posts took first preference. It was extremely hot weather, uncomfortable and tiresome and on many afternoons of duty it was often eight o'clock or even later before I could get away for a meal and a cup of tea. For an hour or so in the mad scramble of the rush hours, morning and afternoon, I had to take over and control the traffic crossing over Whitehall along Horse Guards Avenue through to the Embankment. There were so many things happening with people fainting along the Embankment, and needing to receive help and attention, arguments between taxi drivers and some angry passengers, bus conductors stopping their vehicles seeking assistance with passengers refusing to pay their fare, and on one occasion one citizen collapsing and dying just 20 yards away from me. It was hectic, with never a dull moment, and some serious incident taking place all the time. With so much to do I was often late getting off duty, and very relieved to see the night duty man approaching to take over from me, so that I could get back to the section house to take off my boots, have a cold bath, and a welcome rest.

My first two months as a police officer had been completed, and I realised it was not an easy job either physically or mentally. It was an experience for me to understand the many tasks and duties that were packed into eight hours or so each day on a central London street, unaware what was going to happen next. The forthcoming month for me was to be a tour of night duty, and the first free weekend until 10 p.m. on the Monday night arrived so I decided to travel home to South Wales to see my parents.

I caught the express train from Paddington Station at 9 a.m. on the Saturday morning to arrive at Cardiff at midday and I reached home abut 1.30 p.m. in the afternoon. Everything was quiet when I arrived at Oak Cottage. I had not told them that I was coming down for the weekend, so it would be a surprise. I went around to the back door, and being such a warm day it was wide open, so I quietly walked in. My mother wasn't there, she was probably visiting a neighbour, and my father was sitting in the old armchair fast asleep in the warmth of the lazy afternoon. I did not want to disturb him then, so I sat down to wait for him to wake up. There are occasions in one's life to always remember well, and this was one of them. Eleven years previously in 1936 my late brother Gwyn walked in with me one afternoon to find him sleeping in just the same way. Without disturbing him, Gwyn sat down with his pen and an exercise book and compiled one of his many poems as he glanced across to my sleeping father. In memory of them both I am compelled to rewrite that poem now in the following lines which is entitled, 'The Sleeper'.

> The afternoon wears its sultry hours away
> As if impatient for the new come day.
> The fire burns low as its dying blaze
> Struggles for life under a smoky haze.
> The cat sleeps after a heavy meal,
> Worried by teasing flies in their zeal.
> The day's toil is done; gone the day's care,
> Contentedly he rests in the old armchair,
> Every sinew relaxed in the sweet repose,
> Of blissful sleep to forget the world's woes.
> Chin rests on hand, the lined face
> As if touched on the cheek by an Angel's grace
> Wears a somnolent smile of divine content
> As on pleasant dreams the mind is intent
> Through the pouting lips the bated breath
> Beats a gentle tune to the time of stealth
> As if the escaping air gasps from the cheek
> Liberty in the open space to seek.
> The smile deepens and a longer sigh
> Tells of beautiful sights to the now blind eye
> Only dreams fulfil his life's vain hope,
> His fears and trials are not difficult to cope.
> But alas! a disturbing sound, the sleeper's awake
> A different expression upon a furrowed face
> No longer in the restful land of dreams
> But in a modern world of real schemes.

With sad memories of my brother, those verses must have been the last lines I saw him write before he went back to Scotland, where he met his sad end. However, I had an enjoyable weekend at home, and I left on the Monday morning to return to London.

My first tour of night duty was varied and interesting; it is truly often said the city of London never sleeps. There were buses on their all-night routes, taxis racing everywhere, big produce lorries rumbling along to the Billingsgate fish and meat markets and Covent Garden fruit, flowers and vegetable markets, the old tram cars were also running, the time had not yet arrived to abolish them. The first editions of all the daily newspapers printed in Fleet Street were available on the streets shortly after midnight and at this time the underworld of London with all its vice and crime begins to show its ugly head. For those first two weeks my posting was once again number two beat, the east side of Whitehall from Charing Cross and Trafalgar Square to Victoria Street. I started to get familiar with the things that went on, and the characters that appeared underneath the arches on the embankment along the river when darkness comes down. To begin with it was my duty to move on all those different, and so often, interesting characters, but I soon found when I was absent from that particular area they would return.

I had to watch the clock after midnight in order to do my relieving for a couple of hours for the men on Trafalgar Square and the rear of Downing Street, to get their meals but with the lighted face of Big Ben and its chimes all through the night, it was no problem. In the small hours of some of those balmy August nights, the mist rose off the river and many times I went to the limit of my territory, the centre of Westminster Bridge, where I could look down to hear the swish of water as the lines of barges were towed up and down the river, their faint lights twinkling through the mist. The first Westminster Bridge was opened in 1750 and I understand that Wordsworth composed his well-known sonnet on that bridge, 'Earth has not anything to show more fair'. He did not see what I could see in my time with such a splendid view, representing such a wide panorama of the river, with its banks shrouded in the mist and the twinkling lights of the skyline above, pierced by the towers and spires of so many familiar buildings and churches outlined against the reflected light in the sky. It gave me a little time to examine unhindered the sculptured statue of Boadicea and her daughters in the big scythe-wheeled chariot pulled by two prancing horses. There the bridge met the west embankment, as I silently wandered down to check the ferry and tourist landing buildings near the bridge.

After the first week along the river, many of those strange and sometimes weird characters, who slept around the cold hard paving, or a vacant bench seat, covered with salvaged newspapers spread out to keep out the cold, began to lose some of their suspicions towards me and we began to exchange a few words. Some of them were chronic alcoholics addicted to methylated spirits and any kind of cheap drink and simply no-hopers. Many of them were drop-outs from society, some of them from well-to-do families, who obtained a few shillings from the drudgery of the dirty kitchen chores in the back areas of many shady cafés and illicit clubs in the back streets of the West End, just to keep them going.

In summer time as it was drawing to an end at that period, their beds were free with the pavements as their pillows, and the drinking fountains their only toiletries. In winter and the bleak nights of late autumn, they could obtain a bed, if they could beat the rush, at the Great Peter Street Salvation Army hostel, for one shilling, complete with a round of bread spread with a watered-down, cheap jam for breakfast. This establishment would come into my night life later and I would get familiar with it when I moved to Rochester Row Police Station. I went through that miserable place, the only way for me to describe it, many, many times after midnight searching for a culprit for some serious offence. Sadly I can only say I had little time for the person who ran the place and the way things went on in that building, so perhaps it would be better to say no more about it.

Many of those characters who lived such a miserable existence at night along the Victoria Embankment, stretching from Blackfriar's Bridge to Westminster Bridge, a distance of between one and a half to two miles, soon became very familiar to me. Many of the absolute no-hopers and chronic alcoholics usually found their resting place in the bombed and gutted warehouses and the wharfs towards London Bridge and the docks area. Usually the better types found their way to Charing Cross and the portable refreshment hut under Hungerford Bridge, dispensing mugs of tea, sandwiches, pies, and rolls. One could usually determine their type of disposition by their conversation, their use of words and expressions, and I soon discovered that many of them were well educated.

One of those 'down and outs' I remember so well, became talkative and friendly with me after a while on that first spell of night duty. He called himself 'John', but he would not disclose his surname, and I had no reason to know it because he had done no wrong. His face was almost hideous and terribly scarred from the result of burns; his hands and lower arms were badly scarred too, and I could only assume that his body must have been burned the same way. He did possess a slight Cockney accent but his speech was fluent with perfect English, and I could only guess he was between 50 and 60 years of age. He did have a number of cronie-type associates but they always slinked away when I came on the scene. With the unpleasant experiences of my young days in the 1920s in South Wales, the oppression, hunger, and poverty and how we tried to help and assist those unfortunates, evicted families and downtrodden souls, my sympathies were with John and I was determined to get more information from him and to find out why he lived that life as a drop-out. It took me almost a week with a hurried half-hour each night in my patrols to get a little more background about him. It happened to be a very wet night and I treated him to a mug of hot tea and a sandwich from the refreshment hut, as we sheltered underneath Charing Cross railway bridge. The cost to me was two shillings. He opened up in his conversation saying that he had never been treated like that before. As I more or less guessed, his awful disfigurement was caused by a German bomb – an oil bomb. His wife and her sister died in the fire and he escaped alive but badly burned. The fiery contents of those awful bombs splashed and stuck to everything like sticky tar, and the fiery hot liquid still seared and burned human flesh, after it was extinguished.

It all happened in the winter of 1943. He was rushed to hospital in a terrible state and he spent nearly two years there with skin grafts, before he was discharged to face the outside world alone. All his other relatives had been killed in the East End, in the Blitz of 1940 and 1941. He had worked in the city area of Bishopsgate but with his shocking disfigurement, his confidence and pride had gone. He could not live a normal life again and, with a scarf muffled around his face he became a loner and a drop-out. On Friday and Saturday nights until two, and often three in the morning he washed up and cleared up the mess in the rear kitchen areas of Frith Street Maltese Café in Soho, earning thirty shillings and obtaining two meals each night. In daylight hours he hid away in the bombed warehouses along the river. When darkness came down he emerged to join the haunts of the other characters along the embankments. To me, when I heard his story, this was another travesty, another shocking affair, to end so sadly and suddenly. During the second week of September 1947, a colleague PC

269

John Scott, a huge powerful six-foot-nine-inch south Londoner, residing at the section house, and doing night duty in that area, informed me that one of the 'Charing Cross dregs' asked him to tell me that John had 'jumped the river'. I immediately knew and understood what that meant. He had thrown himself over the embankment wall into the river. The following day I went along to the Horseferry Road Mortuary to see the attendant, with whom, incidentally, I became very friendly in the months ahead, on duty around that area. When I made inquiries about John and I saw his badly scarred body, the comment I received was, 'Just another unknown stiff from the river.' I was told he had been fished out of the river by the river police and was unidentifiable. I must mention also that any member of the river police who recovered a body from the water was paid a bonus of five pounds, if he simply placed his hand into the clothed body to seek means of identification, and this was a task that I was to experience later. My next mission was to see the coroner's assistant, another officer from Rochester Row Station, and to inform him of all the information I had gained from John. His hospital inquiries soon traced him, and he was identified by the hospital staff for the purpose of the inquest. My two shillings for a mug of tea and a sandwich had helped to solve another mystery of that unfortunate individual.

During September I had two weeks of duty at the rear of Number 10 Downing Street, on Horse Guards Parade. There were two officers posted there at all times, a security post covering all the rear wall of the gardens, to the stone steps at the top end of Downing Street. On day duty and finishing at 2 p.m. it gave me the time and the opportunity to get to Stamford Bridge football ground, the Chelsea football team's home ground on alternate Saturdays, for voluntary duty on the ground. I was able to see the big game and to earn the sum of three pounds for my services, paid by the football ground management. The game usually commenced at 3 p.m. and I was back at the section house to get my tea by 5.15 p.m. It was an easy way to spend Saturday afternoon and to get paid for it.

To complete the month my duties were on Trafalgar Square, covering the whole of the square and once again two officers were on duty there at all times. On the Strand corner of the square, there is a small police post built into the column, complete with a telephone and peep hole vision slits, to keep the whole square under observation. It was a very convenient place often for a few minutes break, away from the maddening crowds, with all their problems, the traffic and the dirty pigeons.

270

All day long the square thronged with people, visitors and tourists, and gave no time for laziness, or relaxation, as there was something happening or going wrong all the time. There were people falling and injuring themselves, sneak thieves and pickpockets, traffic snarls, and hold ups, accidents, and pedestrians getting knocked down, and it was a long tiring day. Very often, too, when the traffic became so heavy with hold ups and build ups, as we possessed a key to the traffic signal lights control box, we could alter the seconds time delay on the different controlled stops and intersections, to speed up a line of traffic that was moving too slowly and to turn them off completely to allow royalty and high foreign dignitaries to speed through unhindered.

October 1947 arrived, the beginning of unpleasant weather and heavy rain followed by fogs, but fairly light ones only at that time, the worst were to come. The dreadful pea-soup smog was something I had never experienced before and was soon to find out what it was like on the streets of that city. The first two weeks gave me a change of hours, 8 a.m. to 4 p.m. on traffic duty at Marlborough Gate in the Mall. This was to be my first spell of continuous point duty for eight long hours unbroken, except for a half-hour meal break. The man on the beat did his best to give a ten minute break, morning and afternoon, but he became tied up with so many duties, incidents, and hold ups one could never rely on him getting to you, so I just had to carry on. When conditions became desperate one simply left it to sort itself out uncontrolled, and took refuge in the public conveniences on the park side nearby, to sit down for a short break in the attendant's room. By the end of each day and as the afternoon dragged on, one's arms got tired and weary, each movement and signal felt as if lead weights were attached to one's elbows and arms and it was such a relief to break off at the end of each shift. The most unpleasant and uncomfortable thing for me was during the long periods of heavy rain. With my arms raised hundreds of times continuously throughout those long downpours, although the white gauntlet prevented the water from running down the tunic sleeve, shedding it onto the oilskin traffic coat, after many hours those cold raindrops inevitably found their way down my arm, trickling to the armpit, down the side of my body and down my leg to the boot, and I am sure everyone knows on such a cold day to feel icy water seeping down your bare warm skin is not a pleasant experience.

The last two weeks of October, day shift and afternoon shift involved me in many different duties around the Cannon Row jurisdiction. I did a few days working as an aid to the palace police, relieving one of their members on the sick list. I spent one period on the main palace front gates and another, for the first time, inside the side entrance at the bottom of Constitution Hill where the boundary wall and fence runs along Constitution Hill. This was the area where the German bombs hit the outbuildings of the palace structure causing quite a lot of damage. Inside the gate also was the main exit from the bomb shelters that led down a concrete stairway to the labyrinth beneath the palace. This was one area I did not have the privilege of viewing, the huge steel entrance door was always locked. I did have access to all the gardens around the lake, the steps to the ballroom at the rear and all the big glassed-in area of the swimming pool.

During the final week I came back to the beat to be involved in my first big arrest for robbery with violence, on a wet dark night in Green Park. This park, just like all the other parks of central London, was a haven for vice, thieves, prostitutes and pimps on those dark winter nights. Extending from a considerable length of Piccadilly to Constitution Hill and Hyde Park Corner it is a big area for one man to cover. The time was almost 9 p.m. on a Friday night just south of the Piccadilly roadway and I was concealed in among the trees off one of the pathways. In my dark uniform no one could see me in the rain and the gloom, but all my vision ahead was silhouetted against the street lights of Piccadilly, the illuminated buses and headlights of the streams of traffic moving along that road. Approximately 30 yards from where I stood, with my brightly lit background, I saw an attacking brute strike down another person hurrying through the park, and I took off at full pelt through the trees. I had almost reached the pair, one on the ground, after being struck down, and the attacker hurriedly trying to grab his wallet and possessions, when he attempted to run away. I kicked his legs away beneath him, he crashed to the ground, and I jammed my boot down on his neck. I then pulled him to his feet warning him that if he resisted he would suffer the consequences, slapped his arm up the back quickly, with my right arm beneath to grab his collar. He winced in pain with the hold and I warned him again if he struggled, as he was under arrest, that I would jam my fingers up his nostrils forcing back his head to cause him more pain, and he became subdued. The victim was hurt but he seemed to be all right. I asked him to pick up his scattered possessions, and the cosh, which turned out to be a six-inch length of lead pipe, and to accompany me as I frogmarched my man to the Hyde Park Corner Police post, always manned at night time by one police officer. A telephone call brought the police van around to transport us to Cannon Row. The accused person was cautioned in the familiar way: 'You are not obliged to say anything, but if you do, anything you say may be taken down in writing and given in evidence.' He was charged with robbery of 45 pounds, the contents of the wallet, a pocket watch and a ring valued at 200 pounds, with violence, and causing grievous bodily harm to the victim, who incidentally had a nasty swelling on his head, a small cut, and a mighty headache caused from the blow from the lead pipe. I had to attend Bow Street Magistrates Court for the hearing later. All the criminal cases were conducted by a CID officer and I had to give my evidence of the attack, and the arrest, and the accused pleaded guilty. The maximum sentence a magistrate could impose at that time was six months' imprisonment, and the accused had the option of being committed for trial, or accepting the magistrate's sentence. He chose the latter and received the six months' sentence.

November was to be a very busy month with two big ceremonies, the opening of Parliament, and the royal wedding of Princess Elizabeth on the 20th of the month, with many rehearsals taking place prior to the big event. I prepared, pressed and ironed my dress uniform in readiness, as it was going to be a long tiring month. The first week I was detailed for duty on traffic control at the intersection of Parliament Street and Bridge Street, almost under the tower of Big Ben. It was the unpleasant November weather, drizzling, cold rain, with fog rising and drifting off the river. I was hoping it would not be too heavy and thick, making it very dangerous, smarting the eyes and burning the throat, as the diesel exhaust fumes mixed with the smog, not knowing then that there were far worse experiences to come. Thankfully, 4th November was a fine day for the opening of Parliament and it was to be a much easier day for me. All the traffic lights were turned off and traffic diverted away from the royal procession from Buckingham Palace and all the pomp and ceremony, to the Houses of Parliament. At 5 p.m. after 11 hours of duty, I was glad to get back to my room in Ambrosden House.

On November 19th my schedule was day duty but it was to be the longest period of continuous duty of any day, lasting from 6 a.m. till midnight, 18 continuous hours, because the huge crowds were flocking to the ceremonial route to take up their positions and to remain there all night, camping down with rugs and blankets, to get their front-line view of the procession on the following day. It was to be 1 a.m. that morning of the 20th day, that I reached the section house to get a meal and snatch a few hours' sleep, after which I had to be back on duty at 6 a.m. and then begin another tour of duty for 12 hours until 6 p.m. That night of 19th November 1947 was another one of those periods that will remain fixed in my memory for the remainder of my life; it was just hectic, with all the incidents and happenings that took place. I was expected and called upon to perform the tasks of a doctor, first aid attendant, nursemaid and arbitrator, and they were just a few of them. I can recall that I repaired two broken children's pushers, settled dozens of arguments almost leading to blows and injuries over disputed positions, besides suffering and recording the torments of individuals, the victims of stolen bags, purses and possessions, and I was even called upon to heat a baby's bottle with a stubborn, difficult-to-light spirit stove, by one big fat lady with 8 crying children. Her thermos flask had dropped from her huge hamper of supplies, and broke up on the roadside. Some other kind member of that huge crowd had produced the stove. I was also jeered and catcalled on a number of occasions for removing people from unauthorised and dangerous positions and so it went on and on. What went on after midnight with so many people squabbling for their positions I did not know, but I sympathised with the boys who took over from me in that area. I dealt with two accidents that night, and the casualties had to be taken to hospital after I struggled through the masses to get to the telephone at Trafalgar Square for help. Between 8 p.m. and when I left at midnight, 8 people had fallen or had been pushed into the illuminated pools beneath the fountains on the square, and they too had to be carried away for help and treatment at a first aid post in St Martin-in-the-Fields.

On the early morning of the 20th, I crawled out of bed after being awakened by the section house sergeant at 5 a.m. I had managed to get about three and a half hours' sleep. It was hopeless to try to obtain breakfast with the busloads of hundreds of police from the outer areas filling the canteen. Hours before when I came off duty, I had prepared some filled bread rolls and a Lyons fruit pie and I made my own tea in the dining room with some of the other residents before setting off to Cannon Row, to begin duty and another day at 6 a.m. It was a public holiday. Parliament Square, around the Abbey, and Whitehall was already choked with the huge crowds. Westminster Tube Station was closed, no more people could be accommodated across the Bridge, and into Bridge Street and I had such difficulty getting through to Cannon Row to get to the station.

However, I was told firstly to make my way down Birdcage Walk to Wellington Barracks, to assist the guards being marched out to line the route on both sides of the roads, about five paces apart, and they all had to be in position by 9 a.m. Then my area would be near Admiralty Arch, off Trafalgar Square, at the top end of Horse Guards Parade. I also had to relieve the two men at the rear of Downing Street, for short breaks and meals. A marquee tent had been set up near the arch side of St James's Park, where tea and refreshments could be obtained by all the police around. It was a casualty clearing station and a first aid post, and by mid morning it was working to capacity. That morning when the procession began I saw glimpses of it only, I was occupied with so many things happening all over the place. People were getting pushed and crushed in the throng, others were fainting, they all had to be attended to, and lifted out into the park alongside, either revived or carried to the first aid post for treatment. I succeeded in getting the two meal breaks for the men at the rear of Downing Street all finished by 10 a.m., and my first break and a cup of tea came at 12.30, seven and a half hours after I had crawled out of bed that morning. The crowds began to drift away by 3 p.m. and I went along to Trafalgar Square. It was still crowded there, and just like a garbage dump with all the papers and rubbish left behind by the crowds but the traffic was moving again and the buses were carrying away their full loads.I walked back along the Mall hoping I might get a cup of tea and perhaps give one of the others an opportunity to get one too. A lady with two small children was coming towards me sobbing and crying and of course, I had to inquire what was wrong. She told me her purse had been stolen from her big carry bag as she attended to one of the children. It contained all her money and she had no means of paying her fares to get her back to her home in Surrey. Nothing could be done about the purse, I could only take a description of it and the contents, her name and address, record it in my pocket book and report it. She asked if I could lend her enough to get home and she would repay it later. I did just that and the tears went away, I did my last good deed for the day. I offered her ten shillings, sufficient to get her and the children home. I wrote down my number and address, Cannon Row Police Station, not expecting to be repaid but, sure enough, a few days later there was a letter for me pinned to the notice board containing a postal order for ten shillings, and a note expressing her thanks, so all's well that ends well.

The last days of November dragged on, the weather became cold and miserable as the days of winter were about to begin, and for me the month of December would be another spell of night duty from 10 p.m. to 6 a.m. From memory now it must have been either the 28th or 29th November. It had become very foggy the previous day and warnings were issued that its intensity would increase. We were alerted to be prepared and for me it was to bring the first awful experience of the conditions and dislocations a real London pea-soup fog can cause. I was working the embankment beat taking the place of a colleague on his rostered day off. At two o'clock that day, when I went on duty, visibility had been reduced to about ten feet only, and all the transport depots, taxi cabs, and bus services had been warned to stop running through central London and along each side of the river. The traffic had been reduced to a crawl, nose to tail, bumper to bumper, and all the men abandoned their traffic posts as too dangerous. As darkness came down and the rush hours began, all we could possibly do was to stop everything for periods of ten and fifteen minutes, and line the crossings with torches to get the people across and guide them to the tube stations. The bus numbers were invisible, and it caused confusion everywhere. Parliament Square and Whitehall were still lit with the big gas street lights down the centre. They were all lit at dusk in the old-fashioned way, by the lamplighter, an employee carrying a long pole with a hook and a small flame at one end. The switch, attached to the huge glass domes around the clusters of mantles, was a balanced cross-arm with a small hanging chain at each end and a ring to engage the lamplighter's hook. He pulled it down one side to turn on the gas, and at daylight pulled down the other side to turn off the gas. They were retained to provide the traditional 'Old London' atmosphere, but they were powerful lights, and they could penetrate the fog much better than electricity. On that occasion the lamplighter could not see higher than two feet above his head up the lamp standard. Feeling our way and struggling through the gloom with me as an escort we managed to obtain a ladder from the police station. It was my job to assist him and guide him along from post to post and to watch him disappear up the ladder into the fog to find the switch and light the gas. It seems rather odd and funny now as I think about it, but it was serious and so dangerous at that time such a long time ago. If anyone has experienced the old London pea-soup smog they would never forget it, with all the pollution from the old industries pouring thousands of tons of smoke and soot into the atmosphere, and thousands of coal fires and smoking chimneys. At that time, a person's eyes burned and breathing was difficult, torches and headlights were useless as they would not penetrate the gloom, but just reflected back off the black smog. It settled on one's clothes and skin like a wet soot, and blackened the buildings, glass and windscreens.

By six o'clock that night it brought everything to a complete halt, with visibility nil. I had never seen or experienced anything like it before in my life. Along the left-hand side of Whitehall, and guided only by touching and following contours of the outer walls of public buildings, three of us organised our own system. We grabbed hundreds of confused, frightened, and crying pedestrians trying to find their way, and made them all hold hands or to hang onto one another's coat or some wearing apparel, to form a chain. Touching the boundary walls we brought them down Whitehall across the entrance of Downing Street and along Parliament Street until we found our flashing blue police phone box light. We crossed the road there until contact was made with the buildings on the other side, around the corner and along Bridge Street to Westminster tube station. How many times we did this I cannot remember but I am sure those hundreds of people were glad to reach the tube station to get on their way. About 8 p.m. that same night on one of the return trips I phoned from the blue post asking that the flashing blue light be kept going all night and anyone on hand would ring if there were instructions. I was told that a convoy of traffic had left Victoria, and was crawling up Victoria street, bumper to bumper with two Rochester Row officers, and three municipal employees in the front operating a big paraffin flare. We had to take over at the top of Victoria Street, bring it around Parliament Square, up Whitehall to Trafalgar Square and hand over to a party from C Division. I had never seen the paraffin flares used before anywhere, and operating like a giant blow torch, they were another new experience for me. It was the only instrument that would penetrate the fog and it was effective. What an unpleasant and slow job it turned out to be, the leading vehicles were allowed to move short distances only, while the second flare was ushered along the route behind to bring up the lost convoy. It was 9.30 p.m. that night when we finally reached Trafalgar Square to let the others take over, and I was glad to get away from it. Once again we had the task of finding our way along the building line down to Parliament Street. During those eight hours of continuous duty that day, we were unable to get a meal or a break. How all the others fared I did not know, but I do remember they granted us two hours of overtime payment for our efforts. Going home that night, three of us, Collar, myself and a colleague named Reiby, lost our way in the vicinity of Westminster Catholic Cathedral, when we turned off Victoria Street, believing we had turned into Artillery Row. Probing with a torch and peering closely at numbers and objects, we finally reached the section house at 1.15 a.m. What a day it had been, with burning eyes and a burning throat I was so relieved that the following day was my day off.

My tour of night duty began at the beginning of December. Another year, 1947, was drawing to an end. The Christmas decorations and lights were going up in Regent Street, Oxford Street and throughout the West End, and the huge Christmas tree, which was being presented each year by the people of Norway, with thanks for their liberation from the Nazis, had been erected and set up in Trafalgar Square. With all the masses of pretty lights, the illuminations, and the spectacular display of underwater coloured lights, changing colours every few minutes in the pools and the fountains, the influx of huge crowds increased in the square. It was going to be a full-time job for me. Street barrow boys with their loads of fruit and delicacies became more troublesome, causing obstructions, compelling us to move them on. The cries of the Cockney with his barrow, selling cockles and jellied eels, mixed with the roar of the traffic, and through the night air came the appetising and sweet aroma of roasting chestnuts drifting on the evening breeze from the portable roasting fire of the chestnut man. The flashing neon lights were gradually coming back and even the old Cockney with the barrel organ was on his rounds again. It was approaching three years since the war ended, and things were beginning to settle down to normal conditions once more. I saw a bunch of bananas for the first time since 1939 on display on a street barrow at the enormous price of one pound each! All the theatres and cinemas were booked out with full houses for each performance and it was difficult to get a seat on a booking of more than a week ahead. I checked through my schedule to find I would be on duty Christmas night with a night off on Boxing night. I was yet to know where I would be. I had spent Christmas in so many different places in the past seven years.

The second week of December I was posted for an all-night vigil for six nights in the garden of 10 Downing Street. At that period there was a plain-clothes man and a uniformed officer outside the front door, a plain-clothes officer and a uniformed officer PC, both armed with a pistol inside the premises on the ground floor, and one uniformed officer, at night, at a rear door, to patrol into the garden, which was surrounded by a thick, high stone wall. On the outside of that wall, on Horse Guards Parade a further two police officers patrolled, so security was very strong for this principal residence of the prime minister. I believe considerable alterations have been made to the internal structure of that building since my tours of duty there a long time ago, but I still remember it very well. The first room inside the front door had very few contents, but I do recall adjacent to the door of the adjoining room facing Downing Street there was a prominent high, umbrella-type armchair with a round hood. That chair must have been a priceless antique, made of dark leather, buttoned and pleated all over, and it had occupied that position for many years. With its straight back, to me it was neither beautiful nor comfortable as I sat on it many times and if it no longer adorns that room I guess it would be a priceless treasure now fit for its pride and place in any museum. There was a stairway up to the residential, reception and conference rooms, on the upper floors, and at the end of that first entrance room another door leading to a passage, with typists' offices, and a glassed-over area, leading to the rear door and the garden, and this was my area for my first spell inside that famous residence, 10 Downing Street.

Those December nights were cold and dark, and the garden was illuminated with spotlights. There was not much room to walk around except for the restricted area of the lawn. I could see the whole area from the rear door and the shelter of that doorway and the passage was appreciated. I had become accustomed to those long sleepless nights over the years. My colleagues were very good, besides being relieved for a hot meal at the canteen, there was always someone to give a break for a hot cup of tea. My period of duty was quiet with no incidents, and the prime minister was due to go to the country residence at Chequers for Christmas. Christmas Eve was fairly subdued and quiet also; I was on Trafalgar Square and by midnight all the merrymaking crowds began to drift away, the last buses stopped about 1 a.m., everyone was going home for Christmas Day but I guessed they would make up for it all in a few days' time on New Year's Eve.

I ordered my hot Christmas dinner that early Christmas morning when I went off duty. The conscientious lady who operated the canteen would have it all prepared and waiting for me in the warm oven in the dining room before she left and closed up at 10 p.m., when the night lady came on. Christmas Day I slept until 1.20 p.m. The next day, Boxing Day, I would spend with my sister Edna, but a long, cold Christmas night still awaited me. That Christmas night was, I believe one of the most quiet nights of London, the traffic was still with just a rare taxi moving past, and the silence was broken only with chimes, and the boom of the strikes of Big Ben. After midnight, as a lone, silent figure I wandered around some of the areas steeped in history. I made my way down around the Abbey to study and look at some of the old things, imaged by streetlights. I walked on through the gardens passing the shadowy statue of Sylvia Pankhurst, who bore the banner for women's freedom before the First World War and at the end of those gardens into Dean Stanley Street, and towards the offices of the Board of Trade. This building was purported to have the finest doors in London, and I wanted to see them leisurely with the help of my flashlight. Those enormous doors, I had learned, were 20 feet high and 10 feet wide, and each of the doors weighed two and a half imperial tons. They were all metal and faced on the fronts and backs with silveroid, which is an alloy of nickel and copper, and I understood they took a year and a half to complete, and it was said that nothing like this had been attempted since the bronze gates of the Baptistry in Florence took 30 years to complete in the fourteenth century. I turned down Dean Stanley Street to Smith Square, past the ruined church of St John Westminster, built in 1728, along Church Street to Great College Street, all eerie and silent in those early hours into Boxing Day. This shadowy area had the wall of the Westminster Abbey gardens on the one side, and old seventeenth- or eighteenth-century houses on the other. Some of those houses were once boarding houses for the pupils of Westminster School and Keats the poet lived there for some time. I wandered into Dean's Yard looking around with my old antiquated police lantern, so heavy and cumbersome, and probably still kept as an emergency weapon from the turn of the century. I opened the gate under the centuries-old archway leading to Westminster School, part of which had been hit by German bombs in 1941 and burnt down, some of the same stick of bombs that hit the Houses of Parliament. I found the gateway inscribed with the names of old pupils of the school, the Coat of Arms of Queen Elizabeth, and the date erected in 1734. I understood too that this place was famous for performing Latin Plays at that time of the year, Christmas time, and pancakes were tossed and thrown on Shrove Tuesday. I looked all around, then walked back into Dean's Yard under the archway and opposite the towers of the Abbey. I found the inscription of erection, date of 1735, and designed at that period by Christopher Wren. I continued along the dark path through St Margaret's churchyard, the church so well known for all its high-society weddings. In the darkness I did not know what all the figures and statues represented but I did find the only visible grave and by coincidence I recall well, it was

Alexander Davies, the surname of my ancestors. This unfortunate ancient soul died in the plague and Black Death in 1665. I continued on through Parliament Square with all its statues of dead prime ministers, glistening, and showing up the white pigeon droppings against the streetlights, on to the Guildhall with all its wonderful architecture.

The left-hand side of this wonderful building depicts the signing of Magna Carta and, on the right side Lady Jane Grey, the lady who lost her head on the block, accepting the Crown from the Duke of Northumberland. The assize courts were often held in this building and, as time went on, I did a number of hours' duty outside the door of the court judge, when the court was in session. The authorities must have believed those special, high-ranking judges required special protection as they so often donned the ridiculous medieval Black Cap to send some unfortunate convicted murderer 'to be hanged by the neck until he was dead'.

So, while London slept on Christmas night 1947, and so many people were getting over their over-eating and over-indulgence in the good things of life, my silent footsteps carried me around, through the darkness and the gloom, examining some of the past, disturbed only by the chimes and booming strikes, as Big Ben tolled the hours and the early morning of Boxing Day.

I had just an hour's sleep after getting back to my room that morning, then I went along to Vauxhall Bridge Road for breakfast at an all night café. It seemed the world was starting to wake up after my quiet, undisturbed night. At 10 a.m., carrying presents, I boarded the train at Victoria underground station to visit my sister Edna and to spend the day there. That day was to be Christmas day for just the four of us, sister Edna, her husband Tom, Brian and myself, a lazy day indoors, as the weather was cold, and it was far better on the inside in the warmth and comfort of the living room. It was midnight when I returned to my residence that night and I was able to have a long sleep after a pleasant, enjoyable day. I had only five more nights to complete the month of night duty. January and February were the coldest and most unpleasant months and, thankfully, it would be March before I would be due once again for those long night vigils, unless something unforeseen was to happen.

Thursday 31st December arrived, with New Year's Eve turning into 1948, and it would be a long night for me going on duty at 10 p.m. on Trafalgar Square to face all the crowds, the revelry and troubles, as midnight approached and the final twelfth strike of Big Ben brought in the new year. I was hoping the problems of that night would not

281

involve me too much, as it was my long weekend till Monday, and I was looking forward to catching the train at 9 a.m. on Friday at Paddington to take me home for a break to visit my parents in South Wales, but it did not quite turn out that way.

We were reinforced that night with extra men, some Specials as they were referred to, not full-time men, all wearing soft peaked caps. There were two sergeants, a lieutenant, one of the trained officer class which were being phazed out at that time, and an inspector. The superintendent was expecting a bad night and he had prepared for it. When I went on duty at 10 p.m., the whole square leading up towards the West End, the Strand and Charing Cross to the top of Whitehall was choked with people packed in like sardines already causing severe problems with the traffic around the square. In the middle of those huge crowds and the noise and bustle of everything, the glistening giant Christmas tree with all its pretty flashing lights stood out, as people fought their way in and out of the crush, pushing sections of the crowd into the roadways. It became an almost impossible task of dragging fallen spectators from under the wheels and front ends of violently braking buses and taxis. As midnight approached it became worse, the traffic was stopped completely, and the drivers of those vehicles, taxis and late-night buses were furious, abusing everyone as they were unable to move on their way. There were a number of serious accidents and injuries caused by drunks and careless people, dozens had a cold night after being pushed or ducked in the fountain and many were arrested for stupid dangerous pranks, but I succeeded in keeping clear of anything serious. When it was all ended and into the early hours of New Year's Day 1948, scrutinising the deserted areas, accompanied by a colleague and using a police lamp for close examination all around the area, we picked up as I remember, assorted watches, pins, cuff-links, brooches, tie-pins, broken strings of beads, pearls, necklaces, bangles and various articles of clothing, a total of some 73 articles between the two of us. I realised this was going to delay me getting away quickly. I took 35 of those objects for my share to hand in and report and, as I went through them with the station sergeant piece by piece and listing them for the records, each broken object was passed over and dumped in the rubbish container. Using his words, it was a waste of time noting them. One of those articles was an attractive ladies wristwatch, the glass was broken and the hands were missing, from the pounding of so many feet, but it was still ticking away merrily. I recovered it from the rubbish bin and rightly or wrongly, I put it in my pocket and retained it. It was well after 7 a.m. when I finally got away. I explained to the station sergeant my anxiety to get to my train for my weekend off, and he said he would help if I rang him as soon as I was ready at the section house. I borrowed a colleague's bike to get to Ambrosden House and left it in his usual parking area at the rear. I hurriedly changed and got myself ready, had a quick cup of tea, then I rang the station sergeant, and true to his word he had a van waiting on hand to transport me to Paddington Station. I reached the station at ten minutes to nine just giving me time to get my ticket, before the express pulled out. I gave that wristwatch to my sister Edna later. Tom's family were in the jewellery business in the west of England but somehow Tom was the black sheep and out of it, although I never knew the reason. However, his brother repaired the watch for Edna, in return for a good turn rendered previously. Twenty-seven years later in 1975, I paid a visit from Australia to visit Edna. Tom had died some years before and Edna lived outside Chepstow where the giant Severn Suspension Bridge crosses over to the Welsh Border. She still possessed the watch and it was going strongly and keeping perfect time. I can now confess this was the one and only dishonest act I ever committed as a police officer; whether or not it was wrong to retain that broken watch, I do not know.

I arrived at Cardiff about 12.30 p.m. and I went along to see sister Joan at her employment premises about a 100 yards or so from the General Station on my way to Queen Street Station to catch a train up the Rhymney Valley. Joan was the only member of the family living at home with my parents, as Trefor had left and was with the P & O shipping line progressing as a ship's engineer.

It was the first day of January 1948, bleak and cold with a few snow flakes fluttering in the breeze. It would be a change for me to see a welcome hot blazing fire once more at Oak Cottage, just like old times. My mother did all my washing and ironing for me that afternoon so that relieved me of one of my tasks, and I could relax and take it easy until Sunday afternoon for my return to London.

It was at the beginning of 1948, that the administration developed a forward step at last. We were issued with blue collared shirts and black tie, and the tunic would no longer be buttoned and hooked at the neck. It was a start, we could purchase any extras to make provision for a fresh shirt each day and from that period onwards the uniform had a much better appearance with pressed down lapels, a collar and tie. I completed the next two weeks of day and afternoon shifts, then I was scheduled for three fortnightly sessions to complete the months of January and February and to gain more experience, two weeks on the river, with the River Police, two weeks on an area car and two weeks in plain clothes as an aid with the CID.

Those last two weeks of January were wet and bitterly cold with periods of sleet and snow. Inside the cabin of the police launch it was out of the wind and weather with a comfortable soft seat to sit on. There were two regular officers on the launch and their headquarters was Wapping Police Station with access to the river down Wapping Steps. They picked me up each morning of the first week, about ten minutes past 6 a.m. at the Westminster Pier, where all the river tourist boats and buses booked and loaded all their passengers. The first three days were very interesting to me, as everything was new and so different, checking around long stretches of the river, the bombed and gutted warehouses, buildings and docks and anything suspicious on the river. There was a great deal of barge traffic with many of the old residential bargees living on their colourful painted craft. There was not a great deal of shipping. Millions of tons of shipping had been sunk and lost during the war and merchant ships of all countries were depleted as a result. It was slowly improving but it would still take a long time to get back to normal. After those first three days I found it was the most boring job of all, up and down the river, hour after hour, and it was a relief to get back to Wapping for a meal or a short break for a cup of tea. The second week on late turn was even more monotonous in the hours of darkness, but that week did present us with a little more to do, searching the dark murky water with a searchlight, trying to locate members of the public who had decided they were tired of life. We recovered three bodies at different times that week, two of them had jumped off Waterloo Bridge and Black-friars Bridge, the other was a drunken seaman who had fallen over-board after a drinking session. This was the occasion I mentioned previously, when we pulled the body aboard with a grappling hook and I was favoured with the task of searching for its identification to receive the extra bonus of five pounds.

In February 1948, I began the first two weeks as one of the crew of an area car, one week of day shift and a week of afternoon late turn, in order to experience the routine, radio sequence and the procedures of moving from place to place with serious accidents and measure-ments on the location etc., the brawls, stolen vehicles, and calls from other police officers for assistance through the control centre of the information room at Scotland Yard. There were numerous calls and instructions and diversions all over the place sent out from the information room that needed urgent attention. The second week and the late evenings were the busiest times and often it became hectic. I did get involved with one smash and grab raid carried out in the Strand, and we chased one of the offending vehicles but lost it in the conjestion of Chelsea. The siren was not in use at that time, we had a system like a ringing bell, and the term used was 'to gong' any offending vehicle. I spent hours scrutinising lists of registration numbers of stolen vehicles, adding to the list as they came over the radio, memorising letters and checking quickly and trying to pick out the tallying numbers with those letters of offending vehicles in the long lines of traffic. The time flew by so quickly with so much to do to occupy the whole tour of duty.

The final two weeks of that month gave me more experience in plain clothes with the CID. I also spent some time in the fingerprint department of Scotland Yard with its millions of filed prints and learned the procedure for checking specimen prints taken from the scenes of a crime etc. I went through the Police Black Museum: weapons, instruments of torture and macabre objects from ghastly murders and crimes, photographs, weird objects recovered from many horrible deaths and a chamber of horrors very few people have ever seen. I became an observer, attending lots of break-ins and burglaries, a wounding incident and one shocking break-in with violence where the victim was badly hurt, and I learned a great deal. It was a very interesting two weeks and I wondered if I would become eligible for any one of those varied positions as time went on, at the completion of two years' service.

The blustery days of March were about to begin once again for that year of 1948. It brought another tour of night duty for me, and many long nights of quiet vigil on various security and important protection points around the administration area of Cannon Row. Some of those nights in that first week I recall clearly, perhaps as they were the most important responsibility for me as a police officer, as a bodyguard to the man who held the highest office in the country, the prime minister.

In May 1945 in the General Election at the end of the war Churchill had been put out of office and the man elected to lead the Nation was Major Clem Attlee. Mr Attlee was a quiet, sincere man, whom I admired because of his principles. He was the son of a wealthy City of London solicitor, with no money problems. He was educated at Oxford and called to the bar in 1906, and then practised law for just three years, before taking up residence in the East End of London. He lived amongst shocking poverty and squalor and learnt about the extortions of rich landlords, who reaped the profits from rat-infested slums, evictions and bailiff's seizures. He was a Tory just like his family when he went there, but the conditions, the harsh poverty and misery changed him completely and he turned to politics and the Labour Party. He became a Major after the start of the First World War, and he served at Gallipoli, in Mesapotamia, in France and he was severely wounded. He was outspoken against the disaster of Gallipoli and Churchill and ousted him to become prime minister in 1945. When war broke out again in 1939 he refused to join any government of that old millionaire diehard Neville Chamberlain. He was also a close colleague of Aneurin Bevan whom my father knew so well, the member of parliament for one of the adjacent Valleys in South Wales, and the finest orator in Parliament, whose own mother suffered the torments of starvation under the English Tory oppression and exploitation before the turn of the century.

The first three nights of the first week I was posted inside 10 Downing Street armed with a pistol. I had been a marksman with the Smith and Wesson .38 pistol in my unit in the latter years of the war and I could also fire accurately from the hip, so it was nothing new to me. Along with the plain-clothes police officer, the protection of the prime minister was our responsibility. Mr Attlee came down the stairway to that first ground-floor room quite often where his familiar pipe filled the atmosphere with its strong pleasant tobacco aroma. He appeared to me to have the urge to get away from his papers and ledgers upstairs, to talk and converse with someone different from the usual ministers, politicians and diplomats. He would discuss things and events with us both quite confidently, and as he spoke he would pace the floor backwards, and forwards, puffing at the pipe. With so many problems on his mind, all the financial problems of the nation trying to recover from the enormous losses of the war, reforms and adjustments, I did not envy his job. I remember well also that Aneurin Bevan had brought in his bill of massive reforms for the establishment of a National Health Service and National Health Insurance. On those late nights there, and well into the early hours of the next day, as Mr Attlee puffed his pipe, relighting it many times, I asked lots of questions about those schemes, and added my own ideas and proposals in those conversations with the prime minister. Perhaps now I can believe, maybe, some of my ideas and suggestions added to the final completion of that legislation of wonderful social reform. One other important question I recall asking Mr Attlee during those interesting talks, was about decolonisation.

I Become London Bobby PC 175A

On 15th August 1947 India had become an independent country free from the shackles of hundreds of years of English imperial rule and the British Raj. Mr Attlee and his government were the authors of this mighty step forward, so greatly opposed by Churchill and his supporters. The question I asked him personally was, 'Did he have any fears and worries about civil war and awful bloodshed when the country was partitioned into India and Pakistan, and there would be an enormous migration of millions of Moslems out of the new state of India across to the new independent state of Pakistan?' He looked at me, holding the bowl of his pipe behind a fresh puff of smoke, and shaking his head at the same time he said clearly, something I have always remembered, 'You know as well as I know this should have been done years ago.' It was an answer to which I could give no comment; I was in full agreement. For me those nights inside that famous address were an important part of my life, and the most excited person of all was my dear old Dad when I told him all about it. My father was a devoted supporter of Clement Attlee; he would become even more elated when the Bill was introduced to take the coal mines away from the oppressive exploiting companies and bring the reform of all the shocking conditions imposed on the miners for such a long time.

At the beginning of April I searched around some of the secondhand shops looking for a bicycle. It would be such a help to get to and from the station, and would be so much quicker if I was not delayed by queries and requests. Production had almost ceased during the war years except for the forces and the folding bikes for the paratroopers, but at that period, just like motor cars they were coming back and being produced in volume. I went south across the river to Brixton and the market area. I soon found what I required, a bike about nine months old in excellent condition and with a little haggling I bought it for five pounds. It gave me the chance to test it out as I rode all the way back to Victoria. There was a special undercover, secure, parking area at the rear of Ambrosden House, so everything was in order, and I could now get backwards and forwards to Cannon Row quickly. During that month, on my morning tours of duty finishing at 2 p.m., I began to make my living room a little more homely. My room on the top floor at Ambrosden House was approximately 12 feet long and 10 feet wide. It had a comfortable single bed, a wooden chair and a table, with a central heating system radiator at the side of the top end of the bed, and beneath the sill of the window. Being on the top floor, the view out of that window was not very spectacular, just a typical London view looking across at building walls, roofs and of course hundreds of chimney pots everywhere, protruding skywards from the residential buildings around the area. I went scouting around the antiquated secondhand junk stores all over the place until I found three cheap attractive framed pictures and some hooks to hang them on the walls. I was a little out of place without any tools, something I had always had on hand throughout my life, so I gradually obtained the essentials such as a hammer, pliers and a screwdriver, with a few other odds and ends. I bought myself a comfortable chair, a desk top with pigeonholes and some shelves. I got them home by taxi and fitted the desk top on to my table and it turned out most satisfactory and useful. The only time I spent in that room was to sleep and to do reading and writing, as the greater part of the time I was out of it. The bed was made and the room cleaned daily by the charladies. However, I was glad I fixed it up to make it a little more homely, because a short time later in the middle of the month, I received a wonderful surprise with a visit from my brother Trefor, before he left for overseas on one of the P & O ships. It was so nice to see him and it was so convenient, as I had just finished duty at 2 p.m. so we spent the rest of the afternoon and early evening together. When Trefor departed that day it was to be a very long interval before we saw each other. The next time we met was in 1975 – 27 years later, when I was on a visit from Australia; it was to be a long, long time!

As the rainy days of April 1948 made things wet and miserable, into the final week and half way through the spring, I was posted to one afternoon's duty, in the middle of the week, as an aid to the Buckingham Palace police. There was an acute shortage of officers to fulfil all the usual duties because of sickness and bouts of flu. It was a regular daily practice for an inspector, usually accompanied by a sergeant or a constable, just before dusk, to go through Buckingham Palace to inspect and check all the fire points throughout the building. It is such a huge place, that particular task often took more than an hour to complete. On that evening of my tour of duty there, they were so short of men that I was instructed to accompany the inspector through the building. It suited me, something new and quite different, and we covered everything except the main royal suites and bed chambers. Inside the main archway at the front, there is a big quadrangle with the main buildings built around it, with the two wings and the rear all connected by passages, corridors and halls. The inspector was very good, and he was aware that I had never been inside that palacial residence before, so with a palace attendant with us, and he himself knowing the interior so well, he quite often gestured for me to open a door to have a quick look. I was not slow in doing that of course, anxious to scrutinise and have a look inside. I still remember the journey through that exquisite majestic building but with just short glances at everything it was impossible to take it all in. I can say now that I was privileged on that one occasion to look at what millions of people, journalists and reporters would give anything to have an opportunity to see. For me it was a new experience and another part of my varied duties attached to Cannon Row Police Station.

My work during May was varied, the weather was good and I looked forward to summer with the hope that I could go home for a holiday very soon. I had the daily tasks of Marlborough Gate traffic duty from 8 a.m. till 4 p.m. for the first two weeks. Traffic point duty always seemed to take the longest, as time dragged, hour after hour; it was so necessary not to lose concentration. Each hour seemed like half a day, but I had grown accustomed to it all, and I often abandoned the point to let it sort itself out in its own way if the beat man failed to turn up to give me a ten-minute break.

Two other alarming incidents happened in the third week for me to remember vividly. The first was the extraordinary high spring tides, something I had never seen before. A general alarm and alert was raised one mid afternoon as the river rose alarmingly, lapping the top of the embankment walls and actually just spilling over with the breeze. There was an emergency for a couple of hours until the tide turned. If it had come over, causing chaos and flooding it would have been devastating and put parts of the Houses of Parliament in danger. I believe in modern times they have solved the problem with massive boom gates costing tens of millions of pounds to control the high tides in the estuary.

The other incident was a bad accident on the Underground, when one train slammed into the rear of another in the tunnel at the entrance to Westminster Station. In the emergency and once again not thinking about myself, it was the second time, as I mentioned previously, that I used my rolled tunic to support an injured lady's head on the concrete floor. I lost my wallet and ten precious pound notes. It was never going to happen to me again, I had learned my lesson!

June was another month of night duties in the palace gardens and I had one bad night with the smashing of Bravington's jewellery shop windows on Trafalgar Square, which involved me for two hours in Bow Street Court the next day. This brought me up to my holiday and the warm days of summer, and for the first week of July, I could go home to relax.

20

My Meeting with Meg and my Transfers To Rochester Row and Hyde Park

The long days began to turn into summer and I completed my last spell of night duty on the last Friday night of June. At ten minutes after 6 a.m. on the Saturday morning, I was back at the section house to hurriedly prepare for another day. I was going home for a week's holiday. I gave the key of the locking chain of my bike to John Scott for him to use in my absence. I left a note on my table for the cleaning lady to read on Monday morning, to let her know that I would be absent for the week, prepared myself for my departure, locked the room, taking my case with me to have a quick breakfast in the canteen before I caught the Tube to Paddington Station. I was hoping to get there as early as possible in order to get a seat. There were no reservations in those days, one could only hope for the best to get aboard. The old steam trains were always jampacked and that particular express travelled right through to the Irish Ferry Terminal at Fishguard on the Welsh west coast, with just two stops only, at Reading and Newport, until it reached Cardiff. It was such a long time to stand in the corridors; I had experienced it many times before. However, I succeeded in obtaining a good seat so that I could doze quietly for the next three hours. On that journey I left the train at Newport in the old-named county of Monmouthshire, which in modern times has gone and been renamed Gwent. There, I caught the Red and White bus service, which travelled through Risca, Blackwood, Pengam to Bargoed over the bridge opposite Oak Cottage, so when I alighted I was just 50 yards from home and my arrival was shortly after 2.30 p.m. My mother, father, and Joan were at home, all sitting in the garden in the shade of the big beech tree. My father had given up work just the day previously, age and the lung troubles caused by dust from years of toil in the mines and his general health were causing problems and I agreed he deserved a break and a long rest. It was a beautiful day and I quickly joined them to take advantage of that quiet lazy Saturday afternoon. My brother Trefor was overseas as a fully fledged engineer on one of the P & O ships. Joyce's husband, Bill, was still working as a crane driver loading the big wagons on the Bargoed Colliery sidings. Toots' husband, Arthur, had returned to the Tredomen engineering works, a few miles down the valley as a fitter and Toots was working part-time at Loveday's clothing store on the Pengam Square, so everything seemed to be going along quite well.

Those hot summer days of July were wonderful, and the time seemed to pass so quickly as I wandered around the locality with my father, talking and catching up with so many old acquaintances all over the district. The building trade was going well and Joe, the youngest of the Stucky boys, came to see me to try to persuade me to join him on a big building job in the adjacent Sirhowy Valley. I wondered then if I had done the right thing by getting out of it; however, I rejected the temptation to start again.

The last thing I did before returning to London, which I remember well, was to sell my billiard table. I had bought it in 1938, ten years previously, for the price of seven pounds. It was a beautiful table, eight feet by four feet, which clamped and levelled onto an ordinary dining table. It had a complete billiard and snooker set of balls and we had used it a great deal with Trefor and my father, but it was of no use to me any more, so I sold it for the sum of ten pounds. My holiday came to an end and it was time to return to London, to the rush, the crowds, the traffic and the congested city streets. I was to realise my tours of duty from Cannon Row were drawing to an end with a new influx of men about September, so it would fall to me to move on to another area of the division.

Settling back into my routine once more, the remaining weeks of July were pleasant and hot, and for the first time with a collared shirt and tie, we were allowed to discard the tunic. What a relief it was for those long summer days. The influx of tourists to central London was on the increase, the cruise liners were back in operation, and visitors from all over the world were noticeable everywhere. I celebrated another birthday on the 26th of that month putting me into my 29th year. It fell on my rostered day off, so along with my sister Edna, and young Brian, we caught the train to Southend for a very pleasant and enjoyable day visiting Helen Butler, Edna's friend from Bournville, who had married and settled into a seaside cottage in that area.

The warm days of July 1948 turned into August and another spell of duty 8 a.m. till 4 p.m. on traffic control at Marlborough Gate. I was caught out on this occasion having to cope with the enormous flow of traffic, taxis and heavy vehicles making their way to Victoria for the Bank Holiday weekend. It became one of the busiest periods of my service on the Friday and Saturday, coping with thousands of vehicles travelling down the Mall towards Buckingham Palace Road and Victoria. The weather was hot and humid, making it so unpleasant and tiring and to add to my problems no relief came my way to give me a break. In the middle of it all on the Friday mid-afternoon there was a terrific thunderstorm. I abandoned the post having no waterproof equipment on hand, so there was absolute chaos for nearly an hour. When I left at 4.15 p.m. the traffic was still bumper to bumper way back to Trafalgar Square and choked in Pall Mall. What happened to it from then onwards I did not know and I did not care. I complained when going off duty, that I had completed nearly eight and a half hours continuously, with just 30 minutes' absence for a meal, but my complaints got little response. I continued on that posting for two weeks and I was glad to get away from it to spend the next two weeks on late and early turn at Trafalgar Square.

The month of August was drawing to a close, and my duty roster ended on Saturday the 28th giving me the Sunday of the 29th as my day off, so I spent that day with sister Edna, Tom, and young Brian, enjoying a roast dinner and a quite relaxing day before my week commenced once more at 6 a.m. on Monday, 30th August.

Little did I know or realise as I rode my bike on that early morning to Cannon Row, that this particular day would change the direction of my future life. It appeared to be just another work day, another posting, when the detail was read out by the duty sergeant as we assembled that morning. I was with John Collar interchanging on the traffic point and the pedestrian crossings at the intersection of Parliament Street and Bridge Street. It was a little easier, and we could change over after each half-hour spell on the traffic point, to the street crossing.

It must have been about late morning and approaching 11.30 when everything was a little subdued before the pedestrian rush began at 12 noon for the lunchtime rush. I had just come off the traffic point to stand on the pavement at the pedestrian crossover. Out of the crowds of people crossing from the direction of Westminster tube station, as I held up the traffic coming around from Bridge Street and Great George Street, came a tanned young lady, all smiles, holding onto the round hat on her head with her left hand. She approached me, busy with my hands raised and holding up the long line of vehicles, to ask a question I did not quite hear because of the noise. I released the traffic line stepping back on to the footpath to answer the query and what it was all about. The young lady was inquiring the directions to the Guildhall. By coincidence, at that time, the Assize Court was sitting in the Guildhall and a particularly nasty case was in progress, a big murder trial. With this in mind it prompted me to ask if she was in any way connected with that trial. A little puzzled by my question, she said she was looking for the London County Council Education Department in the Guildhall. I realised the confusion and told her she required the Middlesex Guildhall, not the Westminster Guildhall, and she would have to retrace her steps back across Westminster Bridge to find that particular Guildhall building on the left, just across the river. Our conversation was brief: she was looking for a teaching position and, as I stepped back into the road, I mentioned casually that if she was coming back this way to let me know if she found the place and was successful. She went on her way and with the increased rush of people keeping me so busy, the incident temporarily passed out of my mind. A short while later, as I held up the traffic once more, I saw her coming over the crossing. On reaching the footpath I inquired if she had found the department. She thanked me, and said she had found the place easily and once again we had a quick conversation in between my brief spells of halting and releasing the traffic. In my own mind I thought that she was a visiting Canadian but I was corrected when I inquired, to be told she was an Australian. In the course of our continued conversation I asked if she was finding her way around the city, and I offered to show her around when I came off duty at 2 p.m. How strange it all turned out to be. We arranged to meet each other outside Westminster Abbey at 4 p.m. I had doubts, when I made my way to the Abbey dressed in civilian clothes later that afternoon, that she would be there. However, I was wrong, she was there promptly, waiting, and I found out later that she was in two minds about keeping the appointment also. Somehow it was meant to be – it was the beginning of a life-long partnership and, as I write these lines now in the year 1990, we have passed our fortieth wedding anniversary so it has been a long time. That afternoon and evening was a very special occasion as we got acquainted with each other. We caught a bus to Kew Gardens outside west London and then returned to Marble Arch to enjoy a meal at the restaurant as we wandered up Edgware Road. Meg was staying at the YWCA in Tottenham Court Road and we had to be back at those premises before the doors were locked at the restricted time, to wind up a very enjoyable day. The month of August slipped away and I saw Meg regularly that closing month into September before she took up a position at a boys' private school at Reigate in Surrey. I can recall we toured the areas of central London together and got to know each other very well.

For the final week of that month I completed my last security spell of duty from Cannon Row. There were important conferences and meetings going on, involving high-ranking representatives and foreign ministers from various countries around the world, held at Lancaster House, where some of the diplomats were in residence. Lancaster House was just off the Mall and considered the finest private residence in London. It had become the premises of the London Museum but it was used by the government at that time for all the important meetings with overseas dignitaries and my tour of duty was outside the pillars of the impressive front entrance and along Carlton Terrace.

I was notified that week also that my transfer for attachment to Rochester Row Police Station would take place from the last Monday of September 1948. It suited me to change and it was only a short distance from Ambrosden House. It contained the main crime area of Westminster, the residential areas with high-rise blocks of flats and the big stores and shops of Victoria Street. I knew the complete area very well residing in the middle of it and all I required to know was the routes and boundaries of the various beats. There were only two traffic controlled points from this station. The first at the end of the Mall, with the intersections and crossing points of Buckingham Palace Road, Birdcage Walk and all traffic traversing the statue roundabout in front of Buckingham Palace. The other was at the intersection of Victoria Street, Vauxhall Bridge Road, Grosvenor and Buckingham Palace Road to Victoria Station. Rochester Row was a much more friendly station, where everyone knew each other well, away from the high administration and chiefs, and where one could get on with all the daily tasks of police duties away from the security areas. I soon got accustomed to the layouts and the routes of all the various beats, all the stores, shops and businesses over the area. Each weekday, Monday to Friday, it was a transfer point for all convicted persons and prisoners on remand. The police rear yard was secure and could be locked with big doors, the prison vans from various courts pulled

295

in and prisoners were escorted to other vans to take them to their destinations to begin the periods of detention. This occurred each morning making it necessary to return from the beat promptly to assist in escorting and exchanging these detainees as part of the daily duties. I enjoyed my tour of duty at Rochester Row and soon got to know lots of the residents and business people of that area and also many of the children as they were safely escorted across Vauxhall Bridge Road. Many of those children I soon came to know by name and so often they kept for me, or presented to me, a lolly or a biscuit or some small token, in their young friendly way, as they went and returned from school.

I corresponded with Meg regularly as the days turned into the month of October, the weather at that period was apalling with long spells of miserable rain. During the third week of that month, one evening, I was on patrol in Victoria Street casually making my way back to Ambrosden House for my meal break at the canteen. I had passed the big Army and Navy stores to shortcut through Howick Place and the time was a little after 6 p.m. Suddenly one of the attendants from a Victoria Street block came rushing after me, almost breathless, to tell me to come urgently as there had been a serious accident with the elevator in his building. I raced back with him quickly into Victoria Street but the lift doors would not open and the lift had stopped about four feet above the opening. A few people, all trying to talk together, got through to me to say a lady had fallen down the shaft from above. I raced up the stairways to each floor but none of the doors would open until I reached the sixth floor. All the offices were closed and in darkness, only the corridor lights were burning, and all the employees had left. I found the lift shaft area quickly, something had obviously gone wrong with the mechanism. The outer iron grid concertina doors were half open, and the lift entrance doors were fully open, but there was no lift, just the gaping shaft. The attendant meanwhile had raised the alarm and called the fire brigade and the ambulance. I shone my torch down the shaft to see a lady sprawled across the lift between the ropes and wheels. She appeared to be badly hurt, motionless; there were no sounds or cries. She had walked through the open doors to enter the lift which wasn't there and crashed to the bottom. I was wearing a pair of black knitted gloves, in my pocket I carried my bicycle clips, which I hurriedly used to clip back the bottoms of my trousers, dumped my helmet, hitched the torch to my belt, grabbed the nearest steel rope and swung into the shaft with the left and right insides of my boots jammed against the rope below. I slithered down slowly for about three and a half floors in the darkness of the shaft, until the build up of grease on my gloves got too much. I accelerated faster out of control to land with a terrific jolt on the lift top, fortunately missing the woman. I jarred my right wrist badly between the second rope as I landed, tore off my gloves, thick with grease, but in the torchlight tried to make the groaning lady as comfortable as possible, easing and holding her clear of the ropes and wheels of the lift top. In the meantime help had arrived, and a powerful light was directed down the shaft. The lift was hand wound floor to floor but still no doors would open until we reached that sixth floor. The lady was rushed to hospital with two broken legs, a broken pelvis, and a broken arm, besides other injuries. I went along to get my wrist bound and, as I could not write, I dictated my report to John Scott at nine o'clock that night and he wrote it up in my book. For a whole week I could not write and John entered all my notes for me; I even had to make excuses to Meg later why my letters were delayed. I attended the inquiry some time later and all I received was praise for my action, nothing more, it was just part of my daily duties.

I began my first spell of night duty at Rochester Row at the start of November. The patrol cover of all the areas was very thorough, and it was important to ring through promptly if any occurrence or incident happened to take you away from the beat, and again on returning, so that the station knew the beat was temporarily unmanned. With so much to do, it often became difficult too, to report and ring-in at the two allotted ringing-in times through the night. The beats inter-sected at lots of places and my colleague John Scott and I often arranged regular rendezvous through the night in case either of us needed assistance. In the vicinity all around Victoria Street there were bombed buildings, many of which were being repaired with lots of scaffolding around them. I was in Palmer Street after midnight, on one of those occasions, snooping around at the rear of Victoria Street, checking on doors, windows, and entrances, when I saw high up on the upper floor of a building next to one surrounded by scaffolding, a suspicious partly concealed light. I had arranged to meet Scott at 12.30 a.m. at the other junction across Victoria Street with Artillery Row. I had to make the decision whether to ring through from the nearest box for assistance, or wait till I met up with John Scott at the rendezvous. However, I flashed my torch a few times down Artil-lery Row to receive an answering flash that he was in the distance coming my way. Together we went around to where I had seen the suspicious light and we started to climb the scaffold to gain access on to the planked levels around the building. From our position as we gained more height, we could see from the limited lighting it was a silk-stocking warehouse and store, with two intruders helping themselves, filling boxes and carrying them out through a doorway, obviously preparing them to be carted away at an arranged time. My first ring-in time that night was 12.45 a.m. I would be making my way to the blue police box away from the area for an hour or so, and by that time the intruders and the goods would have vanished. Our only access was by way of the bombed building; we had no knowledge at all of the interior and only a concealed flashlight to find our way. However, we decided to take chances and move across the floors of the bombed premises but, unfortunately, this was the wrong decision. We progressed well for a short distance with easy access through two walls almost reaching our target of the warehouse floor; Scott was on my left a yard or so away from me when, having no idea of the condition of the floor, it suddenly gave way beneath me. I went through that floor and the ceiling beneath, feet first, and I hit the floor ten feet below with a jolt; this too collapsed, sending me through another ceiling below to land again on the floor below feet first in a shower of laths, plaster, mortar and timber. I was covered with dust and plaster but unhurt having dropped two floors, as the impact of hitting the middle floor had checked my fall. I looked upwards and I could see Scott two floors above shining his torch down crying out to inquire if I was all right. In the silence of the night my fall had created a noise but I got back to the planked scaffold to meet John coming down from above. We had disturbed our quarry, however. We quickly obtained assistance in a few minutes by dialling the information room; the thieves had gone but all the goods were intact. I went back to the section house for my meal break and cleaned up my uniform. It had been an interesting night.

Another interesting experience came my way during the last week of night duty during November of that year, I can recall it well. Beneath the streets and the whole structure of London, there is a labyrinth and maze of passages, drains, storm-water tunnels, sewer tunnels, gas mains, water mains, and all kinds of connections, besides the underground railway routes and tubes, some of them with their routes constructed below the level of another. There was even an old tram running underground for a long stretch near Holborn and Meg and I travelled along its route a number of times.

As a boy growing up and reading the old publications of the *Boy's*

Magazine, I saw on one occasion a map and a coloured cross-section of the area beneath central London, all the cable lines, pipes, the post office, underground railway, the tube, storm and sewer layouts, everything that went underground and it fascinated me. In the early hours of the morning patrolling the various areas, I frequently got into conversation with different members of all kinds of services. Some of those people were the sewer men, who entered the tunnels for cleaning and maintenance through those quiet hours after midnight, when the system is at its lowest point of usage and all sensible people are supposed to be asleep. Having become acquainted with them, my aim, of course was to descend one of the entrances, hoping I could get an insight into what went on below and tour some of their nightly routes. I did get an invitation to go down, so I had to arrange a time, unofficially of course, between my first ring-in and the period of my second ring-in, pending no other incident happened preventing me from keeping my rendezvous. I told John Scott, we had an understanding between us, and he would know where I was if something unforeseen happened.

At the rear of Victoria Station on a cold, wet, miserable, November night just after 1 a.m., I went down into the sewerage system with my guides. What a wonderful experience it turned out to be. I could hear the rumble and vibration of the nearby tube trains below and feel the tremor of traffic above. All the main passageways were lit above the walkways and some were even tiled. My guide knew every inch of the routes, all of them named or numbered like streets, and he knew every offshoot and connection, and the exact location of the spot above the surface and all the accesses in and out. It was cold, stark and clammy, with a continuous cold draught, which I assumed was a good thing to prevent any build-up of pockets of gas. I spent nearly one and a half hours below on my tour and I was told I could ascend beyond Green Park at Piccadilly, so I had gone a long way from Victoria. Those sewer men did that job all their working lives; perhaps it wasn't as bad and not so dangerous as being a coal miner but it had no attraction for me.

Christmas was drawing nearer once more and the short days were turning towards the end of another year, during that month of December 1948. Meg had told me she was going on another trip to Yorkshire, North Wales, down to Shrewsbury, with a visit to Cardiff during the Christmas break. We experienced snowfalls late that month and it appeared that we might get a White Christmas. I can mention too one privilege and perk that came my way during my periods of

299

police duties. On those cold afternoons and evenings, having come off duty at 2 p.m., I could always go, as frequently as I wished, to the Victoria Palace cinema, free of charge. The manager of that cinema had extended this privilege to all the residents at Ambrosden House and he encouraged us all to go there at any time, with the knowledge that he had someone on hand if there was any trouble, which of course was quite often. All we had to do was to show our warrant card to one of the usherettes, and we would be escorted to a special seat, where they knew to find one of us instantly if there was trouble. That offer was taken up many, many times.

I would not be spending Christmas on night duty this time but my duties would keep me occupied on the afternoons and evenings on late turn until 10 p.m. The Christmas shoppers were crowding everywhere, electricity was still restricted and, although relaxed a little for the Christmas period, the full blaze of shop windows and display stores was limited. There were constant calls each night to brawls and domestic troubles in the Westminster City Council's blocks of high-rise flats, with alcohol usually the cause, leading to violence and abuse. I paid more visits to the Great Peter Street Salvation Army Hostel with alcoholics causing trouble when they were turned away because the place was full. On Christmas Eve there were the usual complaints from shoppers who had lost their possessions or had bags and purses stolen, but I could do little about it, except write out reports. The losers had no hope of getting back their goods. The streets were crowded, buses and taxis full, and the endless streams of pedestrians laden with parcels trudged towards Victoria railway and underground stations.

Just after nine o'clock that Christmas Eve, with so much recorded in my pocket book, I wandered along Buckingham Palace Road and then up Grosvenor Place into the darkness under the high wall of the boundary of Buckingham Palace Gardens, for a break away from it all. At least that is what I thought; that in one half hour or so I could return to the station, hand in my book and go off duty for the end of my day, but it did not turn out that way. I was concealed under the wall almost opposite the intersection across the road that led into Eaton Square which was out of the divisional area. I saw an elderly lady, carrying a parcel, bag and a small suitcase, turn off Grosvenor Place towards the square. A slightly built brute raced up behind her and pushed her violently to the ground, grabbing the lady's possessions and the suitcase, then proceeded to race off down to Eaton Square. He did not know I was across the road in the darkness and

300

he would not be aware either that I could run very quickly. I dashed across the road and, within a short distance in my silent rubber soles, I caught up to him, tapping his ankle from behind sending him crashing to the road. He had the biggest surprise of his life as I frogmarched him back to the distressed lady and together we turned around into Buckingham Palace Road to the side entrance of the police security room for assistance. The police van was there within a few minutes to convey us all to Rochester Row. The culprit was a thirty-year-old Irishman, who was charged and bailed to appear at Marlborough Street Court two days after Christmas. It was an unpleasant Christmas present for him, as he was charged with stealing the lady's parcels, the suitcase containing a Christmas cake and some clothing and her bag containing seven pounds. He went to prison for six months. So on that particular Christmas Eve, instead of me getting away promptly just after 10 p.m., it was almost 11.45 when I finally reached the section house just before the start of Christmas Day 1948.

For the past eight years or so, I had spent my Christmas day in so many different places. I got out of bed that morning at 8 o'clock, so that I could go down to purchase my breakfast and to make arrangements for my lunch, before going on duty at 2 p.m. The canteen lady would close up at 10 a.m.; as she lived south of the river, and I guess she was anxious to get home to be with her family that Christmas Day. It was a cold, snowy afternoon when I walked across to the station with John Scott. I was wearing my greatcoat and police cape all prepared for an unpleasant icy evening as we went out to relieve our counterparts, anxiously waiting to come off duty. It was to be a quiet night and I arranged to meet up with him a number of times during the evening on our rounds, to break up the long hours. During that afternoon too I called into the mortuary to share a cup of tea with the attendant on duty. This abode, perhaps, was a strange place to visit on Christmas afternoon, but he was pleased to have a visitor and a chat to break up his hours till he went off at 6 p.m. He jokingly told me that he had two silent customers in residence, both of them, sadly, had been fished out of the river during the night, either tired of life, or maybe the celebrations of Christmas Eve had been too much for them, so I supposed these unfortunate happenings throughout our lives will never end. He was expecting more visitors at 4 p.m., probably bereaved relatives, who might be able to identify them. That evening with all the snack bars, cafés and restaurants open it appeared to be business as usual, but for me there were no incidents. I did pick up a number of people wandering aimlessly around having had too much of the good life and too much to drink, but I did my good deeds for the day by stopping taxis and making sure they produced enough to pay their fare and bundled them into the vehicles to carry them home. It was a quiet night with revelry and song drifting from the residential buildings, where all were enjoying the Christmas spirit. Through the flurry of falling snow, glistening against the street lights, it was surprising to me to see so many devout Catholics making their way to Westminster Cathedral to celebrate Christmas in their own way. At 10 p.m. exactly I went off duty, and I believe it was one of those very rare days when I had nothing entered in my notebook. It was the end of one more Christmas in my lifetime.

The last day of the year of 1948 was my rostered day off. It was New Year's Eve and I was pleased to be away from all the noise, the merrymakers, and the law breakers that night. I spent a quiet evening in the Victoria Cinema, taking advantage of my free entry and at 10 p.m. it was a meal in a Vauxhall Bridge Road café. By 11.30 p.m., before the revelry of welcoming the New Year, I was fast asleep in bed, to prepare for the last two afternoons of duty Saturday and Sunday, the first and second days of January, before my early morning schedule once again.

The days seemed to slip by as we began the New Year of 1949. Towards the middle of January, I received a phone call from Meg at Victoria Station. I was free of duties at that time fortunately, so I hurried round to the station to meet her, before she left to return to Reigate. From that period onwards I tried to make my visits to Reigate as often as possible each weekend. I usually caught the London Transport Service Green Line coaches from Northumberland Avenue just off Trafalgar Square at 4 p.m., which travelled direct to Reigate Hill, and then taking the last bus, or the 10.20 p.m. train, to return the same night.

During the final week of January, on a cold winter's evening, I became involved with another problem. A youth of 18 years had climbed one of the scaffolds erected around a bomb-damaged building in Victoria Street. Not satisfied with having scaled the structure to the highest point, he began hurling large pieces of concrete, timber and anything movable at pedestrians passing along the street. He was evidently under the influence of drink, and in danger of falling with all his antics, eight floors above the street. I had no intention of attempting to climb the scaffold, so I called for assistance, and alerted the fire brigade to try to bring him down before he killed someone. It took over two hours to eventually placate the man and get him down

302

to street level, as each time anyone got near to him, they were pelted with missiles. He sobered up a little eventually and he was brought down. Fortunately no one was hurt from the falling missiles but a great deal of damage was caused to passing vehicles. He was locked in a cell for the night until he was sober and charged and bailed the following morning. Scott, myself, two other officers and firemen had to attend the court to give evidence but he failed to appear; the wily character gave everyone the slip and made off. The magistrate issued a warrant immediately for his arrest and being the principal concerned I had to carry that warrant at all times until I handed it in when I was transferred to Hyde Park. To my knowledge that young man was never traced. He was fortunate to get away, as the magistrates at that time were considered to be far from lenient.

On 30th January, on one of my visits to Reigate, Meg and I decided to get engaged sometime around her birthday at the end of March or into April. It was at this time also, through a friend of Tom, my sister's husband, that I was offered a job as a foreman with a big north London construction company. I thought it over a great deal. A London police officer's job is no holiday. In fact, until one experiences it, it is a very difficult and tiring occupation; the shift work and night duty often become monotonous and the pay needed much improvement. At the beginning of June I would be eligible to sit the sergeants' promotion examination and I knew I could have passed it easily. But even then there would be a long wait because, like so many other things and the 'old school tie' prominence, I had already discovered it was 'who you know' not 'what you know' that you needed to achieve anything. However, I continued on conscientiously with my duties through the long cold nights of February.

I paid a visit to Bravington's jewellery store at the Strand end of Trafalgar Square, during one of my days off in that month. Having become acquainted and well known to the manager of that establishment, with all the problems and troubles on duty at Trafalgar Square, I did a little coaxing and inquiring about a substantial discount if I purchased a ring for Meg. I eventually obtained a good deal from him, and he agreed to give me 20 per cent discount off any marked price in the shop. I had already obtained another ring from Meg for the correct size and I soon found what she required from the big range. I received the discount, something I cannot ever remember if I told Meg, however its size had to be altered and I picked it up a week later.

My sister Edna had moved, about that period, to a flat in Chelsea, just off the King's Road. It was only a short distance from my area and very convenient for me to go along to pay her a visit. At the end of February 1949 I completed another month of night duty at Rochester Row and that tour of night duty would be the final one for me attached to that station. I was told that I was soon to move on.

During April my mother travelled up from South Wales to stay for a short time with Edna, so it gave me the opportunity to take Meg along to meet her before she left on her planned trip to Switzerland. When she returned from that excursion on 29th April, I presented her with the ring and we became officially engaged. It all happened on an evening in Hyde Park and, unknown to me then, this spot was soon to become a part of my patch covering the whole area of the park.

In the early days of May I made a special visit to the Passport Office to make an application for a passport. As I made out the application and presented the photos and various documents for identification, I began to get worried. When I was demobilised from the army three years previously, I had been transferred to the Army Reserve with no option and no choice. All the troubles in the world were still causing anxieties, the Eastern Bloc countries were still unsettled with Stalin, civil war was raging in China, north and south were at loggerheads in Korea, and the Jew and Arab problems were increasing in Palestine and I was concerned that I might be affected. However, nothing was said, my application was accepted, and I received my passport. My next step was a visit to the shipping offices in Lower Regent Street to put my name down on the list for a passage to Melbourne. They informed me there was a wait of at least six months so I could only hope and accept it. For the whole period of May I carried out my duties on traffic control at the Vauxhall Bridge Road and Victoria Street junction, which suited me well as I had each Sunday off duty and I could travel down to Reigate to meet Meg.

The warm days of June and the beginning of summer of 1949, I was into my third year of service and many of those brought me inside the station on the switchboard and communications duties, but I soon discovered it was much more enjoyable outside on the city streets. In the middle of the month the inevitable happened and I was informed I had to move on to the Hyde Park Police Station. I continued to reside at Ambrosden House but it was a long trip backwards and forwards each day to Hyde Park, and I realised I would soon have to move all my goods and belongings to take up residence on the upper floor of the station. Meg was leaving her position at Reigate when the school year ended in July for the summer vacation and she had planned to go for a tour of Scotland before returning to Australia about the middle of August. I got settled into my new area but it wasn't as busy and interesting as the streets and thoroughfares of the south-west of Westminster, and in the heat of the day with thousands of people relaxing and enjoying themselves, it often became boring to me. I spent many long hours at the Hyde Park Corner entrance gate where Rotton Row ends and the Serpentine and Park Lane ring roads intersect. Almost every taxi in the metropolis cut through these ring roads, because no heavy vehicles were allowed, cars and taxis only. At that period Hyde Park Corner carried almost as much traffic as Hammersmith Broadway and, when there was a breakdown with the lights, it developed into chaos. In later years that corner has changed a great deal, with a modern flyover, and the congestion has eased. I can recall well the one and only incident of me reporting a taxi driver. Impatience and speed caused it all as one driver slightly side-swiped another. Normally it was passed over, one driver simply exchanging numbers and addresses with the other. On that occasion one of them blamed me, and abused me violently, but it was too bad for him as I reported him. His passenger, an irate and angry city businessman, saw everything and even appeared in court voluntarily to support me.

At the close of the month I received a call from Meg at Victoria Station and together we transported some of her excess luggage to sister Edna's place in Chelsea to store, pending her departure on the Scottish tour, and to hold for her until her return to Australia on 18th August 1949. I had instructions also to move out of Ambrosden House, so I obtained the services of a police van once more to move my belongings to Hyde Park. Someone was anxious to take over my room at Ambrosden House, and I left the desk top for him as it was of no use to me any more. John Scott took my pictures to use in his recently obtained flat south of the river and I told him he could have my chair when the time came and I would sell my bike to him for five pounds. I was allotted a room upstairs above the station. It was quite comfortable with an outlook towards the bird sanctuary. I spent little time there except to do my chores, write and sleep. Marble Arch was a short distance away with all the cafés and eating places of Oxford Street and Edgware Road to obtain a meal.

Meg returned from her Scottish tour in August and, as she had resigned from her job and left Reigate permanently, she obtained accommodation temporarily at the YWCA in Tottenham Court Road once again, to prepare for her departure back to Australia on the 18th of that month. I succeeded in getting some time off for a few days before she left and then sadly on the Thursday of that date, I went to St Pancras Station to see her depart and to say goodbye as the train sped away on that first stage of her journey to board the liner back to Melbourne. I was in a quandary after her departure, as I did not know how long it was going to take for me to get a passage, to rejoin her once more. Meg arrived safely back in Tasmania by the middle of September 1949 and much to my surprise I received a letter from her telling me her father had sponsored me under the migrations programme. Australia at that period was desperate for migrants and newcomers. The process accelerated quickly and I was asked to attend Australia House in the Strand as soon as possible for interviews and instructions, and a medical examination. I handed in my passport and they issued me with an Australian Document of Identity and told me to await instructions to depart within six weeks. By coincidence, I was informed about the same time by the P & O shipping line that I could obtain a passage with them on 1st December, so I cancelled it forthwith.

On 30th September 1949, I submitted my compulsory one month resignation to the station superintendent for my release at the end of October. I discovered it was almost as difficult to get out as it was to get in. I was ordered to appear before two separate tribunals during that month to give my reasons for leaving the force and given lectures and advice, as to why I should remain as a serving police officer, but nothing would deter me, I was on my way out for good. I continued on with my duties during October at a low ebb and the final two weeks was night duty. The roadways and paths were well lit throughout the park and I kept clear of all the big expanses of the dark tree-covered areas, to keep out of trouble, and on the Saturday and Sunday nights I remained in the background listening to the dozens of soap box orators at Speaker's Corner till well after midnight. I consequently received notification from Australia House that I was to embark from Liverpool on the SS *Dorsetshire* on 10th November 1949 for which there would be a special boat train from Liverpool Street railway station leaving at 10 a.m. on 9th November.

On 29th October my resignation took effect, so I packed my belongings and then got in touch with John Scott at Rochester Row to come and collect my comfortable chair and the bicycle. When the final things were completed I went to Chelsea to Edna's flat to stay the night, in order to catch the train to South Wales early the next morning. It was the end of my police service, I could look forward to a whole week with my parents to finalise everything before the big unknown step that lay ahead of me. In the meantime I received further news from Meg, that she had made all the plans and arrangements for us to get married on 7th January 1950, so I had approximately eight weeks only to cover that vast distance across the world to be on time for our wedding.

The following morning I caught the South Wales express from Paddington to Cardiff for the last time. I had a full week to relax, to try to see everyone, pack up my personal possessions, and to visit all the old haunts and places that had been so much a part of my life as I grew up. There was a final reunion with my parents, Joan, Joyce and her husband, Toots and her husband and family. My brother Trefor was absent. I did not realise then it would be another 25 years before I would see them all again, except my father, who died in 1957. Sadly, there was one person I omitted to see and he was my uncle, David John Davies, grandfather's son and my mother's brother. I believe he did not want to see me. I had disappointed him years before by not following in his footsteps. He was a patriotic Welshman, the principality, the people, the language, and the culture meant everything to him; all others were outsiders and I was going to leave it all behind.

In the early morning of 8th November 1989, through a swirling mist with its unpleasant cold dampness sending a penetrating chill through my top coat, I walked along Gwerthonor Road with my father and Joan, on her way to work in Cardiff. There was a feeling of sadness in my heart as so many incidents flashed through my mind of what had happened to me along that road in my early years. We reached the old swing kissing gate through to the Black Path, at the top of the Grammar School Hill, and near the old home of the late Eli Bratt. I had to lift my trunk and suitcase over the top, as there was no room to pass through the narrow swing. Struggling down the Black Path with my load I passed once again the old haunted house, still empty and unoccupied, with many of its windows smashed and broken. Thirty yards farther on I stopped briefly, and lowered my trunk to the path, to look across for the last time at what we had always known as 'Dick Turpin's Tree'. This tree, one of the distant giant oaks at the top of our 'jungle', was shaped like a horse and rider, with a smaller bare, dead, branch, in the raised hand of the rider, which moved to hit the horse's head every time there was a puff of wind. This was my last sad sight of our district Gwerthonor, named and translated for centuries as 'Worthy of Praise'.

I boarded the train, shaking hands and saying goodbye to my father as the guard waved his flag for the old steam train to pull away from Pengam station. There was a sob in my father's voice as he wished me well, and the train moved off. Sadly for me, that was the last time I saw my father; he died before I could see him again.

On reaching Cardiff I said goodbye to Joan as I crossed the General Station – it would be another 25 years before I saw her again. I caught the London express at 9 a.m. to Paddington Station and that too was my final journey on that train. I took my cabin trunk, and a taxi, to Liverpool Street Station, so that it could be dispatched that day and loaded on the ship at Liverpool. Carrying my suitcase I went back to Chelsea and Edna's flat, to stay the night before my departure the next morning.

Part Four

A Different Life on the Other Side of the World

21

The Long Sea Voyage

The next morning, 9th November 1949, I got out of bed about 6 a.m. for the start of my long journey. It was another wet miserable day. Tom had to leave for work at 6.30 a.m. so I said goodbye to him early that morning and prepared myself to depart across London to Liverpool Street Station. I did not realise then how difficult it would be to obtain a taxi during the rush hours of a wet morning. It took me over a half hour to get a taxi. I had to walk all the way down to and along the Kings Road, before I finally stopped a vacant cab to take me back to Edna's flat to collect my luggage. Sadly, it was a brief and very hurried goodbye to Edna and I just hoped I could make it through the traffic to catch the train. I finally reached the station just ten minutes before the train steamed out. It was a crowded train, I knew no one, but I succeeded in obtaining a seat, so I was on my way. Late that afternoon, the train steamed into the docks area of Liverpool and, being such a dreary November day, it was already getting dark. With a howling gale driving the cold rain, it was unpleasant, and everyone sought shelter as we waited to board the ship. In the semi-darkness with just the wharf lights for visibility it was difficult to get my first glimpse of the ship and the size of the vessel. I had been allotted a cabin number so I made my way up the gangplank jostling with the other pushing and shoving passengers, cases and luggage, trying to get out of the wind and the driving rain. On board I found my quarters and discovered a little more about the vessel, which was to be my home for the next six and a half weeks. The ship was the SS *Dorsetshire*, which had been chartered from Libby Line. It was an old ship of about 10,000 imperial tons' displacement and during the latter years of the war it had been used as a hospital ship. My cabin was on the port side about eight feet above the water line with a single porthole. There were eight bunks, top and bottom of a fixed set of four double bunks, eight occupants including myself, all single men between the ages of

20 and 30 years, and all kinds of characters as I was soon to find out. Two of them came from the suburbs of Cardiff. I was the first into the cabin and I chose the top bunk with my head one yard from the porthole, because I realised as we went south towards the Equator that the cabin would get stiflingly hot, with little relief from that small porthole. As it was, there was a notice above stating it must be kept shut tightly in all inclement weather, to prevent water entering from the pounding waves.

We all settled into the cabin that evening and got to know each other, and our destinations. Many of them were ex-servicemen and accustomed to roughing it, so we arranged our luggage in the most convenient way to give us all more room. We had no desire to go on deck that night with the appalling weather, as it was an open deck with just a handrail all around and no shelter anywhere. We had to arrange the sittings for our meals, half on the first and half on the second, working it out with the toss of a coin, beginning with the first meal, breakfast the next morning, as the ship was due to sail in the afternoon of that day, 10th November. I recall I slept well that night with the vessel at the wharfside but it was to be so different when we reached the open sea. Breakfast the following morning like all other meals was good; there was a dining room area with fixed tables and seats, the food was brought in containers and each person helped themselves. When the ship moved off that afternoon into a howling gale the whole structure creaked and groaned everywhere, and from every position throughout the entire vessel, it was impossible to get away from the throb and the noise of the engines, but it was something we had to get used to. After leaving Liverpool and heading out into the Irish Sea, we did not realise there was such a stormy passage ahead. Three hours out from port the ship pitched and rolled violently in the storm, every joint in the whole ship seemed to creak even more, everyone was sick and our rolling, lurching ship turned around to steam back to Liverpool. Something was wrong with the engines, so our first start was a failure. We were back in port once again, so one more day was lost. It was the first delay, and there were more to come before we were to reach our destination. Then on the evening of 11th November we set sail again into calmer waters but we were warned to stay below as there was stormy weather ahead until we entered the Mediterranean Sea at Gibraltar.

Our first scheduled stop was to be Alexandria before we entered the Suez Canal. It was a long way and in front of us we had to encounter, at that wintry time of the year, the South Atlantic and the stormiest place of all, the Bay of Biscay. We had to put up with, and stay below for some time, pitching and rolling on our bunks, unable to sleep as the waves smashed against our only lookout, the small cabin porthole. The turnout for meals was very small, and it was evident many were suffering from sea sickness. I wasn't actually sick but very near to it with that awful squirmy feeling that would not go away, and then increasing even more as the ship wallowed in the trenches between the giant swells. All the hatches were closed and sealed, and we could not venture up anywhere to get some fresh air. We were kept well informed over the loudspeaker system of the details of what was happening, our position at all times, and the weather forecast and radio news at fixed times was relayed from the BBC.

Crossing the Bay of Biscay in the terrible storm a big Spanish fishing vessel was foundering and we listened to the incoming radio calls, standing by in case help was needed, but there were other ships in the area, so what a relief it was as soon as we reached calmer waters and the sunshine and entered the Straits of Gibraltar. The blue Mediterranean, as we left behind the giant rock, was calm and beautiful, and moving along the North African side, the sun was warm and relaxing as we left the European winter behind us. It was a pleasure now to stretch and exercise on the deck as we assisted the crew in erecting the white canvas covers over the rear deck in preparation for the hot humid days and nights ahead of us. The old ship was slow, the noisy engines vibrated the deck as she steamed on at the maximum speed possible, and we could see the distant coastline only, now unable to make out any particular place. The starry nights were still rather cool, as we had not yet reached the still heat and humidity of the Middle East and the opportunity to sleep on the deck to enjoy a little of the cooler night air. It became a lazy life from that period onwards. The ship's bridge occupied the central raised area, and we had the front and rear deck each side with all kinds of obstructions everywhere, and the communicating passages each side with the lifeboats slung above. There was a ship's shop open every day to purchase our requirements, the loudspeaker system played popular songs and music all day long, with regular breaks for news broadcasts. Meals were at regular times, so we had plenty of time to read and write, and enjoy the sunshine.

We reached Alexandria with no problems, refuelled and restocked with fresh water and supplies. It was a British base then and I received a letter from my parents; the mail from the ship was dispatched and, after a short stay, we moved on to Port Said to wait for our turn to go through the Suez Canal. The canal had not been widened or deepened at that time, it could accommodate one ship only for long stretches and that ship moved over to halt in a wide part to allow another ship to pass travelling in the opposite direction. At Port Said many colourful Egyptian traders came on board as we waited, all selling their goods and wares, rugs, carpets and souvenirs. In the harbour, too, were many young Egyptian boys, diving for coins thrown overboard by the passengers, catching them skilfully with their teeth before they reached the sea bed. The humidity hit us there and it became difficult to keep cool and even sitting perfectly still it was impossible to stop perspiring. Our cabin became an oven, so it was a pleasure and a relief to get even the slightest evening breeze. It was a slow journey along the waterway, stopping a number of times to allow other ships to pass. The landscape was uninteresting, but we got glimpses of native Egyptians with their donkeys and camels, and received many friendly waves from a few British soldiers at various places along the bank, as it was under the complete control of the British and French at that period. It took a whole day to travel its course until we came into the Red Sea and our next stop at Port Aden.

Two days later, in the heat of the afternoon, we reached the old port of Aden which, in modern times, has become the main port of South Yemen at the entrance of the Red Sea. The staff and the crew of our ship, and all announcements, referred to it as the Crater, and I wondered why, until I found out the reason when I went ashore. It was a British military and naval base and we were to be allowed ashore for the first time since our departure from Liverpool. It was a hot, sultry, humid day when our ship pulled in to the steamer anchorage and there were scores of Arab dhows sailing in all directions with Arab children, beggars and traders flocking to the ship's side all hoping to gain some reward. There were small numbers of administrative buildings there, a big sandy foreshore and beyond, rows of Arab traders in shops, bazaars and stalls, all eagerly awaiting their customers. I could understand then, as we went ashore, why it was called the Crater. The small old town was surrounded on three sides by high, rocky, precipitous crags, so the whole area must have been a crater in olden times. In the blazing heat of the day, with not a breath of wind, the typical eastern smell filled the hot atmosphere permeating everywhere as I wandered along the stores and bazaars. Pestered all the time with so many offerings and so-called bargains, I did buy a set of seven moonstones and a five-pound weight of super quality eastern tea already packed in a small tea chest, labelled to be addressed for dispatch to anywhere in the world. I sent it to my mother and I was pleased to hear later that it arrived safely at its destination. I tried to explore a little around the area, climbing a steep, wide gravel road up towards the high crags, to find a big British military barracks, but it was too hot for me and I was glad to get back to the ship.

By the pale mellow light of a half moon and a brilliant star-studded sky, we set sail once more into the Red Sea for another long unbroken voyage all the way to our next port of call, Colombo, on the island of Ceylon. That night, for the first time, all the occupants of my cabin carried a pillow and a blanket to the rear deck, away from the stifling heat of the cabin, to sleep under the stars on the hard decking, and were lulled into slumber by the throb of the ship's engines as she steamed on through the flat, calm sea. That occasion was the first time that I saw the brilliant red sun rise out of the sea above the horizon at dawn, reflecting its wonderful and spectacular reddish light on every breaking wave and ocean ripple as night turned into day.

One day and a half out from Aden steaming along the Gulf of Aden, we passed our last distant landfall for a long time. Due south of us, we could see the island of Socotra. Following the map and the route outside the purser's office each day with interest, no one seemed to know to whom this island belonged. It was a large island and whether it was part of Ethiopia or Yemen I have never known, however it did not matter. It was out into the wide open Arabian Sea for us for the long trip to Colombo. During many of those long lazy afternoons, under the shade of the canvas covers over the rear deck, we tried our hand at fishing behind the wake of the ship. We used a long line purchased from the ship's shop, often up to a 100 yards behind the ship with a single hook. We lost the hook many times but failed hopelessly to catch anything.

At the beginning of December 1949, in the very early hours of the morning, when the temperature was almost 90 degrees Fahrenheit, we sailed past the breakwater and piloted through the huge harbour to a berth alongside a neglected wooden quay. Everyone was eagerly looking forward to a break to stretch our legs on dry land and we were allowed to spend the whole day ashore, before we sailed again at night for the long unbroken ocean voyage across the Equator, south to Fremantle.

I was anxious to have a good look around to see everything possible in the restricted time of about 10 hours, having to be back on board by 6 p.m. A 8.30 a.m. after breakfast, the two Cardiff boys and I left the ship to begin our hurried tour. We crowded together in a pedal carriage, through the busy streets, dodging donkeys, horses and carts, and barrows, almost deafened with so many vehicle horns, to the oldest part of the city called Pettah. Our pedal driver could speak good English, which was a wonderful help and, when we asked to be taken to some temples, he pedalled us to a place that I faintly remember as Hulls-dorf, which appeared to be a Dutch name, to see a magnificent Buddhist temple, with a difficult name I cannot remember. He was a Buddhist himself and, going through the rituals, he escorted us inside to see the magnificent architecture and carvings and of course the huge gold Buddha. I was disappointed with our next visit in the same crowded suburb, to a Hindu temple, as there appeared to be some kind of ceremony in progress with lots of ringing bells. Our driver protested and would not get off his pedal car or go near the building, so we were unable to go inside. We had to be satisfied simply looking all around the exterior of the wonderful building. We then requested our driver to pedal us back through the native quarters to a suitable place to get a meal. I remember we paid for his meal but he insisted on sitting at another table in another area; perhaps it wasn't done at that time to eat with a European, as the island was still controlled by the British. For that meal I recall having chicken – I assumed it was chicken – with rice, and a bottle of lemonade, but to me it was not very appetising. The temperature was 100 degrees and the chicken was hotly curried, and I wasn't very fond of curry at any time.

Having paid off our driver, we made a tour of the markets with the shrewd operators ready to cheat us at every turn. I believe that I did get one bargain, a pair of carved teak elephant book-ends as a gift for Meg; they were most useful and have been used all through our married life. It was a tiring afternoon trying to see everything as we strolled through the back streets and squalid areas of the crowded city, under the heat of the blazing sun. We were all glad to get back to the ship, exhausted after our day's outing, ready for a cold shower of salt sea water, and some shade. Salt water was used for almost all of the shower facilities, to preserve the fresh water from the ship's tanks for washing and drinking purposes only.

We sailed out of Colombo harbour that night in darkness to begin the three and a half thousand miles south across the Indian Ocean to Fremantle. I was getting anxious and concerned, as the time was slipping by quickly and there still remained the sea passage to Adelaide and Melbourne. I had to get to Tasmania by the first day of the New Year in January. I could only hope to get there in time. Three days later as the vast distance decreased, we lost the sun for the first

316

time, the sky became black, almost turning day into night, as the heaviest rain I had ever seen in my life poured out of the skies, with terrific, fantastic sheets of lightning and roars of thunder. It lasted unabated for three hours and we took advantage of it all, dressed in swimming trunks, to enjoy the fresh, sweet, warm deluge as it swamped the deck. As the lightning moved away and the black overcast sky broke up, I witnessed too for the first time, the giant waterspouts across the ocean and the spectacular display of phosphorescence and St Elmo's Fire, as it danced and sparkled above the tops of the distant waves. It was an amazing sight to experience, something that was only just imaginable before and something I had simply read about in books and magazines. A few hours later we crossed the Equator; preparations for the ceremony had already been completed. A big tarpaulin had been assembled to make a big pool to be filled with sea water for the performance of crossing the line but the huge deluge had filled it with fresh rain water instead which made it even better. The purser was dressed up as King Neptune and everyone was rounded up and dunked whether they were fully clothed or otherwise.

The old ship sailed on, and the days brought us up to the 15th December 1949. Thoughts of Christmas in the heat of the southern summer were strange as December to me all my life had been in the winter time. Then something suddenly went wrong, the vessel slowed and came to a stop, there were problems down below with the engines. We spent the whole day just wallowing and drifting with the currents in the middle of the Indian Ocean. According to the ship's map and the course, we were somewhere west of the Cocos Islands, and another whole day's sailing time was lost. The ship's engineers eventually got things in order and solved the problems, and without any further delays we sailed on. On the morning of 22nd December, we sighted land at last, to move in to anchor at the quarantine area outside Fremantle. We had to wait for the immigration officials to come aboard for the checking and procedures before we were allowed to proceed into Fremantle. It took about three hours to go through all the documentation, checking and preparing for all the passengers leaving the ship in Western Australia, but in the late afternoon the ship moved into Fremantle harbour to berth alongside the wharf with its wooden piles and wharf sheds, so different from the Fremantle development in modern times. Up to this time, as the vessel was British, all transactions and payments at the ship's shop were made in British currency, even the postage stamps on letters were British. On the following morning at 8 a.m., I changed all the English currency in my possession

317

into Australian pounds, shillings and pence at the purser's office. I received 25 Australian shillings for every English pound so I became much better off than I was before.

At 9 a.m. I walked down the gangplank from the ship to step on to Australian dry land for the first time. I had a whole day free to roam, to see all I could in the time and get my first impressions of Australia. It was just two days away from Christmas Day, and it seemed so strange to me experiencing over the century heat rather than freezing cold at that time of year. The harbour area was an untidy place, with the old dilapidated wood wharf and storage sheds, and I crossed over the many rows of railway lines towards the old town in Fremantle. The first things I saw, beyond the railway lines, were the quaint weatherboard cottages complete with verandahs, and the old lounge chairs, or sofa beds, occupying places of honour under the verandahs outside the back door. To add to it all were the rusty iron corrugated roofs, one of them even had an iron chimney. It all intrigued me because I had never seen a home before with a corrugated iron roof; in my building experience it was illegal. I had only known tiles or slate. I walked on to the town's main street, where many of the shops were weatherboard buildings too, but many were the old stone buildings. I noticed something else as well, and this was the shop verandah built out over the footpath to the road, giving cover along the whole street. I recall a small grass and floral reserve, with the roadway all around and bordered with a small hooped iron fence. I sat down on one of the seats to view the passing scene for a few minutes. I saw no male pedestrian without a hat; everyone young and old wore a slouch hat. I could only tell myself it was either the fashion or the rule, or perhaps to keep off the sun.

My next destination was the post office. I had to obtain the necessary Australian stamps and I was unfamiliar with the postage rates to send the two letters in my possession. However, I conversed with a very helpful assistant who inquired where I had come from and my destination, and he recommended a few places in Fremantle to be sure to visit. He said, I remember so well, 'Don't forget to go up the road to have a quick look at Perth.' I was as green as grass, everything was so strange to me. I believed what he had said about Perth being 'just up the road', so I found another suitable shop and I bought a nice sewing case as a present for Meg's mother, then set off 'up the road' to visit Perth.

Much of the area was open space and undeveloped with a few scattered homes along the way, unlike the built-up area it has become in modern times. Every time I inquired the way and how far it was to Perth I seemed to get the same answer, with a gesture pointing the way, 'Just up the road mate.' I did reach Perth, but I made sure I caught the old bus for the return journey. It had been a long tiresome hike in the heat, I must have walked between 10 and 14 miles, teaching me my first lesson that, being familiar with short distances only and not the vast distances of Australia, the common phrase of 'just up the road' could refer to any distance up to hundreds of miles.

Back in Fremantle, I searched for a place to have a meal as I was very hungry. I found a small café, and then consulting the blackboard menu I saw steak and eggs for the price of five shillings and sixpence. Being ignorant of prices, I placed my order. I sat on a bench-type seat at one of the three tables in the establishment and in a short time my order was brought to me. I had another big shock – it was a big dinner plate containing the biggest steak I had ever seen in my life, laced with three eggs, a big plate of bread and butter slices with a pot of tea. For the past ten years I had been accustomed to a tiny portion of meat obtained with a ration card, and before that, it was small cuts of meat because it was so expensive. I have always remembered that steak and I certainly made short work of it. At six o'clock that evening I walked back to the ship, hot, tired and exhausted but it had been an enjoyable day. The ship sailed that night at 9 p.m. in the darkness on its way to Adelaide, the next day would be Christmas Eve.

After we had rounded the south-west corner of Western Australia into the Bight, the old ship developed a permanent list of about 30 degrees to the port side, caused by the huge waves and giant swells rolling in from the Southern Ocean and pounding against the starboard side. It was so inconvenient, everything leaned and slipped with the list, even a cup of tea could only be filled to a half because it spilled over. Some of the giant hollows and trenches were frightening, our cabin port hole was under water all the time, and we had to stay below. As the ship reached the bottom of a trench, we could look up towards the bridge to see the sea higher than the ship, as she lifted and rolled out of it.

It was Christmas Day 1949, and for me another different, unusual place to celebrate; for the last ten years it had been an entirely different situation each year. For Christmas dinner that day with everything on the tilt, we had to hold on to everything securely, to prevent it slipping off to crash to the floor, so we were all pleased to let Christmas pass, to sail on to reach Port Adelaide. It was to be a short stay there,

319

allowing only enough time for the disembarking passengers to get off and once more, to my relief, we steamed on to Melbourne. During the early morning of the last day of December, the ship finally tied up at Port Melbourne. It took the whole day for the authorities to sort everyone out with their different destinations; the Sydney and Queensland passengers would go by rail the following morning. I was the only person to go to Launceston, two others were going to Hobart, and that evening we were informed that our transport would be by air with TAA the next morning. I would be allowed to take my case only with some light hand luggage. My cabin trunk, in the hold of the ship, would be sent on later by sea transport. It was three weeks later when it was finally delivered to me. It concerned me because it contained my wedding suit and it appeared that the suit I wore to leave the ship would have to be used as a replacement.

At 9 a.m. the next morning I was the first customer at the counter of the Port Melbourne post office. I sent a telegram to Meg with the news I had arrived and I was coming over by air that same morning.

I walked quickly back to the ship, collected my luggage and moved into an assembly area on the wharf, all ready to go to the airport. There were just three of us to go to Tasmania, two to Hobart, and myself to Launceston. I had never flown in a passenger aircraft before, my last experience in the air was on board a big glider, one of two gliders towed behind a Wellington bomber on a training exercise in 1943. It was uncanny then with a load of fully equipped soldiers, in the silence of the sky, with just the whistle of the air rushing through the vents. Our cases were taken by a bus to Essendon airfield to get our plane to Launceston. The luggage was taken aboard and we walked out on to the tarmac to get on board a twin propellor aircraft of Trans Australian Airlines, for our flight to Tasmania. It was New Year's Day 1950, the first day of January, and a Saturday morning. I recall it was a bumpy journey from Melbourne taking about an hour and a quarter to arrive at Western Junction airfield, as it was known at that time. I sorted out my case and luggage from the aircraft myself, to board the old transport bus into Launceston. It was all so strange to me. It was a hot day, and the countryside was unfamiliar, the route seemed windy and rough, and the road was in disrepair with pot-holes and rough gravel patches as the bus bumped along the way. I saw the first signs of habitation as we reached Franklin Village, and a few scattered houses along Hobart Road, and the familiar tramlines as the bus stopped to allow a stationary tram to take on a passenger at Six Ways. The bus continued on, along what I was soon to learn as

Talbot Road, then along High Street, and Brisbane Street, to halt outside the terminal of TAA. I got out of the bus there on the corner of George and Brisbane Street and across the road I caught a glimpse of Meg and her parents awaiting my arrival. My long journey from South Wales to London and Liverpool and across the world had ended. I had reached my destination, my strange new environment, and the place that was to be my future home.

22

Settling into My New Life and Marriage

A little excited and feeling lost in my new surroundings I crossed over what I now know as George Street, to greet Meg and to be introduced to her parents. My case and belongings were tied on to the luggage carrier at the rear of the old Plymouth, the family car parked along the street, and we were soon on our way along Paterson Street, over the Gorge Bridge, up the Trevallyn Hill and around the corner at the summit into South Esk Road to number 25, almost at the end of the road overlooking Launceston and the South Esk River. Meg's mother was fussing around; on reaching home she apologised for the tide being out, showing wide expanses of mud and the various boats sitting high and dry in the river bed away from the flowing channel.

Meg soon escorted me along the Gorge side of the house to the flat below. I inspected the renovated kitchen, all cream and green with a new green marble laminex and chrome table, with four chairs to match, the old-fashioned wire meat safe, cream and green canisters with all the added extras to make it pleasing and attractive. Down below I saw the lounge room which contained a single bed and was my sleeping quarters for the week ahead.

After a quick meal I was informed we were setting out immediately to travel to Bridport on the north-east coast, to spend the rest of the weekend camping and I was involved in packing the car with the necessities for a long weekend, Monday being a holiday in lieu of New Year's Day, Saturday. The family car had no boot and everything was carried on a fold-down metal luggage carrier at the rear above the bumper bar, so out came a big wooden box kept for the purpose to tie on to the carrier to carry as much as possible. Over the front seat and into the back of the vehicle was stuffed a double bed mattress, with all the remaining articles, camp stretchers and the two tents. Meg squeezed into one side and her mother on the other. I struggled into the front bench seat to sit sideways in order to get my back against the door, as it was closed from the outside. Fully loaded and cramped inside we set off on our journey to Bridport – my first experience of travelling anywhere in Tasmania. I received a running commentary, as we drove along, from both Meg and her mother, through Newstead over the railway crossing and the old wooden Hoblers Bridge across the North Esk River. At that point the sealed road ended, and it was to be a rough gravel surface until we reached Scottsdale. As we climbed the twisting hill up to Waverley I had to smile, Meg's father, driving the car, put on speed to climb the hill and we suddenly came up behind a slow ancient vehicle with side curtains and a canvas top. He let out an angry exclamation, 'Bust it, he has stopped my run!' I heard that remark many times in the next two hours, because he hated changing the gears down climbing a hill. The route was winding, dusty and narrow, homes were few and far between, and the interior of the car was like a furnace. There were a few scattered houses at Waverley, and then no habitation until we came to the saw-milling areas of Nunamara, Myrtle Park and Targa, and the area of the Myrtle Park School. Then it was a slow drive over the winding sidling, with the continuous sounding of the car horn as we approached each rough, narrow bend with barely room for two vehicles to pass. We finally reached Scottsdale for a ten-minute break out of the hot car and to stretch our legs. The road out of Scottsdale was worse and very bad, sandy, rough and twisting through the bush as we passed Jetsonville, with corrugations and water washouts everywhere and I was glad to cross over the dilapidated, wooden-planked bridge as we entered Bridport, a quiet unspoilt, undeveloped, delightful hamlet at that time.

It was a peaceful, hot Saturday afternoon as we drove along the strip of bitumen in the centre of the road along the main street, then along past the school to find the Priestly's block of bushland which was to be our camping site for the weekend, and my first experience of the scrub and my life in Tasmania.

We received a visit from Charles, George, and Tas Priestly from their parents' farm at North Scottsdale later that afternoon shortly after we had pitched the two tents. I was introduced to all three with the customary brew of afternoon tea and Meg's mother's kiss biscuits. It was followed by the walk down to the beach for my first swim. We had our beach area to ourselves, so different from what I had always known, and the water was wonderful.

It was a beautiful warm evening as we returned to the camp site later. The big cumbersome wooden box was unloaded from the rear carrier of the car to be used as a table and the greater part of its contents placed in the tent under my care. The fire was soon under way once more to brew the tea, boil the potatoes, the freshly podded garden peas, and to heat the saveloys. The big piece of silverside corned beef was brought out of the meat safe hanging in the breeze under a small shady tree. It was the first opportunity for me to sample an Australian saveloy, as I had never seen them before, but with fresh beetroot, garden peas, lettuce and salad, and a big bowl of raspberries and cream it made a wonderful treat. There was no luxury of daylight saving as I had always known it in summer and it was dark by 8 p.m. However, there was a pale half moon to shed a little light that night, and I remember well: it was the first night of the new year 1950, so Meg and I walked the whole length of the beaches from the old wooden, burnt, piled pier to the recreation ground opposite the Bridport Hotel and the mouth of the Brid River. Parts of the burnt pier were still useable by the more adventurous who cared to fish from the remaining charred planks. It was our first opportunity to talk and discuss everything for the coming week, the future, and our wedding planned for the next Saturday. We made our way back to the camp, then settled down to sleep on the narrow camp stretcher that night. The interior of the tent was sprayed with fly spray, from the old tin fly-spray pump. I did not know then it was to be one of the most unexpected, unpleasant nights for me, with those miserable pests, the mosquitoes. All night long I suffered with dive-bombing attacks, and I was glad when daylight arrived although I then suffered the irritation and itch from scores of bites. I was advised to treat the bites and lumps with sap from the stems of bracken fern, an old-fashioned remedy. It eased the irritation temporarily but the itchy bumps remained red and swollen. However, that weekend was different, a new experience for me and so enjoyable despite the bites, but it all came to an end, and once again we journeyed back to Launceston to climb the twisting bends of the Sidling road, and the potholed gravel road from Myrtle Park to Waverley. Early the following day, Meg and I walked down the steep garden of 25 South Esk Road and the Gorge steps on our way to the city. I had to get to the Commonwealth Bank to see if my money had been transferred from the British post office savings account. Meg went shopping and to inquire about an electric stove to replace the one in the flat, operated by gas from the town supply, and I tried to find my way around until the bank opened for

324

business at 10 a.m. My money had come through much to my relief and, with the currency exchange transaction at that time, I found that my financial assets totalled 491 pounds, which was a lot of money, considering the basic wage was about five pounds per week. Meg found the wedding ring she required and I recall I bought a 'Little Nipper' mantle radio for a wedding present and she purchased a white, tubular bakelite standard lamp which, incidentally, is still in use after over 40 years. It has suffered the exchange of a number of lampshades in that time, and many running repairs, but it still lights up regularly each evening.

Our wedding had been arranged for the forthcoming Saturday, 7th January at the Paterson Street Methodist Church, so we had to pay an urgent evening visit to the minister to finalise all the procedures. Meg had already arranged a number of bridesmaids to escort her, two cousins, Margaret Waldron and Beth Lawrence, and Audrey O'May a fellow teacher from Exeter State School. I was completely alone, not knowing anyone, so I asked Peter Badcock, the fiancé of Margaret to be my best man. Peter agreed willingly to do the honours and he planned to come along early on the Saturday morning to collect me to go to his mother's home in Abbot Street until it was time to proceed to the church.

My cabin trunk, which was to have been delivered to me promptly by sea, had not turned up by the Friday evening, and it contained the greater part of my possessions including my wedding suit. I had to wear another blue-striped suit which I had packed in my suitcase, so everything was in order, although not quite what I had planned it to be.

Peter arrived at 9.30 a.m. that Saturday, and it was the first time I had experienced a state of nerves. For the previous ten years I had often experienced that sinking feeling in the stomach but never at any time, even in the most dangerous situation, had I suffered nerves. I tried to remain as calm and cool as possible, but this was so strange and different for me, to be nervous. The morning soon passed by at Peter's home as we drank numerous cups of tea, talked about everything with his mother, wandered around the garden and relaxed at different times in the shade, until it was time for us to depart.

Everything went well at our wedding ceremony. Meg arrived on time, all the photographs were taken, and we proceeded along to Brisbane House in Brisbane Street, where Meg's parents had arranged the reception. Brisbane House stood out prominently overlooking City Park, so different from the changed area of the present day with hotels and motels covering the whole area, completely blocking out Brisbane House and covering all the old gardens that once lined Brisbane Street. It was a busy time for me being introduced to everyone present and trying to remember each person's name.

It was a wonderful reception and, when all the formalities, the thanks and the speeches had come to an end, Meg's brother had arranged, supposedly in secret, to transport us out to the Perth Hotel to begin our honeymoon. Then at last, we thought on reaching our destination and depositing our cases in our room, we were away from everyone and alone, but not knowing the ordeal and pranks that were to take place that evening. After we had settled into our room we came down that evening into the dining room of the hotel for our tea, all prepared for a quiet meal, and we sat at one of the tables to await service. Suddenly, completely ignorant of everything, in burst a neighbour from South Esk Road, Meg's brothers and others. They had all booked a round table purposely to join us for tea and to begin the interruptions for the remainder of the evening.

In the meantime Meg's brother, Stretton, had formed a conspiracy with the local policeman, obtained a ladder and climbed in through the window of our room to short sheet the bed, raid the suitcases, to tie everything into knots, and to display all our possessions around the room with stockings, and underwear hanging over pictures, bedrails and walls. My pyjamas were tied into dozens of knots, and Meg's clothes received the same treatment, with confetti in every pocket and crease, all unknown to us as we laughed and talked around the dining room table. However, when the meal ended they left and we returned to our room to discover all the mess and the pranks they had played on us both. It took us a long time to get everything straightened out and to put everything back in order, and clean up the mess. It had been a long day and night when we eventually got to bed about 11.30 p.m. But there was to be no peace for us then. A barrage of small stones and gravel began peppering the front window, with laughter, catcalls and heckling from the street below. The gang had returned and conspired with the local constable once again to give us a further reception. It all went on past midnight, then towards the end, one of the larger stones smashed one of the panes of glass in the window, shattering the glass everywhere. This seemed to subdue them, the noise stopped and they finally went away.

The next morning when I settled and paid the bill, I received another account for one pound five shillings for the broken window. Reluctantly I paid it and had to accept it in good fun. When we returned home to South Esk Road after our honeymoon and I told them all about the bill for the broken window, there were roars of laughter; I still get my leg pulled after all the passing years. I had discovered the true meaning of the Australian term 'Tin Kettling' and all the pranks connected with it on a wedding night, but we laughed and accepted it all in good fun.

The next morning, 8th January, we were both ready by 10 a.m. waiting to be picked up by Meg's Uncle Frank and Aunt Hebe to be taken to Hobart to stay with them at Newtown, to give us a base to go on various excursions and trips in Hobart and Southern Tasmania. The immaculate small dark green Morris 10 soon arrived, our cases had to be packed carefully in their special allotted places, everything had to be exact with Aunt Hebe's fussing over everything, and then we set off on the journey to Hobart.

We were well looked after at Aunt Hebe's home in Newtown and we made various trips around Hobart, to the Huon and Channel area, with a one day's outing with Meg's cousins, Des and Barbara Briggs, to the New Norfolk and Salmon Ponds trout hatcheries. The time seemed to fly but it all had to come to an end as we returned to Launceston to settle into our flat at 25 South Esk Road.

About that period, the start of 1950, Launceston began to progress from its quiet country-town atmosphere, and the building industry began to boom. As the population increased, new sub-divisions were opened up, the trams ceased to run from Six Ways along Hobart Road as the concrete road development was in progress to Quarantine Road in preparation for the latest trolley buses.

I was offered a position by Jack Waldron, with Meg's father in his furniture store in George Street. Furniture was in short supply and there was such a huge demand for the lower-priced items, some of it was sold off the delivery truck in Cameron Street before it was unloaded and carried into the store. Meg continued in her job temporarily as a teacher at Exeter Area School, travelling down each morning on the bus from the bottom of the Gorge Steps.

Into February of that year, the days were tiring and hot, and there was very little time to do all the things I wished to do. I tried to save every penny possible as we would soon have to find a home of our own. Meg's parents were considering putting the house up for sale and moving elsewhere. As the days turned into autumn I was asked by a former tenant at South Esk Road to play soccer once again. I considered it for some time wondering if my leg would accept the strain once more. However, I gave it a try and went to practise and

327

training with the Waterside team from Invermay, agreeing to play for them that season. The game was at a very low ebb, and had little support in Tasmania at that time. I played each Saturday afternoon and we became the premier team in the north. I represented the north a number of times playing in Hobart and I had two games playing for Tasmania against Victoria and New South Wales.

At the beginning of September 1950, the house was put up for sale so we had to find another place to live. Through a local real estate company I found the place which to me was ideal. It was situated on Bald Hill at Trevallyn, with the rear garden bordering the reserve overlooking Launceston. The house was not completed, some of the rooms were not plastered, the laundry was not finished and there were many other things to do. The price was 3,750 pounds and I knew I could have soon put it in order to make it an impressive home after it was taken over. My total savings were then 1,122 pounds, and in my eagerness, believing I could easily obtain the remaining amount on loan of just 2,600 pounds, I signed the contract of sale to purchase the place, and I paid 100 pounds deposit.

I soon discovered mortgage loans, at that time, were very restricted and tight and a deposit of at least one-third of the valuation was required, so I needed another 200 pounds for the deposit before I could qualify for the small loan as the property had been valued at 3,900 pounds. I desperately tried all the finance outlets possible, I was unknown and on my own with no one to turn to, and I failed to meet the contract date for settlement. As a result I lost my precious one hundred pounds paid in as a deposit to the real estate firm. Two days later that same real estate business resold the house for 4,000 pounds getting 'two bites of the cherry'. I felt disappointed, angry and bitter, and that same firm carries on business in Launceston up to this day. I had learned another lesson the hard way.

I was in dire straits after my loss and I was desperate to find a place to make a home but there was very little property available except in the high price bracket; together we looked around but everything offered was unsuitable and poor value. Through another real estate agency we inspected a place at Kings Meadows, 50 yards or so from Hobart Road and the main transport route. At that period, there was a row of concrete block cottages along Hobart Road from the Kings Meadows grocery and store at the junction of Risely Street, to Blaydon Street. In this street the homes from numbers 2 to 13 were built on both sides to Guy Street, the whole area beyond being undeveloped with a few scattered homes only. It was a new area, and we inspected and made arrangements to buy number 11, a two-bed-roomed home with a tiny kitchen, for the price of 3,000 pounds.

I did not intend to get caught a second time; Meg's father agreed to lend me 200 pounds to make up the shortfall on the one-third deposit and I obtained a loan for the remainder from the Permanent Building Society to be repaid within five years. I signed the contract for sale and happily it went through with no obstructions or hassles, allowing us to take over and move in on Launceston Show day 1950.

In October also, our first daughter, Christine, was born so we then had extra commitments moving into our new home. There was so much to do to get it in order. It was just a bare house with nothing laid out, no paths, or entrance drive, no garden and only dry hard ground, overgrown with weeds, high grass and twitch, with masses and masses of thick layers of onion twitch bulbs and roots. I remember now well that first week, I purchased a garden spade with the last of my savings to start work on improving things. The price of that spade was three pounds, or to be correct, two pounds nineteen shillings and elevenpence, leaving me flat broke until I received my next pay. All I possessed was one penny in change. To add to our predicament, we received an unhappy comment from Meg's mother, to the effect that Meg was going such a long way out of Launceston to live in 'the bush', as this is what our new location was referred to at that time. I was worried too about my financial position and I suffered pangs of homesickness, so I tried to get over it by working Saturdays and Sundays and from daylight to darkness to get myself back on my feet.

Christmas 1950 arrived and I received payment, at long last, from the superannuation contributions paid in and overdue to me from the London police. It wasn't very much but it was a big help enabling us to obtain extra things for the house, through the shop at a discounted price. On this occasion for the Christmas break we accompanied Meg's parents to Coles Bay, on the east coast, to camp on the beach with the family and Meg's two brothers. There were no more than a half-dozen buildings there in 1950, plus the old weatherboard chalet; the area was very isolated and undeveloped and the terrible rough roadtrack in the area was shocking. However, we set up the family encampment on the beautiful beach, a short distance below the chalet, along with Dudley and Stretton. The owner of the chalet had the audacity to demand rent for our spot on a public beach expecting to reap a reward from the few people who ventured into the area, but he was promptly told to 'jump in the lake'. Our greatest problem was water; we had to get our requirements from a small murky creek, which was discoloured and unpleasant, so every drop had to be boiled, but we put up with it.

Christmas Day was beautiful and in the afternoon, along with the two boys, I climbed over the Hazards and descended down to the complete solitude and the isolation of beautiful Wine Glass Bay. We did something there, impossible nowadays, and long gone, unlikely ever to return. We dangled a baited line from the rocks into the wonderful, blue, clear water of the bay, to bring a big Crayfish to the surface, lifting the bait, grabbed its feelers just below the surface and pitched it on to the rocks. It was boiled in a kerosene tin that evening, on the camp fire and we all made short work of it for our tea. That night the mosquitoes were terrible again, despite our spray. Christine was in the lift-out body of the pram; thankfully she was protected with a muslin net but I suffered again, for they seemed to have a special liking for me.

The following day, in the sultry late afternoon, we were hit with a violent electrical storm. The sky became as black as ink as the torrential rain rolled in from the sea soaking and drenching everything. The tent leaked badly and it turned cold and unpleasant. We were getting a taste of all weather, with a further disaster to come.

The short holiday came to an end, and it was time to move out to travel back to Launceston and home. We packed up all the family possessions into the car with everyone sorted out as comfortably as possible to prepare for the shocking trip along the terrible track until we reached the main road to Swansea, and then a further 50 miles of corrugated, rough, twisting road via Lake Leake to Campbelltown. We had almost reached the main road, when the old Plymouth car lurched into a culvert and stopped dead, with the motor still racing but it had no traction or power and would not move. Fortunately, Meg's brothers, Dudley and Stretton, were leading the way and realising we were not following, they returned to find us broken down and unable to move. There was nothing wrong with the vehicle's motor and the trouble was soon diagnosed. The car had sustained a broken half-shaft axle. We used all our manpower to push it to the side of the track in order to jack it up and remove the two rear wheels to push out the two broken pieces of the shaft. Stranded by the side of the track, the two boys took the broken shaft to Swansea to try to find out if they were able to get it welded as a temporary repair to get us back to Launceston, but it was a holiday and it was impossible to obtain a replacement. We walked out along the track the remaining distance to the main road hoping to obtain a lift back to Launceston.

It was our lucky day after all – Meg, myself and baby Christine, wrapped up in a bundle, received a lift with a passing vehicle all the way home to Kings Meadows; we were so glad to get back after a long, hot, bumpy ride.

The boys succeeded in getting the shaft welded and fitted it back on the car and Meg's father drove it back without mishap early the next day. Our first visit to Cole's Bay was wonderful despite all the problems and I did not realise then it would be another 40 years before we visited the place again, to find so much development there and a first class road instead of a track, so different from that Christmas in 1950.

We turned into the year of 1951 and, for the remaining months of summer and autumn, I had to concentrate towards getting our home the way we wanted it. We had occupied the place for three months. The greater part of the block was so hard it was impossible to turn it over by hand to set out the garden until the rains came to soften the earth. My first objective was to build a small garage to store and keep some of our things.

I submitted a plan to the council which delayed the project for a further 14 days until their meeting was held. It was approved and referred to as a cycle shed. I mixed and laid the cement floor by hand, the weatherboards were obtained from Jim Morrell's secondhand building yard, the doors and the roofing iron came from 25 South Esk Road, Meg's parents' home, being the front extension of the old garage building, which I dismantled before the place was sold. This extension had a dirt floor, the timber was useless and rotted but I salvaged the old roofing iron and the rafters which were all carted to Kings Meadows on George Lewis' ancient Chev 4 truck. By the end of February, I completed my project, so I had a small garage complete with a makeshift workbench to help me along my way. Each Thursday fortnight from that time onwards I managed to slip away to the Webster's Mart for a short time to pick up a few bargains as they came available. At 10 a.m. the first items of what they classed as junk articles were put up for auction. I obtained many boxes and cartons of 'rubbish' from people's throw outs and deceased estates for the price of two, five and ten shilling lots. There were many treasures among them and I built up my collection of all kinds of useful tools and articles, including saws, hammers, nails, screws and bolts.

I disregarded the remainder of the junk and I soon became self-sufficient with the majority of the things I needed for all the jobs I wanted to do. Ironically it cost me more in cartage in George Lewis'

331

truck than the prices I paid for my successful bids, but it was worth every penny to get myself started.

The furniture business was booming at that period, with increasing numbers of migrants and the expanding building trade also added to employment as the state moved progressively forward. The big hydro-electric schemes were at full capacity with so many ethnic groups doing their two years of compulsory employment fulfilling their migrant agreements and it was difficult at times to obtain supplies to keep up with the demand. At various intervals of two or three weeks, we tried to fill Ray Hughes' big transport vehicle with bedroom and lounge suites, and all oddments of furniture, to transport to Hobart to keep up the supplies.

Jack Waldron, with two other stores in Hobart, took over the store of Keating and Allen in Wellington Street and Meg's younger brother Dudley, who was soon to get married, took control of the place. Meg's parents too had sold the old home in South Esk Road and then settled in Rocklyn Place in West Launceston.

In 1952, we decided to extend our home to give us a third bedroom as more room was needed. Once again I submitted my plans to the council building department for approval but there was another delay as the building inspector was ill and absent for two weeks, with further loss of time for me to mix and pour the foundations by the end of October of that year. The next weekend, the start of November, was the usual long weekend holiday, so I prepared to commence my building project then.

In order to take advantage of that weekend holiday, Meg's parents were going to Stonehenge and Dalmeny Park, to stay at the Darlings' property, where Meg had once boarded, for the weekend break. Meg and baby Christine would go along too and I would be free to get on with my job. I had erected the timber wall framing by the Saturday of their departure and removed all the weatherboards off the dining room exterior adjoining my new room. It was six o'clock on the Saturday evening, when the weather turned southerly bringing torrential rain and high winds. I was caught unawares and all I could do was to prop all the roofing iron against the uncovered wall to protect it and stack all my surplus timber against it to hold it in position from the rain and wind. It was a howling gale, with incessant torrential rain, and I was up all night long, trying to keep the iron in position to protect my wall.

The heavy rain and wind continued all day Sunday and Sunday night; flood warnings were issued over the radio and the Midland

Highway was closed at Ross. It stopped raining on Monday morning, leaving water everywhere. The family returned from the Midlands in the old Plymouth car which had been towed across the creek near the Andover turnoff, and then held up for three hours at Ross, waiting to cross the single-file wooden ramp which was used as a standby in order to get in to Ross. They eventually arrived home about 7.00 p.m. to find me waiting anxiously, not having been able to do any work at all.

Each week regularly without fail my mother sent on to me the *Reynold's News* or the *Sunday Express* newspaper to enable me to keep up with events and news, and in many of the vacant areas and spaces, my father wrote lots of titbits and comments. It worried me a great deal as I could read between the lines that he was a sick man and suffering the torments of pain after a lifetime of hard work. My sisters, too, all wrote to me regularly, so I was fully aware of all the family news.

Into the winter months of 1952, we purchased various books by mail through a book club, and in the comfort of the lounge with a cheery warm fire many of them I read out loud so that Meg and I could follow the story together. The radio serials were very popular at that period and we tried to follow each episode. It was a very wet winter and I had obtained a big truckload of she-oak firewood from the Rigby Brothers at Upper Esk and Mathinna so we were comfortable. We had no paths or driveway during that winter, just a block of cement hurriedly laid from the back door to the laundry to replace the duckboards put down by the owner to avoid the sticky wet soil. I had stockpiled loads of gravel and materials at the side of the block in preparation for laying my concrete at the end of the winter. Each Sunday evening, it became a ritual to have tea at Rocklyn Place, the shop and residence of Stretton in High Street, or Dudley's home in St John Street.

I am adding here a few statistics in some quotes from the *Tasmanian Newsletter* issued at Tasmania House in the Strand off Trafalgar Square in London:

At the beginning of 1950 there were 29 persons receiving unemployment benefit in Tasmania, 28 men and one woman. The basic wage had been increased by three shillings making the minimum wage for an unskilled worker, five pounds eighteen shillings per week; also, radio telephones with a range of 20 to 30 miles were installed in 9 taxis in Launceston, the first city in Australia to have such a service . . . Sixty years ago, the Rev R W Dale visited Australia. He crossed the Straits and sojourned amongst the Tasmanians. He found them leading – or thought he did – an ideal kind of life free from ambition, anxiety, or the passion for money-making, a life with leisure for the enjoyment of the charities of home, for the love of nature, and for all the higher intellectual and moral interests. [A charming picture, but one which greater experience would probably have modified!]

Christmas 1952 arrived and I had resided in Launceston for three years. All the old pangs of homesickness had gone, I had settled into my new life and accepted the change of seasons, Christmas in the heat of summer with no more snow and winter in July. We stayed at home over the Christmas break. Clem, Meg's father, took his two weeks' holiday and, I would take mine in January when he returned. After his two weeks' camping holiday he was pleased and full of enthusiasm for a shack he had bought behind the post office for a bargain price. Our holiday too was to be spent at Bridport and Meg had made all the arrangements to board at a Miss Perkins' home in May Street. Clem asked me to inspect his newly acquired shack while we were there and to offer my opinion, with suggestions and comments about the place. We travelled to Bridport on the bus with baby Christine. It was very hot and dusty over the rough gravel road and over the narrow winding sidling but, after our bone-shaking journey, we arrived safely at the Bridport shop, and made our way to Miss Perkins' home. Miss Perkins was rather a quaint, eccentric spinster and I don't think she had ever taken boarders before, because it appeared to be a new experience for her and something different for us. We cooked and prepared all the meals and she was always ready to join us. I don't think she had experienced such treats before.

One hot leisurely afternoon we walked along to find the shack that Meg's father had spoken of. Very little ground was built on at that time and we walked through the scrub at the rear of the top shop to Henry Street, and into the open ground beyond. The shack, ancient, neglected and almost ready to fall down, was situated all alone among the high grass on a large block of ground directly behind, and adjoining, the post office and the Bridport Hotel. It was all open, unfenced paddock with no other buildings around and just one boundary, paling fence to Ken Scott's shack fronting Henry Street. The land was owned by Mr Charles Bennett, a tough, hardworking, elderly gentleman who had built the Bridport Hotel. In 1911 Mr Barnett had transported, on a dray pulled by two horses all the way from Derby in the north-east, a timber tin-miner's hut and set it up on a few timber stumps at the top end of the block adjoining the old well that he had sunk to supply fresh water to the hotel. He had added a tin and stone fireplace and erected a tin chimney. The front facing west had two tiny windows approximately 12 inches square. The rear, facing the sea, had been extended with a lean-to with trellis on three sides, all on rusty hinges, so that they could be propped up with a timber support. This old, quaint and interesting building was used and rented by the warden of the municipality of Scottsdale, Mr Bricky Rose. From the junction of Henry Street that tough wonderful old man Charles Barnett, almost 90 years of age, had begun to dig out a new access road with a pick, shovel and wheelbarrow, which was to become eventually Barnett Crescent. On the south side of the run-down shack, stood the old Dunny with its old wooden seat and bucket, the door hanging precariously on a rusty broken hinge and dragging the earth; it remained permanently ajar, and would not close. Any occupant sitting on the throne could enjoy the view across Anderson Bay and watch the breaking waves rolling into the Brid River. This important establishment was covered and overgrown with the climbing hop, with its masses of full cotton blooms adorning every cobweb and protruding nail.

When I returned to Launceston and back at work once more, we discussed the shack and I agreed it had lots of potential. By coincidence, the next day Reeman and Manning's Motor Garage was to expand along George Street, opposite the furniture store. A wonderful part of Launceston's cultural history was about to be destroyed, all the old Georgian houses along the street were about to be demolished. I watched the demolition workers wreck those buildings, stacking onto the bonfires wonderful newel posts, banister rails, treads and risers and thick wide architraves and then restoking them with old timbers imported and brought here by the early settlers. I suggested to Clem that we inquire about the windows, before they were smashed and destroyed, as they would be useful to install in his newly acquired shack. Each window with its upper and lower lift sash had six panes, one foot by nine inches in Georgian fashion. Clem rushed over as they began ripping out the windows, and succeeded in obtaining five windows intact, a total of ten sashes, for the price of four pounds. I went over too and ripped out the sash cord pulleys. Those pulleys were cast iron and made in England in 1830, with a brass pulley wheel, and a solid brass face plate recessed over the wheel into the frame, imported and installed to add grace and charm to those old

Georgian houses. Some of those cast-iron framed pulleys broke as I removed them but I obtained seven intact. Over the years I have used five of those sash cord pulleys, two of them I have kept as souvenirs and I still possess them, little pieces of old Launceston town. The historic windows purchased by Clem, Meg's father, were soon to become installed and part of the Percy holiday home, and adorned with a cut-out timber nameplate made by me.

But there was more, a little extra from the cultural history of Launceston town and Australia. At the rear of the dilapidated areas of Waldron's Furniture store, and behind the Cornwall Hotel, was the cottage that once belonged to the founder of Melbourne, John Batman. It was a broken-down dangerous warehouse-type brick and stone building and adjoining it was tumbledown and falling to pieces, with some of the framed timbers still standing and a shingle raftered roof, all overgrown once again with climbing kapok and hops. In the frame was a four-panelled door suspended by two heavy and badly rusted cast iron hinges, held in position with handmade dog nails. One of the panels was missing but I soon discovered under the crazed old paint the timber was solid cedar. I carefully dismantled that old door and it was transported on George Lewis' old truck to my home at Kings Meadows. I repaired and replaced that missing panel with the cedar timber from a drawer made by the Jones' family, who made furniture and bedroom suites on the old site at the end of Cameron Street before it was demolished to become Finney's Funeral premises and chapel. The door was taken to Bridport and, to whom it may interest, this front door, from John Batman's Cottage, is hanging and used as the back door at Blue Mist, Barnett Crescent, Bridport.

The winter of 1953 was very wet with so much heavy rain, and we experienced problems with the adjacent creek flooding Blaydon Street. With so much flood water entering the sewers from illegal new connections as the region expanded, the area at the entrance to Hobart Road became a filthy mess. I caught the daily bus service in Hobart Road each morning to make a change at Six Ways to another vehicle until the new trolley buses were introduced. I made every effort to obtain every possible odd job that I could find in order to supplement my income to pay off my mortgage and improve my finances. We organised a working bee with Meg's father and the two boys to put the Bridport shack in order to be made useable as a holiday cottage. The untidy old place was strengthened with extra studs, the windows from George Street were installed and hinged, allowing them all to open outwards, and sheets of tempered masonite were sawn into 12-

336

inch strips to use as wide weatherboards. John Batman's door was installed on the back entrance porch to make the place secure and lockable. Extra iron was added to improve the garage and Charles Barnett's original well was filled in and the ground levelled to make a better clearance to the ancient toilet. I made two double-decker bunks for the spare room, flock mattresses were added from the shop, the house was painted ice blue and then christened by Meg's mother, Myrtle, with the name of 'Blue Mist'.

Up to this time I had paid every penny I could afford off my debts and finally by the middle of March my mortgage was discharged, and the 200 pounds loan from Meg's father was repaid and I was free from debt. It was a big relief to me for I could now endeavour to try to obtain my own transport, a small vehicle of our own, with all the extra convenience of getting from place to place and transport to and from work. I still possessed a British Army driving licence from 1941 but it was mislaid, and I could not recall what I had done with it. They told me this would make it easy to obtain a Tasmanian licence. I wrote to my mother, who found it and conscientiously sent it out to me in a package with lots of army buttons and regalia. Regretfully one important souvenir of my past life was missing, as she had disposed of my army battledress and, with it, my sewn-on, secret, screw-top button containing the tiny compass which had helped me so much during the war.

At the beginning of July 1954, I found the vehicle I thought would suit me, at a secondhand car yard, Superior Cars in Wellington Street. It was a 1943 Morris 10 horsepower, green sedan in good order, clean and well looked after. I paid a deposit of 50 pounds and arranged to pay the balance and pick it up the following week. On 22nd July, Alan Lewis, the son of old George Lewis the local carrier, came along with me to the police station for a driving test to obtain my licence. The police station was situated then at the end of Wellington Street. We drove up Wellington Street to Glen Dhu School and back to the station. I paid my ten shillings' fee, signed the lift-out insignificant top copy piece of paper in the police licence book, countersigned by the constable, and I had my licence for the following twelve months, till 1st August 1955. The following week I had to extend the length of my cycle shed to accommodate the vehicle and it now became a garage. It made a wonderful difference as I was now able to get around without worrying about catching buses and we were able to carry many of the things we had to transport. Everything at that time was obtainable in the town; bread and milk were delivered to the door each day but the majority of our groceries were purchased from Stretton's shop, Meg's brother, in High Street and all other items were carried home from central Launceston.

In September of that year, 1954, Roslyn, our second daughter, was born and Meg and the baby were both fit and well; Christine was almost four years old, growing up, progressing very well, and soon to be able to start school. I received another pleasant surprise, a letter from my brother Trefor posted in Japan to tell me his P & O ship was coming to Melbourne and it raised my hopes that I might possibly meet him again after our last reunion in London in 1949.

One week before Christmas 1954 I received an unexpected phone call at the shop, the telephone number that I had forwarded to Trefor. He was in Melbourne, his ship had docked for just 24 hours but he was unable to come over to see me because of the hurried departure. I spoke to him for about five minutes giving him all the news and events. It was his only trip into Australian waters en route to New Zealand so it was to be another 20 years before I saw him to speak to again.

For the holiday break that Christmas we went to Bridport. We cleaned up the overgrown grounds around the shack with Clem, Meg's father, spent many of the early mornings fishing with Ken Scott and Lindsay Gofton, the neighbours, and lazed on the beach in the sun into the New Year of 1955.

I received lots of cards and news from my sisters and mother in Wales, who were experiencing big falls of snow as we enjoyed the warm sun. The notes and titbits on the vacant spaces of the newspapers sent on to me were getting fewer, and I realised my father was beginning to fail; he was suffering much more as he approached his seventieth birthday.

Christine started school at the Glen Dhu Infant School at the beginning of the new school year, and there were some tears on that first day, but she soon settled into the new routine. It was most convenient for me to take her to school in the Morris car on my way to work and Meg was able to meet her at the bus stop in Hobart Road each afternoon at the end of the school day.

That year, to, brought some bad news to me from Wales. My old boyhood friend, Billy Crane, was found dead, suddenly, at such a young age. Bill and I had been close mates ever since I could walk and all the incidents, problems and frightening events in our early schooldays came flooding back to me, with all the troubles and scrapes we shared together as we grew up. Poor Billy had passed away.

338

William George Crane, his full name, was five months older than I. He was short and tubby, happy-go-lucky and always prepared to join in with any of the pranks that mischievous boys got up to. He could not run very fast due to his build, and it disadvantaged him on many occasions. How well I remember him getting stuck in the thorny boundary hedge and cornered by the farm dog once when we raided the Gwaled-y-Waen pear orchard up Angel Lane, bordering the stick woods across the river. He suffered and endured the subsequent flogging all alone and would not disclose the names of the other culprits like myself and others. One other incident I shall never forget for the rest of my life. We were both about eight years old and, in order to become a recognised and fully fledged member of the Vere Street clique of boys, it was compulsory to perform some extraordinary feat of initiation. The task allocated to Billy and me was to walk through the Pengam Graveyard together on a black winter's night, from the main entrance right through to the river. We were allowed to use a bicycle lamp, the old square type with the two-pronged terminal square battery, which was such a poor light. We were escorted to the entrance by some of the members of the gang and instructed to meet up with four boys. Mooking and Snowy Pryce, and the Richards twins, waiting at the footbridge across the river, beyond the far boundary. There were no industry skylights, as we set off into that weird, frightening, black atmosphere, our small miserable light providing the only assurance to show us the way over the gravemounds past the headstones and the tall tombstones. Billy, behind me, holding fast on to my jersey, started to whimper and shake with fear, and I was just as frightened too! I pulled Billy's cap down over his eyes so that he could not see, and I did the same just allowing a small space to look at the ground and the narrow spaces between the graves. Two ashen-faced, frightened small boys, we stumbled on, Billy's whimper now turned to cries and sobs, as we finally reached the limit of that burial ground and the boundary fence. We clambered through the fence and I grabbed Billy's arm to break into a run over the broken ground, the refuse from an old level that had been picked over for small pieces of coal. We heard the sound of the fast-flowing river at last and picked out the path to the footbridge; our nightmare journey had been fulfilled. The following day Billy was absent from school; Fred, his brother, said he wasn't very well but we had earned our right to be accepted by the Vere Street boys.

The only time Billy ever visited those burial grounds again was to adorn the grave of our old antagonist Noah Thomas, with brother

Fred, and ironically it was I who helped them both to pick the bunches of the blue-purple flowers of the deadly nightshade across the railway lines in the Charity Woods.

In 1986 as I wandered around the Gwerthonor district reminiscing about days gone by, I was told that Edith, the oldest girl, and the last of the Crane family, was still living in Margaret Street, one of the steep streets that ran downhill off Gwerthonor Place. I found out where she lived and I knocked at her front door. My knock was answered by Edith personally; I did not say anything, and she looked at me for a few seconds then burst into tears. 'Ron!' she said, 'it can't be you.' I had a long talk and a cup of tea with her that afternoon; she was nearly seventy-five years old at that time. My sister Joan informed me afterwards that she died about six months after my call, the Crane family having then all passed on.

23

The Closing Years of the 1950s and My Father's Death

In the summer of 1956, after spending a few days at Gordon Darling's property, Dalmeny Park, at Stonehenge in the Midlands, we were invited by Meg's Uncle Roy Briggs for a few days' stay at their shack in Dodges Ferry. The area was a very quiet isolated place, unspoiled and beautiful, just like all the other coastal areas of Tasmania, with a rough gravel road, little better than a track in some places. Roslyn was just starting to walk and with our big load, the old Morris car faithfully carried us along on our journey from the Midlands. We soon found the shack from our directions on some higher ground fronting the sea. A rail track ran from the block over the scrub and the rocks down to the water. A small four-wheeled trolley hitched to a winch with a long wire rope carried a ten-feet-long heavy rowing boat all ready to run out and launch into the sea. The cousins, Des and Barbara, were there with Jenny their daughter, so the children had a wonderful time with a small three-feet long-bottomed boat in the shallow water and the reeds along the edge of the beach. That same afternoon we launched the rowing boat and with Uncle Roy we rowed out into the channel to catch some fish for supper. We caught so many cod in just half an hour we had to return otherwise we could have overloaded the boat. What a contrast now 40 years later. I doubt whether it would be possible to catch any fish at all in that locality, which is now such a built-up area with hundreds of permanent and holiday homes.

On our return journey home we decided to drive up the winding gravel east coast highway and then travel through Levendale to Woodsdale and Oatlands back to the Midland Highway. I regretted it when we encountered the shocking conditions. The road from Levendale was a horror stretch, potholed and broken, and for the greater part covered with loose stones and boulders. After travelling some miles along that terrible track, trying desperately to avoid so many dips, holes and large stones, one of the leaves on our right rear spring snapped and the rear end of our vehicle listed and dropped. We continued on, but before we reached Woodsdale a leaf in the other rear spring broke also, allowing the rear end to level a little with jars and bumps continuously shaking and rattling our small vehicle. There was worse to come; after passing through Woodsdale the constant pounding of stones on the underside of the car severed the brake hydraulics pipe, we lost all the fluid and had no brakes. The remaining 85 miles to Kings Meadows was a slow unnerving drive with just the handbrake to control the vehicle; it took a long time and we were relieved to get home without any further problems. I worked on our vehicle into the early hours of Monday morning fixing the brakes and removing the springs. I carried both the springs in a sack bag on the bus into town that Monday morning up to Jacksons Springs in Cameron Street with the consolation that they would be repaired and ready for the forthcoming Friday. I carried them home once more that Friday evening and refitted them onto the car. On Saturday morning Jim Kennedy came along to help me remove the pistons to fit new oil rings, and the car was completed and mobile once again with new life and power.

On 25th November 1957, I received more tragic news. The first information came from sister Toots on 18th November that my father had died on the 10th of that month. A post mortem had already been performed on his body and he had been cremated according to his wishes before they informed me of the sad news. I suppose there are many occasions in one's journey through life when one almost chokes with emotion as the lump in the throat becomes almost intolerable, and for me this was one of them. As I remember him now, I believe there are no words in this language to fulfil the true praise that I could give my late father. I spent the first 20 years or so of my life only under the guidance of my father but I have always followed his ways, wisdom and beliefs throughout my life. Everyone knew him so well in the whole district. He was always in attendance at all the local meetings putting forward his point of view in arguments and discussions, and there are many things I could never forget regarding his prowess and skills in so many ways. He was always calm and resolute, there were few times he raised his voice, and the number of times he showed his anger, I remember them all. He was a fine athlete, a brilliant cricketer, and a wonderful soccer player.

Our local sportsground was shaped like a saucer with a small flat area in the centre, the main Great Western Railway on the one side with the aerial buckets ropeway and the rail sidings on the other. The last thing the English bureaucrats would do was to spend money on any sporting facility for the Welsh Rabble. On one occasion during the 1920s I was a spectator with my brother Gwyn sitting on the high side of that saucer bowl watching my father batting for the village team in a cricket match. He had reached his half century, and with the next ball he gave it a huge hit high over the saucer boundary through the compartment window of a passing speeding steam passenger train. The game was abandoned as they did not have another ball. I recall that incident well; my brother turned to his exercise book and pencil, recording the scores and in a matter of minutes wrote the following lines, tore out the page, and gave it to me. I can now rewrite those lines 65 years later:

> Greensward lined by a seething crowd,
> A sea of faces with earnest frown.
> Sudden hushed silence of anticipation
> Time passes, with slow deliberation.
> The gruelling sun shines gaily down
> Undisturbed my Man's pleasure round.
> Backs bent, and with intensive sight
> Strained upon lonely mortal with shining bat,
> He takes 'centre' and earnestly looks around
> The 'on' and 'off' of that battleground,
> Then makes his stand to await
> The fiery ball that decides his fate.
> The bowler bounds with speedy run
> A leap at the wicket, the delivery done,
> The speeding sphere hurls with truth,
> Then – a flash of colour, red ball, green turf
> Yellow bat and flashing arms,
> A sickening click! a shout of alarm!
> 'How's that' – the umpire signals 'out'.
> The crowd lean back with a sigh
> Then burst forth with a lusty cry!
> Cheers for bowler, sympathy for batsman.
> An age of waiting, a second in time,
> Displays hope, fear, success, defeat
> In the clean air of the sportmanship
> And not in the gambler's game of how to live.

My father always attempted to change the subject when asked a question about his early life, although I did get a little scattered information during our long discussions and conversations on occasions, sitting by a big coal fire under the living room gaslight, long after midnight, into the early hours of the next day. I understood that his family lived in a tithe cottage, the cruel feudal system whereby one tenth of all produce grown by a tenant had to be provided for the clergy. This was changed to rent in 1836, and I believe it was collected by the state 100 years later in 1936 on behalf of the church. They owned nothing, could be evicted at any time, no repairs were ever carried out, facilities were primitive, and any improvements were their own responsibility. He began his apprenticeship as a black-smith at the age of 14 and he was brutally kicked and horsewhipped for any fault or mistake. He slept for the greater part of the time in the stables where they kept the horses waiting to be shod. Just before his fifteenth birthday in 1900 he ran away to Bristol, to try to emigrate on a ship to the United States but he was turned away as a minor. His sister Dot, ten years older than my father, had succeeded in absconding from the drudgery of the kitchen service with the upper class rich in 1895, and in getting across to a new life in America. Poor Dad was brutally horsewhipped when he returned for deserting his job, some of the scars and pain, he said, he would carry to his grave. He was paid two shillings weekly with three meagre meals daily, threepence was deducted by his violent employer for the use of his tools and he slept in the stables except on Saturday nights into the Sabbath. His miserable earnings he gave to his parents. He suffered and endured this work for two more years, until his mother died and his father died also in terrible pain from appendicitis. He was alone and the youngest of the family. He conspired with three other boys from the village and they all abandoned their miserable, oppressive occupations and set off together to walk to South Wales. They found their way into the Rhymney Valley all finding work and accom-modation at Bargoed, and the Gwerthonor area of Gilfach. My father soon became friendly with the Davies family and Dai 'Wasp' my mother's brother. He married in 1909 and in 1919 my life began.

There was one other incident too for me to always remember when I saw him moved to his greatest anger of my youth, and I was frightened when I heard that he was threatened to be put in jail for obstructing and then standing up for the rights of a fellow member of the local community. That person was a colourful character, an honest family man with the name of Herbie Thomas, residing in the

344

Gwerthonor area. There were four children in the family, Mabel, Muriel, Leonard and Vivian. Vivian was my age and in the same class at school of Miss Doris Davies-Black – at Gilfach Boys School, just prior to the general strike of 1926. It was a Monday morning, Vivian was in tears and sobbing and Miss Davies was trying to find out what was wrong. Vivian between his sobs blurted out that his dad had been taken away to jail in the Black Maria. During the lunch break I told my father that Herbie had been carted off to jail by Noah Thomas. Puzzled by what I had said, my father went off immediately to find out all about it, because he knew that Herbie was a sick man. He was paid a meagre allowance on what they termed as 'Lloyd George' at that time with no job and unable to work, with a miserable subsistence allowance to feed the children.

The Churchill and Baldwin English Tory regime had instituted a cruel means test, giving the investigating overlords power to enter any recipient's home unannounced, to examine the subsistence and living conditions of a family. At 8.30 a.m. that Monday morning two Means Test officials escorted by Noah Thomas, burst into Herbie's home. Herbie being unwell was in bed, Mrs Thomas, his wife, was at the fireplace attending to a cast iron pot and its contents boiling on the coal fire. They seized the pot which contained a pig's head being prepared for the week's food and poured out the contents into the adjoining scullery sink. The two bureaucrats entered and recorded the details in their record book and continued on their rounds for the next victim and consequently all payment was stopped to Herbie's family for two weeks. That pig's head was considered sufficient to feed the whole family for that period.

In the meantime Noah Thomas was questioning and interrogating Herbie's wife, who maintained that the pig's head had been given to them by old man Mathews, from Gwerthonor ISAF, the Mathews' farm. Noah Thomas ordered Herbie out of bed, and detained him, accusing him of stealing the pig's head. He sent for the Black Maria and carted him off to Bargoed police cells. My father spoke to Herbie's wife to try to find out what was wrong, and she told him the whole story. On the day previously, the Sunday, Mrs Thomas, Muriel and Leonard, had helped the Mathews' grandsons to muck-out the line of pigsties that ran along the lane down to the head of our 'jungle'. Their reward for the work was a pig's head. So, concerned, my father missed that afternoon's work shift and the news spread quickly around the district. When we all came out of school that afternoon, he organised Leonard, Muriel, the Mathews' grandsons, and Mrs Thomas, with Old

345

Mathews' in his horse and cart and a crowd of angry neighbours including myself and our schoolmates to proceed to the police station. I had never seen my father so angry in my life and as a young boy I was frightened as he was ordered off the area and threatened with arrest for organising a riot. Herbie was released with not even an apology. I recall too in 1940 after Churchill's speech, referring to Hitler and his forces of evil, he said to me then, 'We have been forced to contend with his forces of evil all our lives.'

I remember the last time I saw the Black Maria, the miserable, steel-banded wooden van, pulled by a black horse, and much feared by us. In 1927, the old horse that pulled that vehicle ended its days, to be sent for slaughter at the knacker's yard, and the van was sold at an auction. I believe it was purchased by a farmer from the upper reaches of the valley where I hoped, just like all the other small boys who were threatened and frightened to be carried off inside it, it finally ended its unhappy life.

In 1958 with so much competition and extravagant spending by its proprietor, the furniture business in Hobart started to decline. The son and daughter came into the business and further spending sprees devastated the profits. In 1959 Clem, Meg's father, was told his services would no longer be required and one of the shops was closed. In the winter of that same year the other store situated a short distance below the post office closed its doors for the last time and Ossie Johnson, who managed the business, came to Launceston to take over. I was getting tired of it all. It was carpet and floor coverings that kept the place going and I was doing all the selling, cutting, planning, and laying of it all. Things were going from bad to worse. So many times I would arrive at the shop just after 8.30 a.m. to find the premises locked and closed, the manager was absent and I was unable to get in. The person concerned would be working for himself at one of the local butchers, cutting and preparing the meat for the day's sales, while I waited to get in to open for business, and to get on with my job, often as late as 9.45 a.m. I would return on many occasions also from a carpet installation to find the premises locked, with a note on the door 'Back in half an hour'. There was no one in attendance and no sales. There was no cash left in the till to provide change on various cash sales and often I provided the necessary change from my own pocket, and then got confused with the amount due back to me. On numerous occasions too I had to borrow money from Virieux' fruit and snack bar next door, in order to carry on, the manager being absent. The business was heading downhill, heading into bankruptcy.

At home I had started to modify and extend our kitchen to make it roomier and bigger, moving the sink and stove, and plans were submitted and approved by the council. We were expecting our third member of the family and Meg went into hospital in July 1959 for the birth of our son Gwyn. It was 30th July 1959 and I did not know it was to be a worrying time, and such a difficult birth for Meg. On that particular morning I had obtained a big order from the Newstead Hotel and it was absolutely essential to keep the business going, no one else was concerned or worried. I was caught between two decisions, three suites had to be carpeted and completed by 5 p.m. for incoming guests or lose the sale, and I had to get to the Queen Victoria Hospital to Meg.

I had had enough. I did not intend to go on in this way any more. I succeeded in finding John, the proprietor's son, at the home of his girlfriend. We both went to Herbert Street in Invermay to seek a German immigrant, who did various upholstery jobs for the establishment and then, I got them both to come with me to the hotel as my assistants. Everything had to be carried out of the apartments, the new carpet laid and then everything replaced. Working all day without a break the job was completed by 5.30 p.m. just in time for the guests. I received no thanks for it. I had had enough, my mind was made up, I was getting out before the business folded up. It was the beginning of the end of Waldron's furniture business. I gave a week's notice that I was leaving the job after nearly ten and a half years. I received no pro-rata long-service holiday pay, as there were no funds to make the payment. I was the loser. I had no problem getting another position and ten days later I commenced my new employment with Young's Furniture Store in Wellington Street.

The Kings Meadows area was expanding rapidly in the 1960s and the Kings Meadows High School was built which was a big advantage to us; Christine would soon be attending high school there, just a short distance away.

We extended our kitchen and the garage at that period too, as our family had increased. On 14th December 1962, just before Christmas, Meg's mother, Myrtle, died after a short illness. It was a sad occasion before the festive season and an upsetting time but we did all go to Bridport once again for a quiet holiday. I recall too while camping alongside Morris' General Store at Swansea in November 1963 attending the annual fishing competition with Dudley and Stretton, Meg's

347

brothers, we 'borrowed' some electric power at the local service station to operate the electric radio on the Saturday evening, and heard the announcement that President Kennedy has been assassinated. I spent six days also locked up and isolated in the old wing of the Cornwall Hotel on jury service. This dormitory wing at the rear of Waldron's furniture store was demolished and later rebuilt. It was the murder trial of an Invermay resident. A rifle was discharged in a struggle with a storekeeper whom he had accused of intimidating his daughter. I learned a little more of the secret side of a jury room and the unmovable prejudices of the other members of the jury, while trying to sort out and investigate every piece of evidence.

I stayed at Young's for three years and generated a lot of business and sales for them but, just like all other family businesses there were too many in authority. Finally I had cross words with one of them over a particular carpet job and gave my notice to quit, which brought to an end my involvement with the furniture business in Launceston.

Towards the end of 1963 I began work with a firm of solicitors known as Archer Hall Waterhouse and Campbell in Holyman House, Brisbane Street, and I remained with them until Christmas 1974.

In March 1967 we received news from my sister Edna's son, Brian, that he was in Sydney and coming to Tasmania. The last time I saw him he was a small child in London in 1949. He had grown up and was serving as the radio operator in a 20,000-ton freighter and actually sailing into the Tamar River, to load a big consignment of aluminium ingots from the Comalco works at Bell Bay. On the Friday evening we raced down to Bell Bay in our Austin car to try to contact him.

We received a clearance from the gate security to drive down to the wharf where the ship was moored. In the darkness with everything quiet and no activity anywhere, we went up the gangplank and found two members of the crew fishing from the bow. They had hooked two fish with their efforts, and by the light of a torch, we could see one was a flathead, the other was a toadfish. In unfamiliar waters they knew nothing about them, inquiring from us what kind of fish they were. Perhaps it was worthwhile that I gave them a timely warning not to eat the toadfish. However, they contacted Brian for us, and he obtained permission from the captain for leave of absence to travel home with us until Monday morning, while the vessel was loading. There were quite a number of jealous comments from other members of the crew. We drove home for a pleasant weekend and Meg drove him back to the ship on Monday morning as I went off to work.

In October 1967 there was more sad news. Clem, Meg's father, collapsed and died from a heart attack. He had remarried, sold his home and lived with his new wife in Phillip Street. There were problems with this marriage but he tried to hide his unhappiness. As a result of his death the three residential premises he owned in Welman Street and the shack at Bridport passed in equal shares to Meg and her two brothers. There was a stipulation that his widow was to be paid 56 Australian dollars (£30) per month for the rest of her life, an amount equivalent to the old age pension at that period, from the rents generated from the three flats in Welman Street. We experienced all kinds of problems with those premises, the rents weren't paid, and many of them made moonlight departures leaving myself and the boys to work continuously to repair the damages and keep the places in order. At the end of 1969, fed up with so much maintenance and supervision, they agreed to sell the properties. They sold for a bargain, through an agent; two complete two-bedroomed houses and a two-storey nine-roomed home for the sum of 13,000 dollars (£7,000).

After all the expenses were paid the residue of 10,000 dollars (about £5,500) was invested to pay for the monthly income of the new Mrs Percy. To show how costs rose with inflation and other factors, 20 years later those three houses, all on one title, were sold for nearly 200,000 dollars or £110,000.

We continued to share the seaside shack at Bridport, paying the rates from the surplus proceeds of the investment and then, in March 1970, Meg purchased her two brothers' shares and the cottage became our property.

In 1969, too, Christine left home to travel and reside in Perth, West Australia, to continue her career as a commercial artist, and Roslyn was in training at the Launceston General Hospital to become a nursing sister.

I had built a speed boat and a trailer for our fishing and recreational purposes and we enjoyed many weekends of leisure. From April 1970 onwards and the next six months, I made a complete new set of windows for the holiday cottage at Bridport. Every Friday evening alone with Gwyn, then almost eleven years old, we towed the trailer fully loaded with materials to completely renovate the premises. We removed all the old hinged Georgian sashes and boards and reclad the exterior and renovated the interior. I found all kinds of interesting newspapers and periodicals, old bottles and objects of the pre First World War era, 1911 and 1912, in the walls behind the plywood lining. I submitted our plans to the Scottsdale Council, which were quickly

349

approved, to add a new bathroom and toilet, another bedroom and a new garage, with new fencing around the back making it completely private for the first time. In 1970, too, Christine returned from West Australia and in March of that year she was married to Graeme Jones at the Cosgrove Park Chapel.

In 1974 Gwyn began his apprenticeship at the Gravelly Beach boatyard to become a shipwright and boat builder. Roslyn was nearing the completion of her nurses training, and Christine was married living in Raymond Street with Graeme and their young son Jarrod. As a result there appeared to be no interest any more in the holiday cottage at Bridport, so we put it up for sale. With the oil crisis of the 1970s and the downturn in the economy, I became redundant and I lost my job at Christmastime 1974. I had reached the period of my life when it was time to make a nostalgic visit to Wales to meet up with all my family once again after an absence of 25 years.

We had obtained a passage on the magnificent cruise ship *Ocean Monarch*, on its final voyage to Southampton before it was stripped of all its beautiful panelling, fixtures, fittings and contents, and sent to be broken up. Roslyn and cousin Pat were leaving, bound for Europe in January 1975, and we planned to meet up with them at Southampton when we arrived. In the meantime, I had obtained a temporary job for three months at Hutton's Abattoir in St Leonards. It suited me perfectly as we were due to sail from Sydney on Anzac Day 1975. Roslyn has completed her training to became a nursing sister and she was awarded the Oakes Memorial Gold Medal, voted as the nurse with the best bedside nursing care. Gwyn had arranged to board at the Exeter Hotel in our absence – we were disturbed at leaving him alone, but it worked out well; everything was in order.

350

24

My Return Journey

On Friday morning, 25th April 1975, Meg's brother and wife, Stretton and Bet drove us to the Launceston airport for our flight to Sydney. Christine, Jarrod, Gwyn and friends were there to see us go. We arrived at Sydney airport on a cold blustery day, after a night of very heavy rain. The bus from the terminal could only take us a short distance, all the routes were closed in preparation for the day's long procession and Anzac marches. We did find a taxi that took us on a long roundabout route eventually to reach Circular Quay and the overseas shipping terminal. We succeeded in depositing our luggage at the ship, and then spent the time visiting the Opera House, the city and the arcades, the parks and the Hilton Hotel. Everything else was closed, due to the Anzac Day holiday. It rained again that evening making things miserable, so we obtained a meal at the Circular Quay Café, then got on board about 8 p.m., with the ship due to sail at 2 a.m. for New Zealand.

We located the comfortable cabin with all our own private facilities, on the ship's port side, sorted out our luggage and sat up awaiting our departure at 2 a.m. Much to our disappointment the sailing was delayed until noon the next day, 26th April. Finally our journey began, out through Sydney Heads and, as the Australian coastline disappeared we had six long weeks ahead across the Tasman, the Pacific and the Atlantic, before we would reach our destination.

At 10.30 a.m. on 29th April, the ship berthed at Auckland and in the afternoon we left the ship for a bus tour. We drove through the borough of Newmarket to Cornwall Park, and the reserve skirting the slopes of One Tree Hill through the residential district of Hillsborough and the natural bush, with wonderful views of the city and the surrounding harbours. We returned through the Henderson Valley and the Western suburbs of Auckland to the ship for our journey to Fiji.

On Friday, 2nd May, just before midday, the ship tied up at Suva. We set off in the afternoon through the markets and the shops, around the stalls looking for a replacement camera for Roslyn. We had received news from her that the campervan they were using had been broken into, in Italy, and her camera was stolen. The ship had a further delay of 24 hours, so our stay extended to three days, giving us extra time to see lots of native ceremonies and a whole afternoon in the Olympic swimming pool. We lost another day crossing the international date line as we sailed on to the Cook Islands, then the ship anchored off the lush tropical island of Raratonga. The natives came aboard from their big outrigger canoes to entertain us with their traditional songs and dances, all dressed in their grass skirts, garlanded with masses of pink and cream frangipani.

Thursday, 8th May, brought us to anchor at Tahiti, a tropical paradise. It was a hot sultry day as we made an excursion around the island with all its tropical fruits, beautiful flowers and glistening high waterfalls pouring out of the crater-lake. Hundreds of coconut palms everywhere were bound with sheets of tin. The explanation they gave was that the tin prevented the rats eating the coconuts. They had bred in plague proportions after being introduced from visiting ships. I saw Captain Cook's memorial erected at the place of his fatal wounding and enjoyed the hot black volcanic sands as I cooled off in the surf. I can always remember papa mousse the giant orange, so delicious and sweet. As we left Tahiti behind, after a wonderful and enjoyable stay, we passed dozens of atolls and low-lying islands on our way across the Pacific to the Panama Canal.

During the early evening of 18th May, we passed the distant Cocos Island and our crossing of the Pacific was nearing its end. The following morning I saw the coastline of Central America for the first time, and the next day would bring us into Balboa and the entrance of the Panama Canal. We enjoyed a small tour of the Balboa area, through the Morgan's Gardens, named after that Welsh Buccaneer and rogue Captain Morgan, the Chinese Gardens, and the Summit Experimental gardens, a jungle forest reserve, with many magnificent and cultivated wild orchids. An unofficial enthusiastic and patriotic Panamanian gatecrashed our party there to voluntarily show off his country to us as visitors. We drove through the canal zone communities of Balboa and Ancon to sight see Panama City. We went into the magnificent interior of the church of the Golden Altar, saw the presidential palace, and the French plaza commemorating the French attempt to build the canal through Panama, the wonderful flat arch of Santo Domingo and the Statue of Vasco Nunex de Balboa. We visited the residential districts of Bella Vista Punta Paitilla, with magnificent panoramic views of Panama City and Panama Bay, then the ruins of Old Panama founded in 1510, but sacked and burned by that rogue and vagabond Captain Henry Morgan in 1671.

It gave us some time for shopping in Panama City, and our small party, Meg, myself, and two New Zealanders, strayed off the main city street area hoping to see some of the native quarters. The back areas were choked waist high with garbage and many startled residents came out waving frantically to us to return and get out of the place with gestures and cries in Spanish. It was too dangerous to go further, so we beat a hasty retreat to the city centre.

We left Panama City and sailed through the canal to our next port of call, the Dutch Shell Island of Curacao off the coast of the South American country of Venezuela. It was 6 a.m. when the ship berthed, allowing us a half day to look around, so we hired a taxi to Willemstad, about six and a half miles away. I was very impressed with the development of that small island with one of the largest oil refineries in the world. We visited the picturesque floating markets where the traders from the Venezuelan mainland bring all their produce and wares for sale. It was the first time I had seen the enormous cooking bananas and so many other central American fruits.

One and a half hours late on our schedule that day we cruised along the coast of Venezuela then north to the island of Trinidad, and the ship anchored off the Port of Spain, the chief port and town of the island to disembark, and take on more passengers, moving again through the Caribbean to the island of Barbados.

It was 25th May 1975, a Sunday and the ship berthed at Bridgetown. At this time there appeared to be problems amongst the passengers, as many began to suffer with gyppy tummy, sickness and diarrhoea, with violent pains in the stomach. Meg was becoming a victim, experiencing the sharp pains as we set out at 9 a.m. boarding a local bus to visit the poorer native areas and the sugar cane regions. On the return journey Meg was sick and fortunately my cotton sun hat came to the rescue to avoid embarrassment and soiling of the local bus. Up to this time I was all right but my turn was soon to come. In the afternoon we hired a taxi along the highway to view the Hilton, the Welcome Inn, and the Crane Hotels, fronting the magnificent beaches with their crystal white sands, then to return to the ship across the calm Caribbean and into the Atlantic. I suddenly caught the tummy bug and became violently sick with uncontrollable diarrhoea. I could not eat or drink anything and I began to lose weight. Those trouble-some waters, normally stormy and rough, were exceptionally calm which helped a great deal.

From the 25th to the 31st May, we still enjoyed the sunshine lazing on the decks. We sighted the island of Sao Miguel and its sister island of Santa Maria of the Azores Archipelago. Our ship slowly entered the port of Ponta Delgada on Sao Miguel and tied up at the wharf. I had always heard so much about those lonely islands in the South Atlantic but I never ever believed that some day I would actually visit them. In the morning we walked through the old town, back into the sixteenth century, full of ancient historic churches, buildings and forts. There were narrow cobblestoned roads, tiny footpaths, and overhang-ing stone verandahs, and everyone greeted our arrival with the con-tinuous deafening noise of blowing car and vehicle horns. The whole countryside rises up to the high central crater with its magnificent twin blue lakes and rich cultivated ridges and valleys everywhere. The entire area, as far as the eye could see, was cultivated, and every possible square metre was utilised, divided up like a patchwork quilt into small fields, all surrounded by miles and miles of dry stone walls, several feet thick, and often as high as nine feet, to protect them from the sea winds, growing produce from all over the world, from pineapples to tea. I was informed that the temperatures never fell below 13 degrees Celsius in winter and rarely exceeded 22 degrees in summer. We took a coach tour that day also, through Ponta Delgada North to the Ribeira Grande and the second next important town on the island with all its quaint sixteenth-century Portuguese buildings. We ascended the Aguade Pou ridge of mountains then on to the highest mountain in the central range to view the magnificent breath-taking Lake of Fire. On our return we stopped in Ribeira Grande to view some of those old stone buildings from the past, then on through several picturesque villages to the Aruda pineapple plantation where they distilled and manufactured all kinds of liqueurs, through the delightful village of Faja De Baixo to Ponta Delgada. We enjoyed other views of the Furnas Valley with its varieties of hot springs and the rich thermal station and all its volcanic phenomena. I picked some locally grown tea and Meg went to see a local wedding with all its garlands and masses of flowers. There was an abundance of every-thing, vegetables, fruits, fish, seafoods, unlimited resources everywhere, huge gardens of every kind of flower and shrub, tobacco and vines, dairy and wool products and papermaking.

It was the first day of June, the start of the northern summer, as we sailed out of Ponta Delgada, north-east into the cold grey Atlantic towards the English Channel. I was improving each day from the stomach ailments but I had lost a lot of weight. The weather turned cold, as we progressed north and we soon began to pass many ships leaving the English Channel. It was a wonderful sunset on the evening of the third day of June 1975, and we could see the far distant white cliffs of the English coast. My unforgettable repeat journey began, but much more leisurely this time, exactly 35 years and two weeks later, heading for the coast of Holland, and the area which was Hook Van Holland in 1940.

I was up at dawn the following morning as the ship approached the Dutch coast to enter the River Scheldt to Rotterdam. I climbed the highest vantage point I could find, a lifeboat above the deck, armed with a pair of binoculars. It was a cold, overcast, miserable, grey, day as I scanned every possible view around. The long steel girder pier with its gantry cranes, as I knew it, jutting far out into the sea, had gone. It was now all big wharf buildings and long lines of tied-up ships, the entry to Europort, the biggest port in the world. I was disappointed I could not even see the small town of the Hook, if it still existed, obscured by so many wharf buildings. The sky above was black with clouds, so different from long ago, as my mind pictured those screaming black Nazi stukas diving out of the sun as their bombs plunged down around us.

Our ship sailed on towards Rotterdam among many other ships on the move everywhere. The visible shoreline was all wharfs, buildings and warehouses until we reached our berth. We walked into the city centre, and everything seemed normal. There were so many new buildings but no visible evidence of that devastating Nazi bombing 35 years previously, the first mass bombing of a western city in the Second World War. I could still recall the huge fiery glow in the night sky as we came in from the sea. We obtained some guilders for dollars at a bank, but we found everything was so expensive. Our first jolt was paying 1.50 Australian dollars (80p) for a small glass of lemonade. We did purchase a few souvenirs, but I was pleased to get back on board and anxious to move on to the last leg of our voyage back to the English Channel and our destination Southampton.

We sailed that evening down through the crowded waterway, still cold, overcast, and blustery, and it was to be our last night's sleep on board that beautiful ship. I had little sleep that night as we did not have many more miles to go. It had been a long enjoyable voyage.

355

All our luggage was packed and our remaining possessions secured in bags and parcels.

It was a Thursday morning, 5th June, and the ship seemed to go so slowly around the Isle of Wight heading for Southampton water. To me it brought back more memories, exactly 31 years previously, of when I was in a security camp at Gosford a few miles away waiting to move out from that area on a tank-landing ship for the invasion of Nazi Europe. There was no apprehension or tension on this occasion, but a feeling of excitement, warmth, and pleasure just to get ashore.

We scanned the waiting crowds of people behind the barriers anxiously seeking a sighting of Roslyn and Pat awaiting our arrival, but there was no sign of them anywhere. Wondering if they had made it to the time of arrival, with all the changed dates and delays of the ship, we made inquiries from the railway information guides who had come on board, about the times etc. of a train to Cardiff. It seemed such a long time; the ship was inspected and cleared by the Customs, there were auctions and sales of fittings, furniture and fixtures, but finally just after 1 p.m., we were allowed to disembark. We got ashore, through the immigration checks, then were delayed again when our cases were opened and searched by the Customs. We got through the barriers at last to search the faces in the crowds. We were greeted by an old familiar face and she called out, 'The girls are here.' It was Kay, Meg's friend and ex-matron from Reigate school and we were quickly reunited with Roslyn and Pat. I carried our heavy cases some distance to the parked Volkswagen campervan which they had christened with the name of Vera. It greeted us with the painted laughing face on the spare tyre cover bolted to the front end with the word 'Smile' displayed in a semi-circle below. We all boarded the van and drove north-east to Winchester to return Kay to her home, where the two girls had stayed overnight.

It was a warm pleasant summer's afternoon and after a hurried stay with so much to talk about we set off for South Wales. We stopped briefly in a shady green country lane in Wiltshire for a quick cup of tea, then continued on to join the motorway to Wales. Late that afternoon we crossed the new Severn suspension bridge and turned off to Chepstow to find and surprise my sister Edna. Edna was living in a big mobile home, in a beautiful country area a short distance from the River Wye, where it joins the Severn Estuary with the giant bridge spanning both high above. We gave her a wonderful surprise and a wonderful reunion after my hurried departure in London on that awful wet November morning in 1949. Incidentally, that battered old wristwatch, trodden upon by hundreds of feet, which I salvaged from the rubbish bin and had given to Edna to repair, was still being worn and was going well after nearly 27 years.

We drove on our way once more to join the motorway into Wales and, as we reached the end of the access ramp, there ahead of me on a big placard was the sign I had eagerly waited to see for so long: *Croesio-i-Cymru* – Welcome to Wales.

25

Croesio-i-Cymru

It was evening but still daylight in summer time till 10.15 p.m., as we travelled with the fast-moving traffic through the county of Monmouthshire, which had since changed its name to Gwent. We passed the exit to Newport, but everything seemed so strange to me as I searched ahead for the exit sign to turn off to Caerphilly. It was 8.45 p.m. and at last we reached our turn-off point from the Cardiff-bound motorway. In ten more minutes we would reach familiar territory and Caerphilly town, this is what I thought, but everything had changed so much I was confused. We passed the ancient rambling old castle to head north what I thought was up the Rhymney Valley. After a few more miles we had to turn back, we were heading for the town of Bedwas, and not the route I required, but we soon found our correct road. We entered the old mining village of Llanbradach, and everything was peaceful and quiet, the derelict colliery had long closed down, many of the old stone-terraced cottages were empty, abandoned and condemned as they were unsafe. After so many years of mining the areas were subsiding, and the cottages evacuated.

We soon arrived at Ystrad Mynach, and everything became familiar and clear to me there, as we drove on through the town to turn left towards Hengoed. The massive high stone viaduct with its 16 giant arches across the valley came into view. It carried the railway no longer: that too had long been torn up, dismantled and scrapped, each end was now blocked with high barbed-wire barriers standing out against the sky background. We had almost reached our destination. The main road traversed through one of those big arches to take us on to that sadly depressed village that I knew so well a long time ago, the village of Tiy-r-beth. The conditions, hardships, misery and poverty inflicted on so many inhabitants, many of them my schoolmates in the 1920s, would be something I would never forget. On this occasion the houses lining the road, and as far into the village streets

358

that I could see, had all been spruced up with woodwork fresh with paint and various coloured front doors. The route ahead was fronted with warehouses and buildings which appeared to be a small trading estate, and not before time, my innermost thoughts quickly prompted me.

The village Glan-y-nant came into view, maybe that name was no longer used, it was always Pengam, perhaps it became common to all the old railways and referred to as Pengam (glam) and across the river as Pengam (mon). We stopped at the traffic lights at the crossroads with the long hill past Lewis' Grammar School, ahead up to the bridge opposite Oak Cottage – traffic lights at Pengam! We must be in a modern world!

My thoughts drifted to that intersection and the old road descending to the river bridge. It was along that road that Billy Crane, at nine years old, fell out of a tree and broke his wrist trying to reach the bird's nest of the rare yellow hammer, and what ever happened to the steam hammer to which its enterprising owner had fitted a small chopper to its base, to chop the wood blocks into 12 one-inch square sticks, to be bound with wire, and sold to kindle the household coal fires?

The jerk of the van moving forward as the lights changed brought me out of my dream as we climbed the hill past Lewis' School. Mutton Trump and the Charity Woods were gone. In their place was black shale, slag and filling, millions of tons of it, right down to the river, no more railway sidings, or shunting areas, just the two up and down main lines under the bridge. Across the river the derelict Britannia mine was silent and still, the distant old eyesore, Aber-Bargoed tip, soaring high above the valley was green, completely covered with pine trees.

We reached the crest to drive slowly over the bridge, then we stopped the vehicle and I climbed out. It was 9.30 p.m. I looked across to Oak Cottage and waved my hand, the family were all outside awaiting our arrival. It had been nearly 26 years since I had seen them and there was a lump in my throat as we drove down to meet them, it was to be a wonderful reunion. I jumped out of the van quickly to embrace my mother, and there were tears in her eyes, as she whispered to me, '*Croesio-i* Ron – welcome home! It's so wonderful to see you again.' She looked frail and aged, years of toil were beginning to tell. Joyce and her husband Gwyn, Joan and Lew, and Toots and Arthur were all there. Trefor would arrive from London on Saturday, and Joan and the family had arranged a big celebration and reunion dinner in the local hall next door on the Saturday evening. We had supper that night and talked into the early hours. Roslyn and Pat slept in the campervan parked outside the top of the garden at the rear; Meg and I had the main front bedroom.

It all seemed so strange to me, I was up early the following morning, Friday, anxious to look around. The huge beech tree had gone, cut down because of age as it had become too dangerous. The giant ash had gone too! And beyond, where old Northcote had his gardens, was a big block of two-storeyed flats, Gummer's Field was no more, that area also was residential flats. At the front of Oak Cottage, below the built-up road to the bridge was a big workshop of new cars, and across the road a service station. Next to the Price's old home were new houses, and two new homes in the old gardens, which were once the pride and joy of our old Gaffer, T C Jones. Things had certainly changed!

I was up early again the next morning. I was concerned about the condition of the campervan. It gave me a little time for a quick inspection; the two girls had travelled thousands of miles with it, all over Europe. The brakes were not very good, the speedometer did not work, the windscreen wipers were just as bad and operated on occasions only, the two front tyres were bald, one of them had a hole in the side wall visibly showing the tube, and how it did not blow out with the air pressure I could not understand. There were no tools at all for a quick repair, to remove a wheel or tighten a nut and, on the majority of starts, due to a problem with the automatic choke it had to be pushed or run down a slope to make the motor fire. With a few borrowed tools we quickly changed the plugs and points, as there were no Volkswagen supplies or agents in the area. However, we drove to Caerphilly in the car with Joan's husband Lew, to the Carfore Supermarket. I obtained a few tools and a wheel brace and I also purchased a two-man Campari nylon tent for our future use. The same afternoon we toured the local areas to see the old places once again. We drove towards Gelligaer, past the old Norman Church and the Cross Inn and along the narrow road track to the mountain road towards Quarry Mawr. The high dry-stone walls across the moors were still there, as sturdy as ever, covered with moss and lichen, and the views were magnificent north and south across the luxurious green valleys. All the distant slag tips that once blotted the landscapes were gone, all covered over and green, after the shocking disaster of slipping and burying an infant's school in terrible circumstances some years before. A new steel security gate barred the entrance track to Quarry

Mawr, and beyond the area was a big open-cut coal mine with many trucks moving their loads along an outlet road. Our old hazelnut grove that once flourished through the thick ferns and bracken was gone, no longer causing shadows against the hillside as I once knew it there, it had all been destroyed with the passing years. Another half mile along the road we got out into the warm afternoon sun to see the breathtaking view down the steep mountain side. Five hundred feet below, deep in the valley, shaded by the steep mountain slopes was the Taff Merthyr mine with its strings of railway lines and loaded wagons. It was still working day and night.

We continued on down into the valley to see Taff Merthyr, and all the hills and slopes to Bedling and Trelewis, then to Pen-y-bryn and the small Cylla valley with the Penalta mine, where I spent some of my early working life, down to Ystrad Mynach and then back to Oak Cottage. It had been a wonderful, memorable and nostalgic trip.

Trefor and his wife Gladys would arrive after midday driving down from London; in the meantime, Gwyn, sister Joyce's husband drove us up the Rhymney Valley through the old mining villages of Deri and Fochriew. The local colliery Grosfaen, once a hive of industry and huge coal production, was shut down, derelict and ugly with its torn-down buildings and rusting steel frames. My greatest shock was the Rhymney River which, for over a century, was black, evil-smelling, thick with sludge, oil, tar and sewerage. It was flowing fresh and clean. We returned across the mountain roads to Gelligaer, with a brief stop at Toots' home in Penpedaerheol, to the Pengam Square, climbing the Grammar School Hill and its right-angled bridge over the railway to Gwerthonor Road. It was wonderful to see and talk to Trefor once again, as we all helped in the preparation of our big reunion party in the hall next door to Oak Cottage. The premises had been built on leasehold land, just like everything else, by the Welsh Baptist group before the turn of the century. Everything was conducted in the Welsh language, with all the hymn books, Bibles, and scriptures also all in Welsh. The old, devoted members had gradually passed on and there was no congregation left, so the place became the Senior Citizen's hall, for all their meetings and recreation activities. At 8 p.m. that evening we had a wonderful welcome home party, and a huge scrumptious meal. The grandchildren, great grandchildren, cousins and the whole family were there with one absentee only, sister Edna, who was unable to attend.

We spent nine days at Oak Cottage with my mother and Joan, with visits and meals to Toots, Joyce and cousin Mair, with exhilarating sightseeing trips to all the old haunts and places, and meeting so many folks from my schooldays. We were invited to an evening at the local workmen's club, which had commenced its business originally at the rear of Lew Walters' shop and home, where we sought peace and quiet as boys from our old tyrant Noah Thomas. At its location next to the Gwerthonor Hotel at that time, it still carried that unpleasant name 'the Nazi'. I visited my old school and was given a conducted tour of honour by the resident caretaker, and I found my photograph with the school Rugby team of 1934, still in its old place hanging on the wall. The old streets of Bargoed town had not changed but many of the shops I knew had gone.

About 14th June, we set out in the campervan to tour England, Scotland and Wales but, as a priority, we first had to get the van roadworthy and in order, so we drove to Chepstow and the Welsh border to a recommended garage and workshop, Bowen's garage. They relined and adjusted the brakes, fitted two new tyres and serviced the vehicle. We were unable to obtain a new cable for the speedometer. It was a big relief for me, the vehicle was now safe and reliable, we just had to watch our speed and stay with the normal flow of the traffic through all the towns and villages. We experienced two afternoons of rain only from 5th June, the date of our arrival, to 31st August, the date of our return to Tasmania. Considering the British weather this was extraordinary. We stayed that night camping in the field behind Edna's mobile home and to tell her all about the reunion in Wales before setting out on our tour.

26

Our Visit Ends and into the 1980s

The old campervan Vera served us very well; we did experience a number of difficult engine starts but mechanically it was excellent and never let us down. We travelled the whole length of England and revisited Thetford and Pickering, both of which had changed so much from the war years. Then into Scotland spending a day in Edinburgh, and we found and visited relatives of Jim Kennedy and Mrs Jean Peck, our neighbour, in Glasgow. We drove north to the extreme end at John-o-Groats and travelled along many of the single-track roads through the Highlands. We camped one night below Ben Lomond and along the shore of Loch Ness, stopped at Gretna Green to re-enter England at Carlyle. The van did a wonderful job through all the steep passes and descents until we reached the Lake District. Our presence wasn't welcomed there and we were ordered to move on, so we drove to the Mersey tunnel, across to Birkenhead and into Wales.

We explored Chester and the North Wales Coast to Bangor crossing the Menai Bridge to Anglesey and our first stop at Llanfair PG, the village station with the longest name. It was 34 years since I saw it last during the war years, little had changed, even Holyhead appeared just the same. We retraced our route to visit Caernarvon and the castle. I inquired from an old resident his knowledge and information about an old wartime colleague of mine by the name of Lewis. It was a stab in the dark and a difficult task with such a common name throughout the districts. I produced an old address and his Christian name. He had known him very well as an employee of the post office, but he told me he had died some years previously so it ended my quest. We toured Snowdonia and through the Llanberis Pass. I had to see Beddgelert to recall the story from my infant days and Welsh history, with the Prince and his dog, Festiniog, and the narrow gauge railway. I climbed down the gorge to see the Ponterwyd Falls and to cross the Parson's Bridge, and on to the Devil's Bridge. The old world came back as I watched the folk fishing from the round coracle boats on the river Tievy, as we camped for the night along its banks.

We spent one afternoon watching events at the Welsh National Eisteddford and continuing on we were welcomed to camp in a Welsh farmer's field for the ridiculous price of 25 pence, and then invited to wash and clean up at the home. What a contrast after being ordered to move on in the snobbish English Lake District.

I enjoyed the sleepy town of Carmarthen, and we drove on through the hills and vales to the Crychan Forest to camp on the mountain top with its wonderful views across the steep grassy slopes, and the folding hills. It was at this spot that evening, with the setting sun reflecting its orange light on every sparkling distant object, as shadows lengthened against the deep green slopes, and a train half hidden by the trees curled its way around the mountainside, that Roslyn, moved by it all, said that some day she would love to donate a seat for everyone to sit and enjoy it all. I wonder will it ever be fulfilled?

The next day was my birthday so we drove on to Brecon to celebrate the occasion at the Bishop's Meadow Restaurant. The old Welsh town of Brecon could never change with its narrow streets, overhanging buildings and quaint shops. Once again I had to visit the museum display of the old Welsh home, the contents, the wares, and the implements, I remembered so well to stir so many of my thoughts and memories of long ago. We crossed the Black Mountains and through the wonderful Beacons, down to Brynmawr. There were many changes there compared with my schooldays. My old railway had gone. It brought back many memories travelling through sleet and snow, on the Brecon and Methyr line, to play rugby at the local school. We did some shopping at the sales in this small town, our vehicle was parked in the street outside one of the terraced houses. The occupant of that house soon came to the front door, which opened onto the narrow footpath. She was dressed in her freshly ironed, neat, Welsh pinafore. Roslyn inquired politely if she had any objection to the van being parked outside her front door. On hearing her accent, so different from anything heard in that area, she was greeted with the familiar Welsh lilt and hospitality, and after a few words, surprised and almost embarrassed, she was invited in for a cup of tea.

We took the moorland and mountain road from Brynmawr to Merthyr, and on to Gelligaer to camp that night alongside the high dry-stone wall 50 yards away from the entrance gate to Quarry Mawr. It was a special pilgrimage for me to rest and sleep, for the last time in my life, at that enjoyable, memorable spot. Early the next morning we were assisted by a passing miner, on his way to work at the Taff Merthyr mine, to push-start our vehicle out of the tall ferns and bracken to continue on to Oak Cottage.

I spent the next few days touring and rambling the neighbourhood. Gwaled-y-waen farm had changed to become a modern country club, and the pear orchard that was such a target of my schooldays, had gone forever. The country lane behind the infants school, which climbed past old Tard Davies' level, the old route for the shire horses and their coal carts, was now a narrow walking track. The magnificent green meadow area and our 'jungle' were still there, but Gypsy Lane, where the bountiful magnificent chestnut trees were cut down and destroyed through the spite and prejudice of Noah Thomas, was now lined with new houses and continuing on along Mathews Lane to Gwerthonor Road. Beyond Maes-y-craig Street and the area I knew as the 'Sloggers' where I once picked winberries, was a big new council estate complete with its own public house. We made another special visit to Abergavenny and the market and a pleasant afternoon at Gwerthonor House, the Price's home, with Janet the last surviving member of the family and the sole occupant at that time.

The two girls, Pat and Roslyn, were now making preparations for their camping tour to Russia and Scandinavia. The campervan was cleaned up and sold, and on the morning of 31st July, Meg, myself and my mother took them to Pengam Station to catch the train to Cardiff, and on to London, to meet the tour. Trefor returned to Wales to take his mother to his home in Epping for a two-week holiday. I said goodbye to her as she left, it was the final farewell, sadly I would never see her again.

For the next four weeks we toured south-west England in a hired car, visiting Edna and relatives in Bristol, with a special visit to Alveston, the birthplace of my father, before returning to South Wales once more. A few more days were spent with my sister Joan at Oak Cottage and around the municipality before setting out for London and our return to Tasmania. We obtained a small bed-sitting room for a few days in Brixton in south London, which enabled us to travel into central London to see and visit some of the old places where my tired feet had carried me around 26 years previously. We then met brother Trefor who took us to his home in Epping to stay for a few days before flying back to Tasmania.

On the evening of 31st August I said goodbye to Trefor at Heathrow airport. The crowded aircraft developed problems, delaying us for ten hours in the desert heat at Bahrein and then another long delay at

Singapore. Tired and exhausted, we were relieved and glad to see the family once again awaiting our arrival at the Launceston airport. The next few days were spent getting everything in order at home and then I started work with Barry Scott at his workshop in Raymond Street.

As the time moved on I started to receive bad news, my sister Edna died, Toots was taken seriously ill and sadly she passed away shortly afterwards. To make it even worse Joyce lost her husband with a fatal heart attack – the members of my family were getting less. On the brighter side, Roslyn was married to John Taylor in March 1978, and Gwyn was married to Ruth in the following April of 1979. It was shortly after this that I received the sad news that Mother had once again tumbled down the stairs at Oak Cottage and she was taken to hospital. It was the saddest blow of all, she never recovered from that fall, on 19th August 1979 she died. According to her wishes just like my father, mother was cremated. How glad I was that I had spent some time with her four years previously giving me the opportunity to say goodbye to her for the last time. It left me with a vision, just like my brother, of that wonderful lady, the vision written in the lines compiled by Gwyn in 1937:

> Gazing upon that intangible face
> so vividly conjured in memory's eye
> Brings emotions that make the pulses race,
> and memories that will for ever lie
> in the depths of the solitary soul,
> unsounded by any other toll.
> Visions of boyhood's halcyon bliss
> the tender affection of Mother's kiss,
> Guidance and care upon her knee
> Graceful chiding given to me,
> Care and sacrifice bountifully given
> until at last I am in despair driven,
> beyond each empty word and phrase
> to thank providence for her tender grace,
> How well I recall those fairest locks
> curling upon that pale broad brow.
> That angelic voice that's calling me now
> Writ on the measured meter of the mind
> her smile will eternally bind.

My thoughts to God and Mother,
For in Heaven they smile at one another.

Mother was the oldest resident of the Gwerthonor district, and the village of Gilfach. She had always been a wealth of information about the entire district, and all the folk born there in her time. Numerous people came to see her seeking some advice about a relative or incident of the past, and she appeared to know the birthdays and the antecedents of so many around the area from the turn of the century. She had achieved her *Hiraeth*, the final utopia of a Welsh patriot; a wonderful lady had passed away.

27

The Final Sentimental Return

In 1986 there were just two members of my original family residing in Wales, sisters Joyce and Joan, with brother Trefor living outside London, in Epping. I had to go back to see them one more time. At the end of June in that year, I departed all alone on a flight to London, for a stay of four weeks. Trefor was there to meet me at London Airport and together we went to his home at Epping in Essex. I stayed two days with Trefor, and he arranged to take me to South Wales and Oak Cottage.

To begin our journey we drove north-east to his holiday cottage near Lowestoft, on the North Sea coast, and we stayed for two more days while I assisted with a few urgent repairs. It was time to set out for Wales, so we drove across to the west of England and the Gloucester area, and across into Monmouthshire through Monmouth until we met up with the Head of the Valleys highway. On this occasion our entry into the Rhymney Valley was from the north and, as we neared the Bargoed area, I was amazed to see some local boys fishing in the Rhymney River, something I never expected to see in my lifetime. We slowly drove under the Bargoed Viaduct to climb the hill and cross the road bridge at the old railway station. Trefor drove the vehicle into Railway Terrace above the station and invited me to get out to view the surrounding scene. The four huge winding wheels and derricks of the Bargoed steam and house coal mines were gone. The huge power station, the washeries, by product works, coke ovens, all the masses of railway lines with the overhead aerial bucket rope-ways were no more, it was an open cleared area, acres of it with the clean river sparkling and rippling through. What I had always known as a vast dirty, smoky, noisy hive of industry had all disappeared for ever. There were many more changes I was soon to discover, as we continued on through Bargoed town, in contrast to my visit eleven years previously.

Joan, my sister was awaiting our arrival at Oak Cottage. She was taking two weeks holiday so that we could visit many of the familiar places together throughout Wales. Trefor stayed for two days before returning home and he arranged to come back to take me to his home before my departure back to Tasmania at the end of the month. I went to see Joyce, and it was wonderful to meet her again. She now lived alone in a flat in Aeron Place, and it was the first time for me to enter that street since the morning of my departure for military service on 5th January 1940. Joyce lived almost opposite the home of Albert Turner, with whom I left on that early, cold, bleak morning into the unknown.

There was one other thing: I was keen to find out about my forebears in Wales. As a young schoolboy in 1926 I could faintly recall my grandfather referring to another signature in his old Welsh Bible, that name was the common insignificant name of William Thomas and it did not mean much to me at that young age. This name I discovered years later at school was Islwyn, one of, if not the greatest, of all Welsh poets of the nineteenth century. I tried desperately to trace back through my memory what he had said about this man. I had a very faint recollection of him telling me he was a fellow member of his Calvinistic Chapel, Y Babell, at Ynys-ddu, and either his cousin or aunt, I could not clearly remember which, was the wife of William Thomas. I told Joan my information, she was very interested also, so she decided we would visit the old Chapel and find Islwyn's grave. When we arrived there we discovered that Y Babell was the centre of the Islwyn memorial society, the Islwyn Museum and Community Hall. I learned a great deal more about him, found his grave, and I purchased Mr Meuric Walters' book, *Islwyn, Man of Mountain*. The contents of that book convinced me, proudly and truly, Islwyn's wife, Martha, whom he married in 1864, was the daughter of my great grandfather's brother Owen, my grandfather's first cousin. I had solved another question I had wondered about all my life.

On our way home to Oak Cottage that day Joan said to me, 'Now you have solved that problem, Ron, I suggest we pay homage to the grave of the grandfather I never knew, and also a sentimental visit to Gwyn's grave at Gelligaer. We must go tomorrow.'

On that particular tomorrow, our visit was delayed; instead I attended the funeral of Bill O'Keefe, one of my old classmates from Gilfach Boys School, and the days of our old Gaffer.

On the following day as we prepared to leave, Joan produced a page from an old school exercise book, which consisted of written

369

lines in my own penmanship writing at a young age in the 1920s. It had my signature, and she asked if I remembered it and what it all meant. In her own sentimental way of keeping everything, she had found it in one of the old books and put it away. I studied it for a long time trying to find an answer why I had written those lines such a long time ago. Suddenly it all came back, an incident from the past. It must have been some time in the year 1927, my brother Gwyn was showing one of his school books to my mother and complaining bitterly about the red pencil cross-outs of one page of his writing by his supervising schoolmaster, and explaining that he had been heavily caned and given two periods of detention. This meant he was compelled to attend school two consecutive Saturday mornings from 9 a.m. till noon, as further punishment for the offensive sentences he had written. Gwyn was eight years senior to me and from my knowledge he had never done a wrong thing in his life. He could speak Welsh fluently and he was a brilliant student of Welsh history. This all puzzled me and my young mind, and I was prejudiced against all those superiors who vented their spleen by vicious canings with the stick. I had to find out more about it and secretly I got hold of Gwyn's exercise book. Gwyn had written a long essay on the iron puddlers and craftsmen during the Napoleonic wars and detailing how so many young Welshmen were shanghaied, chain-ganged and rounded up to fight the English wars and how escapees were often impaled or flogged to death. The essay was marked by a prejudiced English teacher in the absence, through illness, of Gwyn's own form master, resulting in punishment for what he regarded as offensive lines about the English overlords. Consequently, unknown to Gwyn, I got hold of this exercise book, read the essay, and copied the so-called offensive lines. It was a dedication to all those victims as a conclusion to his wonderful essay and I must repeat them again.

To those wonderful folk from the land of my Fathers.
On their memories the sun shall never set,
Nor in the heart of a Welsh born Patriot
shall they be forgotten. We shall continue to remember
that they died from hunger, exploitation, oppression
poverty, misery and the cat-o-nine tails, whilst
the fruits of their seeking in the creation of a
National soul, in culture, Verse and Song.
Cymru Am Byth

370

I could not remember what happened to the copy I wrote, how strange that Joan found it and kept it to turn up again 60 years later. Sentimental Joan had put it away with her treasures, and after my explanation, we set out to visit Gwyn's grave in the Gelligaer churchyard. We had to trace the unmarked site from the church records, as it had almost disappeared after 50 years. We went on to the Pengam cemetery to our grandparents' last resting place, the oak plaque carefully positioned such a long time ago had rotted and almost disintegrated; it appeared time waits for no man.

The next day we were invited to the home of Joan's friends at Maen-Gilfach, so we drove along the mountain road towards Bedlinog. My Quarry Mawr area to my surprise was occupied by an Australian company Pioneer International and the whole site was covered with thousands of tons and huge dumps of gravel, sand, stone, chippings and gradings, and concrete ingredients. We returned to Bargoed and beyond the old park where I picked blackberries, and winberries, was a new grammar school. My old school was still there farther along the road, stark, cold, and forlorn, but it had changed to become a comprehensive secondary school.

For the next two weeks we set off each day to different locations, all the coastal areas from Cardiff to Swansea, and the resorts along the west coast. Two special days were arranged to visit the Abergavenny market and the Brecon Beacons National Park. I had a special enjoyable journey on the Brecon mountain railway, with some of the original bed track which was once the Brecon and Merthyr railway. We visited sister Toots' daughter's home in the beautiful area of Crickhowel to see her children, Kate, Ben and Simon. Arthur, Toots' husband, took me later through the Sirhowy and the Rhondda Valleys, to Newport, Chepstow, and on through the New Forest, and with the 'wonderful' weather it made it all so enjoyable.

Trefor returned just before the end of the month to take me back to London for my return flight to Tasmania. I had one more day with Joyce before my departure and as it all came to an end I spoke to Joan on the telephone from Heathrow Airport. I would never hear her voice, or see her again. Sadly, it was something I did not know at the time.

Shortly after my return to Tasmania Joan was taken ill and her health and condition deteriorated quickly. Tender and wonderful nursing care by Joyce and cousin Mair failed to help her recover and get well. On 21st March 1987 Joan died. It was a sad blow for me, Joan was the youngest of our family and she had helped look after my mother for a long time since my father's death, and had taken over the old home at Oak Cottage. She had worked for the same company in Cardiff for 42 years and become one of the senior management. She had barely two years to go for her retirement and she was planning to come to Tasmania for a holiday as soon as she finished work. Sadly it was a plan she never fulfilled, a dream that never came true. It left me with so many pleasant memories of Joan, right back to her childhood and the numerous times I carried her to school piggy-back, through the deep snow and the winter storms.

28

The End of the Old Family Home

In the December following Joan's death, her husband Lew Thomas passed away after a short illness. The cruelest blow of all was then inflicted on Trefor, Joyce and myself, the last members of our family. The old family home, Oak Cottage, with all its heirlooms, treasures and contents passed to Lew Thomas, with the death of Joan, and as a result of his death, he had willed everything to the Thomas relatives. We did not even know these beneficiaries. Twelve hours after his funeral a huge removal van parked outside the old home, and they swooped like vultures and removed everything. Poor Joyce, elderly, helpless and all alone was abused and ordered off the premises, as the spoils were loaded and taken away. Many of my treasures and war souvenirs left there in trust were simply looted, belongings handed down from my grandfather, all the old treasures of the Alway family owned for so long, oil paintings of Green Meadow and Ryadre by Christine, our daughter, were all carried away. The home occupied by our family for nearly a century was immediately put up for sale for the price of 45,000 pounds. A loan of 1,500 pounds to Joan from my mother in a verbal arrangement in the family towards the purchase of freehold, was never repaid. This sum, with the clear knowledge of Lew Thomas, was to be repaid from the proceeds when Joan retired, 500 pounds each to Toots' two children, and 500 pounds to Brian, Edna's son. There was no one left to challenge and dispute this family agreement, and I was too far away. All this news was sent to me by letters from Joyce. Each time she was near the building there were tears in her eyes to see the huge real estate sign emblazoned across the main entrance, empty and forlorn. Our old home that could tell us so many stories from the past was no more. It was the final conclusion for me and the end of all my connections with Oak Cottage and the Gwerthonor area. The old home was soon sold, and the new owners took up residence probably never to know the warmth and care of the years gone by with the laughter, the joy, and the tears that were found inside those old stone walls.

Time moves on and I have reached the twilight of my life, so perhaps I may be excused for quoting the following lines written about 'One Life' by H. Bonar at the beginning of the nineteenth century:

> Not many lives, but one have we, one, only one!
> How sacred should that one life ever be?
> That narrow span!
> Day after day filled up with blessed toil
> Hour after hour still bringing in new spoil.
> Our being is no shadow of thin air
> No vacant dream!
> No fable of meaning of mystery,
> Tho' strange and solemn may that meaning be.

With all my memories I can add that other meaning – what a strange thing is memory, and hope, one looks backward, the other forward, the one is today, the other is the tomorrow.

In my life I have had many hopes and many dreams. Some have been fulfilled. The majority are gone, shattered, or faded away, so I have well and truly discovered that memories live longer than dreams.